God's City

στη μνήμη του David R. Turner (1960–2003)

The brilliant Byzantist who got me into all this.

God's City

Byzantine Constantinople

Nic Fields

Pen & Sword
MILITARY

First published in Great Britain in 2017 by
Pen & Sword Military
an imprint of
Pen & Sword Books Ltd
47 Church Street
Barnsley
South Yorkshire
S70 2AS

ISBN 978 1 47389 508 9

Typeset in Ehrhardt by
Mac Style, Bridlington, East Yorkshire
Printed and bound in the UK by TJ International Ltd, Padstow

Pen & Sword Books Ltd incorporates the imprints of Pen & Sword
Archaeology, Atlas, Aviation, Battleground, Discovery, Family History,
History, Maritime, Military, Naval, Politics, Railways, Select, Transport,
True Crime, and Fiction, Frontline Books, Leo Cooper, Praetorian Press,
Seaforth Publishing and Wharncliffe.

For a complete list of Pen & Sword titles please contact
PEN & SWORD BOOKS LIMITED
47 Church Street, Barnsley, South Yorkshire, S70 2AS, England
E-mail: enquiries@pen-and-sword.co.uk
Website: www.pen-and-sword.co.uk

Contents

Chapter 1

Pilgrim's Picture

Our story begins with a city, but not with just any city. So, let me begin by assuming, or perhaps merely pretending, that you do not know anything about Byzantine Constantinople. If you already know something, you are welcome to yawn over the following preamble to the city.

Constantinople, throughout its long and turbulent history, has been many things to many peoples: the imperial capital of the Christian Roman or Byzantine empire for over a millennium; the head of a struggling Latin kingdom for five decades; the capital of the Ottoman sultanate for nearly five centuries. To outsiders and visitors such as the Rus', who adopted its Orthodox Church, it was Tsarigrad, the city of the Caesar; to western pilgrims *en route* to the Holy Land, it was the New Jerusalem; to the Arabs, who coveted it, it was *Rumiyyat al-kubra*, Great City of the Romans; to the Northmen, who fought in its armies as mercenaries, it was *Mikligarðr*, the Great City; whereas to the citizens themselves, it was simply the City (Gr. ἡ πόλις). Thessaloniki (the biblical Thessalonica) may be a city, as may Antioch, Alexandria or Ephesos, but when the Constantinopolitans spoke of the City they strictly meant Constantinople. Here, in the Queen of Cities (Gr. *băsíleúousa*), anything else would have been redundant.

It is all too easy for us to assume that once the Roman empire lost the West, and Italy, and the eternal city of Rome itself, it was therefore no longer the Roman empire and had become something else. Yet, the state we are considering had long since ceased to depend on Rome or Italy for it identity. It was still the Roman empire, the *Christian* empire of the civilized (viz. Mediterranean) world, whatever territory it had lost. A place called the 'Byzantine empire' is, in fact, the invention of later French historians, and modern scholars still refer to the 'Byzantines' (from their capital's former name of Byzantium), as we shall continue to do, but they regarded themselves (as did those around them in this part of the world) as the 'Romans' (e.g. Ar. *Rum*) even though they were predominantly Greek speaking. Even today, Greek speakers in Turkey are still known as *Rumlar*, an echo of this Roman past, while the modern Greek word for a certain kind of Greekness is *Rhomiosyni*, 'Romanness'.

Consciously modelled on the *first* Rome, the *second* Rome was a worthy successor to the original capital of the Roman empire. The humanist scholar and antiquarian Pierre Gilles (1490–1555), a French visitor to the Ottoman capital who was searching to discover and reconstruct the topography and antiquities of the long-lost Byzantine capital, writes:

> The ancient city of Constantinople had five palaces, fourteen churches [including the Church of the Holy Apostles], six divine residences of the *Augustae*, three most noble houses, eight baths, two basilicas, four forums, two senates, five granaries, two theatres, two mime theatres, four harbours, one circus [the Hippodrome], four cisterns, four *nymphaea* [public fountains], 322 neighbourhoods, 4,388 large houses, fifty-two porticoes, 153 private baths, twenty public mills, 120 private mills, 117 stairways, five meat markets… the Forum of Augustus [the Augusteon], the Capitol, the Mint and three ports.[1]

The chosen site was that magnificent setting between Europe and Asia protected by the inlet of the Golden Horn to the north, the Bosporus to the east and the Sea of Marmara to the south. The weakest side of what was then occupied by the Greek *polis* of Byzantium was the landward: few natural obstacles stood between this and the vast plains rolling northwest towards the Danube. The emperor Constantinus rebuilt it, enlarged it, repopulated it, and encircled it with excellent walls.

According to Dionysios Byzantii, who was writing before a furious Septimius Severus destroyed his Greek city in 196 following a siege that had dragged on for three years, the original circuit of Byzantium was forty *stadia* in length,[2] expertly constructed, we learn from Herodian, who saw the ruins, 'out of millstone hewn into blocks and fitted together with such close mortises that one might think it was carved from a single block of stone rather than being jointed'.[3] It is possible to gather this from Pausanias, who tells us in his *Guide to Greece*:

> I have not seen the walls of Babylon or the walls of Memnon at Susa in Persia, nor have I heard the account of any eyewitness; but the walls of Ambrossos in Phokis, at Byzantium and at Rhodes, all of them the most strongly fortified places, are not so strong as the Messenian walls [in the Peloponnesus].[4]

We can only wonder what these three Greek gentlemen would have written concerning the land walls of Constantinus had they been fortunate enough to gaze upon them, not to mention the mighty double land walls of Theodosius II.

The new land walls of Constantinus stretched in a great semicircle from the Golden Horn across to the Sea of Marmara,[5] which roughly trebled the area occupied by the old Greek *polis*, while sea walls were added, to link up with those rebuilt by Septimius Severus. A well-travelled visitor would have noted that the newly built Constantinople was emphatically a rival to Rome: a ceremonial Senate, a Capitol, a main forum, a milepost (the Milion) from which all distances in the empire were measured. Constantinople also boasted seven hills and fourteen districts; the same number as its illustrious predecessor Rome, ancient but perhaps not eternal.

The new capital had, therefore, a threefold destiny. By history it was linked to Rome and the Roman empire; by foundation it was the first city of Christendom, by situation and language it was Greek and tied to the Hellenistic world of Alexander the Great of Macedon and to the high intellectual heritage of classical antiquity and classical Greece. Nonetheless, as mentioned above, its emperors and people proudly regarded themselves as *Romaioi*, not *Hellênikés*.[6] This serves to remind us that Alexander, who put paid once and for all to the independence of the free *poleis* of classical Greece (Athens, Sparta, Thebes, Corinth, and the rest) and then blazed his way to the borders of India effectively snuffing out the vast Persian empire as he did so, was a crucial figure in Roman culture. He was the forerunner of the world conquerors of the Roman Republic (Sulla, Lucullus, Pompey, Caesar, and the others), the yardstick of Roman military glory, and eventually the rôle model for successive Roman emperors. More than that, his conquests shaped the world stage not only for the Macedonian and Greek generals that disputed and carved up his conquests after his death, but later for the Romans too, Rome in the process irresistibly rising from a middle-ranking tribal stronghold to the greatest imperial superpower the world had ever known.

Straddling its seven hills and secure behind its elaborate defences, the city of Constantinus, the imperial powerhouse of the later Roman world, was clearly designed to impress outsiders. The scale of its defences and the density and majesty of its skyline, its urban landscape packed with palaces, villas, churches and monuments, must have been striking. And then there were the hordes of bronze and marble masterpieces that had been whisked off from all over the Mediterranean to adorn Constantinople, a brazen attempt to place the new world capital on a cultural par with her more venerable sisters, such as Rome, Alexandria and Athens.

The noonday sun, catching the walls and terraces of some of the finest buildings in the empire, would have flashed like fire from roofs and domes sheathed in burnished bronze. To any traveller approaching from the glistening waters of the Bosporus, the dazzling metropolis – as if heated in a crucible – seemed to rise out of liquid metal. The Norse poet Bölverkr Arnórsson describes the young Haraldr Sigurðarson watching the gleaming roofs of the city on his approach down the Bosporus: 'The excellent king saw the metal-covered roofs of *Mikligarðr* out ahead; many a beautiful ship drew next to the high end of the city'.[7] As the future king of Norway was to soon find out, even at night Constantinople shimmered; it was one of the few cities in the empire to have street lighting. This was a city of golden opportunities, an emporium of golden dreams, ruled by a potential employer rich in worldly wealth and furniture, fat in foodstuffs and padded in soft raiment. We can imagine Haraldr's engaging sense of marvel at the size, scale and splendour of the great city.

Such sights and delights, along with the prosperity and politeness of Constantinople, would have been a source of wonder to any visiting Northman. From as early as the tenth century, Northmen had recorded their impressions of *Mikligarðr* and its splendours, which permeate Old Norse literature and are possibly based on the routine and ceremony of the Constantinopolitan court, something the Varangians would have intimately known. But this is a topic to be taken up in another place. Suffice to say at this moment, in the mediaeval period ultimate sovereignty had an ultimate source – God himself – and the Byzantine emperor could be seen as one of his most distinguished representatives. When seen in this light, the fact that Northmen would have taken service with the most Christian emperor, 'the earthly counterpart and vice-regent of the Christ Pantokrator',[8] is to be expected. Besides, the northern adventurer's thrill of the boundless sea and the lure of its lucrative ports of call were foremost in the minds of these bold predators, while the sword arm was a saleable commodity, naturally. Having been brought up in a heroic tradition, he was willing to fight and die for a noble man he chose as lord, whatever the man's nationality. The Northman was offered a chance to do what he excelled at – fighting and killing – and where could loyal service be more honourable and reward more bounteous than in the sumptuous treasure-city of the Bosporus?

Splendid, almost unimaginable wealth and finery is characteristic of the Byzantine empire in the prose sagas composed on the small, rugged island of Iceland in the middle of the North Atlantic. Most clearly this copiousness is best expressed by a single line from the *Heimskringla*: 'The God of Greece throne is so heavenly rich'.[9] That is the impression given by the mosaic depictions of Christ Pantokrator, which must have appealed particularly to the Northman psyche, being so fond of gold and extravagance. Norse far-travellers who return from that southern empire physically display this fondness, such as the conspicuous showmanship of Bolli Bollason decked out in scarlet silk and gold,[10] the costume of court officials, or Haraldr Sigurðarson's gold ornamented, silken-sailed ship and chests of gold,[11] and Norse visitors to Constantinople see it on display all around them, such as Alexios I Komnenos' splendid gifts to Sigurðr I Magnússon *Jórsalafari* (Jerusalem-traveller).[12] These three Norse heroes we shall meet anon in another book.

It is said that gold is the mother of armies, and in Byzantium the Northmen encountered the only state in mediaeval Europe whose fiscal organization permitted regular paying of mercenaries. The inevitable burden imposed by the retention of mercenary forces was the need for their remuneration – or other form of support – in respect of sword-service rendered. In the smaller and economically weaker early mediaeval European states, the maintenance of large standing armies was simply impossible. In the tenth and the eleventh centuries, armies numbering even 10,000 soldiers were considered very large, and it was difficult to maintain them for a long period of time.[13] By way of a contemporary comparison, the largest number ever mustered by the Latin kingdom of Jerusalem numbered no more than 15,000,[14] and this was a kingdom at war.

It was the Iberian rabbi and world traveller Benjamin of Tudela (1130–73) who once said:

> Wealth like that of Constantinople is not to be found in the whole world. Here also are men learned in all the books of the Greeks, and they eat and drink every man under his vine and his fig-tree.[15]

Similar sentiments were expressed by the humble French knight Robert de Clari, albeit during the systematic looting of Constantinople by the crusaders of the Fourth Crusade:

> Not since the world was made was there ever seen or won so great a treasure or so noble or so rich, nor in the time of Alexander nor in the time of Charlemagne nor before nor after. Nor do I think, myself, that in the forty richest cities of the world there has been so much wealth as was found in Constantinople.[16]

In general, all Latin chroniclers, whatever their views of the Constantinopolitans or their activities in the city, praised Constantinople, and the crusaders of the First Crusade are some of the most enthusiastic. Fulcher de Chartres, chaplain to Baldwin of Edessa (r. 1097–1100) – who was soon destined to be the second king of the Latin kingdom of Jerusalem (r. 1100–18) – spoke of the marvels of Constantinople as an enthralled eyewitness:

> Oh, what an excellent and beautiful city! How many monasteries, and how many palaces there are in it, of wonderful work skilfully fashioned! How many marvellous works are to be seen in the streets and districts of the city! It is a great nuisance to recite what an opulence of all kinds of goods are found there; of gold, of silver, of many kinds of mantles, and of holy relics. In every season, merchants, in frequent sailings, bring to that place everything that man might need. Almost twenty thousand eunuchs, I judge, are kept there continuously.[17]

Even allowing for the mediaeval propensity for exaggerating, this was undoubtedly one of biggest, and certainly the most splendid, cities in Christendom.

As for Fulcher's claim about the number of eunuchs, it does seem excessive, yet we cannot prove him wrong. Eunuchs, castrated males who could normally be recognized by their lack of facial hair, played a significant rôle in Byzantium.

Indeed, the emperors were quite willing to employ eunuchs in their service, even as military commanders: for example, Iustinianus' great general Narses (d. 574) was a Perso-Armenian eunuch (who continued to successfully lead armies in the field into his nineties). This practice, abhorrent as it is to us, was because a eunuch, no matter how powerful, was seen as a safer option as no eunuch could hope to become emperor. Indeed, fear of usurpation appears to have also played a rôle in Narses' promotion. Where Prokopios of Caesarea Palestinae only insinuated, his continuer Agathias made it plain that the non-campaigning Iustinianus felt threatened by the growing popularity of his other top-flight general, Belisarius.[18]

Still, Fulcher's figure would have included those serving the great houses of the city as well as the imperial court. Obviously for Fulcher, an unsophisticated westerner primarily acquainted with the cities of Chartres and Orléans, and whose sojourn was lengthy, Constantinople made a lasting impression.

The *Gesta francorum et aliorum Hierosolymitanorum* ('Deeds of the Franks and Other Jerusalemers') was a popular work written by a crusader who followed Bohémond of Taranto, and later continued to Jerusalem with other crusader contingents when his lord remained at Antioch. Anyway, our anonymous author whole heartedly agreed with Fulcher's view of Constantinople and considers the city the centre of the mercantile world:

> O how great a city! How noble! How pleasant! How full of churches and palaces created with wondrous skill! What spectacles! What fabulous things are contained in her, worked in gold and marble![19]

A great city indeed, given the fact that the population of Constantinople at this time may have well reached the half-a-million mark, a very impressive establishment given that royal Paris, the strongest and largest city west of Constantinople, had fewer than 100,000 inhabitants. Curiously enough, mediaeval Paris was considered – in wisdom, might and holiness – a new Athens, Rome and Jerusalem, and by virtue of its university alone, the theological arbiter of Europe, it was the 'Athens of Europe'; the Goddess of Wisdom, it was said, after leaving Athens and then Rome, had made it her home. Yet, there never was a city like Constantinople, the guardian of the narrow straits of the Hellespont and the keeper of the black waters of the Euxine. As Benjamin of Tudela pointed out, 'there is no other [city] like it in all the countries, except Baghdad',[20] an observation added after his stay in the Mesopotamian city at a later stage of his worldly travels.

Girded by its mighty walls, Constantinople excited awe, admiration and not a little apprehensive amongst westerners, especially when they are not welcome. Take, for example, the vivid insight provided by the pen of Geoffrey of Villehardouin (d. 1212), a leading member and historian of the Fourth Crusade:

I can assure you that all those who have never seen Constantinople before gazed very intently upon the city, having never imagined there could be so fine a place in the entire world. They noted the high walls and lofty towers encircling it, and its rich palaces and tall churches, of which there was so many that no one would have believed it to be true if he had not seen it with his own eyes, and viewed the length and breadth of that city which reigns supreme over all others. There was indeed no man so brave and daring that his flesh did not shudder at the sight.[21]

As a centre of power and influence, the dazzling metropolis of Constantinople must have seemed to possess a magnetic attraction, constantly attracting people from a diversity of linguistic, religious, cultural, and regional backgrounds. But how does one describe Constantinople to someone who has never been there and never will?

Half a millennium ago Pierre Gilles rightly concluded the following about Constantinople: 'It seems to me that while other cities may be mortal, this one will remain as long as there are men on earth'.[22] He was a visitor to the city during the golden age of the Ottoman empire, and at the time of the Frenchman's arrival in 1544 Constantinople (the name continued to be used by Greeks and even some Turks until the establishment of the Turkish Republic in 1923) was the largest and wealthiest city in Europe. Its nearly 700,000 inhabitants rivalled the combined populations of Venice, Palermo, Messina, Catania and Naples, significant cities at the time. It was the Mediterranean capital, and home to a truly international population of diverse origins, much as it had been in the golden age of the Byzantine empire. At that time Constantinople had been indisputably the greatest metropolis in the Christian world, and for some belonged to the world of fable and faerie, a promised land, a never-never land, a faraway land seen through the gauze of fabulous fairy tales revealing an occasional nugget of reality. Such otherworldly perceptions the modern mind will find difficult to understand, rooted as they are in the mental attitudes of mediaeval people. But this outline description is only a small part of our story.

Chapter 2

Before Constantine

Any history of Constantinople must start with the history of the Bosporus, the narrow sea channel dividing Europe from Asia. As Pierre Gilles so eloquently points out, the Bosporus is 'the first creator of Byzantium greater more important than Byzas, the founder of the City'.[1] In the following passage he sums up the predominant importance of this 'Strait that Purpasses all straits' by the epigram: 'The Bosporus with one key opens and closes two worlds, two seas'.[2] How spot on he was.

Crossing of the Cow

The Bosporus (Gr. Βόσπορος) is so named by the Greeks because Io, the daughter of the river god Inachos, crossed here from Europe to Asia.[3] Poor Io had been transformed into a white cow (Gr. βός) by the supreme god Zeus, who coveted her but needed to hide her from his long-suffering wife, the domineering Hera. He was a serial adulterer, a husband who habitually strayed due to his sensual nature. She, however, was not taken in by his chicanery, and had Io in her bovine form guarded by Argos Panoptes, a giant with a hundred eyes. Of these eyes, only two would sleep at any one time, so that Argos could remain watchful with the other ninety-eight. Not to be outdone by his jealous wife, Zeus sent Hermes, who was always ready to support his father in his extramarital escapades, to Argos, with an order to kill the ever vigilant giant.

The cunning Hermes disguised himself as a cowherd and was able to close all of Argos' hundred eyes by playing sweet melodies on his flute. As soon as Argos had fallen asleep, Hermes crushed him with a boulder, cut off his head, and released Io. Hera was furious. She, having placed Argos' eyes in the tail of a peacock as a constant reminder of his foul murder, set a gadfly to sting Io and chase her all over the world. During her frantic four-legged globetrotting, poor Io plunged into the waters that separate Europe from Asia and bequeathed them the name by which they have ever since been known, Bosporus, or Crossing of the Cow.[4]

The next event in the legendary history of the Bosporus is the passage of the Argonauts on their way to Kolchis at the far end of the Euxine, today's Black Sea, to seek a golden fleece. This was the pelt of the golden ram upon which Phrixos and Helle had flown to Kolchis. The royal twins were fleeing from their wicked stepmother Ino. Along the way, Helle fell off the ram and drowned in the sea that was named for her – Hellespont. Phrixos was able to reach Kolchis and stayed there at the court of Æetes. The golden fleece of the ram was hung up in a grove of Ares and guarded by a sleepless dragon.

The fifty Argonauts sailed on the *Argo*, a ship built by Argus (with the help of Athena) and captained by Iason of Iolkos in Thessaly. A band of young Greek champions, each of the Argonauts were excellent warriors. They included Castor and Polydeuces (twin brothers of Helen), Peleus (father of Achilles), Atalanta (virgin huntress), Orpheus (famed poet and musician), Zetes and Kalais (winged sons of Boreas, the north wind), and even the greatest hero of all, the powerful Herakles. The expedition took place some years before the Trojan War.[5] With regards to the Bosporus and the Argonauts, many of their stop off points along the way were recorded, among which the sanctuary of Zeus *Oúrios*, of Poseidon, or of the twelve gods.

The sanctuary of Zeus *Oúrios*, his epithet means 'granter of fair winds',[6] stood at the northern end of the Bosporus, probably on the Asiatic shore near the entrance to the strait as one approached from the Euxine.[7] Tucked away in the British Museum is an inscribed stone base.[8] It once supported a votive statue of Zeus *Oúrios* from his Bosporus sanctuary and sings his praises in elegiac verse:

> The mariner who sets his sail / For the Blue Eddies, where the gale / Rolls a big breaker on the sand, / Or backward bound for fatherland / Would cross the Aegean – let him call / From poop to Pilot of us all, / Zeus of the Fair Breeze, aye and put / His cakes before the statue's foot; / For here above the watery waste / Antipatros' son Philon placed / The god who meets us as we roam / With promise of safe voyage home.[9]

As to which shore this popular mariner's cult stood, tradition was twofold. The second-century BC Greek historian Polybios, describing the Asiatic shore of the Bosporus, begins with 'Hieron, at which place they say that Iason on his return from Kolchis first sacrificed to the twelve gods'.[10] Pomponius Mela, writing under the emperor Claudius (r. AD 41–54), puts it more curtly: 'The god of the temple is Zeus, its founder is Iason'.[11] But Timosthenes of Rhodes, who commanded the Egyptian fleet of Ptolemaios II Philadelphos (r. 285–246), makes the altar to the Twelve Gods a dedication of the hero Phrixos.[12] However, Dionysios Byzantii, our local historian, recognizes *two* sanctuaries, one on the European, the other on the Asiatic, side of the strait. Of the former he notes: 'They say that here Iason sacrificed to the twelve gods'.[13] Of the latter he states: 'Hieron, the "sanctuary" was built by Phrixos, son of Nephele and Athamas, on his voyage to Kolchis'.[14] The founder was, then, either

Iason or Phrixos. Both attributions amount to much the same thing. For Iason was son of Æson, son of Kretheus, son of Aiolos, while Phrixos was son of Athamas, son of Aiolos. Zeus *Oúrios*, of course, was but a later cultic manifestation of Aiolos himself, the ruler of the winds.

What is important to understand is that when coming to new places, Greek colonists invariably brought with them their ancestral gods. Several of these *lieux de mémoire* have therefore been duplicated, commonly as a result of the competition between Byzantion and its rival colony across the water, Chalcedon (see below). Such stories, dating prior to the foundation of Byzantium and Chalcedon, are essentially legends retailed by ancient authors to add value to their establishment through the combination of human and divine phenomena. In this type of story most of the time it is impossible to know where myth and legend ends and history begins. Once myth and history are intertwined, it is no easy task to separate them again over the passage of time. So much for the mythical narrative.

Physically speaking, the Bosporus measures some thirty-two kilometres long, running in the general direction south-south-west to north-north-east from the Sea of Marmara to the Black Sea. The narrowest passage, 700 metres wide, is between the two Ottoman fortresses, Anadolu Hisarı (built by Beyazit I *Yıldırım* in 1394) and Rumeli Hisarı (by Mehmet II in 1452). It was here that Dareios I chose to construct his bridge of boats, designed by the Greek engineer Mandrokles of Samos, when in 512 BC he led his Persian army against the Scythians. While his army crossed the Great King watched from a stone throne cut into the cliff above the waters of the Bosporus.[15] Further north from this crossing point is the widest passage, some 3.4 kilometres wide, between the two lighthouses of Rumeli Feneri (near the village of Büyükdere) and Anaduli Feneri.

One geomorphologic theory is that the Bosporus originally followed the line of a prehistoric river valley and that the sea channel we now know was formed in about 5600 BC when the rising waters of the Mediterranean and the Sea of Marmara breached through to the Black Sea, which at the time was a low-lying body of fresh water. Some people think that the resulting massive flooding of the northern shores of the Black Sea is the historic basis for the flood stories found in the *Epic of Gilgamesh* and Noah's Flood in the Bible. Another theory holds that the deep and jagged cleft of the Bosporus was formed as part of a cataclysmic earthquake caused by movement in the nearby African and the Eurasian tectonic plates. This theory is supported by the appearance of the opposing shores of the Bosporus, which seem to fit each other like the pieces of a jigsaw puzzle. In fact, from a geological point of view, the zone is still notoriously active.

The narrow sea channel has a depth that varies from thirteen to 110 metres in midstream with an average of sixty-five metres. It has two strong currents, the upper one flowing from the Black Sea in a southerly direction to the Sea of Marmara, and the lower one in the opposite direction. The predominant surface current flows at a rate of three to five kilometres per hour, but because of the sinuosity of the channel, eddies producing strong reverse currents flow along most of the indentations of the shore. A very strong wind may reverse the main surface current and make it flow toward the Black Sea, in which case the counter eddies also change their direction. The sub-surface current lies at a depth of about forty metres, and this is so strong that fishing nets can sometimes drag boats north against the surface flow. And then there are the occasional storms that lash it and the impregnable fogs that envelop it. When you consider some 80,000 vessels pass through the Bosporus annually, 10 per cent of which are crude oil or liquefied natural gas tankers, this maritime waterway is one tricky customer when it comes to navigating its winding waters. One wonders if Zeus *Oúrios* is still doing business with Bosporus navigators.

What's in a name?

Byzantion, Byzantium, Constantinople, Stamboul, Istanbul, the names change but the city remains. Byzantion, as the Greeks knew it, was born of humble origins, the earliest human settlement on the west side of the Bosporus dating from the thirteenth century BC and there has been a Greek city there since the seventh century BC. Byzantion maintained independence as a city-state, or *polis*, until it was annexed by Dareios I in 512 BC into the Persian empire, who saw the site as the optimal location to construct a pontoon bridge crossing into Europe as Byzantion was situated at the narrowest point in the Bosporus strait. Persian rule lasted until 478 BC, when, as part of the Greek counterattack to the recent invasion of Greece by Xerxes, a Greek coalition army led by the Spartan *stratêgos* Pausanias captured Byzantion.

Pausanias was soon recalled by the authorities in Sparta from his post after they received complaints of his overbearing behaviour. When he departed for home, Byzantion and other *poleis* in the region placed themselves under the aegis of Athens. Pausanias was acquitted of charges, though not reinstated to his command. However, Pausanias decided otherwise and returned privately to Byzantion, seized the *polis* and, in contrast to Spartan custom and practice, set himself up as its tyrant.[16] Finally expelled forcibly from Byzantion by the Athenians, Pausanias was alleged to have adopted the manners and dress of a Persian satrap. Worse still, not only did Pausanias lead a lavish and comfortable existence at Byzantion, he also appears to have entered into an alliance with the Persian Great King.[17] Wishing to avoid suspicion, Pausanias returned home to Sparta only to be imprisoned. Escaping from his confinement, he was finally cornered in the temple of Athena of the Brazen House, where he was walled up and left to starve to death.[18] Somewhat of an inglorious end for the glorious victor of Plataia.

Byzantion remained an independent, yet subordinate, state under the Athenians, although in 440 BC it joined Samos in a revolt against Athenian domination, but in the following year they gave up the attempt and resumed their tributary status. It was during these troubled times that Byzantion, the gateway to the north Aegean, became a major player in the Mediterranean world when it went to war with Athens against Sparta 431 BC, the conflict we know as the Peloponnesian War (431–404 BC). However, in 411 BC Byzantion revolted once again against Athens, allying itself with Sparta,[19] but three years later the Byzantines and their Spartan allies were defeated in a naval engagement in the Hellespont. Alcibiades, who commanded the Athenian fleet, soon afterwards took control of Byzantion and then was welcomed home in triumph and given full command by land and sea.[20] Within six months the brilliant but reckless Alcibiades had been rejected once again by the Athenians, a decision that was to cost them dearly.

After the defeat of Athens, Byzantion was garrisoned by Sparta and it was still under a Spartan governor when Xenophon and the remnants of the Ten Thousand arrived at its gates in 400 BC. Xenophon and his mercenary comrades were so inhospitably treated that in retaliation they forced their way into the *polis* and, according to Xenophon, would have sacked it but for the pacifying effect of one of his speeches.[21] During the first half of the fourth century BC, Byzantion was once again in enforced alliance with Athens, which imposed a 10 per cent toll on all ships passing through the Bosporus.[22] In the year 364 BC, however, the Byzantines placed themselves under the command of the brilliant Theban *stratêgos* Epameinondas,[23] joining him in his war against the Athenians. In spite of this, the Athenians, through the preaching of Demosthenes,[24] put aside their former hostility to the Byzantines, made an alliance, and sent out a naval contingent to Byzantion when it was invested by Philip II of Macedon in the summer of 340 BC. But the Byzantines fought well and successfully held off the Macedonians in a year-long siege, which included the first recorded use of the torsion-powered catapult. After his final assault was betrayed by inopportunely barking dogs, and despite all his ingenuity in military matters, Philip broke off the siege.[25]

Despite their spirit defence against Philip, the Byzantines had enough good sense not to resist his son, Alexander the Great. Soon after Alexander's victory at the Granikos in 334 BC, the *polis* capitulated and opened its gates to the Macedonians. After Alexander's sudden demise in 323 BC, Byzantion was involved in the collapse and dismemberment of his empire and the subsequent eastward expansion of Rome. From the very beginning of its history Byzantion was an important centre for trade and commerce – the Athenians were very much dependent on grain imports from Scythia – and noted for its wine and fisheries. Not all the wine was exported, apparently, for the Byzantines had the reputation of being inveterate boozers. From the end of the fourth century BC we have the earliest societal descriptions of

Byzantion, which refers to the *polis* as a rowdy port full of winos and villains. The Athenian dramatist Menander (d. 292/1 BC), in his comedy *Auletris* ('The Flute Girl'), delights his theatre audience with the statement that Byzantion is populated with sottish merchants. Says one of the characters in his play:

> Byzantion makes all the traders tipsy. The whole night through for your sake we were drinking, and, thinks 'twas very strong wine too. At any rate I got up with a head on for four.[26]

But then greed became the ruling policy of the *polis*.

In the year 220 BC Rhodes went to war with Byzantion to protect the freedom of the seas; the Byzantines were levying dues from ships sailing onto the Black Sea.[27] The naval war ended when Byzantion agreed to abolish the duty they had introduced.[28] In the year 179 BC Byzantion was captured by the combined naval forces of Rhodes, Pergamon and Bithynia. A century later Byzantion was a pawn in the titanic struggle between Mithridates VI Eupator, king of Pontus, and Rome. After the final victory of Rome, Byzantium, as the Romans called it, became its client state, and thereby enjoyed the fruits of some three centuries of quiet prosperity under the mantle of *pax Romana*.

The three seas

It is true to say, the Mediterranean was the Greeks' first love. It was their home sea, offering a convenient space that could be used for colonization and commerce. Byzantion's geographical situation was superb, and it was the judicious Polybios who sagely observes that

> the site of Byzantion is as regards to the sea more favourable to security and prosperity than that of any *polis* in the world known to us… The Greeks, then, would entirely lose all this commerce or it would be quite unprofitable to them, if the Byzantines were disposed to be deliberately unfriendly to them.[29]

Even Septimius Severus (r. 193–211), after taking the city in 196 in a long and bitter siege that resulted in great destruction (its citizens had supported a rival candidate in the civil war that made him emperor), was quick to rebuild the ancient *polis* so as to benefit from the commercial and strategic importance of Byzantium's location.

It was through its waterways that Constantinople was to manifest its true nature. Perched on a triangular peninsula at the extremity of the flat-lands of Thrace, the city was a place formed by nature for command. Strategically situated at the narrow crossing from Europe to Asia, the city watched over the profitable sea-lane between the Mediterranean and the Euxine, a region that provided fish, grain, honey, wax and costly furs. To its south was the Propontis, today's Sea of Marmara, while to its northeast was the deep, virtually tide-less, seawater harbour still known as the Golden Horn.[30] Northward from the tip of the city ran the Bosporus, joining the Euxine to the Sea of Marmara, and thence through the Hellespont of antiquity, today's Dardanelles, the strategic narrows flanked by the fatal shores of Gallipoli and Troy, to the Mediterranean. The shining sea was visible from almost anywhere in Constantinople, and in the eloquent words of Prokopios of Caesarea Palestinae its watery surrounds formed a 'garland around the city',[31] a sentiment repeated by Pierre Gilles when he says 'Constantinople is washed on three sides by the sea'.[32]

A Greek poet might have once compared Constantinople, the Queen of Cities, with a ship moored at the intersection of two continents, Europe and Asia, and two seas, the Mediterranean and the Euxine, yet believe it not the importance of this prime location was not immediately realized. During the seventh century BC the *poleis* of Greece were busily taking to their agile boats and planting colonies along the seaboard of Anatolia, but Kyzikos (near Bandırma) and Lampsakos (Lapseki) had both become important before Byzantion was even founded. So had Chalcedon (Kadıköy), on the Asiatic side of the Bosporus, for Herodotos says that the foundation of Chalcedon antedated that of Byzantion by seventeen years.[33] Incidentally, both were colonies of one of Athens' neighbours, Megara.

According to tradition, Byzantion was founded in the first-half of the seven century BC, perhaps in 668/7 BC, by the eponymous chief of the colonists, Byzas of Megara.[34] Both traditions have been disputed, and archaeological evidence on the site of the ancient acropolis (now occupied by the Topkapı Sarayı) puts the establishment of the colony a generation later. It is Herodotos who also reports that the Persian general Megabazos, who was in Byzantion in the year 511 BC or thereabout, observed that the colonists of Chalcedon must have been blind at the time to miss the superior spot just across the water.[35] Naturally enough, in later years this judgement was appropriated by the priests of the shrine of Pythian Apollo at Delphi, while the Chalcedonian blindness was repeatedly noted in all kinds of literary records. Both Strabo and Tacitus, for example, recount the expedition from Megara consulted the oracle there before setting out in their boats and were instructed to build 'opposite to the land of the blind men'.[36] Being blind, the previous band of Megarian colonists apparently did not detect that Byzantion's physical setting in relation to its surrounding waters was to be its most important advantage.

Chapter 3

Holy Queen

T here is a fascinating eighteenth-century egg-tempera on wood icon, which stands a little under a metre in height, to be found in a private collection in Athens. According to the fragmentary inscription on the back, the image represents the siege of Constantinople by the Turkic Avars in 626. Like the Huns before them, the Turkic Avars, who are actually depicted in the icon as Ottoman Turks (who now rule Constantinople), were Inner Asian horse warriors. A supranational federation, they, too, shared the Huns' grand ambitions and ruthless drive. With a vocation for destruction, nomadic groupings like the Huns and the Avars swallowed the variety of smaller tribal clans within their sphere of influence, with terror and booty providing the necessary cement. Their existence, therefore, required regular warfare, and their hard-nosed warlords had the manpower to overrun the defences of even major cities.

Yet, the destruction of Constantinople by the Avars (and their Slav and Sasanian allies) was averted only by the military skills of the soldier emperor Herakleios (r. 610–41) or, as was otherwise claimed and is clearly alluded to in this icon, by the Virgin Mary. In fact, the emperor was not present, being far away from Constantinople on a military expedition in the territory of the Sasanians, and had even declined to return to protect his capital.

In the year 626, Tuesday 29 July, Constantinople was saved, as the pious Constantinopolitans firmly believed, by the intercession of the Virgin and her miracle-working icon. The siege had lasted a mere seven days – *seven days* – for on 7 August the Avars abruptly lifted their operations and departed in haste. All Constantinopolitans, from the senior nobles to the most humble citizens, rejoiced and celebrated their deliverance from evil, attributing the auspicious outcome to the direct intervention of the Virgin Mary: how else could it have been so? For, according to the eyewitness account of Theodore Synkellos, the Virgin Mary was clearly seen walking on the city walls and engaging in hand-to-hand fighting with the pagan besiegers, and by her actions she 'preserved her subjects safe and sound, and devastated the enemy masses'.[1] But how was this so?

The image on our eighteenth-century icon has Constantinople besieged on land and by sea, while on the anachronistically cannon-festooned city walls Sergios, patriarch of Constantinople (r. 610–58), presides with attendant clergy over the procession of the icons of Christ Pantokrator and the Virgin Hodegetria.[2] According to the written tradition, the second icon was regarded as a portrait of the Mother and Child painted during their lifetime by the apostle Luke and sent to Constantinople in the fifth century to the virgin empress Pulcheria by her sister-in-law, the empress Eudokia.[3] True or not, what is important is the fact that the Hodegetria icon was greatly venerated by the Constantinopolitans. In the words of our eyewitness, the patriarch 'beseeched God and the Virgin to keep the city, the lighthouse of the law of the Christians, intact, because it is to be feared that with her even the lessons of the mystery of Christ could run into extreme danger'.[4] The patriarch and his retinue then paraded 'around all the ramparts of the city, and he showed the icon, as an invincible weapon, towards the nebulous troops of darkness and the phalanxes of the West [the Avars]'.[5]

However, Bissera Pentcheva reckons, even though images of the Virgin were placed on the city walls to ward off the enemy attacks, the object carried by the patriarch was an *acheiropoietos* (viz. not made by human hands) of Christ, not a Marian icon.[6] Her argument is based on the premise that 'Theodore Synkellos promotes the belief that the patriarch Sergios ensured the Byzantine victory by raising the image of Christ'.[7] In an earlier paper, Pentcheva notes that the 'Byzantine Virgin thus appeared to have acted in a manner similar to the pagan goddess of war [Pallas Athena]. Her help was perceived to have been manifested in her physical appearance, not through her icon'.[8] A second contemporary source, the *Chronicon paschale*, does not mention icons of any sort,[9] but its anonymous author does say that in the crucial moment of the siege 'the impious *khagan* [the Avar warlord]... saw a woman with an august bearing running along the walls'.[10] This figure could be identified with the Virgin Mary, who, according to Theodore Synkellos, appears in person and fights for the Constantinopolitans.[11]

It seems that the notion of a public procession around the city walls with Marian icons during the siege of 626 was an altered perception of the past that came about at a much later date, possibly around the second half of the tenth century, but once it did, it triggered the creation of a powerful myth that linked the panel with the early history of Constantinople, the Avar siege included.[12] Notwithstanding, whether by personal presence and engagement in battle or by her assistance realized through her icons (more specifically the Hodegetria), this was looked upon by the Constantinopolitans as a Marian miracle. Whether a miracle occurred or not is immaterial. What is important to note is the Constantinopolitans devoutly believed in the Virgin Mary and her ability to aid them in times of extreme peril. Miracles and faith in the Virgin have grown unfashionable. Even so, we should not allow an anti-spiritual bias in the study of mediaeval history to prevent us from accepting the fact that the possibility of the miraculous was exceptionally strong in an age so very different from our own. The mediaeval mind could readily adapt itself to ideas which, to a modern, rigorously analytical mind, might appear mutually inconsistent.

In the year 860 the Constantinopolitans needed another Marian miracle. In the absence of the emperor, Michael III (r. 842–67), and his navy, dreaded for its use of Greek fire, the Rus' under the princes of Kiev swept down and occupied the waters around Constantinople. Having rushed back to the city from Anatolia, where he had been fighting the Arabs, the emperor immediately retired to the church of the Virgin Mary of Blachernai, situated on imperial land just outside the land walls at that time. There, on the advice of the patriarch of Constantinople, Photios (r. 858–67, 877–86), her outer veil,[13] a precious relic, was carried from the sanctuary and symbolically dipped in the sea. A seasonal tempest scattered the fleet of the 'godless *Rhôs*',[14] thereby removing the threat to the city, and this was joyously ascribed to the direct intervention of the holy Mother of God.[15]

The divine general

A curious point: for over a millennium the Virgin Mary, 'she who bore the One Who is God', has been a heavenly patron of Christian war and Marian relics and images has been used to claim legitimacy. Not only did her sacred icon apparently serve as a supernatural weapon to fend off the destruction of Constantinople by the Avars, or her holy veil that of the Rus' too, but her banner led the army of the First Crusade across Anatolia.[16] In a moment of crisis the emperor Basil II (r. 976–1025) took an icon of the Theometor (Mother of God) in his hand in the battle against the usurper Bardas Phokas on 13 April 989, at Abydos.[17] Facing insurmountable difficulties at the battle of Beroë (Stara Zagora) in 1122, John II Komnenos (r. 1118–43) looked 'upon the icon of the Mother of God and, wailing loudly and gesturing pitifully, shed tears hotter than the sweat of battle'.[18] According to Michael Psellos, this was 'the icon of the Theometor, the image which Roman emperors habitually carried with them on campaign as a guide and guardian of all the army'.[19] This supernatural protector of Byzantine emperors in battle was probably an icon from the Blachernai church, called the Blachernitissa.[20] The icon was called 'general', 'guard and general', 'guardian of all the army', 'invincible weapon', 'invincible co-general', 'invincible ally', and 'unconquerable fellow general of the emperor'.[21]

Clearly, the Blachernitissa was not linked to the protection of Constantinople but to imperial victory and military expeditions outside the city. It was that other famous icon of the Virgin Mary, the Hodegetria, which remained in Constantinople as a guardian. Niketas Choniates (d. 1217), who was present in the city during the siege by the armies of western Christendom, wrote that the Constantinopolitans regarded this icon of the Virgin Mary as the emperor's 'fellow general'.[22] Taken by the crusaders in a cavalry skirmish outside the walls of Constantinople,[23] the holy relic was to be given to the Cistercian abbey of Cîtreaux in the county of Champagne. Robert de Clari wrote of the Byzantines *vis-à-vis* this particular icon:

> They have so great faith in this icon that they fully believe that no one who carries it in battle can be defeated, and we believe that it was because Mourtzouphlos had no right to carry it that he was defeated.[24]

The sinister Mourtzouphlos ('the traitor',[25] as Robert de Clari dubbed him) had just overthrown Alexios IV Angelos (r. 1203–4) in his bid for the throne, succeeding in that quest to rule as Alexios V Doukas (r. 1204). Mourtzouphlos, whose nickname referred to his bushy black eyebrows, would reign (and live) long enough to regret his treachery.

Universal and unchanging war deity

Outside our topic of study there are many historical examples of the Virgin Mary in the context of war. Three of the many will suffice here.

A nineteen-year-old virgin, believing herself to have received visions from God, and believing God to have called her to war, was burnt at the stake by the English as a heretic. To some, Jeanne d'Arc was a witness to the one true faith. To others, she was a deluded fantasist, a flush-faced demagogue using God to inspire acts of extreme violence. Almost two years after she had died so cruelly, a servant of the Byzantine emperor John VIII Palaiologos (r. 1425–48) asked a Burgundian visitor whether it was true that Jeanne d'Arc had been captured by the English. 'It seemed to the Greeks an impossible thing', the Burgundian nobleman reported, and when he told them what had become of her, they were 'filled with wonder'.[26] Wonder, indeed. For at the sacred abbey of Saint-Dennis, Jeanne d'Arc had hung as a votive offering before the image of the Virgin Mary 'an entire suit of white armour, of the sort for a man-at-arms, with a sword won before the city of Paris'.[27] The sword was of a prisoner Jeanne had captured in the assault on the walls of Paris, while Jean Chartier, the official chronicler of the reign of Charles VII, reported that the armour was the very armour in which she had been injured during that assault.[28]

The naval victory of Lepanto (7 October 1571) was attributed to the intercession of the Virgin Mary, specifically through the Rosary. From Rome Pius V (r. 1566–72), the very same pope who had just gone and excommunicated Elizabeth I of England for schism, believing that the Holy League fleet was a poor match for the Ottoman armada, had asked all of Catholic Europe to pray for a Christian victory at sea, and it was the papal banner depicting the Blessed Virgin that had led the bickering Catholics during the battle to victory against the Ottoman fleet.

In the *Historia Brittonum*, compiled in the ninth century by the Welsh monk, Nennius, there is a list of twelve victories of Arthur (if he ever existed), which ends with the victory at Badon Hill where Arthur slays 960 men in a single charge. Arthur's twelve battles are named after obscurely named rivers, forests, mountains and cities, and it is generally agreed that the passage is based on a Welsh war song. It is battle number eight that interests us here:

> The eighth battle was in *Guinnion* fort,[29] and in it Arthur carried the image of the holy Mary, the everlasting Virgin, on his shield,[30] and the heathen were put to flight on that day, and there was great slaughter upon them, through the power of Jesus Christ and the power of the holy Virgin Mary, his mother.[31]

Unlike King Arthur, the Virgin Mary is gone from the Anglo-speaking world, though some of us may remember her very well from plaster statues in Roman Catholic churches, blue and white, looking down and away, merciful and implacable at once. For those of other persuasions, however, the veneration of Virgin Mary is dismissed as a contemptible Roman Catholic doctrine, a recrudescence of paganism clothed in Christian garb.

In other parts of the modern world, however, the Virgin still remains powerful, proof that there are still those who are prepared to march behind her sacred person, even willing to die for her. She has always been light and dark – a Manichaean deity. Thus, in more recent memory, the Virgin Mary has presided over the Maronite Christians cause, the dominant sect in Lebanon before the civil war. During this long, slow sectarian war (1975–90) between the coastal Christianized people and the Muslim in-landers, the Maronite militiamen, who modelled themselves on the Latin crusaders, went into battle with crosses sewn on their combat fatigues and icons of the Virgin Mary glued to their rifle butts.

Sectarian wars are nasty affairs, especially when 'sect' means an ethnic group as much as a religion. The goal was to wipe out the other tribe. Such wars break down on ethnic lines simply because religion is almost always adopted by an entire tribe, and used to distinguish 'our' group from 'their' group. Cultures are not in the business of promoting diversity. We humans tend to focus on our differences rather than our similarities. In other words, standard human behaviour. So, the Maronites saw the conflict as a matter of either us or them, a war of extermination on both sides, nobody playing nice – and they were right. In a sectarian war, the whole group is a military unit. Tribal all the way, this kind of war is about what military bureaucrats call 'unit cohesion'. And if it does not cohere, it may not be around very long. To further ensure Maronite cohesion and success in tribal battle, it was not unusual for a priest to offer up on their behalf prayers to the Virgin. Then and now, the Virgin Mary is seen as a sign of divine right for victory.

Mother's mercy

Those of a Protestant background may look upon the Virgin Mary as nothing more than a bit player, a young Jewish girl who made a cameo appearance in the Christmas pageant, then quickly faded into the background. A Protestant may well argue that Mary was an incidental participant in the incarnation, not much more than an incubator for Jesus Christ, or even go so far as to argue that Mary was perhaps an example of Christian obedience and submission. Most Protestant exegetes begin with the premise that Mariology cannot be proven in scripture.

In contrast, Orthodox theology regards the Virgin Mary as the 'crown of creation and the supreme-created embodiment of human nobility'.[32] Through her God became man for the salvation of humankind, and thus she was crucial factor in linking man with God. For in her Christ took human form, through the regular 'natural' process. Two of the four canonical gospels describe how the archangel Gabriel announced to Mary that she would bear the Son of God.[33] This is termed the annunciation (Gr. *evangelismos*), an indication that good news was being proclaimed to the Virgin. She reacts with humility and free will to accept God's command. Mary, by virtue of her marriage to Joseph, was a member of the house of David, and David is said to have descended from Seth, the child of Adam and Eve. Here, a parallel was drawn in popular piety and in hymnology between the Old Eve, who of free will disobeyed God, and the New Eve, who of her own free will obeyed the wish of God. The Virgin is the subject of important liturgical hymns, such as the Akathistos hymn, sung at the Feast of the Annunciation (25 March) and during Lent. Narrative artistic representations of Christ's mother focus on her conception and childhood or her Koimesis (her Dormition, or eternal sleep).[34] Most images of the Virgin stress her rôle as Christ's Mother, showing her standing or seated and holding her infant son.

Whether Orthodox, Roman Catholic or other,[35] we are habitually taught that the Virgin Mary embodied boundless maternal love, always ready to mediate on behalf of human sinners to soften her son's judgement. Take, for instance, the Deësis, or intercession scene, an iconographical type in which Christ is flanked by the Virgin Mary and John the Baptist, who are depicted interceding with him on behalf of mankind. The Deësis was originally understood as witnessing Christ's divinity. By the mid eleventh century the scene began to signify primarily intercession, a change attested by a poem by John Mauropous, metropolitan of Euchaïta, for the emperor Constantinus IX Monomachos (r. 1042–55).[36]

There is a superb thirteenth-century gold tesserae mosaic example of the Deësis in the south gallery of Hagia Sophia, Istanbul. Here, John (identified as Ὁ ΠΡΟΔΡΟΜ[ΟΣ], the 'Forerunner') is shown to the right, an expression of agonized grief on his ascetic face. His clothes are of camel's hair. On the left the young and wistful Virgin (identified as ΜΡ ΘΥ, Μήτηρ Θεοῦ) her head inclines towards Christ but casts her gaze shyly downward. Between them, a compassionate Christ holds up his right hand in a gesture of blessing, judge and saviour at the end of time. Though two-thirds of the mosaic are now lost, this panel represents one of the very highest points of European mediaeval art, achieving a synthesis of colour, light, and shade with a spiritual intensity virtually unknown outside Byzantium. In Byzantine culture, a human being can only admit his or her sins; he or she cannot supplicate with Christ. Only the Theometor, John the Baptist, and the saints can take human confession and bring it to a higher level of intercession before Christ. Hence the Virgin plays a central rôle in establishing the contact between the faithful and Christ, as in this superlative panel. In the private sphere, on the other hand, the panel was probably the focus of litanies and prayers for the deceased, and its images played an active rôle. The panel undoubtedly gave a tangible form to ideas of death and salvation.

The Virgin was the ever merciful, ever dependable source of comfort, full of compassion for human frailty, caring nothing for laws and judges, ready to respond to anyone in trouble. We are habitually told, too, that warfare is historically a predominantly male pursuit. As anyone who remembers the stunningly beautiful but unfaithful Helen of Homeric legend knows, men have marched to war throughout history under the banner of women. History is, after all, full of such irony. 'History never repeats itself', once observed Voltaire, 'man always does'. Many will regard this observation as being tinged with both realism and pessimism. Yet, if accepted as true, and it is hard to argue with Voltaire, his words would seem to condemn mankind to an endless cycle of mistakes. In the end, Voltaire is to be like Kassandra, the Trojan princess who was given the gift to see the future but was cursed never to be believed.

The Third Œcumenical Synod (Ephesos in 431) was the first and last time that the Holy Catholic and Apostolic Church attempted to define the Virgin Mary in doctrinal terms – it was believed that the Virgin had lived at Ephesos and had been taken up to heaven from there. In many respects, the rôle of the Virgin in the Church – then as now – is a personal, an inner affair, which does not like critique and conjecture. Indeed, the Virgin was never a theme of the public preaching of the apostles, unlike her son who was glorified from the rooftops. Yet – and this is my main point – one of the consequences of this unwillingness to dogmatize the mystery of the Virgin is that the devotions given to her have been many and manifold over the centuries. In the Byzantine world, the Virgin Mary embodied masculine power rather than maternal tenderness. Known as the Mother of God, Theometor or Theotokos, she was central to Byzantine spirituality as one of its most important religious figures. As the mediator between suffering mankind and Christ and the heavenly patroness of Constantinople, she was widely venerated not only as a merciful mother but as a virgin warrior too, becoming a guarantor of military victory and hence of imperial authority. In this setting the figure of the

Mother of God rose to become the protectoress of city and state, whose unbeatable power stemmed from her paradoxical virginal motherhood and motherly sacrifice.

Mary's mantra

The Akathistos hymn on the Virgin Mary, one of the most influential texts in Byzantine literature, played an important rôle in the liturgical rituals of the time, and is still sung in the Orthodox churches today. Attributed to the deacon Romanos of Emesa (Homs), legend has it that when he arrived in Constantinople from his native Syria in the reign of Anastasius I (r. 491–518), he stood on the pulpit ready to deliver a sermon when the Virgin Mary appeared and gave him a scroll to swallow. With the scroll came the gift of poetry, which Romanos immediately put to good effect. He has been known since then as Romanos the Melodist.

The Akathistos hymn's twenty-four stanzas tell of the incarnation and birth of Christ, then praise the numerous powers of the Virgin Mary, and end with an address to the Virgin for help and protection. The text combines concepts issuing from the Old and New testaments and patristic literature on the Virgin Mary, on the one hand, and the ideology of imperial victory, on the other. In fact, the hymn is a lasting example of how the Theotokos offered victory and protection through the powers of her virginal motherhood.

Each odd-numbered stanza includes multiply salutations (*charetismoi*) to the Virgin Mary, introduced by the word 'hail'. The use of *charetismoi* became popular in hymns written during and after the Third Œcumenical Synod. Some of these salutations draw on the tradition of acclamations addressed to the emperor on his triumphal return from military expeditions. In the penultimate stanza Mary is called 'the precious diadem of pious kings', an 'immovable tower of the Church', and 'an impregnable wall of the kingdom', while her 'trophies are raised up' and 'enemies fall'.[37] Each metaphor, based on attributes or symbols of power, tie the figure of the Virgin to the imperial sphere.

The presentation of Mary as a protectoress of the city and bringer of victory recalls the tradition civic deities Tyche and Victoria. Tyche wore a mural crown and held a *cornucopia*, alluding to her powers to protect the city and ensure its prosperity, while Victoria placed a wreath of victory on the triumphant emperor's head. Yet, the militant and triumphant image of Mary recalls the virgin warrior goddess Athena. She was worshipped as a goddess of war, among many other functions, and was known as the *nikêphóros* ('bringer of victory'), *pánoplos* ('[the one] in full armour'), *polioûchos* ('city protector'), *prómachos* ('first-in-battle'), and *pulaimáchos* ('fighter at the gates'). As both a virgin and a mother, Mary in the Byzantine perception rose to become the invincible commander of the Christian Roman army and the divine protector of the metropolis of Christendom.

Chapter 4

Impregnable Walls

Now we shall fast rewind to January 395, the month Theodosius I passed away. At the time, he was the undisputed ruler of the whole Roman world, East and West alike. However, the dying emperor had recognized that the task was beyond one man and so bequeathed the East, with its court at Constantinople, to his elder son Arcadius (r. 395–408), about eighteen years of age, and the West to the younger son, Honorius (r. 395–423), not yet eleven years old, with its court not at Rome but in its final secluded refuge at Ravenna on the Adriatic coast of Italy. They remained emperors for thirteen and twenty-eight years respectively. Arcadius was puny, somnolent, and slow of speech. Honorius was pious and gentle, but inept and mulishly obstinate, conveniently cloistered both from invaders and from the realities outside his palace.

Obviously the task of governing the two parts devolved upon others. In accordance with Theodosius' wishes, Honorius was placed under the care of the late emperor's close adviser and friend, the Romano-Vandal Flavius Stilicho. Among the many important members of the intrigued ridden entourage of Arcadius was the Gothic commander Gaïnas, who had high ambitions of becoming in the East what Stilicho already was in the West. Never again were the two parts to be fully united under one ruler, though the concept of unity did not disappear and indeed was esteemed. In August of 410 abandoned Rome fell to Alaric,[1] the able warlord of the Visigoths who had broken into rebellion on the death of Theodosius. The damage and the long-term effects of the Visigoth sack of Rome were trifling, but the psychological effects of the blow were immense. The end of the world seemed at hand. Meanwhile, in the East, the Huns poised a growing threat to Constantinople whose wealth and population were continually growing.

The feeble Arcadius died young, and gave way to his infant son, Theodosius II (r. 408–50). The latter grew up to be a retiring and relatively inconsequential figure in almost everything but ecclesiastical affairs. He was dominated alternatively by his elder and more forceful sister Pulcheria, and by his cultured but overtly ambitious wife, Eudokia, as well as by various advisers and courtiers. Some of them, however, were exceedingly capable men. One such man was Anthemius, the *praefectus praetorio orientis*, Praetorian Prefect of the East. According to a law in the *codex Theodosianus*, in the year 413 Anthemius, at the time acting as the regent for the thirteen-year-old emperor, ordered the construction of a new series of land walls, a kilometre or so west of those of Constantinus.[2]

Gateways

The new land walls stretched from the Blachernai quarter on the Golden Horn to the Studion quarter on the Sea of Marmara in a gently convex curve, marching a distance of 6.67 kilometres as they did so, rising and descending with the inequalities of the terrain. Ten gateways pierced the new land walls: one below the Blachernai palace named the Gate of Xylokerkon; another named the Gate of Adrianople; the Gate of Saint Romanos on the brow of the Seventh Hill; the Gate of Rhegion; and the Gate of Selymbria; to name but five.

Also incorporated into the Theodosian walls was the Golden Gate,[3] the triumphal arch that had been built by Theodosius I in 391 on the Roman road leading to the city known as the Via Egnatia.[4] At the time, of course, the Theodosian walls had not been built, so the triumphal arch, as was customary, stood proudly alone on the Via Egnatia. Its name derived from the fact that three gates (viz. the usual triple arcade consisting of a large central archway flanked by two smaller ones) across the outer entrance was covered with gold plate. Four huge copper elephants stood guard over the gateway,[5] while two great marble towers flanked it. All around, decorating the gateway and towers were marble panels carved with a hotchpotch of classical scenes, such as the labours of Herakles, the classical hero *par excellence*, and the deeds of Perseus.[6] Probably taken originally from a public building or villa of some importance, they had been chosen for their beauty rather than any intrinsic meaning. Over the inside main portal was the Latin inscription HAEC LOCA THEVDOSIVS DECORAT POST FATA TYRANNI (Theodosius decorates this place after the death of the tyrant), the 'tyrant' being the western usurper Magnus Maximus (r. 383–8), defeated twice in battle, at Siscia and Poetovio, and beheaded at Aquileia.[7]

Even after being incorporated within the Theodosian walls, the Golden Gate was several times the scene of triumphal entries by victorious emperors. Thus, Herakleios (r. 610–41) in 629 after his defeat of the Sasanians; Constantinus V Kopronymos (r. 741–75), Basil I (r. 867–86) and Basil II (r. 976–1025) after their victories over the Bulghars; John I Tzimiskès (r. 969-76) after his defeat of the Rus' (Gk. Ῥῶς); Theophilos (r. 829-42) and his son Michael III (r. 842–67) after their victories over the Arabs. Possibly the most emotionally charged of triumphal entries was the one that took place on 15 August 1261, when Michael VIII Palaiologos (r. 1259–82) rode through the Golden Gate on a splendid white stallion after Constantinople was regained from the Latins. But that was the last time an emperor of Byzantium was to ride in triumph through the Golden Gate, for the history of the empire in its last two centuries was one of military decline, and then by then the gateway had been walled up for good.

Curtains and towers

Stronger, thicker and taller than any others, the new land walls of Theodosius II were built of limestone blocks, divided at intervals by bands of narrow bricks, five deep, the whole filled with concrete. Projecting from the main wall were ninety-six towers, each eighteen to twenty metres high and set at an average interval of fifty-five metres, of which over seventy were square and the rest polygonal. Each tower consisted of an upper and lower chamber. The lower chamber opened straight into the city, and in times of peace was often rented out to the adjacent property-owners: otherwise, they were used as guardrooms. For reasons of security, the upper chamber could only be entered via the parapet-walk, which was reached by a flight of steps; these were usually located near the main gates. Comparatively large windows looked out from each wall of the towers, thus allowing the defenders good fields of vision and fire, while another flight of steps led up to the battlemented roofs. The curtain walls were ten metres high externally and twelve metres high internally, and 4.7 metres thick at its base and 4.5 metres thick at its apex. The land walls overseen by Anthemius survive today as the inner wall of the fortification line.

Double walls and moat

What follows now in our story of the Theodosian walls is a natural disaster, which helps us to identify the two distinct phases of the land walls of Constantinople. The capital was, and still is, part of an active seismic zone. During the small hours of Sunday, 27 January 447, a severe earthquake reduced sections of the new land walls to jumble heaps of brick and stone and fifty-seven of its ninety-six towers fell.[8] The story gets worse, for Attila the Hun, the so-called self-styled Scourge of God,[9] had recently defeated the eastern field army in a series of running battles and was now advancing on the capital, laying waste Thrace with fire and sword as he came. Theodosius II resorted to pious chants so as to move 'Holy God' to support the Roman cause and protect the city. As some of the barefooted, penitent ruler's closest advisers quietly observed, it would take more than a miracle to repair the walls before Attila reached Constantinople.

Indeed, there was one man who had no intention of waiting for God (or even the Virgin Mary) to come to Constantinople's rescue, the new *praefectus praetorio orientis*, Flavius Constantinus. Utilizing 16,000 of the city's populace under the direction of the two circus factions, the Blues and the Greens, he ensued the walls were quickly repaired. Yet, the strength of any fortification consists less in massiveness than in design. Thus was the case at Constantinople. For not only was this repair work finished within two months but a new wall, the *proteichisma*, 8.5 metres high and some two metres thick, was built between the fosse and the main wall. This outer wall was studded with ninety-six towers alternating in position with those of the main wall, each ten to twelve metres high; in general, these towers were either square or crescent-shaped in turn. Between the main and the outer walls there was a passage, called the *peribolos*, which varied from fifteen to twenty metres in breadth, and stood about five metres above the level of the city. This additional defence not only provided a killing-ground between the main and outer walls, but also served as an area for the movement of defenders between the two walls. Beyond the outer wall was a paved terrace, the *parateichion*, bounded on the outside by the counter-scarp of the broad fosse, which featured a 1.5 metre-high battlement. With a width of twenty metres, the primary purpose of the *parateichion* was to increase the distance between the besieged and the besiegers.

The fosse itself was originally about ten metres deep, twenty metres wide and riveted with stone. Once, it was believed that sections of the fosse could be flooded with water to form a wet-moat if the city was threatened. However, nowadays there is a general agreement that the sections were not flooded with water: the width and depth of the fosse in itself constituted a strong line of defence, hampering the attempts of the besiegers to draw near to the walls with siege towers and battering rams.[10] The only important argument for a wet-moat as against a dry-moat was mining operations were sometimes prevented when the outermost fosse was dug deep and filled with water. Mines were dug down beneath the foundations of walls or, as in this case, moats, and enlarged with wooden supports, which could then be torn out with cables or, more usually, burned. Either of these methods could easily collapse a portion of the moat.

Double gateways

As before, ten gateways pierced the refurbished Theodosian walls, the Golden Gate included, all of them, the Golden Gate excluded, sharing a common design.[11] All were double gateways because they had to pierce two walls. The inner gateway, being the principal one, was built into the main wall of the Theodosian line. Two large towers that projected far beyond the main wall guarded all the gateways. The towers were of very similar design to the towers found along the length of the walls as described above. Finally, there was a postern gate on the Marmara shore.

A laconic bilingual inscription on Proconnesian marble slabs placed to the left corbel of the outer entrance of the *Yeni Mevlanihane Kapısı*, as it is called in Turkish, what was then the Gate of Rhegion, records this remarkable feat of renewal and addition:

GREEK: In sixty days, by order of the sceptre-loving emperor, Constantinus the *eparchos* added wall to wall.

LATIN: By command of Theodosius, in less than two months, Constantinus
               erected triumphantly, these strong walls. Scarcely   could   Pallas
               have built so quickly so strong a citadel.[12]

A third couplet survives in the *Anthologia Palatina*.[13] The Constantinopolitans had
learned from experience and had strengthened their metropolis beyond Attila's
expectations. Attila and his horde would have been confronted not by enticing gaps
in a ruined wall, but by the whole restored and impregnable edifice, regular and
regimented in outline, broken up only by the demands of topography.

Sea walls

Under Theodosius II, the sea wall circuit was completed to join the new land walls.
They were repaired and heightened under Theophilos (r. 829–42), suffering at that
time from their age and the action of the sea.[14] The sea walls ran for a distance of
sixteen kilometres. From the top of the Golden Horn to the Acropolis point, now
usually known as Saray Point (Tk. *Sarayburnu*), there was a single line of walls, ten
metres high, studded with 110 towers at regular intervals, and pierced by sixteen sea
gates. From the Acropolis point to Studion, there was a single line of walls, twelve
to fifteen metres high, studded with 188 towers at regular intervals, and pierced by
eleven sea gates. There were also two small fortified harbours, to accommodate light
craft that could not round the Acropolis point into the calm and sheltered waters
of the Golden Horn against the prevailing north wind.[15] The Golden Horn itself
could be sealed off by a great boom, which consisted of an iron chain supported on
wooden floats. No other city in the world had such comprehensive protection.

Against all comers

It can honestly be said that one of the most impressive and intimidating manmade
features of Constantinople were its fortification walls. For ten centuries the forces
of barbarism, Huns (447), Avars (626), Arabs (673–9, 717–18), Bulghars (813, 926),
Rus' (860, 907, 941, 1043), Latin crusaders (1097), were to view these bulwarks
and recoil. The wall-girt city was proof against them all. The Baghdadi traveller
al-Mas'udi (d. 957), though specifically speaking about the Bulghars of his day,
rightly says that it 'is only thanks to their defensive walls that the inhabitants of
Constantinople are able to resist them'.[16]

It would be at the Gate of Saint Romanos (what would become known to the
Turks as *Top Kapı*)[17] that the last Byzantine emperor, Constantinus XI Palaiologos
(r. 1448–53), the ninety-fifth ruler to occupy the throne of Constantinus, would
dismount from his horse and go out to die alongside his soldiers in the winding

sheet of his empire. At the same time, through the Gate of Charisius (what would become known to the Turks as *Edirne Kapısı*), standing on the peak of the Sixth Hill and at the highest point of the land walls, the twenty-one-year-old Mehmet II would enter the once immodest, impregnable imperial city as it fell to his Janissaries, riding a white horse with an iron mace in his hand. A plaque on the southern side of the Edirnekapı commemorates this historic event, but it fails to mention the fact that the young sultan had one explosive advantage that the other besiegers of Constantinople would have envied: the latest military technology had made its noisy and foul-smelling appearance on the battlefield, gunpowder. The sultan's guns opened fire on Constantinople on 1 April 1453, and after some 4,000 shots had been fired, the walls were breached fifty-nine days later, and the Queen of Cities finally fell. But before that fateful Tuesday morning on 29 May 1453, the last firm date in Byzantine Constantinople, 1006 years of Byzantine history would unroll itself behind the mighty Theodosian walls. No other metropolis in the world has such a continuous imperial history.

Chapter 5

Heaven's Approval

Byzantium. Was it Greek or Roman, familiar or hybrid, barbaric or civilized, Oriental – where Oriental could have both a pejorative as well as a more positive slant – or another Other? If we opt for the distorted perspective of arguably the English language's greatest historian, Edward Gibbon, then the whole of Byzantine history was a progressive degeneration from Roman virtue into oriental vice, sleaze, despotism and monasticism, a view he espoused most famously in his superb and never truly superseded *Decline and Fall of the Roman Empire* (1776–88). The Romans, in other words, had gone soft, and become Greeks into the bargain. But that is to beg the question of 'decline'. Because Gibbon knew with hindsight that 'decline' was around the corner, he tended to focus on the negative evidence. Hindsight is easy: even today, Byzantium neither seems to fit very well into European history, its existence seemingly betraying an acute attack of anxiety when it is acknowledged.

In the late eleventh century, Constantinople was the largest and wealthiest city in Christendom, the seat of the Byzantine emperor, Christ's vice-regent on earth, and the centre of a predominately Christian empire, steeped in Greek cultural and artistic influences, yet founded and maintained by a Roman legal and administrative system. Despite the amalgam of Greek and Roman influences, however, its language and culture was definitely Greek. Constantinople truly was the capital of the Roman empire in the *East*, and from its founding under the first Constantinus to its fall under the eleventh and last Constantinus the inhabitants always called themselves *Romaioi*, Romans, not *Hellênikés*, Greeks. Over its millennium-long history the empire and its capital experienced many vicissitudes that included several periods of waxing and waning and more than one 'golden age'.

So, it is a strange kind of degeneracy that resists multiple enemies – including fellow Christians – using all available weapons, which again and again recovers lost provinces, and actively spreads its religion, literacy and manners throughout its Slavic neighbours. Its culture and artistic heritage are abundant in the myriad churches of the Christian East: Greek, Serb, Bulghar, and Russian. Its political will to survive is still eloquently proclaimed in the monumental double land walls of Constantinople, the greatest city fortifications ever built, on which the forces of barbarism (in the eyes of the Byzantines, that is) dashed themselves for a thousand years. Indeed, Byzantium was one of the longest lasting social organizations in history. There was no hope for an empire that had lost the will to prosecute the grand and awful business of adventure. The Byzantine empire was certainly not of that stamp.

Out of anarchy, orderliness

It is essential for us to trespass on to non-Constantinopolitan history of the Byzantium empire as far as it is necessary to explain the progress of Christianity. The tart and tedious verdicts of Voltaire and Gibbon may be well known (and perhaps even believed), namely that Byzantium represented, in Gibbon's immortal words, a 'triumph of barbarism and religion',[1] yet two of the imperial decisions made by Flavius Valerius Constantinus I (better known to posterity as Constantine the Great) changed the course of history: the first was his recognition of Christianity and the other was his foundation of the city, which, with typical lack of modesty, he named after himself, Constantinople (Gr. *Konstantinoúpolis*, L *Constantinopolis*), the *polis* or city of Constantinus. It is the recognition of Christianity that will concern us in this chapter. So, how did this happen?

The previous century and a half leading up to Constantinus had been a time of upheavals and a series of brutal and forgettable soldier emperors sat on the throne. As often as not, they were soon murdered by the men who had put them there in the first place. In fact, very nearly eighty military commanders, either in Rome or in some other part of the empire, were hailed by the imperial title (the distinction between emperor and usurper became increasingly blurred). Between the years 247 and 270 alone, no fewer than thirty such men were acclaimed. Some were too afraid to refuse the offer. It was an age of violence.

These violent grasps at the throne went on until Diocletianus (r. 284–305, d. 311), who believed the empire had grown too large and complex, its enemies too many, to be governed by one man, established the tetrarchy, a fourfold monarchy. This was a system of government in which the leadership was delegated to two co-emperors (each with the title of Augustus) and two sub-emperors (each with the title of Caesar), with ultimately a regular procedure for abdication, replacement, and promotions through the scale. Diocletianus thus re-established imperial stability through a reign of twenty years, which ended in planned retirement. A porphyry statue group now seen as part of the fabric of the Basilica di San Marco, Venice, shows the tetrarchs as squat figures in military dress, one hand on another's shoulder, the other hand grasping an eagle-headed sword. Portrayed not as persons but as identical types, they watch each other's back against usurpation and murder, and shorten the empire's reaction time to external threats. The surviving Latin panegyrics, like that strange collection of gossipy imperial biographies, the

Scriptores Historiae Augustae,[2] emphasize this common loyalty, unity and concord: 'Four rulers of the world they were indeed, brave, wise, kind, generous, respectful to the Senate, friends of the People, moderate, revered, devoted, pious'.[3] Such heavy-handed propaganda betrays the fragility of the new arrangement: the rule of four rested on nothing more solid than consent.

So, despite all his administrative genius and grim determination, the weakness of collegiate rule was that it ignored all logic of heredity and ambitions, of strong armies to have their own strongman as emperor. It only initiated in short order a new phase of the very kind of civil war it had been designed to prevent. True to his aims, Diocletianus abdicated together with his senior colleague Maximian on 1 May 305, and retired to a specially prepared palace at Spalato (Split) to cultivate cabbages, refusing to return to political life thereafter. Yet, his succession arrangements badly faltered because they disregarded the soldiers' strong dynastic loyalties, that is to say, the staunch loyalty of the soldiers of a certain Constantius to his son Constantinus. Out of the collapse of this abortive system would befall the triumph of Constantinus as sole emperor.

Arguably the only late Roman emperor of whom most people have heard, Constantinus was born, out of wedlock, at Naissus (Niš), and rapidly rose by his military skills. His father, Flavius Constantius Chlorus, was a hard grim fighter who had risen through the ranks to first become Caesar during the reign of Diocletianus and then the Augustus of the western half of the Roman empire. On the way he picked up Helena, the daughter of an innkeeper, from Bithynia. Far better known than her partner, she famously went on pilgrimage to Jerusalem aged eighty, where Christian tradition has it she discovered the True Cross. Though their son was destined to become emperor, Constantius Chlorus was later forced to put Helena aside in favour of the more politically appropriate daughter of his boss, Diocletianus.

The division of the empire between four rulers had been excellent in theory, perhaps, but had not worked in practice. Sole rule therefore probably seemed the best alternative; Constantinus certainly thought so. Constantius Chlorus died in the distant province of Britannia on 25 July 306, during a campaign against the Picts. The thirty-three-year-old Constantinus was immediately proclaimed Augustus by his father's loyal army at Eboracum (York).[4] Although in a strong position in Britannia, to the rest of the empire he was just another rebel and had to fight his path to real power from this remote cantonment. In a six-year poker game of alliances and counter alliances Constantinus was to prove the most patient and astute. For instance, he put aside Minerva who had given him his first son, Crispus, and married Fausta, the daughter of Maximian (r. 285–305, d. 310). This was patently a political move.

Champion of Christ?

On 28 October 312, Constantinus defeated Maxentius (r. 306–12), his brother-in-law and chief rival in the West, just outside Rome at Pons Mulvius, the bridge that carried the Via Flaminia across the Tiber. Maxentius' head was placed on a spike and carried through Rome.

Identification of turning points is an understandable temptation, and acceptable provided that the qualifications for each particular date are not forgotten. Pons Mulvius may have initiated the empire's transformation from polytheism to Christianity, but seventeen hundred years after the battle scholars continue to hotly debate the life and impact of the Roman emperor who converted to Christianity and founded a new imperial capital. It was on the eve of this crucial encounter that Constantinus, who had been raised as a pagan polytheist, is reputed to have had a vision of the True Cross in the sky arising from the light of the sun, carrying the message 'By this sign you will be the victor'. Predictably, Pons Mulvius would become one of the most famous (and controversial) battles in Roman history, but that is mainly because of Constantinus' pronouncement afterwards that he owed his victory to the Almighty God of the Christians.[5]

There are three versions of this remarkable story. Some weeks prior to the battle, according to Constantinus' self-proclaimed panegyrist Eusebius bishop of Caesarea Palestinae, the emperor saw a sign in the sky at midday, a cross of light superimposed on the sun. He took this as a sign of victory from the God whose symbol was the cross, testifying that he saw the words 'By this sign you will be the victor' (*hoc signo victor eris* in the Latin of the emperor, but ἐν τούτῳ νίκα, 'By this, conquer!', in the Greek translation of Eusebius) written in stars around said cross. The night before the battle, Christ appeared to him in a dream and instructed him to reproduce the heavenly symbol and use it for protection against the attacks of his enemies. He apparently did so with the desired results. For when the emperor awoke, he commanded the construction of the *labarum* (Gr. λάβαρον): a military standard that Eusebius insists featured the CHI-RHO monogram (XP), the first two Greek letters of Christ's name superimposed (viz. Χριστός).[6] The story would be difficult to believe, Eusebius tells us, except that Constantinus himself swore oaths on the verity of the tale and, he adds, permitted his biographer to view the *labarum* with his own eyes.[7]

Yet, Eusebius was not the imperial confidant he styles himself as being. Furthermore, in a much earlier version of the same story, Eusebius does not mention any such celestial vision, and is content to liken the victory, and in particular the engulfment of Maxentius' fleeing pagan troops in the Tiber, to the fate of pharaoh's chariots at the crossing of the Red Sea.[8]

According to the more credible version, that offered by the man Constantinus had hired as tutor to his son Caesar Crispus,[9] the Latin rhetor and Christian convert Lactantius, the night before the battle Constantinus dreamt that he was advised 'to mark the heavenly sign of God on his the shields of his soldiers' as a divine talisman. On awaking the next morning, he put his faith to the test when he ordered his men to paint the CHI-RHO monogram on their shields. 'Armed with this sign, the army took up its weapons' and was victorious.[10]

This seems to be the sole display of any personal Christianity by Constantinus in Lactantius' pamphlet, composed in 315 or thereabouts, for although the author goes on to cite the decree by Constantinus and Licinius that lifted the persecutions on Christians and gave them freedom to worship, it seems to be an equating of all religions. It must also be taken into account that nowhere in *De mortibus persecutorum* does Lactantius actually claim that Constantinus was a Christian, or does he claim that the emperor was converted as a result of his dream, even though he may have been inclined to believe such a thing was plausible. Rather, his portrayal of Constantinus in his pamphlet is as a *sympathizer* of Christianity, but nevertheless an unwitting agent of the Christian god and recipient of his assistance: God elevated Constantinus in order to end the persecution of his worshippers and depose the persecutors, and offered divine protection in battle in return for token representation on the soldiers' shields.

Though *De mortibus persecutorum* was written relatively soon after Constantinus' victory over Maxentius, Lactantius is not the earliest source for this historical event. A panegyric delivered at Trier in August 313 describes extensively not only Pons Mulvius, but Constantinus' progress from northern Italy to Rome.[11] In his narrative of the events leading up to the famous battle, the anonymous panegyrist mentions neither dreams nor visions; rather, he refers vaguely to 'divine inspiration' in connection to the entire campaign.[12] More explicitly, the panegyrist states that Constantinus ventured over the Alps seeking 'no doubtful victory, but one divinely promised'.[13] This version is certainly similar to Eusebius' first version of events in his *Historia ecclesiastica*, which was written around 313, where he says Constantinus procured the assistance of 'God who is in heaven, and His Word, even Jesus Christ the Saviour of all' prior to the Italian campaign.[14] Likewise, the panegyrist of 313, describing the aftermath of Pons Mulvius, says: 'After the Tiber had swallowed the impious, the same Tiber also snatched up their leader [Maxentius] himself in its whirlpool and devoured him',[15] which ties in nicely with Eusebius' biblical parallel mentioned above.

It is worth noting here that a potpourri of the Pons Mulvius legend is depicted in a miniature from the ninth-century manuscript of the homilies of the fourth-century church father and patriarch of Constantinople (378-81), Gregory I of Nazianzos the Theologian.[16] In the top register Constantinus dreams a vision of the cross; in the middle register, mounted on a white steed, he charges unaccompanied at Pons Mulvius and dispatches with his cavalry spear the fleeing 'pagan usurper' Maxentius. Constantinus' triumph is glorified by the cross shining in the skies above; the words ἐν τούτῳ νίκα are inscribed inside it. Lastly, in the bottom register, we witness his mother, Helena, a sincere Christian, discovering the True Cross, more of which later.

Some scholars have considered the vision in a solar context, such as a solar halo phenomenon called a sun dog, which may have preceded the Christian beliefs later expressed by Constantinus. In particular, Peter Weiss contends that Constantinus actually witnessed a very public meteorological event, specifically

> a *double* ring-halo – in other words, a really spectacular display ... each ring with three mock suns arranged in cross-formation around the sun, tangent arcs or points of intersection with the circle, presumably with a more or less distinct light–cross in the middle.[17]

By this reckoning, it was Apollo who appeared in the sky to Constantinus offering him laurel wreaths, which were 'the three concentrations of light on each halo–ring'.[18]

As we will shortly discuss, Constantinus had a prior celestial vision, that of Apollo in the guise of the supreme sun god, Sol Invictus, the 'Unconquered Sun'. It is argued, therefore, it is this occurrence that was *later* reinterpreted by the emperor as a vision of Christ following a dream-vision on the night before Pons Mulvius. Coins of the emperor depicting him as the companion of Sol Invictus were minted as late as 320/1, eight odd years after the battle. Statuettes of Sol Invictus, carried by standard bearers, appear in three places in bas-reliefs on the Arch of Constantinus in Rome, which was constructed just three years after the battle. But whatever it was that happened to Constantinus before Pons Mulvius, there is no doubt that Constantinus showed conspicuous favour to the Christians, then a vocal if small sect amongst many others, and continued to wear the symbol of Christ against every hostile power he faced.

Crowned by Christ?

Victorious in the West, Constantinus now came to a grudging agreement with the eastern Augustus and last remaining Diocletian tetrarch, Licinius. In February 313 an *entente* only patchily *cordiale* was drawn up in Mediolanum (Milan), one of the empire's imperial centres, where Constantinus' half-sister Constantia was wed to Licinius. Also, on this occasion the two emperors formulated a common religious policy. One of the conditions of the 'Edict of Milan', as it is erroneously called, meant that Christianity was given the status of a recognized religion.[19] As a result, being a Christian was no longer a punishable crime and Christians were now allowed to openly practise their religion. This edict was *not*, it should be noted, the work of Constantinus alone, *nor* did it make Christianity the sole and official state religion.[20] As we shall discuss anon, it was not until later in the fourth century that paganism was overtly persecuted, and not until the end of the century, under Theodosius I, that it became the sole acceptable state faith. What Constantinus and Licinius did was to make Christianity an acceptable religion.

Licinius himself remained a staunch pagan, and relations between the two gradually deteriorated until verbal conflicts became physical. First, they fell out over the appointment of a Caesar in Italy, and they fought two battles by which Constantinus gained control of the Illyrian and Balkan provinces (316–17). Next, they carried on a cold war over religion, with Constantinus expanding support for Christianity and Licinius affirming his loyalty to paganism. The former removed the pagan gods from his coins and allowed the use of Christian motifs thereupon, while the latter emphasized his relationship with Iuppiter and kept Christian signs off his coinage. When Constantinus marched into Licinius' domain to punish some marauding barbarians in Thrace, and Licinius allowed the martyrdom of some Christians, the cold war turned hot. In 323 Constantinus marched eastward, and in two tough, but decisive battles (24 July at Adrianople, and 18 September at Chrysopolis) the following year annihilated his last rival. In the apocalyptic climate of victory, the official line was that Constantinus and Christianity had triumphed over Licinius and paganism.[21]

Initially, yielding to the pleas of Constantia, Constantinus spared the life of his brother-in-law, but some months later he ordered his execution, breaking his solemn oath.[22] Before too long, the younger Licinius, too, fell victim to Constantinus' anger or suspicions. Thereafter, Constantinus ruled the whole empire alone until his death.

Troy–Rome–Constantinople

It was towards the end of 324 when Constantinus decreed Byzantium should become the heart of his empire. Some said that the emperor wanted to move the capital out of self-indulgent pique at Rome's calcified republican and pagan élite. It was certainly noted that the new capital was to bear a Greek name, not a Latin one, and would have an overriding Christian ambience. More plausibly, however, it was a decision made in the light of more prosaic, strategic and logistical reasons. Now 'leader by the grace of God' and sole ruler of an empire that had been divided for forty years, the emperor drew the obvious conclusion that Rome was no longer a suitable capital for ruling it. As the centre of imperial power moved eastwards, Rome increasingly appeared an anachronism and, more damningly, a monetary liability and a political irrelevance. Besides, in the West it had already been superseded by imperial centres (the term 'capitals' is misleading) in Mediolanum (Milan), from where Gaul and the Rhine was quicker to reach, and the frontier city of Treveri (Trier).

However, even if Rome was a little past its prime and living off its bygone glory, a quick look at a map would have shown that Byzantium was the ideal site for simultaneous supervision of the empire's two vital riverine frontiers, the two that consistently gave it the most headaches, namely the Rhine–Danube line in the north and the Euphrates in the east. What is more, the great advantage of Byzas' site was its defensibility, surrounded as it was by water on three sides, while to the west a relatively short stretch of fortifications could be erected. The building project began on 4 November 326, when Constantinus, on foot and spear in hand, personally traced out the limits of his new city.[23]

Progress was so rapid that the capital, 'The New Rome which is Constantinople',[24] was formally dedicated to the Holy Trinity and (according to later tradition) to the Mother of God on 11 May 330,[25] the feast day of the Christian martyr Saint Mocius, just in time for Constantinus' jubilee. The anonymous author of the *Origo Constantini imperatoris* reported 'Constantinus renamed Byzantium after himself on account of the memory of his notable victory. He adorned it … with great magnificence and desired it to be the equal of Rome'.[26] Flavius Eutropius agreed, writing 'he was the first to endeavour to raise the city named after himself to such a height as to make it rival Rome'.[27] Two years later, on 18 May 332, the emperor bravely announced that, as in Rome, free distributions of food would be made to the citizens. At the time, the amount is said to have been 80,000 rations a day, doled out from 117 distribution points around the city.[28] It seems Constantinus' city was fast becoming a metropolis. Sad to say, by the time of his death five years later, though his eponymous metropolis was almost complete, much of the construction work was so shoddy it had to be rebuilt in the reign of his favourite son and heir in the East, Constantius II (r. 337–61).[29]

Constantinus had at first planned to build his new seat of empire at the celebrated spot of ancient Troy (of hallowed memory), from whence the Romans claimed their legendary origin. Indeed, construction work on the Sigeum ridge at Troy was even begun before that at Byzantium, the foundations having been laid and even the fortifications partially erected.[30] At a place still called Yenisehir ('New City') the gates were said to have been visible to seafarers approaching the Hellespont over a century after Constantinus' day, and parts of the walls were still seen by Elizabethan travellers.[31] Today, a ramble along the ridge reveals not a trace remaining. The situation would have offered as much natural splendour as that of Constantinople, and been more convenient. But the reason why it was abandoned, albeit after the erection of part of the walls, is obvious: by then, the great bay that had been the *raison d'être* for Troy's existence for over three millennia had silted up and ceased to exist – Troy no longer guarded and controlled the entrance to 'the hard-running passage of Helle'.[32]

The Romans had a very particular interest in Troy, tracing their ancestry back to the legendary Trojan prince and hero Aeneas. According to post-Homeric legend, which was marvellously taken up and developed by that Augustan literary genius, Virgil (70–19 BC), Aeneas not only survived the sack of Troy but also fled to Latium in Italy. As a result, the Romans viewed Aeneas as their progenitor and believed Troy to be the 'mother city' of Rome. This belief is well documented on coins of Iulius Caesar, whose clan, the *gens Iulia*, developed their political ideology by claiming Ascanius Iulus, son of Aeneas, as eponymous founder and thus descent from his divine grandmother Venus. On the Ides of March 44 BC, after a century of civil wars, chaos and corruption, Caesar was assassinated by Brutus and Cassius in the name of liberty and the Republic. His heir was his nineteen-year-old grand-nephew and adopted son, Octavian, astute, ruthless and determined. Fifteen years later, having promised to avenge Caesar and hunted down every last one of the conspirators, Octavian made himself master of the known world, metamorphosing into Augustus to become the first emperor of Rome. Virgil's *Aeneid* praises Augustus in two ways. First, by telling the story of his great ancestor, the first founder of Rome, in such a way as resembles the story of Augustus himself, its third founder (the second founder being Romulus). The second mode of praise is direct allusion to Augustus in prophecies and visions, notably near the beginning and end of the epic, in the descent of Aeneas to consult his father, Anchises, in the Underworld at the end of book six, and on the prophetic shield of Aeneas depicting the future wars of Rome at the end of book eight.

Slayer of Darkness

Christian or not, the cult of the semi-divine emperor was taken up wholeheartedly by Constantinus. In the centre of the oval Forum of Constantinus stood a towering column of porphyry, made up of cylindrical blocks (seven still stand and go by the local appellation of Çemberlitaş, the Hooped Column) and standing fifty metres tall.[33] It was erected by the emperor to celebrate the dedication of the city as the capital of the empire on 11 May 330. On the column's summit there was a large capital, presumably Corinthian, upon which stood a statue of Constantinus, which once surveyed the world he ruled alone. The statue did not depict him as a humble Christian penitent, but sporting certain attributes of Sol Invictus (his father had followed the cult of Sol Invictus, the supreme sun god of the emperor Aurelianus),[34] the Slayer of Darkness, and so sharing in the divine light and divine power of his protective deity. An unapologetic exercise in exaggeration, the emperor-god was portrayed holding a sceptre in his right hand and a bronze orb, containing a fragment of the True Cross on which Jesus Christ was crucified, in his left hand. He wore a crown adorned with sunrays, which incorporated small pieces of the nails driven through Christ's hands and feet. The orb, of course, signified that the entire world was obedient to him. This colossal portrait of the superhuman Constantinus illustrates the melding of traditional triumphal pagan imagery with Christian elements, demonstrating that the source of imperial authority is the ruler's relationship to the new Christian God. Grandeur and hype are always two sides of the same coin.

The colossus survived until 1106 when it was blown off its porphyry perch in a powerful storm, killing several passers-by in the process.[35] It was not restored but replaced by Manuel I Komnenos (r. 1143–80) with a gilded cross. Underneath this colossal elevation, according to later sixth-century writers, it was said that Constantinus had deposited a curious collection of Christian relics: the hatchet of Noah, the stone from which Moses made the water flow, the crosses of the two common criminals who were crucified with Jesus Christ at Golgotha, the alabaster jar of Mary Magdalene, and the twelve baskets of the miraculous loaves.[36] Also deposited, according to the same writers, was the Palladium of Troy, the city's traditional talisman, a wooden cult image (Gr. *xóanon*) of Pallas Athena that had been brought to the future site of Rome by Aeneas the exiled Trojan.[37] Old and new religions, Roman polytheism and Christian monotheism, or so it was believed, were thus entombed together.[38]

Let us look briefly at two of the supposedly buried objects, one Christian and one pagan, namely the alabaster jar and the wooden cult statue. The first was the alabaster jar containing perfume with which Mary Magdalene was meant to have anointed the feet of Jesus Christ.[39] Surely there is no better illustration of the Church's diminution of the status of women than the manufactured legend of Mary Magdalene as a *harlot*. Although she is nowhere described in the canonical gospels as such, to the Roman Catholic Church she was a prostitute for nearly fourteen hundred years, from the declaration that she *was*, by pope Gregory I in 591,[40] to the eventual admission that she *wasn't* by pope Paul VI in 1969.[41] In truth, her identity was conflated with the *unnamed* sinful woman who does anoint Jesus' feet in the gospel of Luke.[42] This so-called 'composite Mary' has never been accepted by the Eastern Orthodox Church, who sees only Mary the disciple. And there again, there are those who believe Mary Magdalene was the wife of Christ. It is indeed interesting that Mary Magdalene is mentioned on the very eve of Easter, on the threshold of the death and resurrection of Christ.

Naturally, when we think of the pale virgin goddess of war, wisdom and weaving, we think of her virtuoso chryselephantine statue that once stood straight and tall in the Parthenon on the Athenian Acropolis, described albeit rather briefly by the usually enthusiastic traveller Pausanias in the mid-second century, almost six centuries after it had been made.[43] Yet, compared with the gigantic gold and ivory version of Athena that once loomed in the Parthenon, the Palladium of Pallas Athena was only, according to Diodorus Siculus, three cubits tall and made of wood black as pitch with age and oiling. She held a spear in her right hand, and a distaff and spindle in her left. Furthermore, she was not made by human hand at all, but had fallen miraculously to earth from the heavens, landing at Pessinus (a key centre for the cult of the mother goddess Cybelê and of Attis).[44]

It was said that the continued survival of Troy itself depended on the Trojans possession of the Palladium. In fact, there are two divergent myths. When the talisman is stolen from the sacred citadel, so the story goes, Troy will fall, and Aeneas is fated to be the only survivor of the royal house of Troy. The common account has Odysseus and Diomedes, as favourites of grey-eyed Athena, chosen to perform the cloak and dagger theft of the Palladium, which they do with their customary aplomb.[45] The Romans, on the other hand, promoted the story that the two Greek villains carried off a mere replica of the Palladium, which was on public display, and that Aeneas, on the fall of Troy, rescued the authentic ancient image and brought it safe to Italy.[46] It is here that he engages in activities that eventually lead to the founding of the New Troy in Italy, Eternal Rome, which is eventually destined to become New Rome, Constantinople.

Chapter 6

Victory Bringer

G olgotha, the Place of the Skull, was also said to be the burial place of Adam. One tradition goes that Seth, the son of Adam, had received three seeds from the angel who guarded the gates of Paradise, all from the fateful Tree of Knowledge. These three seeds Seth put in his father's mouth, and three days later Adam died. He was buried, but the seeds took root, and the offspring of one of them would be the tree from which Christ's cross would be made. Thus, the place of the crucifixion, Golgotha, is associated with Adam's tomb, and the wood from the Fall is used by the New Adam (Christ) to redeem the Old Adam and, therefore, mankind.

The Cross of Jesus

The relic accepted by Christians as the wooden cross on which Jesus Christ had been crucified had been discovered in 326, according to post Nicene tradition, by Helena, the pious mother of Constantinus. The True (or Holy) Cross was split into two pieces: one part was sent to Constantinople; the other remained in Jerusalem and was kept at the basilica of the Holy Sepulchre. The piece at Jerusalem was removed by the Sasanians when they took the city in 614, its inhabitants and the relics of Christ's passion being taken into Babylonian captivity. Eventual peace with Persia meant the return of the spoils taken from Jerusalem, including the piece of the True Cross, which the emperor Herakleios (r. 610–41) reinstalled in its rightful place in a grand ceremony at Easter 630. Following the Arab invasion later that century it was divided again and a large section was found by the crusaders soon after they took the city in 1099.

Arnulf Malecorne, the first Latin patriarch of Jerusalem, had the Orthodox priests who were in possession of the True Cross tortured in order to reveal its location. The relic that Arnulf discovered was a small fragment of wood embedded in a golden cross, and it became the most sacred relic of the Latin kingdom of Jerusalem. It was housed in the basilica of the Holy Sepulchre under the protection of the Latin patriarch, who marched with it ahead of the army before every battle. After its capture by Salah ad-Din (Saladin) bin Ayyub, sultan of Egypt (r. 1169–93), at Qarn Hattin in northern Palestine on 4 July 1187, the True Cross disappears from the historical record. Though some Christian rulers, such as Isaakos II Angelos, Richard Cœur de Lion, and Tamar, queen of Georgia, sought to ransom it from Saladin, the True Cross was last seen being paraded through the streets of Damascus upside down by the victors, the symbol of the cross epitomizing Christianity for the Muslims. At present, the Orthodox Church displays a small True Cross relic in the so-called Greek Treasury at the foot of Golgotha, within the basilica of the Holy Sepulchre.

Eusebius, bishop of Caesarea Palestinae, did not refer to the True Cross in his *Vita Constantini*, and it was Ambrose, bishop of Mediolanum (r. 374–97), who was responsible for linking the legend of its discovery to Helena. His Latin account, which is a funeral oration for Theodosius I (25 February 395), is the earliest version and thought to be the most original rendering of this divine event. According to Ambrose, Helena found the *titulus*, the wooden plague bearing the inscription IESVS NAZARENVS REX IDVDAEORVM, which Pontius Pilate had ordered to be attached to Jesus' cross,[1] along with 'three crosses in disarray'. Helena also found the nails of the Crucifixion, which she sent to Constantinople.[2] Writing two years after Ambrose, Rufinus of Aquileia adds that a piece of the cross itself was sent to Constantinus in Constantinople.[3] According to bishop Theodoretos of Kyrrhos (Kurus, southern Turkey), who was writing in the fifth century:

> She [Helena] had part of the cross of our Saviour conveyed to the palace. The rest was enclosed in a covering of silver, and committed to the care of the bishop of the city, whom she exhorted to preserve it carefully, in order that it might be transmitted uninjured to posterity.[4]

Among the most valuable relics still to be found at the monastery of Megisti Lavras on Mount Athos is a piece of the True Cross, which may or may not be the same piece that went to Constantinople. According to the sacred tradition of the Orthodox Church, the True Cross was made from three different types of wood: cedar, pine and cypress. This is an allusion to a verse in Isaiah: 'The glory of Lebanon will come to you, the pine, the fir and the cypress together, to adorn the place of my sanctuary; and I will glorify the place of my feet'.[5] The link between this verse and the Crucifixion lies in the words, 'the place of my feet', which is interpreted as referring to the *suppendaneum*, the foot rest on which Christ's feet were nailed, as depicted in the Orthodox cross. There is a tradition that the three trees from which the True Cross was constructed grew together in one spot. A traditional Orthodox icon depicts Lot, the nephew of Abraham, watering the trees. These trees were subsequently used to construct the Temple in Jerusalem ('to adorn the place of my sanctuary'). Later, during Herod's reconstruction of the Temple, the wood from these trees was removed and discarded, eventually being used to construct the cross on which Jesus was crucified ('and I will glorify the place of my feet').

Like the relics of John the Baptist's head, the abundance of fragments from the True Cross have been used as arguments against the authenticity of Christian relics in general. However, a study by Anatole Frolow has shown that far fewer fragments of the True Cross are known than one would expect.[6] Today, only about a thousand pieces, mostly very small fragments, are thought to survive. Still, the complicated history of the True Cross, or indeed its authenticity, is in many ways immaterial, because most Christians believe in its veracity. Because Christ's body was assumed into heaven, there were no bones left as relics, and items closely associated with his presence on earth were, therefore, highly prized, and none more so than this most sacred and venerable cross of wood, which had been drenched in the blood of Christ.

The sign

And thus it came to be, the most powerful wonder-working charm – the Sign of the Cross. Thence, the cross was one of the most important objects carried by the Byzantine army in battle and triumph, the standard of the cross regularly preceded the army into war, and the recovery of lost military crosses and their subsequent dedication in Hagia Sophia was a prominent state occasion, a cause for public celebration. About the sign of Christ, the late fourth-century poet and lawyer Prudentius says:

> 'Christ' was represented on the purple *labarum* with gems on gold, 'Christ' was written as a symbol on their shields, and the cross blazed forth fixed atop their standards.[7]

The first item, the *labarum*, was apparently a creation of Constantinus. The emperor, we are told by Eusebius, viewed a 'cross-shaped trophy' in the sky,[8] and later that night in his sleep Christ presented him 'the sign which had appeared in the sky, and urged him to make himself a copy of the sign which had appeared in the sky'.[9] Eusebius then provides an extensive description of the copy of the sign that the emperor was apparently instructed to make on the morning of Pons Mulvius:

> Then he summoned goldsmiths and jewellers, sat down among them, and explained the shape of the sign, and gave them instructions about copying it in gold and precious stones. This was something which the emperor himself once saw fit to let me also set eyes on, God vouchsafing even this. It was constructed to the following design. A tall poll plated with gold had a transverse bar

forming the shape of a cross. Up at the extreme top a wreath woven of precious stones and gold had been fastened. On it two letters, intimating by its first characters the name 'Christ', formed the monogram of the Saviour's title, *rho* [P] being intersected in the middle by *chi* [X]. These letters the emperor also used to wear upon his helmet in later times. From the transverse bar, which was bisected by the pole, hung suspended a cloth, an imperial tapestry covered with a pattern of precious stones fastened together, which glittered with shafts of light, and interwoven with much gold, producing an impression of indescribable beauty on those who saw it. This banner then, attached to the bar, was given equal dimensions of length and breadth. But the upright pole, which extended upwards a long way from its lower end, below the trophy of the cross and near the top of the tapestry delineated, carried the golden head-and-shoulders portrait of the God beloved emperor, and likewise of his sons. This saving sign was always used by the emperor for protection against every opposing and hostile force, and he commanded replicas of it to lead all his armies.[10]

Eusebius, as frequently noted by scholars, is not describing the *labarum* as it appeared on the day of the battle. In essence, that *labarum* would have been a makeshift affair; probably a long thrusting spear made into a cross with a perpendicular bar. There was neither a golden wreath encrusted with precious stones perched on top nor a CHI-RHO monogram adorning the said wreath. As Cameron and Hall sharply but rightly say in their commentary on the *Vita Constantini*: 'Constantine sees a cross. Nothing in the text suggests that he sees a *chi-rho* emblem at this point. When Eusebius describes the *labarum* or battle-standard later, the chief shape is the long upright and the cross-piece, making a simple cross'.[11] Thus it was the cross – not the CHI-RHO – that constituted the central element of the Pons Mulvius *labarum*.

As previously mentioned, in his earlier work, the *Historia ecclesiastica*, Eusebius does not appear to have been aware of any story about a vision, stating simply that Constantinus adopted the Christian god as his protector before marching against Maxentius.[12] Nevertheless, even this early and writing in the East, Eusebius demonstrates knowledge that in the West the emperor had made special use of the cross in his imperial representation, specifically as a military instrument. In his description of the aftermath of Pons Mulvius, Eusebius states that a statue of Constantinus was erected in a very conspicuous location in Rome, with the emperor holding 'the trophy of the Saviour's Passion', also termed 'the Saviour's sign', with an attending inscription explaining that it was by means of 'this salutary sign' that Rome was liberated from tyranny:

[A]nd straightway he gave orders that the trophy of the Saviour's Passion should be set up in the hand of his own statue; and indeed when they set him in the most public place in Rome holding the Saviour's sign in his right hand, he bade them engrave this very inscription in these words in the Latin tongue: 'By this salutary sign, the true proof of bravery, I saved and delivered your city from the yoke of the tyrant; and moreover I freed and restored to their ancient fame and splendour both the senate and the people of the Romans'.[13]

It is reasonable to assume that by 'the trophy of the Saviour's Passion' Eusebius can only be referring to the cross, and that 'the Saviour's sign' and 'salutary sign' are epithets for the cross as well. If Eusebius seems at all vague here as to the nature of the symbol, he is much more explicit in the corresponding passage in *Vita Constantini*:

He announced to all people in large lettering and inscriptions the sign of the Saviour, setting this up in the middle of the imperial city as a great trophy of victory over his enemies, explicitly inscribing this in indelible letters as the salvific sign of the authority of Rome and the protection of the whole empire. He therefore immediately ordered a tall pole to be erected in the shape of a cross in the hand of a statue made to represent himself, and this text to be inscribed upon it word for word in Latin: 'By this salutary sign, the true proof of valour, I liberated your city, saved from the tyrant's yoke; moreover the Senate and people of Rome I liberated and restored to their ancient splendour and brilliance.' The God beloved emperor, proudly confessing in this way the victory-bringing cross, was entirely open in making the Son of God known to the Romans.[14]

The particular context here, which is absent from the earlier *Historia ecclesiastica*, suggests that the 'sign' held in the hand of the statue was similar to, if not the same as, the product of the 'vision' used by Constantinus in the battle. The simplicity of the description of the monumental 'sign' – compared to the *labarum* seen much later by Eusebius – indicates that this was some form of prototype, an early and basic construction, which Constantinus would ornament and elaborate in the years to come.

We will now return to the earlier quotation from Prudentius. The last item mentioned by him was known as a cross-standard, and a number of these would have been carried into battle.[15] Cross-standards should be identified with large processional cross, such as the late tenth-century bejewelled example at the aforementioned Megisti Lavras. This bears a Greek inscription on its back side that addresses the cross as a weapon: '[...] and with the weapon (τῷ ὅπλον) of the cross strike down our enemies'.[16] On the same side is also inscribed, in Greek, a verse from Psalm 45: 'Let your sharp arrows pierce the hearts of the king's enemies; let the nations fall beneath your feet'.[17] It was also customary to carry a bejewelled cross, the *basilikòs staurós*, before the emperors during military expeditions.[18] In addition, small pectoral crosses were likely privately worn by the soldiers.[19] It was a true sign of victory. The battle cry was 'The cross has become victorious',[20] which evoked the paradigmatic victory of Constantinus. The cross was also called 'victory bringer'.[21] An eleventh-century prayer before battle encourages the soldiers to recall the memory of Constantinus and his victorious cross:

> To Constantinus, the first Christian emperor, you [God] showed the divine cross in the skies and said: 'Take courage, in this you will be victorious!' Through the power of the cross, O Lord, now give victory, strength, divine might to your army, since you are merciful [...] Lord, save your people and bless your inheritance, bestow on the emperors victories against the barbarians, protecting your state through the cross.[22]

Eusebius highlights the function and efficacy of the *labarum* in battle, emphasizing also the prestige of those chosen to safeguard the miraculous standard. 'These things', Eusebius writes, 'the emperor himself recounted to the present writer in a moment of leisure long after the events, adding a noteworthy miracle to his account', namely, an extraordinary tale of how the *labarum* offered protection from projectiles in battle, which would strike the slender pole of the standard, but never its faithful bearer.[23]

Through Constantinus' decisive victory at Pons Mulvius, the cross acquired a military rôle. Thereafter the Christian God assisted his pious servants, whether in civil war as at Mursa in the early autumn of 351, where the victory of Constantius II (r. 337–61) in an incredibly bloody battle – of the 36,000 rebels engaged, 20,000 were reported killed with Constantius' losses reported to be 30,000 – was signalled by the appearance of a cross in the sky at Jerusalem,[24] or by foreign adventures as in the remarkable re-conquest of North Africa launched by Iustinianus in 533, which was guaranteed by a bishop's dream and Christian omens.[25]

Chapter 7

Sacred Space

From an occidental point of view, the reign of Iustinianus may seem a brief aside in the long history of Europe, a failed attempt to resurrect an empire already dead. Yet, it clearly was the ambition of Iustinianus to re-establish the unity of the old pagan Roman empire and rule once more over the whole of the Mediterranean basin. By the sheer brilliance of his generals, most notably Belisarius and Narses, and by a lavish expenditure of men, money and matériel, he came within a measurable distance of accomplishing his ends; by the time he had taken his last breath on 14 November 565 the frontiers of the Christian Roman empire stretched from the banks of the Euphrates to the Pillars of Herakles. The emperor is praised effusively by the contemporary historian Prokopios of Caesarea Palestinae for his territorial gains, his religious policy, his legal codification – in sum, for having 'wedded the whole state to a life of prosperity'.[1]

The eunuch general

In 552, Iustinianus despatched an army to Italy and to return Rome (for the fifth time during his reign)[2] to the control of the empire. This imperial army was led by the Perso-Armenian eunuch Narses,[3] now well over seventy years of age. Pious, popular, with an easy-going personality, he was without much genuine military experience. Nevertheless, having served faithfully as the *praepositus sacri cubiculi* or grand chamberlain, the top post available to a court eunuch, Narses had the emperor's confidence and full support. As events proved, Narses was a commander of true genius. It is also said that he never engaged in battle without the consent of the Virgin Mary, to which he was especially devoted.[4] In a swift campaign of just two years Narses crushed the power of the Goths. In his victory speech, Narses compared the steadfast courage of his men with their Roman forefathers.[5] This was odd as the army was made up of almost entirely of Gepid, Lombard and Heruli mercenaries, whose general, before the battle at Taginae (Prokopios' Busta Gallorum), had incited them by 'holding in the air bracelets and necklaces and golden bridles on poles and displaying certain other incentives to bravery in the coming struggle'.[6] Then, Narses went further and led his men to fabled Rome to indulge in that most Roman of victory celebrations, the triumph.

Yet, it is a mid sixth-century ivory plaque, the well-known Barberini Ivory currently at the Louvre,[7] which presents one of the most eloquent visual expressions of this older imperial scheme. In the central panel of this originally five-part composite, the equestrian Iustinianus, crowned, armed and victorious, looks towards the viewer as his mount rears energetically. His power, validated through his military triumphs, ultimately issues from Christ, set at the centre of a disc of light supported on both sides by flying angels. Holding a cross-sceptre, Christ offers his blessing to his earthly representative, the emperor. Three smaller Victoria figures bring wreaths: one hovers above the curve of the horse's mane; the second rises from the lower horizontal frieze; and the third is the statuette brought by a cuirassed general to his triumphant emperor. Beneath his horse a full-bodied woman representing fertility and earthly plenty cradles fruits in her lap as she touches the emperor's boot in a gesture of supportive subservience. The message of this is clear: imperial legitimacy is divinely confirmed and secured by victories in war.

The new reality

Within fifty years of Iustinianus' death, his western conquests (except for Venice, Ravenna and southern Italy) had been lost. Just fourteen years after the barbarian army of Narses enjoyed their Roman triumph, Rome fell to the barbarians again, this time finally. Elsewhere, the Slavs overran Greece, while the eastern frontier witnessed constant warfare. The main enemy was Sasanian Persia, and the two empires slugged it out at the beginning of the seventh century. The nadir of this period was the sovereignty of the tyrant Phokas (r. 602–10) whose brutal and shameful excesses led to popular revolt and the accession of the soldier emperor Herakleios (r. 610–41), whose reign saw the consolidation of a new reality, and, seen retrospectively, may be said to represent the real dividing line between the old Roman world and what we today consider the Byzantine empire. By the time of Herakleios Latin seems to have died out all but completely in the empire, even in administrative usage, its last stronghold. In fact, the linguistic shift had already begun during Iustinianus' time, for in his *Novellae constitutiones*, the decrees issued between the years 535 and 564, it was decreed by the emperor that Greek should be the language of state. It was the inevitable outcome of a long process. Iustinianus' pre-eminent general, Belisarius, was a Latin speaker from Illyricum, as was the emperor himself, but the general's *assessor* or legal secretary, Prokopios, was a highly educated Greek speaker from Caesarea Palestinae, and by universal agreement, considered the last of the great historians in the classical Greek tradition. Prokopios and many others – but probably not the emperor himself – were at home in both Greek and Latin, but increasingly Greek had become the common language of Constantinople. Those who had mastered Latin, such as John the Lydian, could feel aggrieved that its use was declining even in the prefectural office.[8]

The empire could no longer avoid acknowledging its complete hellenization even on the official level. The emperor now adopted once and for all the title of *basileús*. Originally the old Greek word for 'king', this title might be translated as 'emperor'. The actual Greek equivalent for the old Latin word for 'emperor', imperator, however, was *autokrátôr*. These two titles, *basileús* and *autokrátôr*, now became the emperor's formal style, translated more literally as 'king and emperor', as well as 'emperor and autocrat'. Indeed, the new assumption of the title *basileús* has even been taken to celebrate Herakleios' triumph over the *Basileús Basileúôn*, the King of Kings of Persia. Yet, it would be a mistake to over emphasize the influx of Persian ideas and autocracy from this period. The trappings of eastern monarchy had already been introduced by Diocletianus and Constantinus; Herakleios added little in this respect.

In truth, there had been too much change over too long a period for a lasting imperial restoration of the old pagan empire and its mores, and Iustinianus' resources were not sufficient for this gigantic task. Worst still, the human price of these grandiose imperial endeavours was tyranny and oppression and the collapse of his other great hopes, those of fiscal and social reform.

There was another drain on the emperor's resources, one that he considered every bit as essential: his grandiose building programme. For Iustinianus was by any other yardstick a great builder and his handiwork can be found adorning damp Ravenna in the West to dry Mount Sinai in the East. But his singular contribution was to Constantinople itself, building or rebuilding thirty-three of the imperial capital's churches and monasteries. Yet, all these ecclesiastical monuments pale beside the splendour of his achievement in the church of Hagia Sophia,[9] the liturgical centre of Constantinople, of Byzantine and of the Holy Catholic and Apostolic world, the supreme focal point of Christian worship in the *oikouménê*, or inhabited world. By the turn of the sixth century Constantinople had become the melting-pot of ideas from both the East and the West, and the culmination of this synthesis is most strikingly apparent in Hagia Sophia. Although a unique monument whose proportions and breathtaking sense of space under the massive dome would never be repeated, this fusion of the traditional western basilica with the domed structure of the Near East, namely the mastery of constructing a circular dome upon a rectangular building, was to establish a canon for Byzantine ecclesiastical architecture in the centuries to come. Hagia Sophia stands as the supreme creation of Byzantine architecture.

The Great Church

Although there are no architectural remains confirming its existence, it is said the first Hagia Sophia was constructed on the site of an ancient pagan temple. Hagia Sophia underwent two phases of construction before attaining its present state,

Iustinianus' Hagia Sophia being the third church to occupy the hallowed site. The first was erected during the reign of Constantius II (r. 337–61), and was open for services on 15 February 360. Although very little is known about the original church, it is assumed that it was a basilica-type edifice with a rectangular floor plan, semi-circular apse and timbered roof. It was burnt down on 9 June 404 during a riot by the supporters of John Chrysostomos, the patriarch of Constantinople (r. 397–404, d. 407), who had been jostled out of his See by the empress Eudoxia, the wife of Arcadius, whom he had unwisely denounced in a sermon as Jezebel.[10]

Its replacement was built by the pious Theodosius II and dedicated on 10 October 415, an edifice again constructed in the basilica-style. The remains of this church show that five steps led to a monumental entrance porch. Including the imperial gate, there were three doorways in the church's colonnaded façade. The remaining architectural fragments of the Theodosian church show that this too was a building of monumental proportions, comparable in size and grandeur to Iustinianus' church. It was to suffer the same fate as its predecessor, being burnt down during the Nika riots of 13–18 January 532 when the Blues and the Greens, in a rare reversal of the usual state of affairs, united in defiance of Iustinianus' attempts to bring the restless circus factions to heel.

The Nika riots were named so because the united factions adopted as their joint battle cry the pregnant watchword νίκα, 'conquer'. To fulfil their stated purpose, Hypatius, a nephew of the previous emperor but one, Anastasius I (r. 491–518), was promptly elevated to the purple against his will and carried by the jubilant mob to the Hippodrome. In an era without plastic bullets or tear gas, the hysteria of a street rabble braying for vengeance inspired immediate terror. On Iustinianus' orders Belisarius brought into the city loyal troops, most of them Thracians and Goths with no allegiance to either of the circus factions. These trapped the poorly armed rioters within the Hippodrome and put an end to the unrest with a slaughter in which, it is claimed by Prokopios, more than 30,000 partisans were slain.[11] The emperor of a day met a martyr's death. There is an ancient tradition that the circus partisans were buried where they fell and that their bones still inhabit the site. Prokopios, commenting on the destruction of the second Hagia Sophia by the rioters, observed that 'God permitted them to accomplish this impiety, foreseeing into what an object of beauty this shrine was destined to be transformed'.[12] Another eyewitness, however, looked back on a city 'uninhabitable because of dust, smoke and stench of materials being reduced to ashes, striking pathetic dread in those who beheld it'.[13]

In the meantime, as the smoke and dust settled on the ruins of its gutted predecessor, Iustinianus, ensconced in the labyrinth that was the Great Palace, put in motion his grand scheme to build a replacement of his own for it. Unusually, the emperor chose two distinguished Greek mathematicians, Anthemius of Tralles and Isidorus of Miletos, to design and build his great church.[14] Unlike the typical builders of their day, Anthemius and Isidorus approached the design of the third Hagia Sophia from a theoretical perspective, their remarkable vision not blinkered by the constraints of empirical building practice. Anthemius was one of the most distinguished mathematicians and physicists of the age, and Isidorus the greatest geometer of antiquity who had been the director of the Academy in Athens before this brilliant Platonic institution was closed by Iustinianus just three years previously.

Although Anthemius died shortly after work had begun on the edifice, it was completed by Isidorus in less than six years – no fewer than 10,000 men had worked on the project at what must have been a frantic pace under the emperor's impatient and, at times, irritating supervision – and was ready for dedicated by the emperor and the patriarch of Constantinople on the feast day of the Protomartyr Saint Stephen, 26 December 537. On entering his new cathedral, Iustinianus is said to have exclaimed: 'Glory to God who has thought me worthy to finish this work. Solomon, I have surpassed you!'[15] Hagia Sophia was raised as a grand monument of Iustinianus' glory and piety as a zealous Christian sovereign.

The ground plan of Hagia Sophia exhibits a rectangle 70 by 79.30 metres, that is to say, the standard Romano–Byzantine basilica plan. Yet, no internal observer is conscious of this squareness. Instead, the observer sees an enormous nave ending in an apse with the whole crowned with a vast central dome,[16] the symbol of the Dome of Heaven. With its ring of forty arched windows, the dome appears to float on air above the mighty vaults. 'In height it rises to the very heavens', Prokopios effervesces.[17] In reality, the 31.36 metre-diameter dome, soaring to a height of 55.6 metres above the marble floor – that is, about the height of a fifteen-storey building – was the largest open vaulted interior in the ancient and mediaeval world.[18] With forty ribs radiating out from its crown, the dome is based upon four robust, central piers and rests upon four massive arches poised upon them, the circle between the arches being translated into the square of the building beneath by four enormous curved triangular segments called pendentives. The dome is flanked by two half-domes based on secondary piers to the east and west. Only the four main piers are built of solid masonry and lead; the walls and remaining supports are of red brick and mortar, the exterior of which was not originally plastered over and whitewashed as it is today.

Space was what was important in a church, not the actual physical structure that enclosed that space. As such, little thought was given to elaborating the exterior, impressive though it was with its huge dome, curves and powerful vertical lines. Attention was paid to the creation of a visual play of space and lighting, which the viewer participated in rather than witnessed. Since space and lighting were composed so as to symbolize the earthly and heavenly kingdoms, the decoration followed a fixed iconographic programme. So, lavishness was the keynote of the interior decoration and, in spite of much remodelling and major repairs the church has undergone, Hagia Sophia still offers an unmatched spectacle, from its polychrome stone pavement to the crown of the nave vaults.

A remarkable wealth of costly, colourful material was deployed in its decoration (and construction): eight great monoliths of green Molossian from Thessaly line the nave; eight great monoliths in porphyry, from Egyptian Thebes, stand in the four exedrae; one-hundred-and-four monolithic columns in Proconnesian marble (soft grey stone streaked with black) quarried on the island of Prokonnesos in the Sea of Marmara, forty in the nave and sixty-four in the galleries. The capitals of these columns are absolutely splendid. There are several different types, but all are alike in having the surface decoration of acanthus and palm foliage deeply undercut so that they produce an effect of white lace on a dark background; it is possible they were once gilded. The commonest of the capitals – those of the nave and gallery arcades – are generally known as the bowl type: ionic volutes support a decorated abacus beneath which the bowl-shaped body of the capital is adorned with acanthus leaves, in the centre of which in front and back is a medallion containing a monogram. The monograms give the names of Iustinianus and Theodora and the imperial titles *basileús* and *augóusta*.

The marble floor is made of Proconnesian marble, which was book-matched, meaning the plaques were sawn across the black veins and arranged in pairs whose pattern thus creates a continuous wavelike design. Likewise, some of the walls are lined with panels of carefully chosen and contrasted marbles: white marble from Lakonia, pale green from Euboia, rose-red and white from Phyrigia, crocus-yellow from Numidia, and one from the Pyrenees, 'the product of the Celtic crags, like milk poured on the flesh of glittering black', in the evocative words of one observer, Paul the Silentiary.[19] In order to obtain the elaborate symmetrical patterns of each panel, the thin blocks of marble were sawn in two, sometimes four, and opened out like a book and placed back-to-back like giant butterfly wings to best display their beautiful patterns. Observers, both ancient and modern, respond as patients do to the ink blots of a Rorschach test by finding in the veined marble panels likenesses of men and animals, devils and angels.

Other walls were once decorated with gold tesserae mosaics. These panels were fixed as follows. Over the structural brickwork of the surface to be covered, two rough layers of plaster (lime and hay) were spread. On this a third layer of finer stuff (lime and marble dust), which was slow setting, was applied. Before this third layer was dry the main lines of the mosaic figures or subject were sketched on in tone with a fine brush. The mosaic cubes (known as tesserae) were then pressed one-third to one-half into this form at odd angles to create an image that shimmered when sun or candlelight fell upon it. The backgrounds of these mosaics were universally formed of gold tesserae, while the figures and subjects were composed of cubes of many colours and gradations of tone. The principal coloured tesserae were cut out of sheets of opaque coloured glass, while the lighter ones – flesh tints, etc. – were of marble. The gold tesserae for the backgrounds were made from gold leaf that had been laid upon glass, a thin transparent film was then spread over the top and the whole annealed into one solid mass. A figure's outline was executed by the craftsman, while backgrounds and the inner masses would be the chore of his apprentices.

These mosaic panels, studded with the images of Christ with his saints and his emperors and empresses of Constantinople, would have shimmered in the light of a myriad lamps and candles. The original church fittings, according to Prokopios, were of equal splendour: 40,000 pounds of silver were employed in the bema,[20] and the actual high altar was an extraordinary piece of craftsmanship made from a blend of precious metals and studded with gems; rich hangings in the aisles and the galleries; gates of bronze, often silvered. Nothing of this richness remains of course, for it has been plundered as the wartime spoils of many nations.

God's gifts: the city and the Church

In the south vestibule of Hagia Sophia is a superb mosaic of the end of the tenth century. In it is portrayed, as it were, the heritage of the Christian imperial tradition, as the Byzantines understood it. The Virgin Mary sits enthroned in glory, the infant Christ on her lap, receiving from two emperors their choicest offerings. On her left is Constantinus, the first Christian emperor, the founder of the Christian imperial polity. The inscription by him reads 'Constantinus the Great Emperor among the Saints'. Represented in his hands in quaintly stylized form is his offering: Constantinople, the imperial metropolis guarded by God, the seat of the Christian imperial mission, and the special beneficiary of the Virgin's protection. But on her right stands Iustinianus, 'the illustrious *basileús*', as the mosaic inscription labels him. In his hands, again in miniature stylized representation is his contribution: Hagia Sophia, the supreme centre of Christian worship in the *oikouménē*, or inhabited world.

The City and the Church, these were the two imperial accomplishments that the tenth-century Constantinopolitans remembered as their sovereigns' greatest achievements, at least as represented here, and also worthy enough to be offered to the Theometor herself. Under Iustinianus, the Church was apparently served by 525 clergy, and these included eighty priests and 150 deacons, rightly so as the liturgical centre of Constantinople. Yet, at the same time the Church served as the very pivot of life in the Queen of Cities. Within its hallowed walls were enacted centuries of human drama, triumph, violence, piety, everyday routine, unheard-of spectacle, and heartbreaking disaster, all of which made up the long and fascinating story of the Christian civilization which called this splendid edifice its *Megalé ekklêsía*, the Great Church.

Chapter 8

Pious Autocrats

We have just made mention of Iustinianus' zealous Christianity, so it seems an appropriate time for us to take a closer look at the unique position held by the Byzantine emperor in the Church. For their part, the main preoccupation of the earlier Roman emperors was civil order and the loyalty of the army – they could not care less about which gods their subjects followed or did not follow. The only expectation that was placed on all was their support for the state and the status quo. Constantinus was to change all that. For when Constantinus adopted the Christian God, the God of mercy, love and justice, as his divine companion and granter of victory, a move justified by successes at Pons Mulvius and then over Licinius, he let loose a philosophy that was to pervade every aspect of political, social, cultural and, of course, religious life, right up to the twentieth century. But that is all with the benefit of hindsight.

The Thirteenth Apostle

Because it was not until his death was only a matter of days away that Constantinus was reputedly baptized a Christian and thus cleansed of all sin, the nature of his conversion and his affiliation to Christianity has been hotly debated. Apparently, Constantinus had wanted to imitate Christ by being baptized in the river Jordan,[1] but in view of his approaching death it was too late for that now. The honour of baptising the dying emperor fell to Eusebius, bishop of Nicomedia (not to be confused with the bishop writer from Caesarea Palestinae). Not everyone was happy with this choice, as there were rumours that Eusebius was a follower of the doctrine of Arius, the presbyter of Alexandria, more of which later.

The emperor was to take his last breath on 22 May 337 in the thirty-first year of his reign and sixty-fifth year of his life. His day of passing was the Pentecost, the Christian festival fifty days after the crucifixion celebrating the descent of the Holy Spirit upon the disciples of Christ, now to be known as the apostles (Gr. *apostoloi*, messengers), empowering them to begin the evangelization of the Roman empire for Christ, that is to say, to establish churches, officiate the mysteries, and transmit the New Law. It could not have been a more auspicious day for the death of the first Christian emperor.

As he had wished, Constantinus was laid to rest in the church of Hagioi Apostoloi, the Holy Apostles, which he had built for himself on the Fourth Hill, the highest hill of his city. The core of the church was a heroön; the nearest Constantinus ever came to providing his new city with a shrine. In the heroön there were twelve small sarcophagi bearing the names of the apostles. As the emperor's Christian biographer Eusebius of Caesarea Palestinae tells us, by placing his sarcophagus in the centre of the others, six either side, he was declaring himself the Thirteenth Apostle, an interesting detail.[2] Socrates Scholasticus adds that the body of Constantinus (he had died at his summer palace in Nicaea) was placed in a gold coffin, which was then borne into the capital and interned in the church,[3] the gold coffin being placed inside a porphyry sarcophagus, probably one and the same Eusebius mentions surrounded by those consecrated to the memory of the apostles. Under the sponsorship of his son Constantius II (r. 337–61), Constantinus' body was moved from its original burial site at the centre of the memorials of the twelve apostles to an adjacent location where his successors were also then laid to rest.[4] Clearly, the son did not fully approve of his father's funereal fancy. By the by, Pierre Gilles, when he was visiting the spot where the church formerly stood, saw a porphyry sarcophagus, empty and lidless, 'which the Greeks and Turks say is that of Constantine the Great'.[5]

In his satirical fantasy *Caesares*, Flavius Claudius Iulianus (better known to history as Julian the Apostate, the one who had renounced Christianity) portrays his uncle Constantinus as a sensualist in every sense. It is the occasion of the Saturnalia, December 361, and a contest is being held between the Roman emperors, with Alexander the Great called in as an extra contestant, in the presence of the assembled gods. In a brutally witty passage, when asked to pick a god, Constantinus runs first to Pleasure who leads him to Dissolution and finally to Jesus who offers to wash away his sins.[6] Such sarcastic scorn is readily taken up by Voltaire, who with his customary wit writes:

> This is how he [Constantinus] reasoned: baptism purifies everything; I can therefore kill my wife, my son and all my relations; after which I shall have myself baptized and I shall go to heaven; and in fact that is just what he did.[7]

Are we really to believe like Voltaire that Constantinus was such a despicable opportunist?

Servant of God?

To some of my readers, religion is probably right up there with the parliamentary system of liberal democracy as an expression of collective idiocy. To others, it is the comforting belief that there is something greater moving all the pieces around. The former may detest people who exploit other people by taking advantage of their spiritual weaknesses, their need to believe in something that is unexplainable in order to make their lives more bearable. Yet the latter may see it as strength, their lives being happier when they believe that God was responsible for the cosmos and all that goes with it. That being said, creation is probably overrated. After all, God made the world in only six days and rested on the seventh. A rush job like Constantinus' Constantinople, if you will, the end product exhibiting signs of substandard workmanship.

With his usual flair for elegant irony, Edward Gibbon put it best when he wondered why the Romans, who were so tolerant of every religion, would take after such a moral and just peoples as the Christians with such ferocity. After all, the paganism of the Roman state was willing to be all things to all men. Being polytheistic, it was multiple and versatile. It was very far from exclusive. Nor was it generally intolerant. True, it had developed intolerance to the Christians, because the Christians, since they owed loyalty to a higher master, seemed to be denying the sufficient minimum loyalty to the emperor and the nation. As a child of the eighteenth-century Enlightenment Gibbon was no fan of Christianity, but he was also no hater. Like Voltaire (whom Gibbon knew and admired), what seemed to him the hypocrisy of the Christian ideal as opposed to natural human functioning was his particular dislike, and it is this problem that runs through his history. For Gibbon it was Constantinus' adoption of Christianity that assisted a process of decline by finally abandoning earlier Roman values.

So, was it sincere piety and personal faith that prompted Constantinus' actions? Or was it something more prosaic? It all depends on how one chooses to weigh the evidence. To some, he saw the advance of the Christian faith as essential to Rome's glorious future and himself as the key player in God's cosmic plan. To others, he was a wily politician whose main agenda was to reunite and strengthen a fragmented and failing empire, who embraced a faith offering practical advantages in a period of crisis. Yet, to others, his alleged conversion was not a religious epiphany but another example of the shift of emphasis from the troubled western part of the empire to the more prosperous, albeit more theological, eastern part. And then there are those who see only Constantinus' cold and terrible lust for naked power, a reference to the stories of the emperor's murder of his then-wife Fausta and his twenty-one-year-old bastard son Crispus, to name only a few. Zosimos, for instance, states that Constantinus' inability to find 'pagan' forms of absolution led him to Christianity, which promises forgiveness for every sort of wickedness.[8] However, Zosimos was a follower of the emperor Iulianus (r. 361–3) and an avid enemy of Constantinus on account of his religion. Such prejudices render the details surrounding these two particular family deaths difficult to discern, made even more so as they are tinged by rumours of a sexual relationship between the two, but appear to have their origins in a dynastic dispute. It seems that Fausta had accused Crispus, the apple of his father's eye and therefore a threat to any of Constantinus' other children, of treason. When the truth emerged, only after the execution of his son, Fausta was done away with in an overheated bathhouse.[9]

Constantinus was not raised a Christian. When he had to respond to yet another Frankish raid across the Rhine, he sought guidance from his father's preferred god, the gifted Apollo. He had a vision of light. So, in 310, an anonymous panegyrist suggested that Constantinus saw Apollo in the guise of Sol Invictus who had become his divine protector,[10] and, as previously mentioned, he continued to put Sol Invictus on his coins until as late as 320/1. On the other hand, Eusebius later contended that the emperor had a vision and a dream in which he saw Christ not Apollo,[11] as did Paul on the road to Damascus: 'About noon, O King [Herod Agrippa] as I was on the road, I saw a light from heaven, brighter than the sun, blazing around me and my companions'.[12] A voice calls out and addresses Paul personally by his Hebrew name, Saul. When Paul asks to whom the voice belongs, the reply is, 'I am Jesus'. All those accompanying him are affected by the experience, either seeing the light but not hearing the voice, or vice versa.[13]

By breaking down the various elements of Constantinus' 'vision' we can see that certain similarities with the common details of Paul's experience on the road to Damascus. First, Constantinus is also on the road ('somewhere', Eusebius indicates); second, he is accompanied by his army; third, it is around midday; fourth, the 'vision' appears in the sky; fifth, it is in the form of a dazzling formation of light; sixth, there is not only a discernible symbol, but also a form of dialogue ('ἐν τούτῳ νίκᾳ'), although Constantinus is unsure as to the identity of the deity; seventh, Constantinus' entire army become witnesses to the marvel and are struck with amazement together with their emperor; and finally, as he sleeps, Christ appears to Constantinus in person and reiterates the instruction given in the celestial 'vision'.[14]

We must, of course, understand that Eusebius was a diehard Christian apologist who intentionally went out of his way to defend his faith against fierce assaults by those who favoured classical paganism. His *Historia ecclesiastica* lauds the emperor as a great man of God, too humble to accept the praises bestowed upon him for ending the terrible tyranny against Christians. He refers to Constantinus' reverence for the most high as 'inborn'. This notion certainly was not lost on later Church fathers. Thus, for instance, Theodoretos bishop of Kyrrhos, who was writing around the mid fifth century and familiar enough with Eusebius to mention him specifically in the prologue of his *Historia ecclesiastica*, refers to Constantinus as 'the emperor worthy of all praise, who obtained his calling "neither from men nor through men", but from heaven, like the divine apostle'.[15]

Eusebius' adoration of the emperor would produce that other document of praise, the *Vita Constantini*. As eulogistic portraiture, his focus is simply those elements that, in his opinion, made Constantinus a laudable emperor. To this end, anything less than praiseworthy, such as the executions of Crispus and Fausta, is decisively omitted. However, the message that permeates the entire text is not simply that Constantinus was a great emperor, but a great Christian emperor. It has been pointed out that as early as the Synod of Arles, in 314, Constantinus referred to himself as the *famulus Dei*, servant of God,[16] a phrase used of Moses in the Septuagint,[17] and one that became a favourite of his. Indeed, Eusebius compares Constantinus to Moses, both patriarchs, both national leaders.[18] He even adds that Constantinus was so hostile to pagan monuments that he took care that they should be destroyed throughout the empire and decreed by law that pagan temples should be torn down.[19]

This is certainly not the Constantinus we have come to understand from the standpoint of retrospection. However, when viewing the *Vita Constantini* as a whole, it is overwhelmingly clear that Eusebius strove to represent Constantinus as 'chosen' by the Christian god to be the sole ruler of the Roman empire and in that capacity to convert the predominantly 'pagan' population to Christianity, at various times assuming the guise of Moses, Paul, and Christ, in addition to being equal to the apostles.

Constantinus' God

Then as now, conversion to Christianity presupposed an acquaintance with its most basic teachings and worldview. The more formal conversion process included three parts: first, a spiritual and mental 'turning away' from other gods and exclusive attachment to the creator God and his incarnate Son Jesus Christ as the one true God; second, formal instruction in the new faith; and third, public acceptance of the rule of faith, or creed, together with baptism. To mention the example of the author of *The Confessions*, Augustine, bishop of Hippo Regius (now Annaba in Algeria), the first part, the actual turning away from classical paganism, could be a process of years gradually achieved through some type of repeated or on-going contact with Christians and their message.

We return, therefore, to the question of Constantinus' delayed baptism. Already a century earlier, Tertullian's writings clearly indicated that baptism was viewed by many as an initiation rite that cleansed a person from past sins, but not future ones. In fact, it made future sins even more difficult to erase. This made for a very real dilemma for a Christian emperor who knew that in the coming years his official duties would include taking part in battle, ordering executions, and overseeing justly a predominantly pagan population and governmental system. It has been proposed that it is this above all that led Constantinus to delay his own baptism for twenty-five years.[20] Needless to say, the non-baptized or catechumens were not allowed to share in or even view the celebration of the sacrament, or to take full part in the worship of the Christian community.

Whether or not Constantinus designedly opted to forego baptism and the public participation in church life that his baptism would have allowed, the Roman Catholic Church came to have a much more positive view of the emperor, viewing him as a hero for ending the era of persecution and championing the faith. The Orthodox Church went even further, for he is hailed as the second founder of Christendom, and referred in their liturgy as the Equal to the Apostles (Gr. *isapóstolos*), or sometimes the Thirteenth Apostle. Such veneration, be it Roman Catholic or Orthodox, is not by virtue of any religious authority, but because Constantinus was instrumental in the dissemination of Christ's teachings to the universal Roman empire.[21] Whatever the reason or reasons may have been, and many ingenious hypotheses have been advanced, the prosaic fact remains that Constantinus took the step. Moreover, Christian or not, it does not matter, for this change, which effected the entire course of history, was not due to a dramatic attack of piety on the part of Constantinus but was driven by the direct material interests of the imperial system he represented. In other words, part of his consolidation of a strong dynastic régime militarily, economically, fiscally and administratively.

Reconstructing Constantinus' doctrine of God depends heavily on which of his theological statements are given priority, for it is not always clear how and whether everything he says actually coheres. In the beginning, the imperial agenda and ecclesiastical conviction shared common interests, but while one strived for the widest possible acceptability of the doctrine of God, the other strived for the appropriateness of it. Is this not a simple matter of politics versus faith?

Whatever Constantinus' true motives, one thing is certain, as a result he decided, after gaining complete control of the empire in 324, that the Christian religion should take the most favoured status in the empire. Moreover, his deathbed baptism left little doubt about how Constantinus wanted to be perceived – as the first Christian Roman emperor. Indeed, by his death the radical transformation of the Roman world was virtually complete. The most conspicuous signs of change to men of the time (depending on their viewpoint), were security of frontiers; a mighty, bejewelled emperor ruling the world from his new and splendid capital in the East; the new religion of Christ, visible everywhere in the building of churches and the influential figures of bishops, zipping about their affairs like court officials; the thriving country estates and villas of the local magnates; the fat jobs in the civil service, the proliferating new titles, uniforms and dignities; locust-like army of bureaucrats with their endless headcounts and tax reckonings; the tightening of servitude on the poor man and the peasant. The gap between Christianity's ruling principle, namely the life of the spirit and of the after world was superior to the here and now, and material life on earth is the great pitfall of Christendom.

Returning to those self-important bishops and their new public rôle, in particular in the service of Constantinus' son Constantius II (r. 337–61), Ammianus writes:

> The plain and simple religion of the Christians was bedevilled by Constantius with old wives' fancies. Instead of trying to settle matters he raised complicated issues which led to much dissension, and as this spread more widely he fed it with verbal argument. Public transport hurried throngs of bishops hither and thither to attend what they call synods, and by his attempts to impose conformity Constantius only succeeded in hamstringing the post service.[22]

Now Ammianus, a pagan soldier, was relatively nonchalant about religious matters, capable of being equally scathing about pagans and Christians alike. Nevertheless, seeing the first stages of this development, and watching the new imperial churches under construction, many pagan subjects of Constantinus himself must have shared Ammianus' exasperation.

Divided Church

Without Constantinus' conversion, what would have become of Christianity? To quote the eminent French mediaevalist Ferdinand Lot:

> Let us imagine that the king of France decided to convert to Protestantism, the religion of a small minority of his subjects. Fired with pious zeal against 'idolatry', he would have destroyed or allowed to fall into ruin all the most venerated sanctuaries of the kingdom, the abbey at Saint-Denis, Reims cathedral, the crown of thorns, the Sainte-Chapelle. That still only gives a faint idea of the frenzy that took hold of the Roman emperors in the fourth century.[23]

But Christianity did not become the state religion without coming to some arrangement with the politics and society of the Roman empire. Christianity itself had to accept many compromises too.

To his dismay Constantinus soon discovered that there was a lack of unity within the Church. In the province of Africa, specifically, there were those who took a rigorist position towards the *lapsi*, namely those of the clergy who had shown a lack of faith during the recent great persecution, and those who took a more moderate, forgiving position. The former eventually became known as the Donatists, after Donatus, whom they elected as their bishop. In April of 313 the rigorists presented to Constantinus their grievance against Caecilian, the bishop of Carthage. Constantinus convened a synod of bishops to hear the complaint; the synod met in Rome's Lateran Council and is known as the Synod of Rome.

When the synod ruled in favour of Caecilian, the Donatists appealed to Constantinus again. In response to the appeal Constantinus convened a larger synod of thirty-three bishops, who met at Arles in southern Gaul on 1 August 314. This synod, too, ruled against the Donatists, and again they refused to submit. Constantinus attempted, unsuccessfully, to suppress them, even threatening to go to North Africa and sort them out personally; only the coming war with Licinius prevented him from doing so. A separatist Donatist church possessed considerable strength in North Africa over the next century or so, and the Donatist schism was still a major difficulty there in Augustine's day, when severe repressive measures were enforced by the Synod of Carthage in 411.

The Nicene God

In all matters concerning God, you have to believe, not reason. If you reason, God vanishes like a mouthful of smoke. Yet for Constantinus this was not enough; the emperor wanted reason. He had been driven to the verge of despair by the bickering of the bishops, and longed for unity and conformity so that his 'unknown God' could be placated. Having embraced the faith of the Christians, Constantinus was now faced with major theological disputes between the Christian clergy of his empire. Vexed that pagans were using these differences to deride his religion and his brethren, Constantinus hosted some 270 bishops and many more lesser clergy in his lakeside summer palace at Nicaea (İznık) the First Œcumenical (Universal) Synod of the bishops of the Church, what became known as the Synod of Nicaea I (20 May to 19 June 325).[24] As Eusebius describes, Constantinus 'himself proceeded through the midst of the assembly, like some heavenly messenger of God, clothed in raiment which glittered as it were with rays of light, reflecting the glowing radiance of a purple robe, and adorned with the brilliant splendour of gold and precious stones'.[25] Seated 'on a small chair of gold',[26] the emperor was present as the overseer and presiding official, but did not cast any official vote. His prime aim was to settle these disputes and to establish a unity of belief and practice among Christians.

The major controversy was theological, and was focused upon the relationship of Christ the Son to God the Father. Arius, a presbyter of the Alexandrian church in Egypt, had recently been maintaining that Christ had been born in time, was a mutable creature that did not fully share in the divine essence, and thus should be seen as subordinate to the Father. Alexander, his bishop, had opposed this teaching asserting that Christ was the eternal Word of God, the Logos, shared fully in the divine essence, and therefore should be worshipped as equal to the Father. Both

Arius and Alexander had appealed to episcopal leaders outside Egypt for their positions, and had divided the faithful on this central issue of Christianity by the time Constantinus had conquered the East. The emperor also noticed that some Christians in Syria and Palestine were still holding the Easter festival according to the date in the Jewish calendar as opposed to the majority of the faithful who celebrated it as a movable feast based upon astronomical calculations.

Constantinus clearly wanted the Church to be a unified *state* organization. He had no time for what he saw as the petty theological squabbles between bishops, and his biographer Eusebius promotes with his ever busy pen the idea of ecclesiastic concord, 'one unanimous opinion shared by all'.[27] The truth was otherwise. The emperor foisted the Nicaean Creed on the synod as a supposed compromise. Six of the bishops refused to sign the Nicaean Creed as the official statement of belief for the Holy Catholic and Apostolic Church of the Roman empire, and these, among them Arius, were packed off into exile as heretics. What is more, eleven bishops apparently did sign the documents, but 'with hand only, not heart'.[28] Nonetheless, bickering bishops or not, the Synod of Nicene did issue a creed that confessed the consubstantiality of the Father and the Son, and stated in no uncertain terms:

> We believe in one God, the Father Almighty, Maker of all things visible and invisible. And in one Lord Jesus Christ, the Son of God, begotten of the Father the only-begotten; that is, of the essence of the Father, God of God, Light of Light, very God of very God, begotten, not made, being of one substance (ὁμοούσιον) with the Father; by whom all things were made both in heaven and on earth; who for us men, and for our salvation, came down and was incarnate and was made man; he suffered, and the third day he rose again, ascended into heaven; from thence he shall come to judge the quick and the dead. And in the Holy Spirit. But those who say: 'There was a time when he was not'; and 'He was not before he was made'; and 'He was made out of nothing', or 'He is of another substance' or 'essence', or 'The Son of God is created', or 'changeable', or 'alterable' – they are condemned by the holy catholic and apostolic Church.[29]

Again, on the positive side, as most of the bishops present at the synod were Roman patriots and Christian zealots, they likewise agreed to the suggestion of their imperial champion of avoiding the Jewish method for dating Easter, and accepting the western tradition of celebrating their most important festival on the first Sunday after the first full moon of the spring equinox – honouring the day that Christ had arisen rather than the date.

Nicene I was a real watershed. Nevertheless, the actual outcome of this synod may have been rather disappointing to Constantinus, for the theological disputes kept dragging on and on. In fact, when the emperor died, the Arian controversy, a topic for later discussion, was only gaining momentum. Arianism had been condemned by the synod. What was decreed in the synod, however, did not always happen in practice. This dogma had to be condemned more decisively at the Second Œcumenical Synod (Constantinople I in 381). As a result, the Arian challenge to the divinity of Christ had been officially repulsed, and the imperial development of the Trinitarian equation of the Son to the Father was finally assured. It is true that Arian factions of dissent continued within the empire after 381, such as that which flourished in Mediolanum (Milan) around empress Iustina, the mother of Valentinianus II (r. 375–92) and the foe of that city's bishop, Ambrose. For the most part, however, Arianism was on its way to complete extinction among the peoples of the empire by the end of the fourth century.

Militant Christianity

Constantinus' actions had thereby raised a relatively small and non-influential Christian community to a dominant position in the state, and following three decrees of Theodosius I (r. 379–95) forbidding pagan sacrifice and pagan cult, Christianity would become the empire's only official religion in November 392.[30]

The son of an able but disgraced *magister militum*, Theodosius' own military prowess had caught the eye of the militarily inept Gratianus (r. 367–83), who despatched him off with to command the Illyrian army to deal with the various barbarian confederations making regular excursions across the Danube into Roman territory. After scoring some impressive victories on the battlefield, Gratianus gave Theodosius the ultimate reward by crowning him co-emperor and formal successor to Valens (r. 364–78), Gratianus' Arian uncle who had recently been violently killed at Adrianople while fighting against the Goths. Theodosius, a Nicene Christian, then went on to conclude a treaty with the Goths in October 382. This apparently assigned them lands in northern Dacia and Thrace, between the Danube and the Balkan mountains, in return for military service as *foederati* under their own leaders. Under the terms of the treaty they were also to be settled as a group, to be exempt from taxation and to receive a yearly payment.[31] The frontier along the lower Danube, their own area of settlement, was thus protected by the Visigoths themselves. The benefit, in principle at least, was that this settlement created a buffer zone for the Romans, a solution that seemed workable at the time. In the following years Theodosius put down the rebellions headed by two western usurpers, firstly Magnus Maximus (r. 383–8) and then, literally with a little help from the weather (and the Visigoths), by Flavius Eugenius (r. 392–4). As Pacatus eulogizes, in his panegyric to Theodosius of 389, the admission of the Goths into Roman service is 'to supply soldiers for your camps and farmers for our lands'.[32]

During the waning years of his life Theodosius became the first Roman emperor to turn full circle on the issue of religious tolerance. After centuries of Christian persecution and then another three quarters of a century whereby Christians and pagans coexisted more or less peacefully, Theodosius began the active persecution and steady elimination of all non-Christian sects and their temples. Indeed, his three edicts not only decreed the total union between state and Church, but also proclaimed Orthodox Christianity (i.e. the faith as proclaimed at Nicaea I) as the only proper worship due to God. The word orthodox comes from the Greek *orthos* (correct) and *doxía* (belief) and implies a purity of doctrinal teaching inherited from Christ and the Holy Catholic and Apostolic Church (viz. the Early Church devoid of all manner of disunity, as founded by Christ and handed by Him to the care of the apostles). Semantics aside, even though the ban was neither complete nor universally applied, the pagan cause was definitely discredited when Eugenius was defeated in September 394.

Christian chroniclers understandably interpreted the final battle at the Frigidus (somewhere in today's Vipava valley, Slovenia),[33] between Sirmium and Aquileia, as a divine judgement on the pagans:

> It may perhaps be hard for the pagans to believe what happened; for it was discovered that, after the prayer that the emperor [Theodosius] poured out to God, such a fierce wind arose as to turn the weapons of the enemy back on those who hurled them. When the wind persisted with great force and every missile launched by the enemy was foiled, their spirit gave way, or rather it was shattered by divine power.[34]

This was certainly an unforeseen climatic event or, in Christian parlance, a God-given miracle. On the second day of the battle, just as the two armies were about to engage, 'an indescribably great windstorm suddenly began to blow violently into the faces of the enemy'.[35] Christian cant aside, the two-day battle on the banks of the Frigidus had been a costly but total victory for Theodosius. In the immediate aftermath, Eugenius was captured and brought before the emperor in shackles. His pleas for mercy went unanswered and he was beheaded; the severed head of the former professor of rhetoric was displayed in the victor's camp.[36] The western provinces quickly submitted to Theodosius. A mere five months later he was dead. As for Eugenius, though himself a Christian, he was the last emperor to support Roman polytheism; during his brief rule, the altar and statue of the goddess Victory was again restored to the Curia – they had been removed in 382 by Gratianus – and private funds were provided for the restoration of many pagan ceremonies, temples and sacrifices.[37]

The grim Theodosius was to be revered as 'the Great' by the Orthodox Church because of the uncompromising Christian orthodoxy – he was certainly the bane of heretics – that characterized his imperial programme, which included those three edicts proscribing paganism, bringing to an end, among other changes, a thousand years of that strongest link with the pre-Christian world, the Olympic Games. That was followed at Olympia almost immediately by the conversion of one of the more suitable buildings into a Christian church, and it is unthinkable that the Games were permitted to coexist with a Christian community and Christian worship. While festivals and ceremonies acquired a new Christian colour, pagan temples began to fall into disrepair, aided by the vandalism of Christians: did not Augustine himself exult over the destruction of pagan temples?

In April 390, Butheric, a favoured Gothic *magister militum* in command of Illyricum and based in Thessaloniki, had a popular charioteer imprisoned for a homosexual offence; he had attempted to rape a cupbearer.[38] Christian attitudes to homosexual sex were more extreme than those of its parent religion, Judaism. The Church's view on the matter was founded in the scripture: 'Do not lie with a man as one would with a woman; that is detestable'.[39] Eventually, the Church's condemnation of any type of non-procreative sexual intercourse brought about the outlawing of homosexuality and an edict of Theodosius that very year threatened with public burning the forcing or selling of males into prostitution.[40] Behind this edict lay not a disgust of prostitution, but the fact that the body of a man would be used in homosexual intercourse in the same way as that of a woman. And that was unacceptable, for as our arch-Christian convert Augustine would later make clear, 'the body of a man is as superior to that of a woman as the soul is to the body'.[41]

In the meantime, the people of Thessaloniki demanded the charioteer's released and, as Butheric bluntly refused, a riot followed. This resulted in the unruly mob lynching him and a number of Roman officials. An enraged Theodosius, then resident in Mediolanum (Milan), ordered units of the Illyrian army to herd the citizens of the city into the hippodrome, its largest edifice, and have them butchered in revenge.[42] Sickened by the senseless massacre of some 7,000 people, Ambrose, the bishop of Mediolanum, denied the emperor communion and publicly humiliated him for the atrocity.[43]

Stunned, Theodosius accepted full responsibility and went on a month-long period of penance during which time he sought to appease the Church (and Ambrose) by enacting a number of steps designed to sweep all traces of paganism from the empire. Now empowered with state and Church sanction, Christian mobs took to the streets all across the empire to lynch influential pagans and destroy their temples. The orgy of sectarian violence culminated in 391 with the patriarch of Alexandria, Theophilos (r. 385–412), who incited his own posse to strip the famous Serapeum, the temple of the Hellenistic Egyptian god Serapis, of its sacred treasures, burnt thousands of scrolls housed within and finally razed it to the ground. Along with the anti-pagan legislation, the senseless destruction of the

Serapeum, described by Ammianus as 'next to the Capitol, which is the symbol of the eternity of immemorial Rome, the most magnificent building in the whole world',[44] provoked high feelings. It was against this background that the rebellion was raised against Theodosius under that obscure teacher of rhetoric Eugenius.

The execution in 408 of Flavius Stilicho, Romano-Vandal generalissimo, who had become Theodosius' *magister peditum praesentalis*, was immediately followed by a law excluding pagans from the army – since their loyalty was no longer regarded as secure. Thereafter, acts of repression against the pagans continued well into the four-thirties. On his accession as pope, Leo I (r. 440–61), he who confronted Attila, declared that 'Truth, which is simple and one, does not admit variety'. In the same spirit, in 448, Theodosius II (r. 408–50) started to burn pagan books: 'all the volumes that move God to wrath and that harm the soul we do not want to come to men's hearing'.[45] Such pious barbarism resulted in the destruction of the works of the Neoplatonic philosopher Porphyrios of Tyre (d. c. 305) and other literary opponents of Christianity.

All this is a far cry from what Jesus Christ would have desired. Any Church he would have established in his name would have been remained poor, and powerless, and modest. It would have wielded no earthly authority except that of love. It would not have cast anyone out. It would have owned no property and made no laws. It would not have condemned, but only have forgiven. There would have been no ecclesiastical princes with profligate lifestyles or gilded palaces with marble walls and polished floors, or guards standing at ornate doors. His Church would have been like a tree with its roots deep in the soil, offering shelter to all and sundry and giving blossom in the spring and shade in the summer and fruit in season.

Chapter 9

Holy Prince

We live in different times. Until the middle decades of the last century, a general but unstated assumption survived that theology, beliefs and rituals of Christianity were sufficiently well known to readers as to need no explanation. For a post-Christian twenty-first-century readership, living as it does in a sceptical and self-centred age, an age of chatty social media and crisp sound bites, it seems necessary (regardless of the author's own beliefs) to provide definitions and explanations of the various elements of Christian belief and liturgy, which practising Christians would take for granted.

The coming of Christianity that led to the rise of the Christian Roman empire was a far more complex and subtle one than is commonly appreciated, even by practising Christians, and understanding it requires first of all stepping back in time to the turn of the common era, as well as a shift in geographical location from Constantinople to what was to become known as the Holy Land.

Naturally, my critics will bleat that I am going well beyond the province of Constantinople, so be it. For our emphasis now shifts to Jesus of Nazareth (c. 5 BC– AD 33). Jewish nonconformist and itinerant preacher, by accepted tradition Jesus was born in the Roman province of Iudaea in the reign of Augustus. His mission to reform what he saw as corruption in the Jewish faith caused conflict with the religious hierarchy and led to his arrest and trial by the Roman authorities. He was executed in Jerusalem, by crucifixion, during the reign of Tiberius and the governorship of Pontius Pilate (AD 26–36/7), an equestrian prefect who later served at Vienna (Vienne) in Gallia Lugdunensis. Reportedly, though no fault was found in him, the prefect acquiesced to the demands of the Sanhedrin to put him to death. After his death and subsequent reports of his resurrection, followers of Christ developed his teachings into a new faith, independent of Judaism but keeping much of its scriptures.

Christianity evolved out of Jewish teachings and traditions in Palestine during the first half of the first century. Jewish religious tradition had long insisted an anointed leader known as the Messiah – Hebrew for Anointed One, translated into the Greek as *Christós*, Christ – would re-establish the Israeli kingdom of David and Solomon, and bring peace to mankind. It was not quite clear how or when this Messiah would reveal himself, but his appearance had at times been associated with the end of the world and the reconstruction of a new Eden and a New Age.

In search of the Anointed One

It is notoriously difficult to know anything for sure about the founder of a world religion. In the case of Jesus Christ, scholars are presented with that most dangerous of tools, a little knowledge, inevitably of a disputed nature. Indeed, apart from the four short gospels in the canon of the New Testament, whose evidence is partly repetitive and partly contradictory, few facts are known about his life. It should be understood that the gospels of Matthew and Luke are an elaboration based on the earlier and much shorter allegorical account of the life of Jesus in the Gospel of Mark, which was written somewhere around AD 65 or AD 70. Matthew and Luke were produced ten or fifteen years later, while John was the last of the canonical accounts, written near the end of first century, around AD 90 or AD 95. These dates are ten to twenty years earlier than more sceptical scholars would accept. Furthermore, it should be understood, too, that several gospels had been written by disciples of Jesus during the centuries following his death, but only the four aforementioned were authorized by the Synod of Nicaea I in 325 for inclusion in the Bible.

Thus, for a man who has made the most impact on human history, there is no historical document that mentions him, and there is no trace whatsoever to him in Roman literary sources – a subject of Augustus, then Tiberius – that would be contemporary with him, the great literary age of the nation of which Jesus was a subject. It was a time when writers flourished, historians, poets, orators, critics and travellers abounded. Yet, not one mentions the name of Jesus Christ, much less any incident in his life. His significance beggars that of any emperor, and the continuous rôle of Rome itself as the hub of occidental history is in large part his legacy. Nor did he even attract major notice from the Jewish writers of the period, such as Josephus or Philo. Neither is there any reference to him in the earliest Christian writings, including those of Paul. The total absence of contemporary evidence for the historical Jesus should be allowed to speak for itself. Where would Jesus be if the gospels had not been written?

In a lapidary remark on his great *Encyclopédie*, Voltaire said: 'Twenty folio volumes will never make a revolution. It is the little portable volumes of thirty *sous* that are to be feared. Had the gospel cost twelve hundred *sesterces* the Christian religion would never had been established'.[1] True, indeed. The four gospels outline the ministry of Jesus, which began in Galilee on the shores of Lake Tiberias and reached as far as Jerusalem many kilometres to the south. It is hard to imagine that we can realize Jesus by reading the gospels. For his personal teaching is known only from a score of parables, from his sayings during the various incidents and miracles of his ministry, from his talks with some or all of the twelve disciples he chose from among local fishermen and workers, and from a handful of key pronouncements: his Sermon on the Mount, his answers in the Temple and at his trial, his discourse at the Last Supper, his words on the Cross.

Christian tradition states that Christ was proclaimed as the Messiah by the angels at the Nativity, the long-foretold saviour of the Jewish scriptures, but he reduced the vast corpus of those scriptures to two simple commandments:

> Jesus replied: 'Love the Lord your God with all your heart and with all your heart and with all your soul and with your entire mind [Deuteronomy 6:5]'. This is the first and greatest commandment. And the second is like it: 'Love your neighbour as yourself [Leviticus 19:18]'. All the Law and the Prophets hang on these two commandments.[2]

Jesus himself never refuted this claim, but at the same time called himself the Son of Man to stress his commitment to all mankind (and not just to the house of David) as Son of God (more about this supposed title later). Consequently, his teachings were seen as valid since they are those of the incarnate Word of God Himself, who was crucified, died and then rose from the dead.

Jesus did not challenge the secular authorities,[3] stressing before Pontius Pilate 'My kingdom is not of this world'.[4] When he died, he left no organization, neither Church nor priesthood, nor political testament, nor doctrine, indeed, just the enigmatic instruction to his disciples: 'If anyone would come after me, he must deny himself and take up his cross and follow me. For whoever wants to save his life[5] will lose it, but whoever loses his life for me will find it'.[6]

Mythical Jesus

We are all probably familiar with the word euhemerism, yet most of us have never heard of Euhemeros, a Greek mythographer who held a position at the court of Kassandros of Macedon (r. 305–297 BC). It was he who first theorized that the Greek gods who lived at the summit of Mount Olympus were defied kings, heroes or conquerors, and their myths were based on legends sprung from accounts of real people and events. Zeus, for example, was a mortal king of Crete who had been a great empire builder, and his tomb (complete with inscription) was shown to visitors near Knossos.[7] It is said the past is already written, the ink already dry, but for Euhemeros mythology was nothing more than history in disguise.

So many might be surprised that they too are euhemerists on the subject of Jesus Christ. That is to say, though they may not believe Jesus was the divine Christ that Christians venerate as the Son of God and saviour of the world, and may regard accounts of the miracles and wonders attending him as mere legendary accretion, nevertheless they certainly believe there had to have been a central figure that began Christianity.

Perhaps Jesus was just a wandering teacher or an exorcist, an apocalyptic prophet or a zealot who opposed the Roman overlords. Perhaps he was all these things, or even a composite of several such early first-century figures, but at any rate, surely there had to be *somebody* at the original core of Christianity, arguably the most famous individual in human history. All this seems to be a perfectly reasonable, completely natural assumption to make.

By way of an apposite comparison, we know more about the prophet Muhammad than we do about Jesus Christ. His neighbours in Byzantine Syria got to hear about him within two years of his death at the latest. A Greek text written during the Arab invasion of Syria mentions 'a false prophet has appeared among the Saracens' and dismisses him as an impostor on the grounds that prophets do not come 'with sword and chariot'.[8] It thus conveys the impression that Muhammad was actively leading the invasion. The *Doctrina Jacobi nuper baptizati* ('Teaching of Jacob') is a Greek Christian anti-Jewish polemical tract set in Carthage. It supposedly records a discussion that took place on 13 July 634 between a Jew forced to convert to Christianity, Jacob, and some Jews on the conditions of the Byzantine empire in the light of the recent Arab conquests, and how they should proceed as he had done, convert to Christianity. This non-Muslim source gives us pretty irrefutable evidence that Muhammad was a historical figure. In stark contrast, on Arabic coins and inscriptions, and in papyri and other documental evidence in the language, Muhammad only appears some fifty years after his death (whatever its exact date).

The silence of Paul

That Christianity should have become the official religion of the Roman empire could hardly have been foreseen. For generations of believers in later times, the triumph of Christianity was simply the will of God. It was not seriously questioned or analysed, for this was a world that believed in miracles and that God was active in the world. But for many Romans in the early centuries it must have presented a real puzzle. Jesus was long regarded as an obscure, local phenomenon. His followers, whose beliefs were confused by outsiders with Judaism, were unlikely candidates to found a religion of universal appeal. The fact was the underlying spirit of Christianity was essentially alien to Roman tradition. The faith of slaves and simple fishermen offered no advantage for class or sectional interest. Their gospels, which made such a clear distinction between the spiritual kingdom of God and the rule of Caesar, seemed to have resigned in advance from all secular ambitions. What the gospels told them was that in this new way of life and of communion, called the kingdom of God and born of the heart, there were no nations, but only individuals. In other words, the gospels were an offer, a naïve and tentative offer: 'Would you like to live in a completely new way? Would you like to enjoy spiritual beatitude?' Christians may have been secretive and held themselves apart, yet ironically the spread of their monotheistic faith was greatly facilitated by *pax Romana* and *koine*, the common Greek dialect that was widespread in the East. Within three decades of Christ's crucifixion, Christian communities were established in most of the important cities of the Mediterranean.

The key figure in all this Christianization was without doubt the Greek-speaking Saul of Tarsus (d. c. AD 65), better known to Christians as Saint Paul, whose writings constitute the greater part of the canonical New Testament, and whose journeys were the first pastoral visit of a Christian leader. Born a Jew and educated a Pharisee, he took part in the early Jewish persecutions of Christ's followers. He was present at the stoning of the first Christian martyr, Stephen, in Jerusalem around AD 35. But then, after his sudden conversion on the road to Damascus,[9] he received baptism and became the most energetic proselyte of a more liberal policy, the so-called New Way. His three missionary journeys were the single most important stimulus to its growth. He met with varying success. In Athens, in AD 53, where he established an altar 'To the Unknown God', he was received with hostility by the Jews and with suspicion by the Athenians, the latter a people noted for their quick wits and nimble tongues. He sojourned twice in more congenial company at Corinth where he practised his trade as a tentmaker. On returning to Jerusalem he was accused of transgressing the Jewish Law, but as a Roman citizen appealed for a trial in Rome. He is generally believed to have perished in the imperial capital during the persecutions of Nero.

As the Roman historian Tacitus' makes clear, it was the background of popular hatred that allowed the despotic Nero to seize upon the unpopular Christians, at the time still a small and exceptional minority in Rome, as scapegoats to absolve himself of suspicions that he had ordered the great fire of 18/19 July AD 64, burning, crucifying, and throwing them to the dogs.[10] For Tacitus, the Christians were indeed guilty, and so got their just deserves at the hands of Nero, for their 'abominations' and their 'mischievous superstitions' and their 'hatred of mankind'.[11] Still, the first text to suggest that Nero killed an apostle is the apocryphal *Ascension of Isaiah*, a Christian writing from the second century considered outside the main body of canonical texts. It says: 'The slayer of his mother, who himself is king, will prevent the plant which the Twelve Apostles of the Beloved have planted. Of the Twelve one will be delivered into his hands'.[12]

Thereafter it is Eusebius (d. 339), bishop of Caesarea Palestinae, who first claims that Nero's persecution of the Christians led to the deaths of Peter and Paul, though the emperor did not give any specific orders.[13] As for the manner of death, the good bishop only mentions the beheading of Paul. As for Peter, he is said to have been crucified upside down in Rome during the reign of Nero in the apocryphal *Acts of Peter*, which was written around the turn of the third century and likewise considered outside the main body of canonical texts. By the fourth century, a number of Christian writers were claiming that Nero personally ordered the apostles' deaths.[14] Which brings us to three contentious points about Peter: there is little evidence for the claim that he was bishop of Rome, it is debatable that Jesus had given him primacy over his other apostles (the apostles themselves seem to have been unaware of it), and no one can pretend that Jesus had said anything about Peter and his successors – if they were his successors – becoming rulers of earthly states, the so-called Patrimony of Saint Peter.

Jews, Christians and Muslims believe that their god is active in history and can be experienced in actual events in this world. But did these events really happen or are they *only* myths? Every culture, whether it believes in God with an uppercase G or gods with their lowercase gees, has its myths. There are Egyptian myths, Greek myths, Roman myths, and – yes – even Christian myths. Paul is regarded as the model of conversion to Jesus Christ. Yet, from certain perspectives, however, Paul may be viewed as a tyrannical figure. An extreme view perhaps, but much like Stalin, the Soviet leader who interpreted (or twisted) the word of Karl Marx in order to justify his despotism, destruction and divisiveness, Paul interpreted (or twisted) the word of Jesus Christ to correspond with his own religious ideas. Saint Paul, who is widely respected as an icon of good, and Joseph Stalin, who is generally considered to have been a force of evil, the epitome of the paranoid dictator ruling by his personal whim, both in their interpretations of Christ and Marx respectively differed radically from those that preceded theirs.

Paul's contribution was crucial on two separate accounts. On the one hand, as the self-styled Apostle of the Gentiles, he established the principle that the New Way was not the tribal preserve of Jews, that it was open to all comers: 'There is neither Jew nor Greek, slave nor free, male nor female, for you are all one in Christ Jesus'.[15] On the other hand, he laid the foundation of all subsequent Christian theology. Divine Grace through Christ redeems sinful humanity, whose Resurrection abrogated the Old Law and ushered in the new era of the Spirit. Christ is more than the Messiah: He is the Son of God, identified with the Church in His mystical Body, which is shared by the faithful through Repentance and the Sacraments until the Second Coming. Jesus was uniquely the source of its inspiration, his real work in the world only beginning after his crucifixion, but it was Paul who founded Christianity as a coherent religion.

At its simplest, Christianity may be summed up as 'Jesus Saves'. To expand upon this, the Pauline message is that Jesus Christ was the Son of God, who after a life on earth, was crucified to death; he rose from the dead and ascended into the kingdom of Heaven. The believer is promised salvation from sin, and resurrection into Heaven. This evokes the Pauline text concerning the concept of baptism as sharing in Christ's death in order to share in his risen glory.[16] It can be honestly said that Paul transformed Jesus Christ into a mythical figure. Before Paul, the notion of Jesus Christ as the sacrificed Lamb of the Christians did not exist. In fact, prior to this, the lamb was (and still is) the Passover Lamb of the Hebrews. After Paul, the lamb provided Christians with a twofold meaning. First, the lamb in the arms of the shepherd symbolized the believer, safe in Christ's care, and second, the lamb alone symbolized Christ himself – the symbol of the New Covenant whose sacrifice 'takes away the sins of the world'. When symbolizing Christ, the lamb was usually shown carrying the Cross.

Jesus never called himself *Son of God* as far as I know – but he used to call himself the 'Son of Man'.[17] Paul was not much interested in Jesus' teachings, which he rarely quotes, or in the events of his earthly life. 'Even if we did once know Christ in the flesh', he wrote to his Corinthian converts, 'that is not how we know him now'.[18] What was important, as we touched upon in the previous paragraph, was the 'mystery' of his death and resurrection. The words mystery, mysticism and myth are all related to the Greek *musteion*, 'to close the eyes and mouth'. All refer to experiences that are obscure and ineffable, because they are beyond speech, and relate to the inner rather than the external world. Thus, Paul has nothing to say about his risen Christ that seems to clearly refer to a life on earth. His was a purely spiritual Christ, probably along the lines of the saviour in the original Ascension of Isaiah who descends through successive layers of heavens by dying and rising again in each one.

Paul had transformed Jesus into the timeless, mythical hero who dies (the traditional human victim without spot or blemish offered up as atonement for sin) and is raised to new life. Thus, everybody who went through the initiation of baptism (the traditional transformation by total immersion, which recalls the baptism of Jesus himself in the Jordan) entered into Jesus' death and would share his new life.[19] Jesus was no longer a mere historical figure but a spiritual reality in the lives of Christians by means of ritual and the ethical discipline of living the same selfless life as Jesus himself.[20]

Human nature being what it is, once an idea is common knowledge, there is no power on earth that can put it into question. At the time, Jesus' suffering and death seemed like a horrible tragedy to his followers, but later it was interpreted by Paul as a sacrifice to redeem all people. As Paul himself wrote: 'If indeed we share in his sufferings in order that we may also share in his glory'.[21] Christ became the redeemer, the Lamb of God, the self-sacrificing saviour who takes away the sins of the world.[22] Thus, Christians no longer knew him 'in the flesh' but they would encounter him in other human beings, in the study of scripture, and in that most sacred of Christian rites, the Eucharist.

'Eucharist' is a Greek word for 'thanksgiving', and its Christian use has a double significance: it is the supreme act of Christian thanksgiving; and refers to Jesus' own actions on the occasion of the last supper with his disciples. Essentially, the Eucharist re-enacts symbolically Jesus' taking bread and wine, giving thanks for them, giving them to the disciples to eat and drink, and declaring that they are his body and blood, given as a redeeming sacrifice or the forgiveness of sins.[23] In the celebration of the Eucharist, the priest blesses bread and wine, which are then offered for communion in the transformed state of the body and blood of Christ. The prerequisite for salvation, the rite was clouded by the metaphysics of transubstantiation and was little understood by the ordinary layman, except for the magical powers believed to reside in the consecrated wafer. Christianity, like paganism before it, is a religion of blood and altars.

Pagans and Christians

Pagans considered the Christians as just another cult, and the Christians saw everyone as pagan, even if they worshipped only one god, it was not their God. Though they were of opposing opinions, Christian or pagan, everyone worshipped a God or gods, and to have no religion was entirely unheard of. Still, one of the fundamental contrasts between pagan 'cultic' practices (for want of a better term) and Christianity was the passage from oral culture of myth and conjecture to one based firmly on written texts. For Christianity was pre-eminently a religion of the book. In the first Christian communities, there had already been a significant break with contemporary habits of reading: Christians used the codex, or book, for their scriptural texts, whereas pagans still vastly preferred the scroll. The Christian codex was made of papyrus, not parchment. It made it compact and better suited to people on the move, and it was an easier form in which to refer to and fro between texts. In a sense, the Christian revolution lies at the beginning of the history of the modern book.

While pagan priests and magistrates competed in their *philotomia*, Christians looked upon this as pure vainglory. While civic cults of the empire paid honour to the presiding manifest divinities of the city, the Christian 'city' lay in the kingdom of Heaven and their 'assembly' was the gathering of people of God throughout the world. The cults and myths gave the pagans a focus for their civic patriotism, yet Christians obeyed one law, the same from city to city. Indeed, a person whose loyalties were less engaged by the hometown, or enlarged by travel beyond it, could respond to this idea of a universal assembly. At their festivals, the élite pagan families made distributions to the civic authorities, members of their own ruling class. Christians brought their funds to those in need, men and women, citizen and non-citizen. Christian charity differed in motive from pagan philanthropy: it earned merit in Heaven and sustained that dear to God, the poor. Christianity appealed to the poor because it promised a better life after people died. Moreover, the poor were attracted to a faith that taught poverty was the law of Christ, all people were equal, and no one branch of mankind should rule over another. The idea of 'doing unto others as you would wish them to do unto you' was not alien to pagan ethics, but there was no precedent for the further Christian advice 'to love one's enemies'.

Its birth in Galilee had saved Christianity from being just one more of the innumerable revelations of the Semite. Galilee was Syria's non-Semitic province, contact with which was almost uncleanness for the perfect Jew, it laying alien to Jerusalem. Jesus by choice passed his ministry in intellectual freedom, not among the boorish shelters of a Syrian village, but in the polished streets among fora and colonnaded houses, products of an intense if very exotic provincial and corrupt Greek civilization. The people of this strange land were not Greek – at least not in the majority – but Levantines of sorts, aping a Greek culture, though not the correct commonplace hellenism of the consumed homeland.[24]

Chapter 10

Christian Alternatives

In its origins Christianity was not a European religion. Like Judaism and Islam, which emerged from one womb and all three stem from one and the same ethnic race – whence 'the religions of Abraham' – Christianity came from the Near East. In reality, Europe did not become its main area of concentration until the Arabs' first great rush round the Mediterranean in the century following the death of Muhammad the prophet of Islam.

The three great monotheistic and related Abrahamic religions share far more concepts and traditions than most people care to realize. On a general level, all three believe that God is omniscient, omnipotent, omnibenevolent, that He will one day deliver unto mankind divine retribution, and that He intervenes in the world. Along with the big three, Judaism, Christianity and Islam, some would include the Bahá'i faith too. Yet, the religion Muhammad created is different in one important respect from Judaism or Christianity – it has no 'established church' or priesthood, any pope or central organ for imposing orthodoxy. Muhammad's one overriding principle was that there was no intermediary between God and the individual believer, hence the opposition to idolatry, and the multiplicity of sects and heresies in Islam.

Islam, which comes from the Arab verb 'to submit oneself', whence comes the name Muslim, 'he who submits', demands obedience to Allah, the creator and judge, who determines the fate of all that exists. This is expressed in the formula 'None has the right to be worshipped but Allah, and Muhammad is the Messenger of Allah'. Prayers are obligatory five times a day, an obligatory yearly payment (*zakat*) of a fixed percentage of a Muslim's income for charitable use, fasting is implemented in the month of Ramadan, and at least one pilgrimage to Mecca is required. The fundamentals of the faith are the Qur'an, the words of Allah given to Muhammad and collected into 114 *surahs* or chapters, with 6,219 *ayahs* or verses, the Sunnah, the correct 'Islamic' interpretation of Muhammad's life and doctrine, and the Ijma, the unwritten contract of the faithful whereby matters of policy and dogma are formulated by the people. These are the five pillars of Islam.

Sunni Islam is the larger of the two branches of Islam, the second being Shi`a Islam, which today represents about 10 per cent of the world's Muslims. The fundamental division between Sunni and Shi`a Islam goes back to Muhammad's death. Muslims disagreed as to who should be his successor, or caliph. Some believed that the caliph should be of the prophet's 'house', and preferred his cousin and son-in-law, `Ali ibn Abi Talib. Yet, it was Abu Bakr, dubbed al-Siddiq, the Veracious, a first-generation convert who married one of his daughters to Muhammad, who claimed the caliphate when the prophet died. According to the Shi`a version of the confused, gory mess that followed Muhammad's passing, Abu Bakr was a classic schmoozer, a coward in battle who had used unscrupulous means to gain the caliphate. Naturally for the Shi`a, `Ali is the first legitimate caliph as he had been designated his successor by Muhammad himself. Even the Sunni are not generally thrilled about Abu Bakr, whose caliphate only lasted twenty-seven months and whose descendants turned out to be terrible rulers.

Shi`a Muslims developed a mythical view of the prophet's male descendants, who were their imams. Each imam was an incarnation of the divine *ilm*, knowledge. Thus, for the Shi`a, it is the imam who is appointed by Allah to lead the Muslims. Shi`a Islam held that only a just imam could declare *jihad* for he was infallible and could prevent needless violence and ensure that the *jihad* is properly guided. Nevertheless, it should be understood that the Shi`a Muslims were (and still are) not all of one mind. The majority of them, known as the Ja`fari Shi`a, traced the line of descent of their heads, the Infallible Imams, from `Ali and his heirs by his wife Fatima, the prophet's daughter, to the twelfth imam, Muhammad al-Mahdi. He disappeared from normal history in 940, and they held that he is in occultation (absent, not dead or alive) and will return one day to restore Islam and thereby inaugurate an era of justice and peace. Twelver Shi`ism became the state religion of Iran in the sixteenth century, as it still is today.

A variant claim to legitimacy was made by a fringe group, the Isma'ilis, in the tenth century. A major ideological rival to the Sunni 'Abbasid caliphs of Baghdad, they ended the succession of the Infallible Imams with the seventh, Isma'il ibn Ja'far al-Sadiq, whence their name. As time went on they produced numerous sects, and one of these evolved into the Fatimid caliphate. Its leader, 'Ubaydallah, claimed descent from the Infallible Imams, and began a widespread propaganda against the 'Abbasid caliphate. He finally established himself in North Africa, and there in 910 he assumed the caliphal title of *amir al-mu'minin*, Commander of the Faithful, thereby asserting a claim to supersede the 'Abbasid caliph and to rule over the entire Muslim community. In 969, Egypt was conquered by the Fatimid warriors, and caliph al-Mu'izz, 'Ubaydallah's great-grandson, moved to Cairo, a new city he was building to house his followers and be the capital of a new dynamic Mediterranean state. Both Shi`a and Sunni became locked in an internal battle for supremacy within the Islamic world. Anyway, I digress.

So far as Muhammad was acquainted with Judaism and Christianity, he disapproved of the rigour of their ethics, which were apt to degenerate into a body of mere empty forms, while he also rejected their dogmatic teaching as utterly false.

Above all, he repudiated whatever seemed to him to savour polytheism, including the doctrine of the Trinity. Without a doubt, one of Islam's chief objections towards Christianity must stem from the misunderstandings or antipathy toward the concept of the Trinity, which Muslims often regard as *shirk*, or polytheism, particularly the notion that God is the 'third of three' (a reference to the Holy Spirit) or that Jesus has a 'share in divinity'. Again, there is the objection that Jews and Christians disregarded their own scripture and exhortations by God, and were therefore less righteous than Muslims. Thus, what distinguished the Arab version of monotheism from its Christian and Judaic predecessors was a strong element of puritanism. It was this 'purer' piety that expressed a reaction against the great empires of the Byzantines and the Sasanians.

One God, different varieties

There were many varieties of Christianity within the Early Church (second to fourth century), but once established as the official state religion, the Holy Catholic and Apostolic Church ruthlessly suppressed all those doctrines that were different to it. The question of where the dividing line lay between true faith and heresy was in truth more of a political one than a theological one. As politics was the heart of the matter, it could be argued, indeed, that these theological splits reflected the struggles of power, position and privilege between the four (later five) patriarchies.

All that having been said, however, the nature of Christ was (and still is) the central and most difficult debate in all Christian theology. Again, it could be argued such theological debates meant little to the vast majority of the community, but whether we, with the mindset of a very different, indeed sceptical age, can understand not just the finer points of Byzantine theology, but the nature of the faith in the world that Constantinopolitans inhabited. The Church influenced almost every aspect of life be it political, economic, cultural or social. It was more than just an institution of clergy and officials, for the Church must include everyone baptised in the name of Christ, from the most pious monk to the most heinous villain. Thus, in those days even the citizen on the street took a keen interest in Christ's divine-human reality, the debate over Christology, which, incidentally, ranked in his or her eyes as a recreation only surpassed by the chariot races at the circus.

Trinitarian theology involves the Holy Trinity, while Christology contemplates the process whereby one member of the Holy Trinity, the Logos, (or the Son, the Word) became man (the Incarnation) in Jesus Christ. To be more specific, Christology concerns how the Logos was manifested after the Incarnation. Many Christians had different views as to what Christ was, or how far he was human and how far he was divine. This question was the most controversial theological matter in early Christian history and led to eventual divisions of the Holy Catholic and Apostolic

Church, especially in Syria, Palestine and Egypt from the fifth century. These were known as Christological controversies and they led to the summoning of the œcumenical synods to combat what were considered heresies or misinterpretations of doctrine.

Christology revolves around two elemental questions. First, to what extent was the story of Jesus about a man, a god or a man–god or some other strange combination of the two? Second, was the human element of Jesus subsumed within the godly element or was it separate and equal to it? For some, Jesus lived and died a man; for others he was not, and so on. Thus, the Christological controversy revolves around the one or the two Natures of the Son. Did Christ comprise two Natures, the Human and the Divine, distinct yet somehow united, as the Fourth Œcumenical Synod (Chalcedon in 451) had set forth in the orthodox position? Or was He of one single all-embracing Divine Nature, which submerged any distinct aspects of humanity, as the Monophysites persistently maintained (and still do)? Christology was a matter that rested on interpretations of the Bible, first of all, in different languages, as well as a vast variety of other truth-bearing texts written by Church leaders, emperors, theologians, and monks, most of them devoted to the ideal of one Church and one empire.

The Trinitarian God

Nicaea I, convoked by Constantinus in 325, was the first synod to try and formulate what it was Christians perceived as the relationship between God the Father and God the Son, concluding they were, with the Holy Spirit, each an equal part of the Holy Trinity, three manifestations (or *hypostases*) in one essence. The three manifestations differ only in origin: the Father is without beginning (Unborn), the Son is *generated* by the Father before time (Begotten), and the Holy Spirit *proceeds* only from the Father (Proceeding). The Son, therefore, was *homoousios*, 'of the same substance' as the Father, unlike the Arian belief that the Son was *homoiousios*, 'of like nature' with the Father, that is to say, there was no spiritual equality between the Father and the Son.

Those of an irreligious nature could easily dismiss all this as a ludicrous theological debate over the Greek letter iota, but the Dogma of the Trinity is the foundation of Christian theology and is considered a mystery, which cannot be known by unaided reason apart from Divine revelation. And so it was that this synod, and those œcumenical synods that followed Nicaea I, were regarded as having formulated binding definitions of the faith, which cannot be changed since they were inspired by the Holy Spirit. The Church had been obliged to answer Jewish and pagan polemic by explaining the relationship between the *hypostases* of the Trinity, namely the God of the Old Testament, the incarnate Logos (His Son Jesus Christ), and the

Holy Spirit, the grace of which brought about the baptism of Christ and energised the apostles at Pentecost.[1] To put this into some sort of perspective, Christianity was a monotheistic religion and the Nicene Trinitarian concept of God was considered monotheistic. However, why was it felt necessary to put so much time and trouble into formulating a doctrine in which a single God who is at the same time Three-in-One?

The crux of the problem was to underline both Christ's full divinity and full humanity, for if Christ was just a mere mortal, he could not have pulled off the resurrection, not only of himself but of all mankind. As Gregory (d. 395), bishop of Nyssa, had explained, Father, Son and the Holy Spirit were not objective, ontological facts but simply 'terms we use' to express the way in which the 'unnameable and unspeakable' divine nature adapts itself to the limitations of our human mind.[2] You could not prove the existence of the Trinity by rational means. As Gregory the Theologian (of Nazianzos) had correspondingly said, Trinitarian teaching was designed to remind Christians that they should not even attempt to think of the divine in terms of a simple personality.[3]

Yet, as Voltaire prudently pointed out, 'this unintelligible doctrine is nowhere found in scripture'.[4] Voltaire was a philosopher in the loose sense of the word, what we would call a freethinker: he was a man of great learning who liked to share his opinions with others. He shared them on a vast range of subjects: love, adultery, *haute cuisine*, cannibalism, idealism, government, and so forth. Overwhelmingly through, his concerns were religious. In particular, he had little time for the abstractions of theology (such as consubstantiation) and spent a lot of time telling anyone who would care to listen. Superstition and organized religion is bad; God works through natural laws. 'God I respect', Voltaire wrote in an elegy in response to the 1755 Lisbon earthquake, 'yet I love the universe'.[5]

In a very real sense, the Nicene Creed, which is still seen as the cornerstone of Christian belief, was a construct of the Roman state rather than the inspiration of the Holy Spirit. One does not become the sole Roman emperor, having subjugated all one's rivals as Constantinus had done, without having reasoned carefully. A band of babbling bishops were not going to browbeat over what he considered 'trifling and of little importance'.[6] By a 'petty' matter Constantinus did not refer to issues touching the divinity, but to the incomprehensible efforts being made to explain its nature. After Constantinus religious differences over the nature of the Holy Trinity and Christ – often an expression of political and social conflict within the Christian Roman empire – would continue. Despite such differences, however, theological development raised Jesus from being merely the son of God to become a component part of the Trinity.

The Unitarian God

On the other hand, Arianism, founded by Arius, presbyter of Alexandria, maintained that God could only be monadal, that is to say, he consists of a single eternal unit, or monad. The Son could not be fully part of this 'creature', and not an integral part of the Father. As discussed above, for the Arians the Son was *homoiousios*, 'of like nature', with the Father. The essence of God and Christ the Logos are thus said to be different. Jesus Christ, therefore, was in a sense secondary to God, having been created by the latter for the specific purpose of the Incarnation. Like Unitarians in recent times, Arius was accused of stressing the humanity of Jesus at the expense of his divinity.

After the death of Arius in 336, Constantinus himself was baptized on his deathbed the following year by the Arian bishop Eusebius of Nicomedia. Constantinus left behind three sons, each of whom was given a share of joint power until civil wars reduced them to one survivor. Constantius II, whose brothers Constantinus II and Constans were killed in 340 and 350 respectively, and who was sole emperor from 350 to 361, was himself sympathetic to Arianism. However, the defence of the Nicene Creed and opposition to Arianism was championed most eloquently in the East above all by Athanasius (d. 373), patriarch of Alexandria from 328 and author among many other works of the *De Incarnatione*, one of the greatest works of Trinitarian theology. A difficult and quarrelsome person, Athanasius was not afraid to challenge the state in the person of the emperor over the depreciation of Jesus' godhead; he spent several periods in exile or flight, first in 335, then again in 339, 346, 362, and finally 365. For Athanasius the Nicene Creed was the gold standard of orthodoxy.

Finally, in 381 and again in 388, Arianism was officially proscribed and all its office holders banished. Nevertheless, the Arian brand of Christianity became popular with the German nation. The Germans found it much easier to understand than the Nicene form of Christianity, because the Arian doctrine that the Son must be younger than the Father, and in a sense inferior, corresponded with the paternal structure of their warrior society.

The apple of Christian discord

In absolute contrast to Arianism was Monophysitism, a doctrine that believed the incarnate Christ was fully divine, and thus of *one* nature (Gr. *mónos*, single, and *physis*, nature). Christ's human nature, it was held, was an illusion made to help man back to God. The Monophysites, who had their centres of power within the empire not only in Constantinople but in the Syrian hinterland and the Egyptian monasteries too, thus appeared to deny the full humanity of Christ in his human form on earth. This 'heresy' was repeatedly condemned at the Fourth, Fifth and Sixth Œcumenical synods (Chalcedon in 451, Constantinople II in 553, Constantinople III in 681). It is difficult to avoid the argument that Monophysitism became to a great degree linked with local disaffection in the eastern provinces, especially of Syria and Egypt. Much of the population in these regions was resentful of the distant tyranny of Constantinople, a parvenu both politically and ecclesiastically. Ground down as they were by ever-increasing oppression of the imperial fiscal system, they would therefore snatch at any form of resistance to the central government and everything for which it stood. Up to the present day, Monophysitism, or anti-Chalcedonianism, is largely dominant among the Christians in Egypt, and is clearly part of the national identity of Armenia and Ethiopia.

Its opponents were known as Chalcedonians or dyophysites, namely those who believed in that Christ be viewed as a single *prósôpon* or person in which were united the two (Gr. *dúo*) perfect and distinct natures, the human and the divine, mysteriously working and co-existing together. In 450, the pious Theodosius II fell off his horse and died. His sister Pulcheria allied herself with Anatolius, the new patriarch of Constantinople (r. 449–58), and pope Leo I (r. 440–61). She consolidated her power by marrying Marcianus, who succeeded Theodosius as emperor (r. 450–7). The new emperor decided to solve the Christological impasse: he called the synod that was to end all synods. The Fourth Œcumenical Synod, which met at Chalcedon in 451, was destined to be the touchstone of Christological orthodoxy in the view of Rome and Constantinople; it was also destined to be considered the great betrayal of Christological orthodoxy by much of the Church in the eastern provinces of the empire and the grounds for its separation from them. For Church leaders such as the Antiochene bishops, those three little words – 'in two natures' – made Chalcedon a monumental disaster. Chalcedon was thus a historic watershed.

The Chalcedonian doctrine (viz. the God-Man Christ) for us may seem utterly incomprehensible, since for its understanding it demands the knowledge of a though-world that belongs to a past age. Chalcedonianism only restates a problem and does not solve it, but like the apple of discord it cannot be simply ignored. Thus, the point of contention was whether one should speak of *two* natures in Jesus Christ, as it had been decided at the Synod of Chalcedon, or of only *one* new nature, in which divinity and humanity were joined together. By way of a useful comparison, Protestantism is too coldly logical, for it seems to walk around its God in complete comprehension, rationalism, having rendered its practitioners immune from the divine tug of mysticism. Rationalism, of course, considers reason the sole means of acquiring knowledge, opposing faith in the supernatural or in divine revelation. Still, we should not be blind in modern times to our own gullibility and capacity for superstitious belief.

The human Christ

Finally, Nestorianism. This was the doctrine founded by Nestorius, patriarch of Constantinople (r. 428–31, d. 451), who came from the great Syrian metropolis of Antioch, modern Antakya just inside the southern Turkish border with Syria. This 'heresy' over stressed the humanity of Christ, and thus by reason of his manhood was less divine than the Father, in other words, he was simply the son of Mary who was 'adopted' as God's son and deified after crucifixion. Because Nestorianism appeared to deny the full divinity of Christ, coexistent with his full humanity, it was condemned, and Nestorius was deposed, at the Third Œcumenical Synod (Ephesos in 431). At this synod too, the Virgin Mary was proclaimed Theotokos (Gr. *Theotókos*), literally 'God-bearer', to underscore that Christ was God, and his mother the Mother of God or, more accurately, 'she who bore the One who is God'. The Nestorian position would make her only Christotokos (Gr. *Christotókos*) or the Mother of Christ or, more accurately, 'she who bore One whose Humanity compromised his Divinity'.

Cyril, patriarch of Alexandria (r. 412–44), emerged as the champion of the rival majority Christological tradition as he defended the title Theotokos, yet the Synod of Ephesos was, in fact, the first and last time that the Church attempted to define the Virgin Mary in doctrinal terms. In many respects, the rôle of the Virgin in the Church – then as now – is a personal, an inner affair, which does not like analysis and speculation. One of the consequences of this unwillingness to pry too much into the mystery of the Theotokos is that the devotions given to her have been many and manifold over the centuries. She is proof that humanity could be deified, and thus a soteriological rôle model for future generations. In this respect she is given divine epithets, not as a deity but as a deified human being.

So, justification is not forensic, no matter how those with a reflexive hostility towards the veneration of Mary attempt to spin it. The Old Testament was seen as a mine of pre-figuration for the Virgin Mary; the burning bush,[7] for instance, was interpretation as a representation of her, that is to say, she who was consumed but remained pure. Jacob's dream of a ladder ascending from earth to heaven,[8] to take another example, was seen as a pre-figuration of the Virgin Mary, who would link heaven and earth through Christ. These and other Old Testament passages were used in devotional and iconographical language to affirm the key rôle of the Theotokos in the life of the whole Church. In brief, Marian doctrine permeates the Old Testament, providing depth and colour to the New.

Even today, the Virgin Mary plays an extremely important rôle in the Orthodox Church, where she is most commonly known as the Panayia, or 'All-Holy'. However, for other theologians – and notably the later Muslim ones – the very idea of God having a mother (or a son) was a ridiculous notion. Take, for example, Qur'an 19:35: 'It befits not (the Majesty of) Allah that He should beget a son'.

The 'Christology' of the Qur'an is therefore in close agreement with the Nestorian Church, which was popular in the eastern, Persian, part of Arabia – the limited numbers of Chalcedonians came to be known as Melkites, 'emperor's men'. Likewise, we can look at two sections of the Arabic inscribed on the Dome of the Rock, Jerusalem, that monumental symbol of Islamic power at the centre of Jewish and Christian faiths:

> For (verily) the Messiah, Jesus / son of Mary, (is) the messenger of God, and his Word [Logos], (which) he has infused into Mary, along with his Spirit. / So, believe in God and his messengers, and do not say 'Three' – cease (doing that) / (it would be) better for you. For (verily) God is a unique God – may he be praised – how could he then have a son... O God, bless your messenger and servant Jesus / son of Mary.[9]

Clearly this polemical inscription, dated to 72 AH/AD 692, was directed against the Trinitarian teaching of the followers of Nicaea.[10] To the Muslims, Jesus ('*Isa*) was merely one of the prophets of Allah,[11] though he was the Messiah,[12] and he did perform miracles,[13] unlike Muhammad, and he was sinless,[14] again unlike Muhammad.[15] Incidentally, Mary (*Maryam*) herself is mentioned thirty-four times in the Qur'an, whereas there are only four specific references to the prophet Muhammad.

The political fallout

One of the reasons often cited for the Byzantine's collapse in its eastern provinces of Syria, Palestine and Egypt in the wake of the Arab invasions is that many Christians there felt isolated from the government in Constantinople due to the continuing religious disputes that divided the Monophysites from the Chalcedonian orthodox, who lived mostly in Europe and Anatolia. Because of this rift, the Monophysites and Chalcedonians fell out of communion with each other by refusing to accept the legitimacy of the apostolic succession of each other's bishops.

In order to find some middle ground between the Monophysites and the Chalcedonians, the emperor Herakleios (r. 610–41) and the patriarch of Constantinople Sergios (r. 610–58), like Iustinianus (r. 527–65) before them, tried to strike a compromise so as to unite Monophysites and Chalcedonians. This they did with the dogma of Monoenergism, which was shortly replaced with that of Monotheletism; these doctrines held that there was a single energy or divine will (Gr. *thelesis*) in Jesus Christ. The compromise was rejected by most parties of both sides; the Chalcedonians in particular since one will presuppose one nature, something impossible in the incarnate Christ, who had two natures, one divine and one human.

Under the next emperor, Constans II (r. 641–68), the Chalcedonian opposition found staunch champions in pope Martin I (r. 649–53, d. 655) and the Greek theologian Maximos Confessor (d. 662). The trial of Maximos on charges of treason in 655–6 underscores the difficulties faced by the emperor in enforcing his authority in a rapidly deteriorating empire. Maximos was determined not to allow the secular power of the emperor to encroach on the church's rights to define dogma. See how the theologian describes his conception of the emperor's rights in the following quote:

> None of the emperors were able, through compromising measures, to induce the Fathers, who were theologians, to conform to the heretical teachings of their time. But in strong and compelling voices appropriate to the dogma in question, they declared quite clearly that it is the function of the clergy to discuss and define the 'saving' dogmas of the universal Church. And you said: 'What then? Is not every emperor a Christian and a priest?' To which I respond: 'He is not [a priest], for he does not participate in the sanctuary… he does not baptise…nor does he lay on hands and ordain bishops, priests and deacons… nor does he bear the symbols of the priesthood… as he does bear the symbols of his rule, the crown and the purple robe'.[16]

The whole question of imperial authority in the universal Church would be a major theme in the iconoclastic controversy of the following century.

Ostensibly, the Monthelete 'heresy' was settled when Constantinus IV (r. 668–85) convoked the Sixth Œcumenical Synod (Constantinople III in 681) to condemn of forms of Monophysitism once and for all. This was probably a matter of form, mainly because the recent loss of the eastern provinces to Islam allowed the Church in the rest of the empire to consolidate its predominately Chalcedonian character.

Splitting hairs?

Having looked, albeit rather sketchily, at some of the major 'heresies' that troubled the universal Church and had sophisticated men quibbling and hating each other, even as far to excommunicating each other over differences of opinion regarding dogma, some may ask: What is orthodoxy, anyway?

Orthodoxy is intellectual without being rationalistic. The Orthodox Church is comfortable with mystery, with the things which God chooses not to reveal to us, or which He reveals without explanation. This tradition reaches at least as far back as Clement of Alexandria (BC 150), and encompasses all the defenders of the Nicaean faith in one *ousia* and three *hypostases*, including among many others Hilary of Poitiérs, Basil of Caesarea, Gregory of Nyssa, Gregory of Nazianzos, and Augustine of Hippo. It had been recently argued that divine incomprehensibility was indeed central to those responsible for expounding and defending Nicaean orthodoxy.[17]

In the West, everything has to have an explanation, has to be rigorously defined and endlessly categorized. This is positive theology, and accounts for the western churches seemingly endless need to create systematic theologies. Orthodoxy, by contrast, is an expression of apophatic theology, a spirituality of negation. The two different approaches are best illustrated by their descriptions of God: the West describes God as omnipotent, omniscient, and omnipresent; the Orthodox liturgy describes God as 'ineffable, inconceivable, invisible, incomprehensible, ever existing and eternally the same, you, and your only-begotten Son, and your Holy Spirit'.[18] The western and the eastern approach come from two very different places and lead to two very different conclusions – the one to endless speculation, the other to endless contemplation. Hence, Orthodox tradition was nervous of philosophy. Good churchmen believed in a philosophical training. They used Platonic terms and Aristotelian methodology. But they held that philosophy was incapable of solving divine questions, since God was essentially beyond human knowledge.

Chapter 11

Icon Wars

One of the important developments during the Macedonian dynasty (843–1071) was the organization of a scheme whereby large-scale fresco or mosaic programmes also came to serve theology and cosmology. In other words, the wall surfaces of particular parts of a church building were given over to specific scenes or figures, which together represented a message that could be read by the viewer as well as contemplated. This iconographic programme included the development of what are known as cycles, a series of depictions like a cartoon strip showing the life of Christ, the Virgin, or one of the saints. The location of each iconographical theme in a specific part of the church was dictated by its meaning and symbolism. Thus, on the central dome the viewer always finds Christ Pantokrator, while just below him, on the drum of the dome, are the prophets and / or apostles, the teachers of the faith in the Old and New Testament. The Virgin is often shown with them, along with angels (the heavenly court). These are the holy figures that are with God around his throne, and have borne witness to His Son.

Christ Pantokrator (Gr. *Pantokrátôr*) literally means 'Holder of All', that is to say, Christ as Lord of the Universe, the highest in the heavenly hierarchy. Originally, the title Pantokrator was reserved for God alone. Aside from the one use by Paul,[1] the author of the Book of Revelations is the only New Testament authority to use Pantokrator, and he does so nine times.[2] A later Christological shift, probably in the fourth century, meant the title came to refer to Christ rather than the Creator, and with that Christ Pantokrator is a mild but stern, all-powerful judge of humanity.

Christ Pantokrator is traditionally shown in bust form giving the faithful the benediction with his right hand (the three fingers together signifying the Holy Trinity) and holding a closed book, which represents the four canonical gospels, with his left. Either side of his halo is the Greek Christogram Iς Xς; to the right Iς, the first and last letters of Ἰησούς, Jesus, the left Xς, the first and last letters of Χριστός, Christ. Two additional letters A and Ω, the first and last letters of the Greek alphabet, proclaim Jesus' eternal divinity: 'I am the Alpha and the Omega... who is, and who was, and who is to come, the Almighty'.[3] At the same time, his left eye looks straight at the viewer in the nave, so symbolizing his fully human nature, his right gazes to heaven, so symbolizing his fully divine nature. Put very briefly, the image affirms orthodox belief that Jesus is both human and divine, Saviour and Judge, the ever present Christ the Logos at the head of His Church.

What is an icon?

An icon is a flat panel, usually made of wood, on which is depicted a holy image. In Orthodox culture, it is said that an icon has been 'written' rather than painted, because an icon is much more than a religious painting. Almost everything within an icon has a symbolic meaning.

The word icon comes from Greek εἰκών, *eikôn*, meaning image. The icon was perceived as matter imbued with χάρις, *cháris*, or divine grace. On important feast days, the principal icons of a Church were to be provided with additional oil lamps and candles. 'When illuminated', says Bissera Pentcheva, 'by the trembling flicker of candles and oil lamps rather than the steady and harsh spotlights of museum displays, the painted holy face on the revetted icon sinks and disappears in the shadow'.[4] Such holy faces may represent Christ, the Virgin, the prophets or the saints, or scenes from the Old and New Testament. Along with holy relics, the gospels, and the Cross, icons are venerated (*not* worshipped) by the faithful. In fact, icons are not just venerated, they are addressed: talked to, kissed, prayed to, and hugged. For example, they represent the presence of a saint; not in the wood and the egg-tempera, but – to quote Basil of Caesarea (d. 379) – in that 'the veneration paid to an icon goes to the prototype [the saint]'.[5] In return, the saint will exercise his or her beneficial power through the icon in favour of his or her supplicant.

A patron saint was an extra companion through life who healed hurts, soothed distress, and *in extremis* could make miracles. So, in their original setting, icons are not simply a means of decoration; they constitute a path, ways through which one can contemplate the figure represented and pray or supplicate to him or her. In this manner, one does not worship a saint; saints carry messages to God and might be seen as close friends, intimates who listen to your prayers and send them on. To kiss an icon of a saint is to show love and respect to the saint depicted. As Leo Tolstoy once wrote: 'A good and lofty work of art may be incomprehensible, but not to simple un-perverted peasant labourers (all that is highest is understood by them) – it may be, and often is, unintelligible to erudite, perverted people destitute of religion'.[6] One can only agree with him. Icons are also a theological statement on the divine and on man, on the ultimate goal of our existence. As such, they have been called 'symbols of Orthodoxy'.[7]

Iconoclastic Isaurians

As a new drive was launched in Anatolia by 715, it looked as if the Arabs might at last realize their great dream of capturing the Christian capital. Fortunately, as it was so often able to do, the empire produced another saviour in an hour of great peril. Leo, the *stratêgos* of one of the Anatolian themes, led a successful coup and took the throne. It was a triumph for the Anatolian aristocracy of the empire and for the interests of strong centralized government. It was also a victory for the elements in the empire most capable of organising effective resistance to the enemy. Leo III (r. 717–41) established the Isaurian dynasty that reigned till 802. When in the summer of 717 the Arabs gathered around Constantinople for their greatest siege of it, the empire at last had a leader who could save it. The resistance was brilliantly organized, utilizing all the benefits of the metropolis' defensive advantages, including the wonder weapon Greek fire. As their failure turned to misery and hardship, the Arabs became demoralized; finally abandoning their siege after a year, they withdrew in disorder.

The turbulent seventh century had left the imperial ideology faced with a dilemma: if the emperor was, indeed, the Vicar of Christ and His chosen leader of the Chosen People, how was it that he was constantly being beaten in battle or prone to palace putsches? The emperor Iustinianus II (r. 685–95, 705–11) had even been publicly mutilated in 695. It now seemed that the people were placing more and more faith in concrete manifestations of the divine (icons, relics, holy men etc.) than in the fount of law and authority, the emperor in Constantinople. This may partly explain why Leo III embarked on a crusade to eliminate the use of icons in the everyday devotional life of the Church and of individual Christians. The movement is known as iconoclasm, 'breaking of icons', and was to prove the catalyst out of which the mediaeval Byzantine state was to emerge.

Thus, in the year 726, the iconoclast movement decided that icons should be removed from Byzantine churches. They mistakenly thought that icons were the same as 'graven images', which are not to be made according to the Second Commandment given to Moses. In truth, this was a distorted interpretation of the Second Commandment, which had perhaps arisen as a superstition among Byzantine soldiers who feared that icon veneration had incurred God's displeasure and brought about natural disasters and a long string of losses against the Arabs and the Bulghars. In the same year Leo III issued a decree against icons, and ordered the destruction of an image of Christ over one of the doors of the Chalke, or Brazen House, the grand entrance vestibule of the Great Palace, an act that was fiercely resisted by the citizens.[8] It was, truly, a 'transmutation of all things into ungodliness',[9] as Theodore the Stoudite (759–826), abbot of the Stoudios monastery in Constantinople, characterized it. Theodore was a great partisan of the icon.

Essentially, the iconoclasts regarded icon veneration as idolatrous. They maintained that an image of Christ, to take an extremely important example, can only depict the human nature of His incarnation, but *not* His divine nature; therefore, such an image was improper, since it could not portray Christ as God, as part of the Trinity. Indeed, they proposed that the cross and the perfect Christian were the best 'images' of Christ. An iconoclast mosaic cross can still be seen in the barrel vault of the apse in Hagia Eirene.

Leo III followed a mostly non-violent policy against the opponents of the iconoclasts, the iconodules, 'friends of icons'; taking icons down from places they were visible. But it did not end there. Leo's son and successor, Constantinus V Kopronymos (r. 741–75), was more fierce a persecutor of the iconodules and waged what amount to a war against iconodule monks and leading churchmen. To give theological backing to his iconoclasm, Constantinus convoked a Church synod in 754, the Synod of Hieria, which condemned the 'worship' of images, after which many treasures were broken, burned, chipped from walls or painted over with depictions of trees, birds or animals. It was not enough to persecute iconodules, which included the use of torture and blinding, they had to be shown the error of their ways. This compelled Constantinus to compose his own theological works on the thorny subject of divine images and prototype.

A further affront to Orthodox belief that went beyond the ruling of the Synod of Hieria was Constantinus' increasing disparagement of the saints and the Mother of God. A pamphlet by the patriarch of Constantinople Nikephoros (r. 806–15, d. 829) reads:

He [Constantinus] abolished the use of the title Saint and said the Theotokos could help no one after death, and that the saints had no power of intercession, their martyrdom helping only themselves and saving their own souls from punishment.[10]

It was veneration of the Virgin, however, that most incensed the emperor, until finally it became a punishable offence to even use the common exclamation, 'Mother of God, help me'. A contemporary anecdote about Constantinus V by Theosteriktos, author of the *Life of Saint Niketas of Medikion*, relates:

Taking in his hand a purse full of gold and showing it to all he asked, 'What is it worth?' They replied that it had a great value. He then emptied out the gold and asked, 'What is it worth now?' They said, 'Nothing'. 'So', he said, 'Mary (for the atheist would not call her Theotokos), while she carried Christ within was to be honoured, but after she was delivered she differed in no way from other women'.[11]

One source refers to the church of Blachernai, the principal Constantinopolitan shrine to Virgin Mary, as having been converted into a 'storehouse of fruit and an aviary'.[12] At the Milion, the milestone of the capital from which all distances in the empire were calculated, scenes of the six œcumenical synods were replaced with portrayals of chariot racing and a picture of the emperor's own favourite charioteer.

One of Constantinus' most far reaching reforms, however, involved the reorganization of the military system, the *tagmata*, which provided the emperor with a powerful and loyal fighting force established in and around the capital. It was this small élite standing army led by a caste of professional officers that would implement his sometimes violent policies. As both Constantinus and his father had proved excellent soldiers against both the Arabs and the Bulghars, the army – especially the *tagmata* – now came to iconoclasm with military success and imperial prestige, and the emperor's soldiers proved to be the most fanatical iconoclast of all.

Despite frequent illness Constantinus was a strong military campaigner against the Arabs and the Bulghars. He recovered part of Syria and Armenia from the Arabs, and defeated them at sea, regaining Cyprus. With the ending of the 'Umayyad dynasty in Damascus, the Arabs turned their attentions eastwards. Constantinus, meanwhile, led nine campaigns against the Bulghars, winning a series of victories with his iconoclastic army, culminating at Anchialos in 763. During his final campaign his legs became swollen and he died while being borne back to Constantinople on a litter.

Iconodules fight back

Iconoclasm, however, went against the religious devotions of the majority of the people of all social classes, and with Constantinus' daughter-in-law, the empress Eirene the Athenian (r. 780–802, d. 803), the iconoclasts found their match. Following the sudden death of her husband Leo IV (r. 775–80), who had followed in the theological footsteps of his father, Eirene was able to restore the veneration of images through the agency of the Seventh Œcumenical Synod (Nicaea II in 787), but not before opposition from some of the military and members of the imperial family. On his death, Leo's brothers had quickly moved to depose the young heir, Constantinus VI (r. 780–97, d. 805) and his regent-mother, but the twenty-five-year-old Eirene effectively put down the attempt, arresting and exiling the iconoclast military officers and key civil functionaries who had sided with the conspirators and replaced them with members of her own household.

The first attempt at a synod was held in September of 786 in the basilica of the Holy Apostles in Constantinople. The participants included two legates from Rome and two from Egypt representing the patriarchates of Antioch, Alexandria and Jerusalem, which were already under Arab rule. The empress, however, underestimated the iconoclast sentiments of old-guard bishops, laymen, and soldiers loyal to the former Isaurian emperors. As the synod convened, a mob of armed soldiers from the garrison of Constantinople gathered in the forecourt and, pounding on the doors, shouted threats against the synod. The meeting ended in chaos and Eirene and Constantinus returned to the Great Palace, offering no public response. Biding her time, Eirene understood that success depended on finding a way to secure the military defence of the capital and to draw the teeth of the iconoclast troops. This she managed peacefully by the masterful stroke of ordering the iconoclast army units to Malagina, a traditional meeting place for the army setting off on Arab campaigns. Once there, she had the iconoclast ringleaders paid off and dismissed to their native places, informing them that she had already sent their families home from the capital.

Next, Eirene appointed commanders loyal to herself, and within eight months she had quenched the fiercest support for her husband and father-in-law's theological policies. She proceeded with the Seventh Œcumenical Synod, this time carefully held outside of Constantinople at Nicaea. Presided over by the patriarch of Constantinople Tarasios (784–806), the synod was attended by 400 bishops, monks, and laymen, with 308 bishops signing the declaration of faith by which icon veneration was restored.

Triumph of Orthodoxy

From 787 to 813, the empire was officially iconodule. However, ineffective rule was demonstrated by the emperors of that time, in particular Nikephoros I (r. 802–11), who had been the chief finance officer of Eirene until he overthrew her in a bloodless coup. He made costly and senseless invasions of Bulgaria, which was to eventually cost him his life; the emperor's skull, it is said, was silvered and used as a drinking vessel by the Bulghar khan. This led to a great sense of dissatisfaction, especially during the Bulghar siege of Constantinople in 813. The upshot was the rekindling of the iconoclast controversy, thereby allowing once again an iconoclastic soldier emperor to ascend the throne during a time of distress and defeat.

In the year 815, having defeated the Bulghars, Leo V the Armenian (r. 813–20) sought to repudiate Nicaea II, which had re-established icon veneration, and restore iconoclasm. His reasons for wishing so he stated in the following proclamation:

> For what reasons do the Christians thus suffer, subject to the heathen? It appears to me because of worshipping icons, and nothing else. I therefore desire that these should be destroyed. For behold how those emperors who accepted and worshipped them died either deposed or in battle. Only those who did not worship them died as emperors and were with honour interred in the imperial tombs at the church of the Holy Apostles. Therefore, I decree that I, too, shall follow their example and destroy the icons so that I may live many years… and that this dynasty should last till the fourth and fifth generation.[13]

True to his word, Leo V held a synod in Hagia Sophia to restore iconoclasm, and once again allowed the persecuted of the iconodules, but he himself was assassinated on Christmas Day by supporters of Michael the Amorian, one of his most trusted commanders, who took the throne as Michael II (r. 820–9). The assassins struck off Leo's head, exposing the body naked in the Hippodrome, before placing it on board ship to accompany his wife, Theodosia, into exile. Leo's four sons were castrated. Thereafter, iconoclasm was more of a matter of imposing imperial authority than actually implementing a specific theology on religious images. It was mostly during this period that the 'theology of the icon', peculiar to the Orthodox Church, was developed by theologians such as Theodore the Stoudite and the aforementioned patriarch of Constantinople, Nikephoros.

The last iconoclast emperor was Theophilos (r. 829–42), a gifted ruler and a notable patron of the arts. The emperor was viewed favourably by his subjects. Once a week he would ride from the Great Palace to the church of Blachernai; *en route*, people could wave him down to tell him their woes and to demand justice. He frequently visited the market places in disguise to check that merchants were using fair weights in their sales. It was Theophilos who instituted the throne room that impressed foreign visitors with its golden organ, mechanical birds singing in a tree, mechanical roaring lions, and a throne that ascended to and descended from the ceiling. He probably took a romantic view of iconoclasm as harking back to the glorious days of the Isaurian warrior emperors, Leo III and Constantinus V Kopronymos.

The leaders of the Church looked into the problem and decided that the Commandment about 'graven images' does not refer to Holy images of Christ, the Theotokos, and the saints. So, in the year 843, the empress Theodora, who was acting as regent (r. 842–56, d. 867) for her two-year-old son Michael III (r. 842–67), asked the Church to convoke a synod to restore the icons, which was attended by 367 bishops in Constantinople. The bishops agreed that icons helped to preserve the teachings of the Church and that venerating an icon was not the same as worshiping it. They proclaimed: 'He who venerates the icon, venerates in it the reality for which it stands'.[14] That is, for example, if the icon is an image of a saint, it is the saint that was being honoured, not the picture. Then the empress, her son Michael, the new patriarch of Constantinople Methodios I (842–6) – the iconoclast John VII Grammatikos (r. 838–42) was deposed – and many monks and clergy came in procession to Hagia Sophia and put all the icons again in the church. The day is celebrated to this day every year on the first Sunday in Lent (the Sunday of Orthodoxy).

Storm clouds in the West

Though the iconoclasts were denounced by the Church in 843 as heretics, they did help to rejuvenate and consolidate the prestige and the power of the emperor and the strength of the army, providing the first effective military opposition to the empire's growing list of enemies. Another result of iconoclasm was to weaken ecclesiastical relations between Constantinople and Rome. The latter had remained staunchly iconodule throughout the controversy – the iconodule popes happily painted frescoes and put up mosaics in defiance of the iconoclastic emperors – and had major disagreements with those tough Isaurians Leo III and Constantinus V Kopronymos over taxes and lands in southern Italy. In fact, pope Gregory II (r. 715–31) had excommunicated Leo, and the pope's seven immediate successors including the Syrian Gregory III (r. 731–41) each restated Rome's disapproval of iconoclasm.

Faced with considerable problems closer to home, Rome had to look elsewhere for help – and they found it in the Franks who, unlike many other western peoples, had always been Chalcedonian. The man chosen by pope Leo III (r. 795–812) was Charlemagne (r. 771–814), who ruled most of what is now France, Germany, Austria and northern Italy and was by far the most powerful monarch in western Europe. The Roman pope need the military might of the Frankish king in his fight against heretical doctrines, turbulent warlords, and rival factions in the Church. In a carefully orchestrated act, *Carolus Rex Francorum* was crowned 'the great and peaceful emperor' in Saint Peter's basilica on Christmas day, in the year 800.

This was a direct challenge to the authority of Constantinople, which happened to be ruled by a woman at the time, as the metropolis regarded this (perhaps correctly) as usurpation of a title that belonged to it. There were no legal precedents for a 'barbarian' emperor, and certainly no precedents for the imperial power being bestowed by a pope. Leo III implied that apostolic or divine inspiration had led to the crowning; Charlemagne was therefore 'crowned by God'. This sidestepped the legal aspects of the dramatic Christmas Day coronation, for the combined nations of Europe might have chosen to elect an emperor by some other means. In Constantinople, on the other hand, it was the state that 'elected' an emperor, and coronation by the patriarch of Constantinople was simply a formal ratification of that election. In fact, the first coronation to have taken place in Hagia Sophia, and not the palace chapel or the Hippodrome, occurred in 641. Thus, the actions of Leo III were regarded by the Byzantines as ludicrous and insulting. Because if there was one God, one faith, and one truth, then there could only be one empire and one emperor; surely that emperor ruled in Constantinople, not in Aachen. The claims of Charlemagne's successors, both physical and political, would constitute a bone of contention between Constantinople and the West.

On top of that, Byzantine tradition clung to the belief in the charismatic equality of bishops. None of them, not even the heir of Saint Peter, had the right to impose doctrine. The definition of doctrine was for a œcumenical synod alone, when, as at Pentecost, all the bishops of the Church were represented and the Holy Spirit would descend to inspire them. So, did the pope in Rome enjoy an honorary primacy or an absolute supremacy in the Church? As far as Constantinople was concerned the answer was the first not the second, the Byzantines believing that such powers lay in the Pentarchy of patriarchs, of which Rome was the senior but not the supreme member.

Chapter 12

Purple Born

The emperor in Constantinople was the lawful heir of Augustus and of Constantinus. He also ruled as Christ's vice-regent on earth, and on his death was supposed to 'bear joint rule with the son of God', and automatically became 'of sacred memory'. This close association of the emperor with Christ was heavily emphasized in such ceremonial as the imperial banquets. Philotheos, the author of a banquet treatise at the end of the ninth century, tells us that the emperor imitated the second coming of Christ, while at his table reclined twelve of his friends, on the model of the apostles.[1] The Christian emperor ruling from Constantinople was thus the agent of the supreme power whose government was the government of the universe. His duty was to copy the God of the Christians, his task to establish on earth an imitation (Gr. *mímêsis*) of the Christian Heaven, himself sustained by the Divine Word – the Logos.[2] The Byzantine world was filled with the spirit of *deisidaimonía* – religion, faith, superstition, translate the word how you will.[3]

In theory, therefore, the emperor was chosen from birth to fulfil the will of Heaven, and how he got to the throne was less than important than the fact that he had got there. Emperors were supposed to be elected, chosen by the Senate and the army with the agreement of the people. That was one basis of the emperor's claim to rule. And the other was the choice of God, which was clearly evident by the claimant's successful assumption of power. But since any emperor who controlled both the treasury and the army was, in the eyes of the world, legitimate, and while no one could know the mind of God, the Almighty had a marked tendency to ratify public opinion. As the learned courtier Michael Psellos properly put it: 'It was as they had the sanction of God. Really, of course, their power rested on three factors: the people, the Senate, and the army'.[4] Of course, those not inclined to play the doubting Thomas could argue that the emperor ran the state, and the army, and the treasury, but God ran the emperor.

Once in power, however, an emperor had the right to crown a successor, and during his life time he could establish a dynasty. Hence autocrat, *autokratôr*, was a title used for the reigning emperor, the one who exercised complete control in matters both civil and military. The emperor *autokratôr* was distinguished from co-emperors by his effective exercise of power, power which he could delegate to a chosen official, such as a *stratêgos*, on a temporary and local basis.

Since the end of the Theodosian family rule in 457, the Isaurians were the first to establish a lasting imperial hereditary line (717–802). Their vision of worldly power was expressed in adding to the Great Palace complex a throne room, or *chrysotriklinos* ('golden room'), and a Purple chamber, or *porphyra* (Gr. *porphýra*). It was in the latter that the empress gave birth to the future heirs to the throne. The first Isaurian, Leo III (r. 717–41), built both in an attempt to secure the legitimacy of his new dynasty. His son, Constantinus V Kopronymos (r. 741–75), was the first emperor recognized as *porphyrogennetos*, 'one born in the purple'.

It was now the custom for the imperial children to be born in the *porphyra*, thus taking the title of Porphyrogenitus (Gr. *porphyrogénnêtos*) for males and Porphyrogenita (Gr. *porphyrogénnêtê*) for females. In other words, to be born to an emperor during his reign was a far greater distinction than that of primogeniture. The *porphyra* was a detached building, sometimes called the Boukoleon palace (so named on account of the stone sculpture of a lion in a death struggle with a bull located there),[5] which stood just behind the Boukoleon harbour. By custom, those 'born in the purple' had a legitimate right to the throne. There was a special ceremony for the birth of a child to a reigning emperor. Prayers were offered to God and the Mother of God, beseeching their protection for the imperial infant.[6]

In fact, the Porphyrogeneti were under the special protection of the chaste Mother of God, the mighty guardian of Constantinople. This is indicated by the acclamation chanted on Ascension Day:

O spring of life of the Romans [Byzantines], Virgin, Mother of the divine Logos, you alone march in battle as a fellow fighter on the side of the emperors (born) in the Purple (chamber). They receive the crown from you, for they receive you in the Purple (chamber) as an invincible shield against everything... For they receive you as might that brings victory against the enemies.[7]

This Ascension Day acclamation clearly asserts that the *legitimate* ruler, born in the *porphyra*, receives the imperial crown and military victories from the Virgin Mary.

By the eighth century (not coincidentally marking the establishment of the Isaurian dynasty) Constantinus I was perceived as the *modèle par excellence* of the pious emperor, having been transformed into a semi-legendary Christian hero, if you will. Following the sign of God, he allegedly dedicates his new metropolis to the Mother of God. Indeed, one of the principal effects of the exaltation of the Porphyrogeneti was to convey the illusion of the antiquity and continuity of their 'cult'. The success of this propaganda is reflected clearly in the writings of Liudprand of Cremona. Twice the Lombard envoy repeats the statement that the Purple chamber was built by Constantinus I who desired 'that the successive rulers of his noble family should see the first light of day here, and that all the offspring of his line should be called by the glorious title of Porphyrogenitus'.[8] Liudprand then goes on to refute the view held by 'some people' that Constantinus VII Porphyrogenitus was directly descended from the first Constantinus.

The father of the seventh Constantinus, Leo VI Sapiens, had encountered great difficulties in producing an heir to the throne and thus secures the endurance of the Macedonian dynasty. Only one of his first three wives, who were all short-lived, bore a son and he soon died. Therefore, Leo waited until his new mistress, Zoë Karbonopsina, gave birth to a healthy boy on 3 September 905 before marrying her the following April – thus, Constantinus' title of Porphyrogenitus was somewhat of a pun, he being born out of wedlock, in a manner of speaking. Zoë 'of the coal-black-eyes' was of the same distinguished family as Theophanes Confessor, the chronicler. Nevertheless, this uncanonical fourth marriage (the Church permitted, after a mandatory penance, three marriages, no more) scandalized the state and split the Church hierarchy. The patriarch of Constantinople Nikolaos I Mystikos (r. 901–7, 912–25) lost his office in the fallout, although he reluctantly baptized the fruit of this relationship, the future emperor Constantinus VII Porphyrogenitus.

The matter, known as the Tetragamy affair, was finally settled after the death of the emperor, around 920, but not before Nikolaos, once again the patriarch, had managed to have a gold tesserae mosaic showing Leo prostrate at Christ's feet imploring forgiveness – symbolic of his submission to the Church – over the imperial gate in Hagia Sophia, still visible today. Constantinus himself would co-reign with his father, his uncle Alexander and his mother for thirteen years, then with the 'intruder' Romanos I Lekapenos (r. 919–44) for twenty-six years, to finally rule alone for almost fifteen years.

There can be no doubt that the Constantinopolitan government deliberately fostered the misconception of the extreme antiquity of the Purple chamber and the continuity of the line of the emperors. Into the bargain, a presumptive heir 'born in the purple' signified a major political tool used by emperors to consolidate power. These children, namely royal princesses, were considered to be ordained by Christ and purple was symbolically associated with the imperial persona. The rarity of *porphyrogenitae* and the conditions of their birth determined that these children were major factors in Byzantine diplomatic strategy. The princess Anna Komnene described her *porphyrogenita* birth as, 'he [Alexios I Komnenos] found the empress in the throes of childbirth, in the room set apart long ago for an empress' confinement. Our ancestors called it *porphyra* – hence the world-famous name of *porphyrogennetoi*'.[9]

The untouchable

Not only was the emperor 'purple born', but his position once on the throne was exceedingly elevated and withdrawn too. His formal powers were virtually unlimited. He was, after all, God on earth. He was autocratic ruler of the state, limited only by what his subjects would put up with. It must be understood that though Constantinople was one of the five great patriarchal seats (the others were Rome, Antioch, Alexandria and Jerusalem), and the patriarch there was at least as important as the emperor in religious matters, it was the emperor himself who was the head of the Church as well as being, of course, the head of the state, and he was ostentatiously symbolized by a portentous solemnity, befitting his rôle as God on earth. Since this was his unutterably lordly status, everything relating to him was pronounced sacred. A series of successive edicts even restricted the numbers of those who were entitled to touch his purple robes, and who were permitted to perform their obeisance before His Serenity in person. Those unqualified to obtain such access prostrated themselves before his holy images and portraits instead. To them, the emperor, whatever his human shortcomings, ruled by divine will.

The problem of immoderation at court was a by-product of a deliberate policy of Diocletianus, a pagan emperor. Together with his co-rulers in the Tetrarchy, Diocletianus wanted to stamp his authority on an empire that had teetered on anarchy for too long. He achieved this by transforming the Principate established by Augustus into a palace-centred sacred monarchy, which was quickly followed by the establishment of its alliance with the Christian Church by Constantinus. This imperial structure will persist with little internal change until the last emperor, who is also the last Constantinus, perishes at the taking of Constantinople in 1453.

The emperor therefore became an untouchable figure, closer to the gods than at almost any stage previously, and the court developed a style of eastern obsequiousness that the West had never seen before. This distancing of the emperor from the people he ruled is demonstrated by the conduct of Constantius II, who went so far as to behave like a statue in real life whenever he appeared in public.

> He was like a dummy, gazing straight before him as if his head was in a vice, turning neither right nor left. When a wheel jolted he did not nod, and at no point was he seen to spit or to wipe or rub his face or nose or to move his hand.[10]

Such was Ammianus' eyewitness description of the emperor's state visit to Rome in 357.

The lucky few to gain an audience with the emperor had to do with bended knees and the minutiae of court ceremony, pecking order and bureaucracy soon emerged.

Libanius, the proud Antiochene philosopher and self-professed pagan, sarcastically scribbles:

> There were a thousand cooks, as many barbers and even more butlers. There were swarms of waiters, eunuchs more in number than flies around the flocks in spring and a multitude of drones of every sort and kind.[11]

This lambasting from Libanius reminds us of the witty remarks of an Arkadian ambassador recently returned from the court of the Great King of Persia, Artaxerxes II (r. 404–359 BC). He lost no time in debunking Persian power to his fellow Arkadians by saying that, 'while the king had masses of bakers, cooks, waiters and doorkeepers, all his researches had failed to discover any men capable of standing up to Greeks in battle'.[12] With far too many idle mouths and gourmet chefs, what we are witnessing here are two classic cases of conspicuous consumption. By way of a contrast, we can read a firsthand account of a banquet hosted by the Visigothic king Theodoric II (r. 453–66). One of the guests is the Gallic aristocrat and later bishop of Arverna (Clermont-Ferrand), Sidonius Apollinaris (d. 489), who notes that the food attracts by its skilful cookery, not by its costliness; the platters by their brightness, not by their weight. But the most weighty thing on this royal occasion is the conversation – 'you can find Greek elegance, Gallic plenty, Italian briskness; the dignity of state, the attention of a private home, the ordered discipline of royalty'.[13]

Naturally, there was a downside to all this venality. Every ruler was honorifically described as His Serenity. Yet there was a bitter, unconscious irony about this choice of title, since an emperor's agitations and anxieties were ever-present and harrowing. He was a man constantly navigating the realpolitik required to survive in his dazzling but unforgiving world. He has been described as the man most to be pitied in the entire Byzantine world.

By divine appointment

The bishopric of Rome, described subsequently as the papacy, had enjoyed particular respect from the earliest beginnings of the faith. Christians in the East admitted the special prestige of the See of Saint Peter, yet were reluctant to agree that it had the right to dictate to them or legislate on their behalf. They also maintained that ecclesiastical authority was not vested in any one person, but (with the reservations that certain apostolic sees were entitled to precedence of honour) was assigned by the Scriptures to *all* the bishops, who expressed this authority corporately through their general synods.

Over lunch with the Roman Catholic churchmen accompanying the Fourth Crusade the Orthodox archbishop of Corfu observed, with delicious irony, that 'he knew of no basis for the Roman See's primacy other than the fact that Roman soldiers had crucified Christ'.[14] Eastern tradition could not accept the administrative and disciplinary authority of Rome, believing such powers lay with the Pentarchy of Patriarchs, of which Rome was the senior but not the supreme member; in other words, it was *primus inter pares*, first among equals. This was due to the fact that the bishop of the See of Rome was seen as the successor to Saint Peter, Christ's closest disciple and chief of the apostles ('And I tell you that you are Peter, and on this rock I will build my church, and the gates of Hades will not overcome it').[15] But in the early years the Church had other important apostolic sees, notably the See of Alexandria (associated with Saint Mark) and the See of Antioch (associated with Saint Peter). And with the transfer of the capital of the empire to Constantinople, the bishop of that city, of New Rome, naturally gained immense prestige and importance, which was ratified at the Second Œcumenical Synod (Constantinople I in 381).

The Church thus came to be divided up into five patriarchies, each under an archbishop known as a patriarch (in Rome known by the more common title of pope, from Greek *papas* meaning father). This system came to be known as the pentarchy, and included – in order of honour – Rome, Constantinople, Antioch, Alexandria, and from 451, Jerusalem. Thus, Rome was only considered one partner – albeit an honoured one – amongst five, and the pope *primus inter pares* among the patriarchs – but no more – and his claims to supremacy seemed arrogant and unjustified. And so it was that Byzantine officials informed Liudprand of Cremona in 968, 'that silly blockhead of a pope (*papa fatuus, insulsus*) does not know that the sacred Constantinus [Constantine the Great] transferred to this city [Constantinople] the imperial sceptre, the Senate and all the Roman knighthood ...'[16] The argument recorded by the ambassador for the Holy Roman Emperor clearly expresses the customary Byzantine certitude of the superiority of the Constantinopolitan emperor over any western emperor.

More to the point, since Constantinople was now the city where emperors were born, baptized, betrothed, married, crowned, and were buried, each of these occasions gave rise to significant public ceremonial. Thus, when the emperor passed through his metropolis he rode in a chariot drawn by four white horses or on an ass and, if it was an important occasion, a religious or secular ceremony as the case may be, the route was cleaned and decorated with myrtle, rosemary, box, ivy, and such flowers as were in season, while fragrant perfumes were poured out before his steps.

New normal

It is hard for us to believe that fragrant perfumes, balmy incense and aromatic spices traditionally accompanied imperial and liturgical ceremonies in Constantinople, but such things revealed imperial power as more majestic and awe-inspiring. The most elaborate account of such doings appears in *De ceremoniis* in a section on imperial military campaigns. The extensive list of aromatics therein includes 'ointments, various perfumes, mastic, frankincense, sachar, saffron, musk, amber, bitter aloes moist and dry, pure ground cinnamon of first and second quality, cinnamon wood, and other perfumes'.[17]

With the air heavy with incense, those residents along ceremonial routes would hang their best carpets and tapestries out of the windows. Cheering and applause was forbidden: at intervals along the way priestly choirs were stationed in order to chant hymns composed in the emperor's honour or to glorify his imperial office.

For example, in describing the triumphal procession of John I Tzimiskès, in celebration of his victory over the Rus' in 971, Leo Diakonos recalls that 'the middle of the city . . . was everywhere decorated with purple cloths and, like a bridal chamber, was thickly bedecked with laurel branches and with fabric interwoven with gold'.[18] In a latter passage he briefly describes a subsequent triumphal procession of John Tzimiskès, after his brilliant victories over the Arabs, as going through the 'marketplace' (*ágorá*), viz. the main city thoroughfare known as the Mese (Gr. *Mésê Odós*, Middle Street).[19] Worthy of note is the fact that John Tzimiskès, at the first triumph, placed in the triumphal chariot 'an icon of the Theometor as a protectoress of the city (*polioûchos*), and ordered it to proceed him'.[20] This ostentatious humility of the emperor attests to the divine support, which gives legitimacy to his rule. The Virgin Mary also appears on his official coinage, placing the crown on John Tzimiskès head. Her gesture vouches for the legitimacy of his right to the throne (he was, after all, a usurper) achieved not through being 'born in the purple' but through his victories in war.

Likewise, the triumphal procession of John II Komnenos (r. 1118–43), who was 'born in the purple', in celebration of his victories in 1133, the emperor:

[G]ave instructions that a silver plated chariot be constructed; and the chariot, adorned with semi-precious jewels, was a wonder to behold. When the day designated for the procession had arrived, all manner of gold-embroidered purple cloths decorated the streets. Nor were there missing the framed images of Christ and the saints, fashioned by the weaver's hand, and which one would have said were not woven figures but living beings. Worthy too of admiration were the wooden platforms and scaffoldings set up along both sides of the parade route to hold the spectators. The part of the city that was thus bedecked was that which extended from the eastern gates to the Great Palace. The splendid *quadriga* was pulled by four horses, whiter than snow, with magnificent manes. The emperor did not himself mount the chariot but instead mounted upon it the icon of the Mother of God, in whom he exulted and entrusted his soul. To her as the unconquerable fellow general he attributed his victories, and ordering his chief ministers to take hold of the reins and his closest relations to attend to the chariot, he led the way on foot with the cross held in his hand. In the church of Hagia Sophia, he ascribed his accomplishments to the Lord God and gave thanks before all the people before he entered the palace.[21]

There is no more dramatic picture of how different the world of the Christian Roman empire was from that of the pagan Roman empire. Again, the triumphal procession of Manuel I Komnenos (r. 1143–80), after his victory over the Hungarians in 1168, as described firsthand by Niketas Choniates:

> When the time came for the emperor to join the triumphal procession, he was preceded by a gilded silver chariot drawn by four horses as white as snowflakes, and ensconced on it was the icon of the Mother of God, the invincible ally and unconquerable fellow general of the emperor. The axle did not creak loudly, for it did not carry the dreadful goddess, the pseudo-Virgin Athena, but the true Virgin, who, beyond understanding, bore the Word through the word. Following behind were the emperor's renowned blood relations and all ministers of senatorial rank and illustrious dignitaries who enjoyed the emperor's favour. Next in the line of procession was the most glorious and most great emperor mounted on a stately horse and arrayed in the imperial regalia.[22]

Generally speaking, these imperial events were carefully choreographed spectacles, reproducing the spiritual benefits to the people of having a sovereign who was God on earth.

A gilded, silken world

It is said that the emperor's edicts were written in gold ink on purple parchment (actually always vellum, the higher quality version) and received by his ministers, many of whom were eunuchs, with reverently covered hands. They were formally 'adored' because the association of purple with gold preserved the link between imperial power and divinity. Since they were heavenly and consecrated, breaches of their provisions were sacrilegious, and could be punished accordingly. Amusingly enough, though purple vellum was supposedly restricted for the use of the emperors, Jerome, in a letter of 384 written at Rome, scornfully talks of wealthy Christian women whose parchments 'are dyed purple, gold melted into lettering, manuscripts decked with jewels, while Christ lies at the door naked and dying'.[23]

This fascination with gold can easily be explained by its radiance and glitter, but purple has a more culture-specific meaning in Byzantium. Like gold, it has a changing, mutable character that imitates both fire and turbulent waters. The highest-quality dye was derived from the murex, a marine mollusc, and each batch could differ in hue and saturation. The Greek word for purple (*porphyreos* or *pyravgês*) captures this changing quality; *porphyreos* derives from the colours of the heaving, surging waters of a stormy sea or gushing blood, while *pyravgês* expresses the luminous spectacle of fire. Therefore, unlike the limited English term, the Greek word encompasses a spectrum of hues ranging from rosy red, green, and purple to blue and black.

The only colourfast dye in antiquity went to colour the 'purple clothes' mentioned in the Old Testament.[24] These fabrics had been enormously popular for many centuries all over the Mediterranean, having become – as we would say today – a status symbol, a sure sign of solid wealth and refined taste. Writing around the middle of the first century, the elder Pliny relates that in the days of Cicero (arch-orator, political broker, self-publicist, and social climber) 'double-dyed Tyrian purple fabric was impossible to buy for less than a thousand *denarii* a pound',[25] an outrageous price. At the time Iulius Caesar's legionaries were earning 225 *denarii* per annum. Soon, the emperor Tiberius (r. AD 14–37), whose reign if he had but known it included the crucifixion of Christ, found it necessary to prohibit the wearing of silk, giving as a specific reason that there was too much of a drain on the empire's gold reserve. In our period of study, Tyrian purple, as we call it, was a colour reserved for the imperial household alone, as was brocaded silk. Though wool was the basic material for all hardwearing clothing, with linen the next most common, silk was more plentiful in Constantinople than anywhere except China itself, and was the fabric of choice for all the aristocratic families of the empire.

According to Prokopios, Iustinianus (r. 527–65) himself introduced silkworm breeding in the empire, when with his encouragement monks from India smuggled silk moth larvae from China (Gr. *Tzinitza*) to Constantinople.[26] Silk is spun from the cocoon of silk worms that live on the white mulberry tree in China. Silk production was then a closely guarded secret of the Chinese, and was thought to be harvested by them 'combing fleecy silk from leaves' as per Virgil five centuries before Iustinianus.[27] Possibly as early as the seventh century, the Byzantine silk industry was centred in the capital, and this was maintained for centuries thereafter as a vital part of the Byzantine economy and a state monopoly.

Also for the emperor's exclusive use were scarlet shoes, studded with rich gemstones, like the scarlet buskins (calf-length boots), these shoes were the emblem of imperial majesty. As the usurper emperor Bardas Skleros said, as he stretched out his right foot to reveal his scarlet buskin to the bishop of Nicomedia, 'It is impossible, sir, for a man who has once publicly worn that boot voluntarily to take it off again'.[28] Over a white tunic and purple hose the emperor wore a purple robe which had a large square of cloth-of-gold embroidered on the front and back.

Bejewelled headdresses might be a better description for the crowns and diadems worn by the sovereigns, a custom that had originated in Persia.

The usurpation of imperial prerogatives was not merely treason; it had an element of blasphemy, on account of the emperor's position as Christ's vice-regent on earth. Iustinianus' law code preserves in force a number of laws originally by Theodosius, Arcadius and Honorius forbidding the production and sale of purple cloth for anything other than imperial use. In particular, one clause forbids cloth to be dyed 'with any colour resembling the Imperial purple' and decrees death as punishment for doing so.[29] The section following this affirms that the possession of any purple garments is high treason. Nonetheless, the next clause does allow an amnesty on punishment for possession of such garments, provided that they are surrendered immediately to the imperial treasury.[30] These laws remained in force throughout our period of study with just a single amelioration. Leo VI Sapiens issued a new constitution that allowed the public 'sale of small fragments and scraps of purple cloth, which afford means of ostentation to our subjects'.[31] O lucky subjects.

Chapter 13

Secular Spectacles

Quite clearly, there were many changes to the lives of ordinary citizens of the empire with the advent of the state religion of Christianity and all that entailed. Likewise, the very nature of the office of the ruler that ruled them was transformed. The emperor became an absolute sovereign, surrounded by pomp and ceremonial, bedecked in dazzling splendour that was set off by an ostentatious Constantinopolitan court, and isolated from his subjects. Thereby was he made more lofty and awesome in their eyes, as well as removed to some extent from what we would call nowadays the real world. There was one place in Constantinople, however, where the emperor was exposed to his subjects' scrutiny and, on occasions, their scorn: the Hippodrome.

The Hippodrome

Constantinus I rebuilt and enlarged the original hippodrome constructed by Septimius Severus in 203.[1] The Great Hippodrome was 480 metres long and 117.5 metres wide and it had an estimated capacity of 80,000. On the east side was the imperial loge, the *kathisma*, which was connected to the Great Palace through a spiral staircase, and behind and below were the stables, the *manganon*. The straight northern end of the arena, where the spectators and chariots entered through vaulted passageways, was located about where is now the polychrome fountain of Kaiser Wilhelm II of Germany. The semi-circular southern end, or *sphendone*, is today concealed far beyond the buildings at the south end of the modern square. Down the centre was the *spina*, around which the track ran. Built of stone, it was not more than a few feet high. At each extremity were three cones, marking the turning posts, or *metae*, while just behind was where ovoid-shaped objects, seven in total, were piled one on top of another to indicate the number of laps run in the chariot race. Constantinus VII Porphyrogenitus (r. 913–59) describes the monuments in the Hippodrome on the occasion of the visit to the capital of Arab envoys.[2]

A notable acquisition of Constantinus I was the Serpent Column, which stood near to the temple of Apollo at Delphi where Byzas consulted the oracle before establishing Byzantion.[3] Dedicated to Pythian Apollo to commemorate the defeat of the Persians at Plataia in 479 BC, it was originally composed of three entwined bronze serpents on whose heads rested a golden tripod, which had been made from one-tenth of the portion of the spoils seized from the vanquished.[4] Upon the coils of the serpents were inscribed the names of the thirty-one Greek *poleis* that had 'warred the war' against the Persians.[5] The golden tripod had disappeared long before Constantinus ordered the trophy to be removed from Delphi and relocated on the *spina* of the Hippodrome. In fact, it had been melted down by the Phokians at the onset of the Third Sacred War about 354 BC,[6] and today all that remains is about 5.5 metres of the origin eight-metre column, jagged and broken at the top. One of the serpent heads is to be seen in the Istanbul Archaeological Museum.

Another famous monument transported to Constantinople and re-erected on the *spina* was the top half or so of the red granite obelisk from Karnak in Egypt, variously known as the Obelisk of Theodosius or the Obelisk of Thutmose III. Now only 18.45 metres in height, it was originally thirty metres high, like the Lateran Obelisk, capped with gold, and probably weighed around 455 tons. This impressive monolith was originally commissioned to celebrate the victories of the Eighteenth Dynasty pharaoh Thutmose III (r. 1479–1425 BC). As such, it is carved with hieroglyphs glorifying the warrior pharaoh: 'Thutmose, who crossed the great river of Nahrain [Euphrates] as a mighty conqueror at the head of his army'. This was the pharaoh's victory over the Mitanni, which took place on the banks of the Euphrates in about 1450 BC. Added to the Hippodrome during the reign of Theodosius I (r. 379–95), the obelisk still rests firmly upon four bronze cubes, each forty-five centimetres square, and beneath them is a carved marble plinth with bas-reliefs.

On three faces of the plinth are seen Theodosius, flanked by his two ineffectual sons Arcadius (with the prominent ears) and Honorius, conducting various activities at the Hippodrome from the *kathisma*: attending a triumph, presiding at the races, and receiving tribute. The north face shows Theodosius supervising the actual erection of the obelisk, which is carved in two registers. The lower one contains eighteen figures and two machines. Groups of four men operate each machine by means of levers. In the upper register there are also two machines working in tandem with the lower ones to raise the obelisk. Each one is again operated by four men who wind strong ropes attached to the prone obelisk. There are two epigrams carved on the stylobate of the plinth, one in Latin (east face) and one in Greek (west face), which reminds us of the bilingual character of the capital at this date. Both inscriptions claim that the obelisk was erected in a mere thirty-two days from start to finish, under the supervision of Proklos, the *eparchos* of the City, who two years later fell from favour and was beheaded in the Hippodrome. The *eparchos* of the City was no small fry, and was effectively the governor of Constantinople, his duties including the maintenance of law and order, superintendence of the circus factions, control of the guilds, and above all the supply of grain. In the absence of the emperor, he presided over the imperial supreme court.

Yet, one of the most admired decorations of the Hippodrome must have been the stunning, 'shapely figure of the white-armed, beautiful-ankled, and long-necked Helen, who mustered the entire host of the Hellenes and overthrew Troy', who, though created out of base bronze, 'appeared as fresh as the morning dew, anointed with the moistness of erotic love on her garment, veil, diadem and braid of hair'.[7]

Racing punters

Throughout the empire chariot races were almost an obsession with all social classes, who divided themselves into two circus factions, the Blues and the Greens. The old circus factions (L *factiones*) had been transplanted from old Rome to New Rome. Originally, the charioteers had been organized into four teams, Blues (*vénetoi*), Greens (*prásinoi*), Whites (*leukoi*) and Reds (*roúsioi*), named from the livery the charioteers wore in the chariot races,[8] but eventually the Whites and the Reds melted away, having been incorporated into the Blues and the Greens respectively, by the time of Iustinianus (r. 527–65). We know from a near contemporary source that Anastasius I (r. 491–518) had 'supported the Red faction at Constantinople and took measures against the Greens and the Blues everywhere when they caused disturbances'.[9]

Popular devotion to one or the other of these circus factions involved more than mere sports enthusiasm. Chariot races were the most important events in the life of the ordinary Constantinopolitan, and race days were occasions for excessive gambling, roistering, eating, and shouting – providing a particular kind of excitement and entertainment not available to him in any other facet of his life. The spectator chose a circus colour, and supported it for the sake of the supporting. As a colour partisan, the Constantinopolitan gambled his self esteem on the outcome of the race, and this enthusiastic backing of a racing colour gave him an opportunity for contest, rivalry, and risk that was otherwise denied him in an increasingly authoritarian society.

Attendance to the races was apparently restricted to men. Alan Cameron noted that the *kathisma* was surmounted by a room with grilled windows, from behind which the ladies of the court could watch the events below, 'it not being considered proper for ladies to attend the games in the ordinary way'.[10] In a reference to factional rivalry, the mid sixth-century courtier and historian Prokopios of Caesarea Palestinae commented that women joined the men 'in this holy war', although they never 'go to the public exhibitions at all'.[11] Byzantine women appear, then, to have lost some of the social freedom that Roman women had enjoyed.

Turf wars

The circus factions were also represented, albeit unofficially, by excitable street gangs always spoiling for a fight and prone to acts of hooliganism, and not just in the imperial capital either. 'Every town' wrote Prokopios, who was indignant at this savage passion for the races, 'has in the classes of the people its blue and its green faction'.[12] In 495, for instance, the Greens appealed to Anastasius I for the release of some of their partisans who had been arrested for throwing stones at officials. The emperor grew angry and as a result sent his troops to attack the partisans. The situation escalated until a Green threw a stone at the emperor and he (the Green) was subsequently dismembered by Anastasius' bodyguards, the *Exkoubitoi*. The riot then petered out and in this instance the prisoners were not released.[13] In 501, again during the reign of Anastasius, the Greens ambushed the Blues in Constantinople and butchered 3,000 of them. Four years later, in Antioch, there was a riot caused by the victory of Porphyrios, a popular Green charioteer, who defected from the Blues.[14] In the capital a habitual challenge for the *eparchos* of the City was this rivalry maintained by the two factions, together or separately, which regularly erupted into mayhem.

The most infamous occasion was the Nika riots in 532. There were seven faction members set to be executed (all convicted of murder) but when they were hanged two of the ropes broke and one member from each of the Blues and the Greens escaped. The two factions called for mercy from Iustinianus but he offered no response. The Blues and Greens ended up uniting to set fire to the *praetorium* and then broke the prisoners out of custody.[15]

In 547, during the city's anniversary celebrations on 11 May, the factions got out of control and the *Exkoubitoi* were called in, resulting in heavy loss of life.[16] Much the same occurred in May 562.[17] Other factional riots broke out in October of the same year and in the following year too. On the latter occasion a partisan of the Greens was sentenced to be castrated for raping a girl. While he was being publicly paraded, he was seized and taken into the Hagia Sophia for asylum. After there was much turmoil in the church, Iustinianus decided to grant clemency.[18] There were yet other riots, including one over the proposed debasement of coinage in 553, which forced Iustinianus to perform a hasty U-turn.[19] Little wonder, therefore, to find Prokopios strongly criticizing the emperor for letting the circus factions to get out of hand.[20]

Certain young partisans of the Blues were said by Prokopios to affect a 'weird combination they called the Hun haircut'.[21] This consisted of untrimmed facial hair and head hair shaved at the front and grown long at the back. As for their dress, this was equally bizarre:

[T]he sleeves of their tunics were cut tight about the wrists, while from there to the shoulders they were of an ineffable fullness; thus, whenever they moved their hands, as when applauding at the theatre or encouraging a driver in the hippodrome, these immense sleeves fluttered conspicuously, displaying to the simple public what beautiful and well-developed physiques were these that required such large garments to cover them. They did not consider that by the exaggeration of this dress the meagreness of their stunted bodies appeared all the more noticeable. Their cloaks, trousers, and boots were also different: and these too were called the Hun style, which they imitated.[22]

Prokopios continues, informing his readership that these young Blue partisans would form gangs to engage in night-time muggings and street violence:

Almost all of them carried steel openly from the first, while by day they concealed their two-edged daggers along the thigh under their cloaks. Collecting in gangs as soon as dusk fell, they robbed their betters in the open Forum and in the narrow alleys, snatching from passers by their mantles, belts, gold brooches, and whatever they had in their hands. Some they killed after robbing them, so they could not inform anyone of the assault.[23]

One such hooligan was the future author Menander Protector, who was to write the continuation of Agathias' *Historiae* from 557/8 to the year 582, which in turn was a continuation of *On the Wars*, Prokopios' account of the political history of Iustinianus' reign. The emperor Mauricius (r. 582–602), the supposed author of the military treatise *Stratêgikón*, created new opportunities for aspiring authors and this is was what saved Menander from continuing his life as a lazy young lout. In brief autobiographical remarks in his preface, Menander explains that although his father had received no education, he and his brothers were sent to study law. 'But', he continues:

I did not take up the profession for which I was trained. For I had no desire to plead cases or to haunt the Basileios Stoa and impress the petitioners with my eloquence [a possible jibe against Agathias' pitiful remarks about the difficulties of earning a living].[24] I therefore neglected my career for the disgraceful life of an idle layabout. My interests were the gang fights of the 'colours', the chariot races and the pantomimes, and I even entered the wrestling ring. I sailed with such folly that I not only lost my shirt but also my good sense and my decency.[25]

But when Mauricius who 'loved the Muses, being enthusiastic for poetry and history… offered financial inducements to stimulate slothful intellects',[26] Menander seized the opportunity to turn his life around and began to write his *Historia*. He seems to gloat over his success, which came so much easier to him than to his literary predecessors Agathias and Prokopios.

Us and them

Hooliganism and outrages aside, in the capital these circus factions even had their own spokesmen who formed a link between the emperor and his people, ranged according to their colour in the Hippodrome, a large edifice pivotal to the life of Constantinople. Events in the Hippodrome were often accompanied by the raucous activities of the sport fans. Sometimes the Blues and the Greens would unite to heckle the emperor seated high up in the *kathisma*, with their complaints, voiced in a rhythmical chant, as they did in the devastating Nika riots.

Though it is dangerous to generalize, whereas the Great Palace symbolized an elevated, remote and secretive aspect of imperial power, being a carefully confined and guarded complex accessible to a very select group of dignitaries and foreign ambassadors, the Hippodrome, by contrast, presented a visible and accessible aspect of the imperial power in touch with the city's populace. For it was not only concerned with chariot races, it was also the arena for other major civic events.

Victorious generals celebrated their triumphs here, heretics were burned here, emperors received the approbation of their subjects here and, on occasions the mutilated bodies of fallen rulers were exposed to the derision and ridicule of the capricious mob in this great open space. The Constantinopolitans could show supreme indifference to the emperors; they hailed the victor with acclamations, and dragged to the Hippodrome the corpse of the vanquished. These were 'the wine-bibbing portion of the vulgar masses', as that Niketas Choniates so condescendingly describes them.[27] Granted. The most detestable of all things to the ruling élite was a mob. But popular enfranchisement did not exist, which meant that the 'vulgar masses' were poorly represented, if at all. The only way for their voice to be heard was by taking to the streets and sitting in the Hippodrome. This was the true political and secular heart of Constantinople, the Senate being not much more than a cipher that tended to praise and ratify the whims of the emperors. Here emperors were made and unmade.

In September 1185 emperor Andronikos I Komnenos (r. 1183–5), the last of the Komnenoi, met a particularly grisly fate. At the end of the *coup d'etat* that removed him from power he was found hiding behind casks of wine by the supporters of the new emperor, Isaakos II Angelos (r. 1185–95, 1203–4), cast into prison and grotesquely tortured. One eye was plucked from its socket, his teeth extracted, his beard torn off and his right hand severed. Barely conscious, he was then paraded through the streets of the city on the back of a mangy camel to face the spiteful savagery of the mob. Some threw human and animal excrement at him, others pelted him with stones and a prostitute emptied a pot of her urine over his face. In the Hippodrome Andronikos was hung upside down and had his genitals hacked off. A few of the crowd thrust swords into his mouth, others up his rectum, before finally, mercifully, the poor man expired. After several days, his hacked up body was taken down and thrown into one of the vaults of the Hippodrome.[28] This was surely one of the most public and hideous deaths of the mediaeval age.

Besides such horrible tumults, the Hippodrome, lest we forget, was the locus of regular programmes of chariot racing and other entertainments, 'all of which', Agathias observes, 'tend to have a profoundly disturbing effect on the minds of the young'.[29] On these festive occasions the Hippodrome would shake with the roars of tens of thousands of people. For much of the city's population could be accommodated in the Hippodrome to cheer on their favourite charioteer as he circled the arena's axis, and to raucously root for their preferred faction. Indeed, fans, young and old, became fervently attached to one of the factions, proudly proclaiming themselves 'partisans of the Blues' in the same way, as people today would be fanatical Celtic supporters. Take, for instance, the 'tribal exchange' during a violent clash between the Blue and Green supporters of Constantinople in 561: 'Burn here, burn there, / Not a Green anywhere'. The Greens replied by rushing and stoning the opposition, crying: 'Set alight, set alight, / Not a Blue in sight'.[30]

Obviously, the 'great and the good' often took a negative view of the factions and frequently commented on their lack of loyalty and the senselessness of their actions. Prokopios provides several examples of this. First, he comments that the factions care 'neither for things divine nor human in comparison with conquering in these struggles',[31] and comments on the senselessness of the violence in which they partake, saying:

> They fight against their opponents knowing not for what end they imperil themselves, but knowing well that, even if they overcome their enemy in the fight, the conclusion of the matter for them will be to be carried off straightaway to the prison.[32]

At other times, however, the factions united to heckle the emperor, seated high up in his loge, with their complaints and worries.

The circus factions provided the sole outlet that the populace had for any expression of its opinion or will, and the Hippodrome was the only place where the emperor and his subjects could confront each other directly and regularly. The factions therefore became important and volatile channels for public opinion. Thus, the races could be used to symbolically make religious statements, such as when a charioteer, whose mother happened to be called Mary, fell off his chariot and got back on and the crowd roared: 'The son of Mary has fallen, risen again and is victorious'. However, it should be noted that since the work of Alan Cameron it is now widely believed that neither of the factions had any consistent religious bias or socio-political allegiance,[33] in spite of the fact that they operated in an environment fraught with religious and political controversy.[34] He also successfully disputed the claims made by those scholars who argued that the factions constituted a militia force. With regards to this, Cameron argues that at most 'the factions constituted a small (and unreliable) paramilitary body, based not on the municipal organization of Constantinople as a whole, but on their natural focus in the hippodrome'.[35]

There is one promising instance for making a good case that the circus factions were used as a militia to defend Constantinople, namely during the revolt of Phokas.[36] Because his predecessor had depleted the treasury, the emperor Mauricius had been forced to limit public expenditures and military pay, which earned him much disfavour – on one occasion in the Hippodrome, the spectators shouted lewd verses at him about his numerous illegitimate children. In 602, he ordered his troops to winter in camps north of the Danube in the territory of the Avar, a strategically sound decision, but his troops mutinied. They acclaimed an obscure junior officer named Phokas as their new leader by raising him up on a shield (copied from Germanic coronation ceremonies),[37] a practice that was, in fact, proclaiming him emperor.[38] At first, Mauricius treated the outbreak lightly; he had mastered other mutinies. However, once Mauricius learned that he had lost total control of the army, he turned to the factions to defend the land walls of his capital. 'Then the emperor having armed them [factions] and calmed them with soothing words, ordered them to guard the city walls with the *demarchoi*'.[39] The factions deserted the unpopular Mauricius when it became apparent that defending the walls would consist of taking on the army. With the enemy finally at the gates, the emperor's position collapsed. Eventually, he and four of his sons were captured and brutally murdered. Their heads were displayed in the Hippodrome and their bodies thrown in the sea. Phokas took the throne, beginning a decade of misrule, thuggish brutality and political pandemonium. His excesses would lead to a popular revolt and the accession of the emperor Herakleios (610–41).

Yet, the key piece of evidence (or lack of it in this case) that supports Cameron's argument is as follows: manning the land walls in defence of Constantinople and serving as a militia are two different things. Ordinary citizens can perform the first function, but a city militia, which after all is a military force, requires some basic training for it to perform passably in this rôle. Of that there is absolutely no evidence in our literary sources. In the end, there is no doubt that Cameron is correct in his main thesis—that the circus factions were simply composed of racing fans, official, and competitors, and that the factions were given an official rôle in imperial ceremonies.

A day at the races

The eight minutes and twenty seconds devoted by William Wyler in his 1959 film version of Lewis Wallace's *Ben Hur* to the chariot race have helped to form the popular image of the Roman world to an extent equalled only by the Asterix the Gaul strip-cartoon series. This cinematic masterpiece, despite its niggling inaccuracies, thrillingly conveys the quintessential character and atmosphere of such a grand sporting event. And so it was for those who actually sat in the Hippodrome and experienced the spectacle firsthand. After its establishment as the most popular sport of all social classes, chariot racing became ritualized as part of the ceremonies surrounding the imperial court in Constantinople, and maintained a pre-eminent position until its decline in the twelfth century.[40]

Chariot races were held in the morning as well as the afternoon, while during the midday interval, spectators remained in their seats and were entertained by a wide variety of spectacles, such as wrestling, boxing, acrobatics, bears, singers and mimes. There are nine teams at the start of the race in Wyler's epic version of *Ben Hur*, an improbable number for a chariot race. In fact, four *quadrigae* participated in each race, representing the two colours – Blue and Green. Charioteers drew their starting positions with balls placed in a revolving lot-casting urn,[41] and then raced seven laps around the Hippodrome, making a course of around a couple of kilometres. The number of races presented in one day varied over time. In the sixth century, the standard programme offered twenty-five races, but by the tenth century, this had been drastically reduced to eight.[42]

Once the horses were ready, the white cloth (*mappa*) was dropped, the gates (*ostia*) were sprung, and the teams of horses thundered onto the track. The strategy was to avoid running too fast at the beginning of the race, since seven full laps had to be run, but to try to hold a position close to the *spina* and round the *metae* as closely as possible without hitting them. It has been estimated that teams could temporarily reach speeds of up to about seventy-five kilometres-per-hour when racing up the long side of the *spina*, but they had to slow down considerably before the *metae*, probably to twenty-five kilometres-per-hour.

There were plenty of ways that teams from one stable could foul their opponents during a race, and sometimes even before it started (attempts to dope or poison horses and charioteers were not unknown). Racing techniques were undoubtedly aggressive and ruthless. A charioteer would cut across the path of an adversary's chariot, trying to force it aside and up against the *spina*. Another trick was to hog the inside track, as recorded by Niketas Choniates:

[V]ery close to the eastern turn of the four-horse chariot course called *roúsioi* [Red], statues of charioteers were set up with inscriptions of their chariot-driving skill; by the mere disposition of their hands, they exhorted the charioteers, as they approached the turning post, not to relax the reins but to hold the horses in check and to use the goad continuously and more forcefully, so that, as they wheeled round the turning post in close quarters, they should compel their rival, even though his horses were faster and he a skilled competitor, to drive on the outside of the turn and come in last.[43]

Spectacular, albeit dangerous, collisions were an accepted part of the sport – the technical term was *naufragium*, shipwreck. Such situations were exacerbated by teamwork between charioteers of the same faction. Writing in the fifth century, Sidonius Apollinaris records one such incident:

His horses were brought down, a multitude of intruding legs entered the wheels, and the twelve spokes were crowded, until a crackle came from those crammed spaces and the revolving rim shattered the entangled feet; then he, a fifth victim, flung from his chariot, which fell upon him, caused a mountain of manifold havoc, and blood disfigured his prostrate brow.[44]

Incidentally, Wyler's film shows six out of nine teams totally written off, their luckless drivers mangled to death by speeding chariots, not to mention a soldier being fatally run over.

On the terraces of the Hippodrome the clamour of the cheering and heckling was thunderous as the horses thundered round the course. 'The hoarse roar from applauding partisans stirs the heart, and the contestants, both horse and men, are warmed by the race and chilled by fear', runs the graceful verse of Sidonius Apollinaris.[45] He has provided us with the most detailed and lively account of an amateur chariot race in Ravenna circa 450 won by his friend Consentius, and the conduct differs only very slightly from that of a professional race.[46] Undoubtedly, fans shouted instructions to a charioteer that could not possibly be heard and hurled abuse at rivals. They could follow the progress of a race by watching the egg-shaped counters, and as the race neared its climax the din must have been absolutely deafening as the thousands of spectators were caught up in the adrenalin rush. When the race was finally over, the emperor ceremoniously presented the victorious charioteer with a palm branch and a laurel wreath while the crowds cheered wildly; the more substantial monetary awards for stable and driver would be presented later. The victor would then drive a lap of honour.

The prestige of winning was far more important than the prize, which consisted of money, a cloak, and a wreath, all of which was received from the hand of the emperor.[47] The more famous of the charioteers had their statues erected on the *spina*. Usually, these were bronze statues, presumably each in the likeness of the charioteer, mounted on a marble base, which was decorated by bas-reliefs and inscriptions in Greek on all four sides. Porphyrios, for instance, had seven such statues erected on the *spina*, none of which survive, though the stone bases of two of them are to be seen in the Istanbul Archaeological Museum.[48]

The charioteers

Otherwise known as Kalliopes, Porphyrios was born in Libya in 480. In 507 he was involved in a mob attack on a Jewish synagogue in Antioch:

> A former *factionarius* [the most senior charioteer who drove for either the Blues or Greens] from Constantinople… took over the stable of the Green faction, which was vacant, and was completely victorious…They set fire to it, plundered everything that was in the synagogue and massacred many people, setting up a cross there and turning the site into a *martyrium*.[49]

Such anti-Semitic actions did not damage his career or his popularity. Indeed, Porphyrios was a successful charioteer for more than forty years, his racetrack triumphs spanning the years 500 to 540.

On one of the aforementioned bases, Porphyrios is depicted frontally in a *quadriga*, holding a palm branch in his left hand and a wreath in the right. On the other base, Porphyrios is depicted receiving a wreath of victory from the emperor. Both bases have epigrams that praise him, who must, after the older statue had been erected by the Greens, have switched to the Blues. Other texts include the shouts of the fans ('You can do it, fortune of the Greens'), and the names of ten of the thoroughbred horses our charioteer drove with: Nikopolemos, Radiatos, Pyrrhos, Euthynios, Haliaios, Anthpotos, Kynagos, Pelerios, Aristides, and Palaiastinarches. One epigram, on the older base, in part reads: 'Porphyrios, alone twice gained the splendour of such gifts, not boasting many decades of years, but many hundreds of victories, and all of them akin to the Graces'.[50] On the other base, that erected by the Blues, we can read in Greek:

> To others when they have retired, but to Porphyrios alone while still racing, did the emperor [Anastasius I] give this honour. For often he drove his own horses to victory and then took in hand the team of his adversary, and was again crowned. Hence arose a keen rivalry on the part of the Greens, hence a shout of applause for him, O King, who will give you both to Blues and to Greens.[51]

This epigram describes a feature unique to chariot racing in Constantinople, the *diversium*, which provided an opportunity for the winner of a race in the morning to challenge the loser to a rematch in the afternoon, with horses and chariots exchanged. In this manner, the doubly successful charioteer could demonstrate that his wins were the result of skill, rather than of luck. A prose inscription on the base erected by the Blues declares Porphyrios to be the only charioteer to have won the *diversium* twice, presumably in a single day. Another epigram, however, records that a charioteer by the name of Constantinus later won twenty-five races in the morning and twenty-one by *diversium*.[52] This implies a racing programme of fifty races, but Alan Cameron suggests that this may have been a special occasion, arranged to give this popular charioteer an opportunity to display his talents, and that these races were probably reduced in length.[53]

From these various epigrams, Cameron has discerned Porphyrios' career. His father having left Libya, Porphyrios was reared in Constantinople, where he began racing with the Blue faction while still very young but then changed to the Greens under the emperor Anastasius I (r. 491–518) and back to the Blues under Justin I (r. 518–27). He continued to race even in his sixties and seems to have adopted Kalliopes as his name later in life. As the epigrams proclaim, he was the first charioteer to have his statues erected in the Hippodrome while still competing and the first to have a statue (indeed, at least two) from each faction. Apart from that attack on the Antiochene synagogue, Porphyrios' other off-circus antics included rallying support for Anastasius during the armed revolt of Vitalian in 516. Vitalian, who was partly barbarian in origin, was an able commander exploiting religious discontent among units of the Illyrian army – it appears Anastasius was promoting anti-Chalcedonian, pro-Monophysite policies. The embattled emperor, 'with the Greens to assist him, warred with the furiously raging enemy of the throne'.[54] In appreciation, Anastasius, who, himself, favoured the Reds, restored the privileges of the Greens and permitted them to erect a new statue of Porphyrios.

We should spare a thought for Porphyrios and his fellow sportsmen, who, like prostitutes, made a living with their entire bodies. Charioteers wore little body protection – a lacing of straps around the torso and wrappings of tough leather (*fasciae*) around the legs – and only a small, round helmet (*pileus*) made up of a layer upon layer of tough leather, which was held in place by a chin strap. Their practice of wrapping the reins tightly around their bodies, just below the arms, so they could use their body weight to control the horses was exceedingly dangerous. In the case of accidents they carried a short, curved knife tucked in the straps of the torso lacing, but a charioteer still ran the risk of being dragged and trampled before he could cut himself loose. A charioteer's life could end at the turning point of the circus, 'that goal, ever quickly gained by your hastening car',[55] and it is not uncommon to read on extant grave stones of charioteers the laconic phrase 'killed driving'. It should come as no surprise, therefore, that these daredevils of the circus were elevated to superstar status. Also, as is evident from Porphyrios' *curriculum vitae*, it was perfectly usual for professional charioteers to switch from one faction to another.

The chariots

Roman racing chariots were purposely designed to be as small and lightweight as possible, stripped down affairs estimated to have weighed as little as twenty-five to thirty kilograms. They were made of light hardwoods and afforded little support or protection for the charioteer, who basically had to balance himself on the axle as he drove. The latter was long and straight, but the wheels were small and light, features that helped to stabilize the vehicle as it took sharp bends at speed. The wheels had six or eight spokes and probably thin iron tyres as well. They revolved freely on a fixed axle made of a single piece of hardwood timber. The cab floor was a series of interwoven leather straps, which was not only light but provided some sort of suspension. Rising from the front of the cab was a wooden hoop, which came up to the charioteer's waist. The design gave a wide wheel base and a low centre of gravity.

Originally, racing chariots came in two versions, a two-horse chariot, *biga*, and a four-horse chariot, *quadriga*, adopted from the Greeks. Although slightly slower, the *biga* was more manoeuvrable, and could display the charioteer's driving skills to greater effect. However, it was the *quadriga* that was more popular with racing fans in Constantinople. Since horses were always harnessed abreast, more than four were uncommon. The horses either side of the chariot pole wore a simple harness consisting of a girth around their stomachs and a chest band running forward from the girth. This harness was connected to a wooden yoke projecting from the pole, which sat on the horses' shoulders. The two outside horses wore a similar harness, but where linked to the pole by yoke. Shockingly brutal as the Roman attitude to animals could be, they were also capable of positively sentimental love of animals for their own sake, particularly horses, and even more particularly racehorses. 'Win or lose, we love you, Polidoxus' (*Vincas, non vincas, te amamus Polidoxe*) runs the legend on a mosaic from Constantine in North Africa showing a racehorse of that name.

Plenty of race fans could rattle off the names and pedigrees of the lead horse on a winning team. The best and most experienced horse in a team was usually harnessed on the right side of the yoke, where he could help the other horses negotiate the tight turns. Since chariot races were long and gruelling, stamina and responsiveness to commands were more important than absolute speed. A great many inscriptions commemorating charioteers also include the names of winning horses, as was mentioned above with Porphyrios, and some horses even merited their own inscribed tombstones, such as that which commemorates an African horse named Speudusa, 'Hasty', who was 'speedy as the wind'.[56] Unusually, Speudusa was a mare; most circus racehorses were apparently stallions. Neither were these champion horses forgotten when the victory prizes were awarded. Many depictions show palm branches stuck in the horses' harness. Moreover, at the end of a successful career in the circus a horse could expect not the knackers yard but retirement on a pension: 'Lest the steed that has won many palms should fall, dishonouring his victories, lazily now he crops the meadow grasses', as a much earlier Roman poet once wrote.[57]

As just mentioned, racehorses were normally stallions, stocky and of medium size standing 135 to 155 centimetres high, which makes them slightly smaller than the modern riding horse, but puts them among the largest breeds of antiquity. In performance they were inferior to their modern counterparts only in their ability to jump, which depends very much on the length of the legs. However, the ability to jump was certainly not a requirement for a circus horse. Horses began training as two-year olds, were put into training harness at three, but were not raced until they were at least five years old.

The sport of kings

Not all sports of Byzantium were inherited from Greece or Rome. Persia gave the world polo, and in due course, this horseman's team game made its way to Constantinople, where it became a popular activity of not only the nobility but emperors too. Basil I (r. 867–86) excelled at polo, the alcoholic Alexander (r. 912–13) died of apoplexy during a drunken game of polo, and John I Axouchos of Trebizond (r. 1235–8) died from a fatal injury incurred during a polo match.

The introduction of polo to the Byzantine empire is generally attributed by historians to Theodosius II (r 408–50). The game was known there as *tyzkanion*, presumably a variation of the Persian name, *tschougan*. The field on which Byzantine polo was played was called the *tyzkanisterion*, and Basil I, as an aficionado of the game, caused such a ground to be built within the walls of the Great Palace.

Of particular interest is the form that polo took in Byzantium. According to the most detailed description available, the game resembled nothing so much as lacrosse-on-horseback. John Kinnamos, secretary to Manuel I Komnenos (r. 1143–80), described a game of polo, played in the winter of 1166/7 by his master, as follows:

Some youths who divide themselves equally cast a ball made of leather, comparable to the size of an apple, into some level space which seems right to them when they measure it out. As it lies in the middle like a prize, they charge their horses at full speed toward it, against one another. Each holds in his right hand a stick sufficiently lengthy, but which abruptly terminates in a broad loop which is divided in the middle with cords of gut, dried by time, intertwined with one another in the fashion of a net. Each side makes great haste to sweep it up and get it first to the other end, which from the outset has been assigned to them. Whenever the ball, driven by the sticks, comes to either end, this constitutes victory for that side. Such is this sport, very perilous and dangerous. It is constantly necessary that one participating in it turn backwards and swing his hips, spin the horse in a circle and engage in every sort of race and be carried along in as many types of movement as the ball happens to make.[58]

Clearly, the netted loop at the end of the stick and the skill of sweeping the ball up imply a game in which the ball was gathered or caught, and then thrown with the stick, in contrast with the striking actions employed in the modern mallet version.

Christian overtones

Several principal church festivals were also celebrated in the Hippodrome. The Hippodrome of Meat, the Byzantine equivalent of Shrove Tuesday, marked the last day before Lent on which meat could be consumed. As a replacement of the pagan *Lupercalia*, it also heralded the beginning of spring, and was the occasion for ceremonial chariot races, choral singing, and dancing. The most important national festival of the year was the *Genethliaka*, celebrating the anniversary of the founding of Constantinople. The races held to commemorate this event were known as the Hippodrome of Vegetables. Both the emperor and, the patriarch of Constantinople attended these festivities, and presided over the distribution of vegetables, bread, fish, and cakes to the poor, a variation of the early Roman practice of dispensing *annona civica*, or 'political bread'.

Although ceremonies with a religious component were conducted in the Hippodrome, the Church was a reluctant participant in these rituals. Church leaders held strong moral objections to the secular amusements that had been inherited from pagan Rome, and would have been pleased to see them disappear completely from Constantinopolitan life. But chariot racing was too important to the citizens of Constantinople, and the Church therefore used its victory over paganism to modify the ancient hippodrome ceremonial and give it Christian connotations. Alan Cameron says that: 'One of the main purposes of the religious side of hippodrome ceremonial was to serve as an incentive to religious *solidarity*; to create and foster the all important theme of an emperor appointed by God as the protector of the faithful and champion of orthodoxy'.[59] Races in Constantinople were opened with the emperor making the sign of the Cross, while the crowd hailed him as God's representative and the factions sang hymns. Following the races, victorious charioteers gave thanks at the nearest church.

Closing races

Chariot races in the Hippodrome continued up to the sack of Constantinople by the crusaders of the Fourth Crusade in 1204. To give a couple of examples of this, Leo Diakonos tell us that Nikephoros Phokas, as emperor, organized chariot races, for 'the Byzantines are fonder of spectacles than any other people'.[60] However, on another occasion:

> He also gave orders to his soldiers to descend into the stadium, divide into opposing units, draw their swords, and attack each other in sport, to train in this way for battle. But the inhabitants of Byzantium, who knew nothing of military exercises, were panic-stricken at the flash of the swords, and, frightened by the assault of the soldiers in close quarters and by the clattering [of their arms], in their terror at the novel spectacle they turned to flight and ran to their homes. Quite a few deaths resulted from the shoving and the chaotic rush, as many were trampled underfoot and miserably suffocated.[61]

An earlier emperor, Michael III (r. 842–67), according to the testimony of John Skylitzes, not only took great delight in chariot races, but 'nor did he consider it beneath his dignity to drive a chariot himself'.[62] Apparently, when racing the emperor wore 'the colour of the blues'.[63] Much to the disgust of our already disgusted author, this latter day Nero also had a 'crew of catamites who followed him around, ready for any shameless deed'.[64] The same author castigates another emperor, Constantinus VIII (r. 1025–8), for neglecting the affairs of state, entertaining himself instead 'with chariot races, actors and comedy shows, passing his nights playing silly games'.[65]

The court biographer John Kinnamos mentions races and other amusements be held in the Hippodrome at the festivities of Christmas 1161 in honour of the marriage of Manuel I Komnenos (r. 1143–80) with Maria, daughter of Raymond de Poitiérs and Constance of Antioch.[66] Eighteen years later Ranieri di Monferrato (1162–82) was offered the hand of Maria Porphyrogenita (1152–82), the daughter of Manuel and his first wife Bertha-Eirene of Sulzbach (d. 1159) and second in line to the Constantinopolitan throne. The following year William of Tyre, the Latin chronicler and archbishop of Tyre (1175–86), was present at the grand ceremony and the cleric enthused over the magnificent nuptial splendour and the generous gifts and entertainments the emperor lavished on his own people as well as strangers:

> We may mention the games of the circus, which the inhabitants of Constantinople call hippodromes, and the glorious spectacles of varied nature shown to the people with great pomp during the days of the celebration; the

imperial magnificence of the vestments and the royal robes adorned with a profusion of precious stones and pearls of great weight; the vast amount of gold and silver furniture in the palace of untold value. Words would fail to speak in fitting terms of the valuable draperies adorning the royal abode, to mention the numerous servants and members of the court ...[67]

Ranieri was the brother of Bonifacio, marquis of Monferrato, 'worthy and valiant, and one of the most highly prized of living men'.[68] His petite chivalric court at Monferrato was the resort of artists and troubadours. Related to the French royal house, his family was a family of crusaders, and he himself would be chosen as the leader of the Fourth Crusade. After the capture of Constantinople Baldwin of Flanders, rather than Bonifacio, was elected Latin emperor. Bonifacio was to marry Margaret daughter of Béla II of Hungary, widow of the emperor Isaakos II Angelos, and establish the kingdom of Thessaloniki in Thrace and Macedonia, previously held by Ranieri. Bonifacio was ambushed by the Bulghars in the Rhodopes in September 1207, caught without time to don his armour, and died from an arrow wound in the arm. According to Geoffrey of Villehardouin, his head was cut off and sent to a joyous khan.[69]

When the Iberian rabbi and world traveller Benjamin of Tudela (1130–73) visited Constantinople in the late twelfth century, the city was in a period of decline. Nonetheless, the Byzantine capital remained an immensely prosperous and lively city, and Benjamin describes various entertainments in the Hippodrome, particularly the spectacles taking place there on the 25 December of each year:

Close to the walls of the palace is also a place of amusement belonging to the king, which is called the Hippodrome, and every year on the anniversary of the birth of Jesus the king gives a great entertainment there. And in that place men from all the races of the world come before the king [Manuel I Komnenos] and queen [Maria of Antioch] with jugglery and without jugglery, and they introduce lions, leopards, bears, and wild asses, and they engage them in combat with one another; and the same thing is done with birds. No entertainment like this is to be found in any other land.[70]

Arriving late in 1161 or in the first months of 1162 in the Byzantine capital, Benjamin spent a little over a year there.[71] His description of Constantinople is fairly long.[72] He was deeply impressed by the city's wealth, its wealthy citizens, and its cosmopolitan character. Even so, Benjamin is often prone to exaggeration, as in his description of the clothes, all in silk, worn by the Constantinopolitans. According to the British Library manuscript of his work, he states that the yearly revenue of the Byzantine imperial treasury from amounts to 20,000 *hyperpyra* or gold coins, yet according to another manuscript this was the daily income.[73] Whatever the original version, both figures were at best popular estimates and both quite implausible.

Turkish delights

In time, the civic and political importance of the Hippodrome declined, and by the tenth century, public protests and official ceremonies had moved to the great square in front of the Great Palace. In the mid-eleventh century, the emperors took up residence in the Blachernai palace on the outskirts of the city. This eroded the importance of the Hippodrome even further; then, when it was blackened by fire in 1203 and despoiled by the crusaders one year later, it fell into partial disuse. Although occasional jousting events, polo games, and displays of wild beasts were presented there, by the time Constantinople fell to the Ottoman Turks in 1453, the Hippodrome had long since ceased to be the centre of life in the capital city.

However, following the Ottoman conquest, the Square of the Horses (*At Meydanı*), as it became known, was renovated and reused for feasts and spectacles. One of the most spectacular celebrations enacted there, according to the historiographer to the court of Louis XIII of France (r. 1610–43), Michel Baudier (d. 1645), was that for the circumcision of one of the sultan's sons. After the presentation of gifts, there were mock battles between soldiers dressed as Muslims and Christians, a re-enactment of the siege of Famagusta (taken from the Venetians in 1570), and displays by tumblers, dancers, mountebanks, magicians, wrestlers and performing animals. Then the young prince for whom this had all been arranged was brought to his father's chamber, where he was circumcized by one of the great men of the court in the presence of all the paşas.[74]

At a much earlier circumcision festival in *At Meydanı*, that of 1582, the Guild of Bakers built a small bakery mounted on wheels where bread was kneaded and baked, a feat that won the applause of everyone, including the sultan Murad III, who watched from the comfort of the palace of Ibrahım Paşa (d. 1536). The resulting loaves were scatted among the crowd. Not to be outdone by the bakers, whose guild had a prestigious place in the hierarchy of guilds, the Guild of Kebab Cooks built a mobile kebab kitchen, complete with charcoal grill and a dining area for customers to enjoy freshly grilled shish kebabs (Tk. *şiş kebap*). Then, as now, the Turkish people enjoyed kebabs, and it is said the shish kebab was born over the open fires of the Turkic horse warriors that first invaded Anatolia, who, so as not to burn their fingers, used their swords to grill meat, as they pushed westward from their homelands in Central Asia. Given the obvious simplicity of spit roasting meat over a camp fire, I suspect its genesis is much earlier. Surely the description of skewering small pieces of meat for roasting in Homer's *Odyssey* must count for a proto-shish kebab.[75] Anyway, Homeric or Turkic, Ottoman poets, who wished to describe the pangs of love, compared them to with the ordeal of fire endured by the kebab before becoming cooked.

The chief organizer and planner of the imperial festivities of 1582 on the occasion of the circumcision of the young prince Mehmet, was Uluç Ali Paşa, the Grand Admiral, *kapudan-ı derya*, of the Ottoman fleet. After the naval battle of Lepanto (7 October 1571), where he had commanded the Muslim left, he had succeeded in bringing the remnants of the shattered fleet safely back to harbour in Constantinople, and for his gallant achievement was appointed to this key post. He served as such for fifteen years from 1572 to 1587 during the reigns of Selim II and Murad III. By all accounts the Uluç Ali was by well-earned reputation an outstanding naval tactician, a skill he was to put to good purpose on dry land in *At Meydanı*. One of the highlights of the festivities was a faithful replica of the Süleymaniye mosque, the second largest but by far the finest and most magnificent of imperial mosque complexes in Ottoman Constantinople, executed with great precision by members of the Guild of Architects. Made of wood and ivory, the model was some five metres high and was carried on poles supported on the shoulders of twelve men, six on each side. A man guided the impressive model from the front, while another pushed it from behind.[76] The architect of actual Süleymaniye mosque, the incomparable Sinan, was still alive and would have been among the spectators.

Lasting fifty-two days and nights, making it the longest of Ottoman imperial festivals, the festivities became the occasion for the artisans and craftsman of Ottoman Constantinople to display their ingenuity and skill. While the various guilds of the capital offered the sultan their most precious gifts, they entertained the people who assembled in the *At Meydanı* as well as the state dignitaries and the members of the foreign missions with a procession of colourful pageants each representing a particular craft or trade. All this Ottoman splendour was a complete contrast to the sporting madness of Byzantine Constantinople. We shall be returning to the Ottomans in due course.

Chapter 14

Pious Augustae

We open Chapter 14 with a Byzantine fairytale. Euphrosyne and her stepson the sixteen-year-old Theophilos (r. 829–42) were on good terms, so much so that the young emperor acquiesced to her selection of candidates at the imperial bride show she arranged for him in 830. Born in Constantinople to a good family, exceptionally beautiful and intelligent, Kassiane was among those candidates selected by the dowager empress. According to one tradition, as the young women assembled, she gave Theophilos a golden apple, telling him to offer it to whomever he chose. First drawn to Kassiane, the emperor approached her saying, 'Through a woman came forth the baser things', implying the sin of Eve, to which Kassiane responded, 'And through a woman came forth the better things', recalling the Incarnation.[1] Greatly displeased by her ready wit, Theophilos turns to another contestant, the more demur and silent Theodora of Paphlagonia, and offers her the golden apple.

The sudden turnabout was a godsend for Kassiane who, according to tradition, had already set her sights on monasticism, and she became a renowned abbess, poet, composer of liturgical and non-liturgical verses. She was later canonized. Approximately fifty of her hymns are extant and twenty-three are included in Orthodox services, including the most famous, the hymn of the repentant harlot washing the feet of Christ,[2] which is sung on Tuesday night of Holy Week.

In their proper place

Sounding very much like that staunch republican and guardian of ancient Roman mores, the elder Cato, John Chrysostomos, patriarch of Constantinople (r. 397–404, d. 407), wrote: 'The true ruler is he who masters his passions of anger, envy, and lust, and subordinates everything to the laws of God; who, keeping his mind free, will not let pleasure dominate his soul'.[3] There again, John with the golden mouth, from which he receives his name, was one of the most contentious patriarchs in the history of Byzantium; he would have seen both Church and empire wrecked rather than compromise his principles. Nevertheless, feminine virtues too continued traditional Roman precepts, particularly the ideal of the wife as gentle, modest, and dedicated to family and home. The good empress augmented the properties of the ideal wife with élite largesse: she was pious, philanthropic, humble, and chaste.

It was Prokopios of Caesarea Palestinae who described the ideal imperial bride as 'noblest born, most highly educated, most modest, carefully nurtured, virtuous and beautiful virgins of all the ladies in the whole Roman empire: a maiden, as they say, with upstanding breasts'.[4] So, the imperial public image expected the empress' primary function to be that of flanking the emperor during audiences and receptions, splendid, silent and self-effacing. The empress Theodora of Prokopios' *Anékdota* is none of these things: she is portrayed as the betrayal of all Roman feminine virtues. Indeed, parts are so vitriolic, not to say pornographic (especially chapter nine), that for some time translations from Greek were only available into Latin. As a result, Edward Gibbon wrote about Theodora that 'her arts must be veiled in the obscurity of a learned language',[5] and then went on to quote the passage in Greek with Latin comments. Then again, Gibbon did not entertain a high view of the female sex.

In Theodora, Prokopios created the perfect anti-woman. Rather than a modest and meek Roman matron, Prokopios' empress inverts all the qualities that Roman culture valued in a woman. For us, it is easy to comprehend that Theodora refused to play the subservient rôle normally expected of a Byzantine empress. Theodora, who by all accounts was especially beautiful and extraordinarily intelligent, took a very active rôle in the management of the empire. This was a controversial enough move in itself, but it was rendered vastly more so by the empress' lowly origins. She had grown up as a child of the circus factions to become the capital's best known stage actress – which, in those days, was the same thing as saying she was the capital's most infamous prostitute. This brings us back to Prokopios. He portrayed Theodora as a wanton of the most promiscuous sort, and the reader is unlikely to forget the picture he painted of a stage act that the future empress was said to have performed involving her unmentionable parts, some barley grains, and a gaggle of trained geese.[6]

We may like to note, however, that the later centuries of the empire were to produce many individual empresses of great influence, a particular characteristic of the Byzantine Christian society as it matured. If it is true, as has been suggested, that a civilization may be judged by the way it treats its women, the Byzantine must rank high. Indeed, we may observe in our particular period of study a number of redoubtable women in the imperial family – and not only empresses – who, by virtue of their position, frequently dominated their families, were active in court and possessed both liberty of thought, expression and action, and the ability to utilize such freedom at will, as an appreciation of the life and the loves of the extraordinary empress Zoë clearly reveals. Here is her story.

Zoë's story

After the death of her uncle Basil II, one of the greatest and most powerful of Byzantine rulers, a period of steady decline set in. Under his feeble successors, starting with his sexagenarian brother Constantinus VIII (r. 1025–8), who was the father of Zoë, the state lacked effective control. At the same time, rivalry and factionalism developed between the civilian, court-centred aristocracy of the capital and the landed military nobles of the Anatolian provinces, some of the latter even providing imperial dynasties or great warrior emperors (e.g. the Phokai, the Komnenoi). The vigour of an autocratic régime depends largely upon the character and qualities of the autocrat, and the Byzantine empire was no exception. In this kaleidoscope of Constantinopolitan court politics Zoë was to find herself as the sole ruler of Byzantium.

Empress Zoë Porphyrogenita (979–1050) had been singularly unlucky in love. At the age of twenty-three she was engaged to the Holy Roman Emperor Otto III (996–1002), but he died of a fever before the marriage could be solemnized and Zoë spent the next twenty years confined to the women's quarters of the Great Palace. Her warrior uncle had died three years previously leaving no son to succeed him. Now lingering on his deathbed, her libertine father had no son to succeed him either.[7] Still a virgin, Zoë became once again a moveable asset: a marriage was arranged in haste between Zoë and the sexagenarian senator Romanos Argyros, who relinquished his wife of forty years to accept the union only under extreme duress – to refuse meant losing his eyes – and just in time to become Romanos III Argyros (r. 1028–34) following the death of his new father-in-law on the very day after the wedding.[8] As she was well beyond the age of childbearing, Zoë and Romanos resorted to all kinds of charms, lotions, potions and ointments in an effort to make her pregnant. They had no success and Romanos, tiring of the game, came to hate his new wife.[9]

In the meantime, the spurned Zoë became infatuated with a lowborn Paphlagonian teenager, Michael, the brother of a eunuch, John the Orphanotrophos, who held an important position in the court. An interesting fellow from an equally interesting family, John the Orphanotrophos had been a *protonotarios*, the head of the civil administration of a theme and subordinate only to its military governor, under Basil II.[10] Once in Constantinople John had secured for himself the prestigious office of director of the capital's principal orphanage, the orphanage of Saint Paul situated on the First Hill, hence his moniker 'guardian of the orphans'. He had four brothers: Michael, Niketas, Constantinus and Georgios, the last two like himself being eunuchs. The family came from Paphlagonia, a province that provided the court with many eunuchs, and appears to have been occupied in some disreputable business. George Kedrenos hints that they were even engaged in forgery and other such felonious practices.[11]

In the meantime, having at last awakened to the realization of the joys she had been missing, Zoë seduced the boy and after Romanos conveniently passed on, possibly with the aid of hellebore, married Michael the same evening.[12] It was Good Friday, 12 April 1034. She was fifty-six, he was sixteen. She believed that 'she would have a slave and a servant rather than a husband and an emperor'.[13] She was wrong. She was beautiful, restless, indiscrete, and highly sexed. But Michael never loved Zoë and soon after the marriage, refused to have any physical contact with her. She was banished once again to the women's quarters.[14]

Michael IV (r. 1034–41) had long suffered from epilepsy and the attacks became more frequent and prolonged.[15] He began to deteriorate physically. Though still only in his twenties, he lost his good looks completely and became gross and bloated to the point of semi-paralysis. By the end of 1041 the emperor was obviously dying. His energetic brother the Orphanotrophos was ready and acted swiftly. His one remaining brother with manhood left intact was Constantinus, but he was now as widely hated as John himself. Stephanos, the caulker promoted to command the imperial navy by reason of his marriage to the emperor's sister Mária, had been dead for over a year but had left a son. Thus, before Michael finally passed away on 10 December, Zoë had been brought to the court and induced to adopt the nephew of the Orphanotrophos, he himself being regrettably disqualified from assuming the diadem and the purple. This seemingly unconscious tool of the uncle was called Michael Kalaphates (the cognomen obviously a satirical reference to his father's former lowly trade).[16] This step, however, proved to be his undoing.

Michael V Kalaphates (r. 1041–2) had scarcely sat on the imperial throne of Constantinople before he banished his uncle, to whom he owed everything, to a distant place of exile from which he was never to return.[17] Soon enough it was the turn of Zoë herself. Michael had always hated his foster mother, who he kept under constant surveillance, and about four months after his coronation he accused her of attempted regicide.[18] On 18 April 1042 his personal bodyguard of eunuch 'Scythians' (possibly Pečenegs) dragged her from the women's quarters and she was shut up in a convent on Prinkipo (Büyükada), the Isle of the Prince in the Sea of Marmara. As Michael Psellos wrote, obviously filled with distaste, the old empress, 'the daughter of a most noble family, was dispossessed by a man sprung from the gutter'.[19] It is said that Michael gloated over her shaven tresses as she was bundled away from Constantinople. The departure of the sinister uncle was lamented by no one; but the news of the anointed empress of the great Macedonian house shook Constantinople to its very foundations.

So, Zoë was to have her revenge and none too cold either. She, and her spinster sister Theodora,[20] were much loved by the population of the city who called them familiarly in Greek μάμμαι, the Mothers.[21] Two days later Zoë was hastily brought back from exile, but it was too late. The citizens, now backed by the Church and the nobility, refused to submit any longer to the misrule of the parvenu Paphlagonians, remaining as they did firmly attached to the former legitimate dynasty. What is more, according to the eyewitness testimony of Michael Psellos, 'not even the foreigners and allies whom the emperors are wont to maintain by their side – I am referring to the Scythes from the Taurus [*Tauroskuthai*, viz. Varangians] – were able to restrain their anger ... all were ready to lay down their lives for Zoë'.[22] After a period of terrible rioting in the city, on the evening of 20 April Michael was deposed, publicly blinded and exiled to the monastery of Eleimon on the eastern Aegean island of Chios, a retreat into the religious life being considered the proper place for a dethroned emperor. What God had given, He could take away too.

The late spring of 1042 saw Zoë ruling the empire with Theodora. The two sisters were not only manifestly unfitted to rule, but thoroughly detested one another too. Little surprise, therefore, this period of joint sororal rule was not at all successful, and within two months, at the age of sixty-four, Zoë married again. Her third husband was Constantinus Monomachos, an agreeable and attractive roué to whom, as Constantinus IX (r. 1042–55), poor Theodora was only too happy to surrender her half of the throne and return to monasticism.[23] As emperor, Constantinus IX based all his claims to legitimate power on his family name, Monomachos, 'Lone Fighter', for he lacked both *porphyrogennetos* birth and military victories. There is a Marian icon belonging to the emperor whose silver revetment carries an inscription in the form of rhyme: 'O, Monomachos, fight having me, the invincible one, as a companion in combat'.[24] The Greek text is rhythmically structured on words whose root is μάχη, 'fight'. It is a pun on Monomachos, which Constantinus associates with the Virgin Mary with Victoria; she is the *symmachos* (L *comes*, 'companion'), a traditional epithet of Victoria.

Constantinus had a mistress, Skleraina, and it would appear that Zoë shared her husband with Skleraina in a happy *ménage à la trois* until her death at the age of seventy-two in 1050.[25] Women were almost never identified by a personal name, but usually by their surname, thus the Komnene woman, or, as in this case, the Skleraina, meaning a woman of the Skleros clan. She was, in fact, the niece of his late second wife, Pulcheria, and granddaughter of Bardas Skleros, one of the pretenders who had challenged the young Basil II. Concerning Skleraina, we have a lovely anecdote from the pen of Michael Psellos.[26] When this beautiful Kappodocian mistress of the emperor first appeared by his side in public a courtier expressed his admiration in just two words, οὐ νέμεσις, 'there is no blame'. Skleraina saw the impression created by the quotation, but did not understand: she summoned the courtier to her side and asked for an explanation. But for the court of Constantinople those two words from Homer had sufficed to conjure up the picture of the murmurous aged men on the walls of ancient Troy who gazing at Helen in her divine radiance uttered οὐ νέμεσις but did not complete the quote.[27]

Zoë Porphyrogenita, albeit graced with good looks, was no Helen of Troy. Conversely, we do find analogies to Zoë in the images of Queen Penelope in Homer's *Odyssey*, Princess Draupadi in *Mahâbhârata*, Queen Brünhild in *Nibelungenlied*, and Queen Rhiannon in the Middle Welsh prose tales of the *Mabinogion*, as each of them delivered the kingdom to her spouse (respectively Odysseus, Arjuna, Siegfried and Gunther, and Pwyll). Of course, the exception for Zoë being that she performed this deliverance thrice not once.

Golden glory

On the eastern wall of the south gallery of Hagia Sophia there is an exquisite eleventh-century gold tesserae mosaic. Along with the empress Zoë, it shows her third and final husband, Constantinus IX Monomachos, in full imperial finery; all the details of his vestments and diadem, with its prominent cross and hanging pendula of pearls, would have been carefully copied here.[28] The emperor holds a large moneybag containing gold coins which, as part of the ceremonial of the Church, he would place on the high altar both as part of the coronation ceremony and during the services of Holy Week. The emperor's exceptional status is highlighted by the nimbus around his head. Between the two is the haloed Christ. He is shown enthroned; his right hand is raised in a gesture of benediction, his left holds a gem-studded book of gospels, his face subtly animated in an expression of grave benevolence. At the left the emperor offers the moneybag, and on the right the empress is holding an inscribed scroll. Above the emperor's head an inscription reads: 'Constantinus, in Christ, the Lord Autocrat, the faithful Emperor of the Romans, Monomachos'. Above the head of the empress is the inscription: 'Zoë, the most pious Augusta'. The scroll in her right has the same legend as over the emperor's head, save that the words Autocrat and Monomachos are omitted for want of space.

The general idea expressed in the mosaic is that the earthly ruler and his consort are represented as generous donors, offering to the Divinity a sum of money and a document in the form of a scroll, presumably a *privilegium*, to the Church. The mosaic was situated in a prime location, for the south gallery was directly connected with the patriarchate, and was to serve throughout the eleventh and twelfth centuries as the main meeting place for the Holy Synod. We can imagine the brilliant gold background of the mosaic shining brightly through the haze of incense of the candlelight gallery as the Church hierarchy gathered here to discuss rarefied affairs.

There is nothing exceptional about the theme of the mosaic or its location. Still, every picture, they say, tells a story. No less so with this one. For on closer inspection it is evident that all three heads and the two inscriptions concerning Constantinus have been altered. Constantinus IX Monomachos (r. 1042–55) is the third imperial figure to be shown with Zoë in the mosaic, replacing her second husband, Michael IV (r. 1034–41), who in turn replaced her first husband, Romanos III Argyros (r. 1028–34), who was possibly killed by her. The heads of Christ and Zoë are thought to have been defaced during the brief reign of her adopted son, Michael V Kalaphates (r. 1041–2), who loathed her so much as to have her banished to an island convent.[29] The mosaic in its present state is thus dated to 1042 or shortly thereafter, and so the viewer gazes upon an elderly Zoë with her unwrinkled skin and plump cheeks, her pencilled eyebrows and made-up features, just as the courtier Michael Psellos had known and admired her.

The princess who wanted to be emperor

As readers we all relish a sensation. As readers we want to be stunned and fascinated. Let us turn to one of the most important and influential historiographers of Byzantine literature, Anna Komnene (usually Latinized as Comnena). The firstborn child of the Alexios I Komnenos, Anna was 'born in the purple' on 1 December 1083, two years after her father had deposed the emperor Nikephoros III Botaneiates (r. 1078–81), and at the very young age of eight she was betrothed to Constantinus Doukas, the son of the deposed Michael VII Doukas (r. 1071–8).[30] The engagement was a political one, designed to cement the position of the Doukas family after their support had proved crucial in Alexios' seizure of power. But Anna's hopes of gaining the throne were dashed by Constantinus' death (sometime before 1097), and from then onwards we can clearly see the emerging hatred she held for her younger brother and heir to the throne, John.[31] Clearly Anna craved a higher function than being merely a sexual object, a breeder of children, or a conveyor of privileges and titles.

As we well know, an easy-going and cavalier manufacturing of the facts is typical of many historians both past and present. This is not surprising, since it is the only fig leaf these historians have. This was not so with our Byzantine purple princess, who had studied the authors of classical antiquity, having read Aristotle and Plato, Homer and Demosthenes, the historians and the poets. In the words of a fellow courtly *littérateur*, Niketas Choniates, she 'was ardently devoted to philosophy, the queen of all the sciences, and was educated in every field of learning'.[32] More modern critics have not been so kind. The purist Edward Gibbon, a man not noted for his kind patience towards the female sex, did not like her style, writing that 'an elaborate affectation of rhetoric and science betrays in every page the vanity of a female author'.[33] Tut-tut Mister Gibbon, our erudite Anna you may write down as importunate, nagging, domineering bluestocking, but she certainly knew her stuff.

Anna Komnene had, of course, her prejudices, racial, social and personal, but that does not mean that she was necessarily trying to deceive her audience. Throughout her history her love, affection and admiration for her father and his achievements is unquestionable. Thus, the *Alexiad* pays unfettered homage to Anna's father, and why not? The small, dark and unprepossessing Alexios. He was the nephew of a previous emperor, Isaakos I Komnenos (r. 1057–9), one of the empire's best generals from an aristocratic family of distinguished military leaders, and a man of shrewd and tenacious purpose. The Komnenoi came originally from Komne, near Adrianople, and had estates in the Kastamon district of Anatolia. Isaakos was the son of Manuel Erotikos, a distinguished *eparchos* under Basil II, and he had married Catherine (or Aekaterina) the daughter of John Vladislav, a prince of Bulgaria. The union produced a son, who died young, and a daughter, who retired (along with her mother) to a convent soon after her father's death. Both Isaakos and his brother John had already held high office.

Like his uncle before him, Alexios too was a usurper, a quality that ran in the family. For his daughter the princess also personally interfered in power politics. With her mother Eirene's help, in August 1118, Anna unsuccessfully tried to divert the throne from her brother John to her husband Nikephoros Bryennios. He was either the son or grandson of the Nikephoros Bryennios who had rebelled against Michael VII Doukas and Nikephoros III Botaneiates. Married to Anna by 1097, he had soon risen to become a trusted member of his father-in-law's inner circle, enjoying not only the backing of the emperor, but also of his wife, Eirene Doukaina, who happened to be the cousin of Michael VII Doukas. Anyway, apparently Nikephoros failed to turn up for his own *coup d'état*, to which his wife's reaction was reported as vituperative. 'It is said that *kaisarissa* Anna', writes the chatty Niketas Choniates, 'disgusted with her husband's frivolous behaviour and distraught in her anger, and being a shrew by nature, felt justified in strongly contracting her vagina when Bryennios' penis entered deep inside her, thus causing him great pain'.[34] Probably to the relief of her slothful (and sore) husband, Anna was eventually packed off into comfortable exile at the monastery of Theotokos Kecharitomenes, lingering there until 1143, the year her brother died. Anna herself says absolutely nothing about this failed plot, although she does stress she had been excluded from Constantinople and from her family and friends, living in isolation, not receiving a visitor for thirty years if we are to believe her.[35] It is John Zonaras and Niketas Choniates who later write of Anna's thwarted ambitions to take the throne and her subsequent fate.[36]

The ability to move fast in politics, as in real life, makes you seem flexible, agile and in control. Speed is decisive. This was where Anna's power grab probably stumbled and ultimately failed. When Alexios felt himself at death's door, he slipped his ring into the hand of his son, and pressed him to hurry away and have himself proclaimed emperor at once. Despite their vigilance, mother and daughter failed to notice this, and so father and son were finally able to outwit them. Armed with his father's ring, John hurried to Hagia Sophia where he was crown by the patriarch, after which he returned to his father's palace. Here, the Varangians denied him admittance, until he declared the death of his father to them and showed them his signet ring, whereupon they accepted him as the new emperor and let him in. He was then able to take control of the army and the navy, and duly put down an attempted *coup d'état* by his mother and sister.[37] The stigma of the plot does not appear to have extended fully to Nikephoros Bryennios, who campaigned alongside John II Komnenos shortly before his death in 1138.

Chapter 15

Christian Soldiers

'The vices of Byzantine armies', snipes Edward Gibbon, 'were inherent, their victories accidental'.[1] In occidental eyes the Byzantine state was timid and treacherous, the Byzantine army feeble and unwarlike. The truth is otherwise, as any Northman knew who had made the long journey southward and spent time in the service of the Byzantine emperor. He was at the centre of a large and well-organized state apparatus, more developed and sophisticated even than the Frankish and Anglo-Saxon courts, and infinitely more advanced than anything in Scandinavia. What concerns us in this chapter, therefore, is what exactly the Northmen (or any other foreigner for that matter) encountered when they came into contact with the advanced and superior Byzantine military organization, as well as its complicated diplomatic system.

A preference for peace

Marbled rhetoric aside, the Byzantine empire had a highly sophisticated approach to international politics and military strategy. Unlike most of their contemporaries, the Byzantines learnt very early in their history that winning a battle did not necessarily win a war, and consequently its military policy was essentially defensive when that of the rest of the known world was aggressive. The Arabs, the Pečenegs, the Latin crusaders, and the Bulghars were peoples devoted to war who generally marked their path with fire and sword, yet, despite its limited manpower and frequent internal dissension, the empire effectively resisted and long outlived these warrior nations. Created from the glories of the original Roman empire, the Byzantine empire and the men (and a few women) who ruled it depended upon the diplomatic stratagems that had successfully worked for centuries. Not idly did Michael Psellos say of Michael IV (r. 1034–41) that the emperor kept in check those beyond the frontiers of the empire 'partly by the dispatch of envoys, partly by bribery, partly by annual displays of military strength'.[2]

Unlike western Europe where prowess in battle was a mark of status and distinction, the Byzantines seem to have regarded war as, at best, a distasteful necessity. Byzantine warfare was therefore of a twofold nature – diplomatic, and only at the last resort military. Since diplomacy was far cheaper than brute force as a means of self-protection, it was zealously pursued. In the wise words of Leo VI Sapiens (r. 886–912), 'To master the enemy by wisdom and stratagems seems to me safer and more profitable than to overcome him by violence and force, and than to risk battle face to face'.[3] Constantine IX Monomachos (r. 1042–55) allegedly made peace with the Pečenegs in 1053 because he would not allow Byzantium 'to be cut to pieces from its youth up'.[4] One of the main objections to war, of course, was the danger of losing. 'You should never be enticed into a pitched battle', warned the wise Leo VI, '… success is a matter of luck rather than proven courage'.[5] These imperial attitudes should not be confused with pacifism. Diplomacy is still regarded as one of the Byzantines' foremost skills.

Through much of the mediaeval period the Byzantine empire possessed, together with its unrivalled bureaucracy, a diplomatic and intelligence service that could be matched by few, if any states (besides the Sunni 'Abbasid caliphate at Baghdad), certainly in Christendom. Surpassing its pure political function, diplomacy, whose basic objective was 'divide and rule', was understood to have an intelligence-gathering function. For this reason, Byzantine agents ranged widely, and the authorities in the capital often knew more about other states or peoples than the latter knew about themselves. The emperors used specific strategies in negotiations with foreign powers. Many of these strategies were formulated clearly in *De administrando imperio*, an empirical treatise sponsored by the learned son of Leo VI Sapiens, Constantinus VII Porphyrogenitus (r. 913–59), which was intended to guide his son, the future Romanos II (r. 959–63), and future emperors in their interactions with rival powers.[6] Thus we can read in Anna Komnene praise for her father, Alexios I Komnenos (r. 1081–1118), for only warring with the barbarians when peaceful methods had failed. 'After all', she reasons, 'it is the mark of a bad general, when all is peaceful, to incite his neighbours to war intentionally – for peace is the objective of all wars. Invariably to prefer war instead of peace, to disregard a positive conclusion, is typical of foolish commanders and foolish political leaders, the mark of men who work for the destruction of their own state'.[7] Wise words that still hold true today.

Naturally, the empire's neighbours did not always understand the complex motives of plot and counterplot, flattery and threat, which were essential ingredients of Byzantine international politics, and most tended to regard the diplomatic manoeuvres and skulduggery of the emperor and his ambassadors as underhand and two-faced without appreciating its true politico-military value. Writers of different nations commented scathingly on what they saw as the Byzantines' lack of martial ardour and on the fact they nonetheless often prevailed. The Ottonian cleric and chronicler Thietmar of Merseberg (975–1018) alludes 'to the customary artfulness (*calliditate*) of the Greeks'.[8]

These 'artful' practices require little explanation: the playing-off of one people or state against another; the cultivation of useful friends in foreign courts; the support of rebellious or dissident elements in a foreign power; the support or retention of a claimant to power from a foreign state; the use of spies (ex-prisoners were a good source); the acquisition by various means of client states; the lavish use of money as a diplomatic tool as an alternative to military power or as a means of winning foreign favour. What this all boils down to is the frequent use of subterfuge, spies and, above all, specie. There is no need to remind ourselves that to conceal one's own secrets and to discover those of the opposition can be held to be a most potent factor in the ultimate victory. One tenth-century foreign envoy to Constantinople, Liudprand of Cremona, drew attention to two great assets of the Byzantines. After listing their sundry neighbours, he states that they 'far surpass these people both in wealth (*divitiae*) and wisdom (*sapientia*)'.[9] Naturally, as the envoy of a Byzantine ally in Italy, Liudprand received special treatment when he visited Constantinople in 949. He was received in the Magnaura, an audience hall of the Great Palace, by the emperor, and at the end of his stay he was presented with a pound of gold. Even so, Liudprand, who saw the empire's stance as essentially defensive, had put his finger on the two qualities with which a sedentary civilisation could almost easily defend itself 'against the most ferocious peoples'.

It was one of these 'ferocious peoples', the Turks, who would later on master all the tricks of oriental diplomacy themselves, who complained that the Byzantines had ten tongues and one talent, deceit. The use of deceit is admirably illustrated by Anna Komnene when she recounts her father's intrigues against Bohémond in 1108. Having discovered who were Bohémond's truest followers, Alexios composed letters thanking them for letters, which were in fact utterly fictitious. As Anna relates, the 'play acting had a purpose: if it came to Bohémond's ears that such men were traitorous, that they had been seduced and had made overtures to the emperor, he would at once be thrown into confusion'.[10] The letters of Alexios also promised 'donations, gifts from the emperor and extraordinary inducements'.[11] Naturally, Alexios arranged that these letters to fall into Bohémond's hands. This act of disinformation, however, failed to stir up the hoped for discord in the Italo-Norman camp, for Bohémond seems to have suspected the authenticity of the letters' contents. But it shows what dissension Byzantine diplomacy sought to sow through wealth (even without the actual distribution of gifts) and wisdom (even if it was used in a double-tongued fashion).

The disinherited firstborn son of the Norman warlord Robert Guiscard, Bohémond of Taranto (d. 1111) was to be the founder and first ruler of the independent principality of Antioch (officially proclaimed Bohémond Ier d'Antioche in March 1099) despite Byzantine claims. He had been one of the first crusader leaders to give the oath of fealty to Alexios I Komnenos, expecting to become the leader of the First Crusade in the emperor's service. Disappointed in this, he saw in Antioch a means to realize his ambitions, a city that was significant to Christians as the place where saints Peter and Paul had lived and as one of the five patriarchal seats of the Church. He was captured by the Seljuq Turks near Aleppo in 1100 and imprisoned until ransomed in 1103. The following year he was defeated by the Seljuqs at Harran. In the year 1106 Bohémond travelled back to Europe to fund his campaign against both the Seljuq Turks and the Byzantines, all the while trumpeting the fight against both Greek and Turk alike. 'As he journeyed through Italy and France recruiting help he was responsible more than anyone else for spreading the story that the Byzantine emperor had betrayed the crusaders'.[12]

With a new army Bohémond besieged Durazzo (Dürres) from 1107, but failed to take it. By the Treaty of Devol (signed September 1108) he recognized Byzantine overlordship, swearing under oath that he 'shall be, from this moment, the loyal man (λίζιος άνθρωπος) of Your Majesty and of your much-beloved son, the Lord Emperor John, the Porphyrogenitus'.[13] But what is the good of promises if they are not backed up by deeds? He had readily taken the oath that he would be a faithful vassal, but his promises were like piecrusts and he just as readily broke them. Like his father, Bohémond was a talented and ruthless opportunist, and massively cunning too. The fascinated Anna Komnene had much to say about this tall, muscular, stooping 'habitual rogue'.[14] Indeed, her father was destined to be let down by Bohémond. His promises became a dead letter once he left the emperor's presence, not for Antioch, but for Apulia where he died in March 1111. To complete the story, Tancred de Hauteville, Bohémond's nephew and regent in the principality of Antioch, proved a match for his uncle and a very obstinate and persistent thorn in the empire's expansion eastwards, at least until his death in 1112. He never materialized his uncle's promises and he demonstrated great arrogance and defiance towards Alexios' envoys in Antioch.[15]

Nevertheless, even when dealing with duplicitous, hardboiled individuals such as Bohémond and Tancred, 'jaw-jaw' was still deemed preferable to 'war-war'. The Byzantine preference to the use of 'soft power' for the most part, rather than military conquest, to control their neighbours, is ideally illustrated by one of the predominant themes in Byzantine ceremonial acclamations, namely the emperor's rôle as 'peacemaker' (Gr. eirênopoios). Hailed a mark of strength, not weakness, even the army chanted almost in the same breath 'many years to the triumph-bringing emperors ... many years to the peacemaking emperors'.[16] But against this backdrop of peacemaking through fraud and intrigue there is one essential fact that must not be forgotten; such a policy of threat and bribery inevitably presupposed a strong military establishment. Indeed, when we consider the complex Byzantine military system it is necessary to think more of armies, military institutions, and military administration rather than individual warlords and their followers, which was the norm in western Europe and the Nordic world.

The Macedonians

The Byzantine army of the Macedonian dynasty could certainly wage war in a most businesslike manner when the need arose. The forces led into battle by generals such as Nikephoros Phokas and John Tzimiskès (whom would later become emperors),[17] for instance, were well equipped and trained. Virtually unchanged from the tradition of Roman times was the emphasis on defence, on caution, on constant drilling, on meticulous preparation for campaign and combat, on remaining in formation, and on adaptability and innovation. As heirs of the formidable Roman legions and the defenders of Christendom, the army regarded itself, and rightly so, as the finest fighting force in the known world. No contemporary state possessed a military machine so well organized, nor could any muster on the field of battle, on a sudden exigency, a better appointed army as could the emperor of Constantinople.

One should never equate illiteracy with ignorance, and Basil is a good case in this respect. John Zonaras tells the story, perhaps true, that the future emperor, Basil, poor and down on his luck, first entered Constantinople via the Golden Gate, which had apparently been left open. He was then taken in at a nearby monastery and eventually went on to become emperor.[18] True or not, Basil had risen to high office under the sottish emperor Michael III (r. 842–67) and killed his rival, Bardas Caesar, Michael's uncle and the virtual ruler of the empire.

Theodora (r. 842–56), widow of the Theophilos (r. 829–42), had acted as regent during the minority of her son Michael, who was said to have been introduced to dissolute habits by her brother Bardas. By the time Michael had assumed power in 856, having packed his mother off to a nunnery, he was already notoriously known for excessive drunkenness and outlandish behaviour, appearing in the Hippodrome as a charioteer and burlesquing the religious processions of the clergy.

Clearly debauchery rather than warfare was the emperor's way of life – a most unhappy commander for the field – and recognizing Basil's talents Michael appointed Basil to the post of *protovestiarios*, the official in charge of the imperial wardrobe, and promoted him to the rank of patrician in 864. Within three years this formidable operator would give Michael grave cause to regret his elevation. Basil became co-emperor in 866, and eliminated Michael the following year. It seems Michael had been fond of neat wine, and would, 'when he was drunk, command some very irregular things to be done: one man to have his ears cut off, another his nose and the head of a third'. Evidently the canny Basil 'feared for his own person'.[19]

Basil... he had come from nowhere. Yet the accession of Basil I as *autokratôr* on 24 September 867, however questionable the manner in which it was carried out, inaugurated the greatest and most glorious dynasty ever to occupy the throne of Constantinus. So named after Basil's homeland (in fact, he was an Armenian peasant from the theme of Macedonia), the Macedonian dynasty, which was to last until the death of Basil's great-great-great-granddaughter Theodora on 31 August 1056, numbered among its members some of the most able and dynamic rulers in the long history of the Byzantine empire. Basil I (r. 867–86), whose military triumphs initiated the new era; Leo VI Sapiens (r. 886–912), who, unlike his upstart and unlettered father,[20] was an erudite man with a taste for composing and delivering sermons, and had a sharp eye for administration problems; likewise his son, Constantinus VII Porphyrogenitus (r. 913–59), known in particular as a finished scholar and for his patronage of arts and letters and for his sponsorship of monumental handbooks on Constantinopolitan court ceremony and international diplomacy; the brilliant general and future emperor Nikephoros II Phokas (r. 963–9), whose armies achieved the re-conquest of Crete and Cyprus, the Cilician towns and Antioch,[21] thus breaking the power of the Hamdanid emirate of Aleppo, the Muslim archenemy of Byzantium and earning him the official title 'the pale death of the Saracens';[22] John Tzimiskès, another brilliant general and future emperor, who withstood the challenge of the Kievan Russian prince Sviatoslav for control of the Balkans, and carried Byzantine arms into Palestine; and Basil II (r. 976–1025),[23] the austere and indefatigable soldier statesman, who triumphed over the Bulghars and reduced practically the whole of the Balkans to imperial rule, and extended Byzantine domination over Armenia and northern Syria. The military achievements of these three soldier emperors in particular marked their epoch as the heroic age of the Byzantine empire, 'l'épopèe byzantine' as Gustave-Léon Schlumberger dubbed it. Michael Psellos summed up the whole dynasty's achievements in these memorable words: 'I doubt if any other family was ever so favoured by God as theirs was – a surprising thing, when one reflects on the unlawful manner in which the family fortune was, so to speak, rooted and planted in the ground with murder and bloodshed'.[24]

Organized for war

Already since the eighth century the Byzantines had set up two distinct but mutually supportive mechanisms, the themes, which were clearly defensive in their rôle and whose main objective was to intercept and harass any invading army, while the *tagmata* (see below), based in or near the Great Palace or in the districts about Constantinople, were clearly professional units trained to deliver the final blow to the enemy on a pitched battle. In short, the army consisted of a full-time professional core and a part-time territorial militia.

The military organization of the empire was therefore firmly based on its political division, the system of the themes (Gr. *thémata*). The name is peculiar, and the closest approximation is that theme (Gr. *théma*) was used to denote the 'emplacements' (viz. detachment) of soldiers stationed there to defend it. The themes had evolved during the seventh century, possibly under Herakleios (r. 610–41), in response to urgent problems of defence in Anatolia – so recently retaken from the Sasanians – particularly those caused by the unremitting *razzias* of the Arabs. At first they were merely groupings of provinces across which different armies were based. By 730 or thereabouts they had acquired a clear geographical identity, and by the later eighth century some elements of fiscal as well as military administration were set up on a thematic basis. The number of themes increased as the empire's economic and political situation improved. The *Taktikôn Uspensky*, compiled around 842, lists eighteen generals (Gr. *stratêgoi*) of themes, while the *De thematibus*, compiled a century later, lists twenty-eight.

For a time the military governors of the themes coexisted with the civil governors of the old *provincia* or provinces, which maintained a shadowy existence. Legislation of Leo VI Sapiens, however, put an end to this vestigial survival and imposed uniformity upon the administrative apparatus of the empire as a whole. At the same time he continued the process of dividing the original themes, often vast in extent, into smaller geographical units, which were both more manageable and militarily more defensible.

Defence in depth and defence by fragmentation were the only feasible solutions to the Arab inroads. Small, mobile units of cavalry, well armed, well trained and well led, the excellent thematic cavalry mentioned by Leo VI Sapiens in his military manual *Taktiká*, were the only effective method of defence, and these entailed the multiplication of independent military commands. Each theme, therefore, was under a general (Gr. *stratêgós*) who had at his disposal a rich patrimony of lands, and the revenues from customs and other sources attached to his post. He was also free to exercise the imperial authority according to his conceptions of duty and his acquaintance with the theme he exercised authority over; his sovereign had delegated to him during the term of his office the fullest privileges and rights in the theme, which he was no longer required to administer, as was the case in the former *provincia*, but to govern. The *stratêgós* divided his theme into smaller administrative districts and appointed his own representatives to act as officials therein. Still, his powers were restricted in the sense that the thematic judges and tax collectors reported not to him but directly to the court in Constantinople.

Soldier farmers

The *stratêgós* had under his command, without any restriction, the native soldiers (Gr. *stratiôtai*) who were settled into his theme as soldier farmers in exchange for lands from the imperial demesne, which varied in size according to the holder's rank, in return for compulsory military service. They were attached to the lands surrounding a specific fort, a military camp or a strategic town and these lands provided the economic means for the maintenance of themselves, their families and their military equipment. And the fundamental principle was that these military holdings were inalienable and they remained in the possession of the same family as hereditary, being passed on to the holder's eldest son so long as he took on his father's military obligations.

It was the village commune (Gk. *chôrion*) that provided the empire with its basic tax unit, and as such was the backbone of imperial finances. An eighth-century document known as the *Farmers' Law* (*Nomos georgikos*) outlines the rules and obligations of members of such a commune, and underscores the notion of joint responsibility of the villagers for tax. By the tenth century, this had come to regulate responsibilities of villagers to pay taxes on the land of impoverished neighbours, but also to keep any profit they may have made working the land. This was a very important matter, as famine and war, along with at times excessive taxation, often obliged peasants to abandon their land. Thus, the *Farmers' Law* states:

> If a farmer is too poor to work his own vineyards and takes flight ... let those from whom claims are made by the public treasury gather in the grapes, and the farmer if he returns shall not be entitled to mulch them in the wine.[25]

This principle became important in the institution of the thematic military holdings, for it was these holdings that were given to the soldier farmers. Thus, the policy of the emperors was to discourage large estates, preferring that the land should be held by village communities, many of which paid for their tenancy by providing soldiers for the thematic armies.

Although it is difficult to trace their origins, the military holdings appear to have been established in one form or another by the early ninth century when we find Nikephoros I (r. 802–11) decreeing that:

> Poor farmers [should] be conscripted into the army and to be equipped by fellow farmers who are jointly responsible for the provision of eighteen-and-a-half *nomismata* [sg. *nomisma*, gold coin] to the fisc in lieu of the taxes of the impoverished farmers.[26]

This system enabled the state to have otherwise uncultivated land made profitable and, at the same time, fully equip a soldier for the army at least possible cost to the fisc.

The psychological importance of this system for the morale of the army was recognized by military commanders, such as the author of the anonymous tenth-century manual *De velitatione*, who wrote:

But was is more important than all else…, what arouses their enthusiasm, increases their courage, and incites them to dare what nobody else would dare is the fact that their own households and those of the soldiers serving them and everyone about them possess complete freedom … You will find that this has been legislated by the holy and blessed emperors of old.[27]

Any defect in the system would greatly impair imperial defences, especially in the critical border regions of Asia Minor, which had rapidly expanded with the conquests of Romanos I Lekapenos, Nikephoros II Phokas, and John I Tzimiskès in the tenth century.

These soldier farmers were obliged to report for duty when their officers sent for them, either for defensive or offensive campaigns or for regular training. As far as we can gather, there were no geographic limitations concerning their service or a time-limit of any kind. Apart from an irregular fixed pay (Gr. *róga*) of a modest amount, which varied, of course, over the centuries,[28] they also enjoyed exemption from a number of taxes. Thus, for the most part the empire raised its own soldiers, soldiers whose interests, or so it was expected, were firmly rooted in the areas they were liable to defend. Of these the best came from Armenia, Kappadokia, Isauria, and Thrace. No longer was the empire dependent upon the *foederati* of barbarian soldiery for its defence as the emperors of the late antique Roman empire had been.

Each theme had an obligation to furnish two or three *tourmai*, each of which was divided into a number of *drouggos*, and each *drouggos* into five *banda*, the *bandon* being the basic tactical unit for both infantry and cavalry. It seems apparent, however, that the strength of thematic units differed according to the size and manpower strength of each individual theme. Thus, it is possible to see that a *bandon* strength could, in fact, vary between 200 and 400 men (though a figure as low as fifty is recorded), and the *drouggos* therefore fluctuated between one and two thousand men. It also appears that the original number of *drouggoi* in a *tourma* was five, but later only three; the original *tourma* was therefore originally some 5,000 strong, much like the antique *legio*, and later only 3,000 men.

The commander of a *tourma* was titled *tourmarchos*, the commander of a *drouggos* a *drouggarios*, the commander of a *bandon* a *komes*. The junior officers were respectively *hekakontarchoi*, *pentekontarchoi*, and *dekarchoi*. The last officer commanded a *dekad*, the smallest tactical unit in the Byzantine army. All officers of the rank of *drouggarios* and above were appointed by the emperor and so owed their allegiance to him rather than to individual army commanders. As we would expect, these senior officers were mostly drawn from the aristocracy of the empire which, though not exclusively devoted to war like the nobility of other contemporary nations, was still deeply imbued with the martial spirit; the Byzantine aristocracy was not only schooled in strategy and tactics, but also the in geography and military capabilities of the empire's numerous enemies. Many of these aristocratic houses were powerful landowners in Asia Minor, and some of them even provided imperial dynasties or great soldier emperors (e.g. the Phokai and the Komnenoi). It was not unknown, however, for a man of lowly origins to scale the ladder of military success to the highest commands (e.g. Georgios Maniakes), or even to don the imperial purple (e.g. Basil I).

The professionals

The introduction of the *tagmata* (Gr. *tághmata*) in the mid eighth century surely marks one of the greatest innovations of the Byzantine army's long history. The fundamental distinction between the old thematic and the new tagmatic units is that the soldiers of the *thémata* were part-time soldiers, or they represented a kind of peasant militia scattered in large numbers throughout the Byzantine rural areas. The soldiers of the *tagmata*, however, were clearly professional, highly trained, experienced and very well equipped and paid. As opposed to their thematic counterparts, they were recruited from the *themata* close to the capital and equipped by the state. They were employed as a garrison for Constantinople, and also as a mobile reserve for any urgent military need such as combining with the thematic forces for expeditions. Or, to put it more simply, they provided the emperor with a powerful and loyal force established in and around his capital.

It was Constantinus V Kopronymos (r. 741–75)[29] who first created this small élite force, consisting as it did of six *tagmata*, the three senior of which were cavalry *tagma* named the *Scholai* (Gr. *Skholaí*, 'Schools'), the *Exkoubitoi* (Gr. *'Exkoúbitoi*, 'Sentinels') and the *Arithmos* (Gr. *'Arithmos*, 'Numbers') or *Vigla* (Gr. *Vígla*, 'Watch'). Nikephoros I (r. 802–11) created a fourth cavalry *tagma*, named the *Hikanatoi* (Gr. *Hikanátoi*, 'Worthies'), while John I Tzimiskès (r. 969–76) created a fifth one, the *Athanatoi* (Gr. *'Athánatoi*, 'Immortals'),[30] shortly after his accession. The three junior *tagmata* were infantry units, with the *Noumeroi* (Gr. *Noúmeroi*, 'Bathhouse boys') and 'Walls' (Gr. *tôn Teicheôn*), the last, as the name suggests, manning the Theodosian land walls and generally serving as the permanent garrison troops for the capital, while the *Optimatoi* (Gr. *'Optimátoi*, 'Best') were a support unit responsible for the mules of the baggage train while on campaign.

Every *tagma* had an enrolment of 4,000 men,[31] and each was commanded by a *domestikos* (Gr. *doméstikos*) – bar the commander of the *Arithmos*, who bore the title *droungarios* – with a *topoteretes* (Gr. *topotêretês*) as his second-in-command. By the time of Michael III (r. 842–67) the *domestikos* of the *Scholai* (Gr. *doméstikos tôn Skholôn*) had become senior to all but the *stratêgos* of the Anatolikon theme (Gr. *Théma tôn 'Anatolikôn*), who commanded the largest of the thematic armies (15,000 men in theory), and commander-in-chief in the emperor's absence during the course of the tenth century. The future emperors John Tzimiskès and Alexios Komnenos both held this important high office.

Naturally, only men of good breeding were admitted to these units or young men of foreign extraction with good connections or promise; Turks, Slavs, and Arabs who had been raised as Christians were often to be found in their ranks (as were Latins at a later date). It is hardly surprising, therefore, that we witness the three (later five) cavalry *tagma* rapidly becoming the especial lifeguards of the emperors. The *Scholai*, for instance, were particularly in charge of the defence of the imperial palaces, as well as generally available as guards for the capital. The *Arithmos*, on the other hand, had the duty of night watch over the imperial palaces, while on campaign they provided the guards for the emperor's tent at night as well as conveying his orders. They were apparently also responsible for prisoners-of-war.

Before the mid-tenth century the *tagmata* were stationed in and around the capital. During the reign of Romanos II (r. 959–63), they were divided into eastern and western commands, and correspondingly the office of *domestikos* of the *Scholai* was divided into two, one for the East and one for the West: Nikephoros Phokas was thus made *domestikos* of the *Scholai* for the West, his brother Leo Phokas for the East. This decision was taken after many decades of experience of the western and eastern armies in fighting different enemies in the Balkans and in Asia Minor. Detachments of the *tagmata*, however, were also sent to certain key frontier regions, like Macedonia and Illyria in the Balkans or the Anatolikon theme and the Armeniakon theme in the southern central district and the eastern and northern districts of Asia Minor respectively.

The emperor in Constantinople had also foreign mercenaries in his service, and at times they appear to have been of more importance than the native Byzantine forces. It was very common for emperors to resettle people, and in many cases transport the inhabitants of conquered regions to distant parts of the empire, and settle them there, thereby making them soldier farmers with an obligation to perform military service. It was, of course, a harsh policy, which bore severely on the people involved, but it was often an effective measure for meeting new dangers to which menaced and ravaged parts of the empire were exposed.

Centripetal versus centrifugal

The greater need for troops in the eleventh century had to be met by other than the customary means of relying upon soldier farmers. Thus we find, in the context of the rivalry between the civil and military aristocracy, the rise of the *pronoia* system, whereby the emperor would give personal grants of land to friends in return for the provision by the *proniar* (the receiver of the grant) of military aid in the form of men and supplies. The peasantry on the lands of the *proniar* were known by the term *paroikoi*, locals, a term which became synonymous with the word *ptochoi*, the poor. By the eleventh century, their position regarding the land they tilled was almost comparable to that of a serf, although they were not tied to it to the same extent as were western serfs. The central government attempted to limit the number of *paroikoi* on any single *pronoia* estate by excluding free peasants and soldier farmers from being included therein.

Land was to be held only for the lifetime of the *proniar*, but in time the system became abused with *proniars* using their influence to avoid their military and even their tax obligations. Consequently, much needed resources were squandered on the needs of private estates rather than on the state as a whole. Despite the fact that the emperor was still considered the owner of *all* land, effective ownership now lay in the hands of the landed magnates, *dhynatoi* (literally the 'powerful'), and thus some scholars see this development as an indication of Byzantine feudalism, although the hierarchy of rank and dependence affirmed by oaths of fealty common in the West were never really known in the Byzantine empire, thus differentiating eastern from western feudalism on a crucial point.

The two sources of patronage were the court and the army. Officials employed in and around the court are known as the civil aristocracy, the central government administrators in Constantinople. The generals and officers in the themes are known as the military aristocracy or landed magnates.

The first group consisted primarily of a hierarchy of merit that relied on one's proximity to the emperor or his ministers. Thus, the 'bearer of the imperial inkpot' was at times more important than a high minister. The civil aristocracy, based on a system of officers and ranks at the court, was there to maintain the power and prestige of the emperor, the central authority that kept it in office and pay. It should be noted that Byzantium did not have an aristocracy in the western sense of landed nobility. Many people working at court, for instance, including at times the emperor himself, could be of humble birth. Income more than land and blood defined one's importance, and income was derived almost exclusively from the state.

The second group were mostly made up of the landed military families whose members had over the centuries made up the officer corps of the thematic armies. These families, even by the tenth century, had become immensely wealthy in land, but this did not – unlike the situation in the West – automatically entitle them to a share in power in Constantinople.

A conflict thus arose between the two power groups, with the thematic armies, the power base of the military aristocrats, being looked upon with deep suspicion by the civil aristocrats. This is partly the reason why more funds were being squandered in Constantinople during this period, than being sourced out to the thematic armies. However, as we sometimes see military families siding with the Constantinopolitan court, the rift between civil and military aristocracies is best seen in terms of a clash of thematic centrifugal forces with the centralized imperial ideology.

A good indication of the state of affairs can be found in a passage from the *Chronographia* of Michael Psellos. Constantinus Psellos (1018–78), intellectual giant, sometime monk (Michael was the name he adopted as a monk), provincial magistrate, philosophy professor, political adviser to Constantinus IX Monomachos, gave in his *Chronographia* a lively and colourful description of the events at the court of Constantinople between the years 976 and 1077, writing seven books of imperial prose portraits from Basil II to Michael VII Doukas. His shrewd, in depth analysis of human nature provides us with a vivid account of the vices and the virtues of the major protagonists of the Byzantine empire in the eleventh century. So this particular passage is a first-hand account of the accession of Michael VI in 1056, backed by the civic aristocracy, and the revolt and accession in the following year of Isaakos I Komnenos, who was backed by the military aristocracy:

Apparently the last few emperors were convinced that they were firmly established if the civil element acclaimed them. Indeed, their close relations with these persons were such that the emperors believed the throne was safely ensured beyond all dispute if the civilians were well-disposed. Naturally, therefore, as soon as they took up the sceptre it was to the civil party that they granted the right to speak in their presence before all others... Really of course, their power rested on three factors: the people, the Senate and the army. Yet while they minimized the influence of the military, imperial favours were granted to the other two as soon as a new sovereign acceded. In the case of the aged Michael, the conferring of honours surpassed the bounds of propriety. He promoted individuals, not to the position immediately superior to that they already occupied, but elevated them to the next rank and the one above that... His generosity led to a state of absolute chaos. When this came to the ears of the soldiers, and among them those who held position of command, they came to Byzantium with the equal object of winning honours for themselves... A day was therefore fixed for them to have audience with the emperor and I myself was present on the occasion, standing beside him. The men who came into his presence were noble warriors, men of fine reputation. After bowing to him and making the usual acclamation, they stood, at the emperor's command, awaiting their turn. Now at this juncture he should have taken them aside individually. Instead, he started by finding fault with them *en bloc* – a mean thing to do. Then, having made their leader stand forth in the centre of the group, together with his second-in-command – Isaakos Komnenos was the chief man in the deputation and (Katakalon) Kekaumenos... was the other – he poured out a torrent of abuse on Isaakos. He charged him with... corrupting his army... he had levied the people's money for his own use, and, instead of using his command to win glory, he had made it a pretext for satisfying his personal greed... When his fellow generals tried to defend him, the emperor forbade them even to speak.[32]

Having lost his imperial cool, the emperor was to lose his imperial crown when the dishonoured commanders convinced their chief Isaakos to head a military coup.

The emperor's own

The developments outlined above gradually weakened central authority and consequently led to diminished resources of both soldiers for the army and money for the fisc. Consequently, greater reliance was placed on foreign mercenaries, many quite unreliable, being recruited directly into imperial service, and these included men from nations with which the Macedonian emperors had been in conflict, such as Normans, Frenchmen, Germans, Lombards, Magyars, Rus', Arabs, Turks, Khazars, and of course Northmen. The Persian traveller and geographer Ahmad ibn Rustah, who made the pilgrimage to Mecca in 903, records that 10,000 (clearly an exaggeration) Turks and Khazars accompanied the Byzantine emperor on parade,[33] and since the mid ninth century some mercenary units were indeed stationed in Constantinople, forming part of the lifeguard force there.

The overall name for these troops was the *Hetaireiai* (Gr. *Hetaireiai*), and its commander was the *hetaireiarkhes*, who held the imperial rank of *stratarchos*, and so was counted among the highest officials of the empire. A detachment of the *Hetaireiai* seems to have accompanied the emperor at all times whenever he left the capital, and the importance of the position of *hetaireiarkhes* should be emphasized, crucial for the security of the emperor and his palaces. This is the category from which the Varangian Guard emerged. Records of the twelfth century show that the Varangians serving the emperor used the quarters of the *Exkoubitoi*, known as the *skipt* and inside the Great Palace, and in later centuries they were lodged in the upper floors of a building near the Hippodrome known as the *Numera*, which had been used as a prison during the ninth and tenth centuries.

Queen of battles

Byzantine infantry of the tenth century was divided into two classes, armoured and unarmoured, what we would call heavy and light, with the theoretical makeup of an infantry thousand-man *drouggos* being 400 disciplined spearmen (Gr. *hoplítai*) able to stand firm in the line of battle, 300 archers (Gr. *toxótai*), 200 javelineers and slingers, and a hundred *menavlatoi* (Gr. *menaúatoi*), a new type of foot soldier, selected for their exceptional strength and courage, who formed ahead of the front line to blunt the attack of the enemy.[34] The standard battleline was eight combatants deep, being a rank of *menavlatoi*, four ranks of spearmen, and three ranks of archers. As individual accuracy was *not* sought, on the contrary, archers aimed to deliver an arrow storm, archers would shoot over the heads of the ranks to their front. The principal point to consider here is that three hundred archers shooting in unison must have had a withering effect at close range, but even so, they were expected not to repulse the enemy but to break up the cohesion of their attack.

The heavy infantry, known as *skutatoi* from the large oval shields they carried, were equipped with iron conical helmets with or without aventail (Gr. *kráneia*), body armour (Gr. *lôríkion*) of some type, knee-length mail shirts (Gr. *zábai*) or, as was more common, hip length lamellar corselets (Gr. *klibánia*), the *lamellae* made of iron, horn or leather, with or without sleeves, and knee-length leather boots. Additional protection came by way of heavy leather gauntlets (Gr. *manikélia*), splint vambraces (Gr. *cheiropsella*) for the forearms, and splint greaves (*podopsella*) for the lower legs. Arm and leg protection could be of iron, leather or wood. They carried a long thrusting spear (Gr. *kontárion*), oval shield (Gr. *skoutárion*), which essentially protected the body from shoulder to knee,[35] and a straight double-edged long sword (Gr. *spathíon*). It was a weapon descended from the *spatha* adopted by the antique Romans from the Celts. The *spathíon*, which could measure up to eighty-five to ninety centimetres in length,[36] was less commonly suspended from a belt than hung from a baldric or transverse shoulder strap 'in the Roman fashion', as the author emperor Leo says.[37] When worn on a baldric, the sword would hang vertically down the left leg. However, according to Nikephoros Phokas, this was not the preferred method of wearing the *spathíon* by foot soldiers, for he says they favoured 'belt-hung swords'.[38] When worn so, the *spathíon* was suspended from the waist belt by two straps attached to one end of scabbard, and so hung at a slight angle to the horizontally beside the left leg. In this position, the *spathíon* could be drawn from the scabbard directly into an engagement, whether a cut or parry, to supplement the shield.[39]

Those soldiers who could not afford metal or lamellar body armour usually substituted it for a knee-length double felt or thickly quilted cotton coat (Gr. *bambákion*) that came with or without a hood and wide, half-length sleeves tied to the shoulders by strong laces. *Skutatoi banda* normally deployed eight or sixteen men to a file,[40] the better armoured men obviously being stationed to the front. This is implied by Leo VI Sapiens, who says the first two ranks of *skutatoi* wore *zábai* or *klibánia*, the other six plus ranks wore the *bambákion*.[41] Each *bandon* was easily identified by its distinctive shield blazons.

Most of the light infantry, known as *psiloi*, were archers, though some were equipped with javelin (Gr. *âkóntion*) or sling (Gr. *sphendónê*). The archers carried on a baldric a combined bow case/quiver of forty arrows.[42] It was a round-bottomed cylinder with the arrows inserted point downwards (in contrast to the cavalry quiver). Because the recurve composite bow was drawn with the thumb, the strongest digit, the arrow was fletched with four feathers. The bowstring rested on a thumb ring, which protected the thumb. The flights were a symmetrical crescent shape and fairly small. In the late tenth century the Byzantine infantry bow was capable of sending an arrow more than 300 metres with a killing distance of perhaps 200 metres.[43] The draw weight of recurve composite bows can be substantially over a hundred pounds (45 kgf).

To permit maximum mobility *psiloi* carried little in the way of armour or additional weapons. Nonetheless, most wore linen corselets or leather jerkins, some even went as far to don a helmet, and they usually carried a short sword or an axe (Gr. *tzikoúrion*) in addition to the recurve composite bow and bow case/quiver or javelins or sling.

Generally speaking, tactics in our period of study were uncomplicated – infantry tactics especially so – and a fundamental attribute of Byzantine infantry tactics outlined in the military treatises was their simplicity. Their formation was stationary, very straightforward and hence well suited to their defensive rôle, as were their battle deployment. Each type of foot soldier had one specific task to perform in this defensive system designed to force attacking horsemen to ride through a hail of arrows, stones and javelins into a wall of spearmen.

La arme blanche

Though scholars now generally agree that cavalry were not the only effective part of the Byzantine army, 'long-range fire, cavalry mobility, and the weight in defence and attack of well-drilled infantry' being part and parcel of the most successful Byzantine armies,[44] the fighting edge of any tenth-century Byzantine force was its disciplined *kataphraktoi* (Gr. *katáphraktoi*), which symbolized the power of Christian Constantinople in the same way the legionaries had represented the might of pagan Rome. In characteristic forthright declaration, the pious Nikephoros Phokas affirmed that the commander 'with 5,000 or 6,000 mounted warriors and the aid of God will stand in need of nothing more'.[45] A bit of an exaggeration perhaps, but God or no God, the *kataphraktoi* employed by Nikephoros Phokas were surely a force to be reckoned with, the army's *force de frappe*. But what about *klibanophoroi* or 'boiler-boys'?

These were true *kataphraktoi*. They are recorded for the first time at the battle of al-Hadath (Adata), northern Mesopotamia, in 954. The army was commanded by Bardas Phokas, the father of Nikephoros Phokas, the future emperor. The contemporary Muslim poet Abu ar-Tayyib al-Mutanabbi (b. 915) alludes to these super heavyweight fellows in his eulogy to the victor that day, Sayf al-Dawla of Aleppo:

The enemy [Byzantines] came at you [Sayf], hauling their weapons as if they travelled on legless horses. / When their ranks caught the light, their swords remained unseen, since their (mail) shirts and turbans [helmets] were also made from steel.[46]

Interestingly enough for us, among the auxiliary troops on that fateful day were a band of Rus', a warrior race we shall meet in another book.[47]

The stout mounts of the *katáphraktoi* wore a full *klibánion* made of hardened ox-hide *lamellae*, split at the front for ease of movement and covering the whole horse to its knees. The horseman too was covered from head to toe in armour: a conical iron helmet, mail hood two or three layers thick to cover the face; full body lamellar *klibánion* to elbows and knees; and the forearms and lower legs protected by splint-metal vambraces and greaves. To guard against concussion as well as penetration the horseman could opt to wear over his body armour a padded and quilted, long surcoat (Gr. *epiloríkion*), made of 'coarse silk (*koukoulíon*) or cotton (*bambakíon*) as thick as can be stitched together',[48] and it clear from pictorial representations that the *epiloríkion* was a fairly common item of clothing. The *epiloríkion* was padded strong enough to act as a defence by itself, and it was known that raw silk, with its tight weave, was very effective against arrow punctures. A heavy, woollen cloak for cold weather, which also served as a blanket, was rolled up and strapped behind the saddle.

Though they carried *kontós* and *spathíon*, their primary weapon was the large mace known as a *bardoukion* (Gr. *bardoúkion*, 'sledgehammer'), used for smashing through the centre of the enemy battleline. A weapon of no compromise, this was an all-metal mace of hexagonal type. Nikephoros Phokas calls them 'iron staffs',[49] and they were furnished of beaten iron plaques and topped with a massive iron head with sharpened, ridged edges. This is probably the *rabdobastakis* mentioned in the epic poem of border warfare *Digenes Akrites*.[50] A second weapon was the *paramêrion*, a single-edged, slightly curved sword of Avar influence. Its handling characteristics were indistinguishable from a straight sword. The fundamental advantage was that a single-edged curved blade was very much easier to make than the equivalent straight blade. Much less forging was required, so the risk of flaws being forged into the blade was reduced. This factor, among others, was why this sword type originated with the horse tribes of the Eurasian steppes. The *paramêrion* was worn slung from a baldric attached at two points on the inside curve of the scabbard, and so hung at a slight angle to the horizontal beside the thigh (which is the very meaning of its name). An extra sword is described as a *spathíon*, similar to the straight double-edged sword used by the infantry but slightly longer.[51]

The helmet could be topped with a horsehair plume, dyed a distinctive hue for each *bandon*. A cavalry *bandon* was usually drawn up in rows five horsemen deep. Each *bandon* had its own pennant, with a recognizable symbol or letter, as identification.[52] The tenth-century military manuals of Nikephoros Phokas and Nikephoros Ouranos, recommend that friends and relations should not be split up, but kept together in each *bandon*, sharing quarters, meals and duties with each other.[53]

McGreer notes that, after the war against the Rus' in 971, the *katáphraktoi* are not mentioned again, except in penny packets in Syria.[54] Evidently being very expensive to train, equip and maintain, and the offensive phase of this period having played out, *katáphraktoi* passed out of use about 1025.

Foreign imports

In the mid eleventh century the line of the Macedonian dynasty (867–1056) was exhausted, leaving imperial power open to the aspirations of the civil aristocracy in the capital and the military aristocracy in the themes. Only in 1081 did Alexios Komnenos bring an end to this period of unrest, seize the imperial throne, rebuff the resistance of the civil aristocracy, and establish his family as the new imperial dynasty, which would then rule for more than a century. However, by 1081 the Byzantine empire was no longer the fearsome and vigorous beast it had been in 1025. When Basil II died in that year, he left a full treasury. He also left a formidable all arms army capable of conducting empire-making battles and wars. When Alexios came to rule, there was little of the soldiery, or of the public purse which to pay them. So, the army that Alexios deployed against the Normans in 1108 was different in both structure and composition than that which Romanos IV Diogenes had gathered for his Turkish campaigns that culminated in Mantzikert. The old thematic and tagmatic units, indigenous troops that formed the backbone of the Byzantine army's structure for centuries were largely replaced by foreign mercenaries, large bodies of paid troops of any ethnic background hired for long-term military service.

During the tenth and early eleventh centuries, when their army was at the zenith of its power and efficiency, the Byzantines were able to recapture much of the territory lost to the Arabs and the Bulghars. The army's increased potency and effectiveness was rooted in the efforts of such soldier emperors as Nikephoros II Phokas and Basil II to employ more heavily armed soldiery, such as the *kataphraktoi*, of which some mention has already been made, and to perfect combined infantry and cavalry tactics. At the same time, however, the army's structure and composition began to change; command was centralized at Constantinople, and the growing presence of mercenaries of diverse ethnic origins, already a fashion in the tenth century, became even more pronounced in the following century as a result of the declining strength of the thematic armies.

Despite this trend, however, it was the débâcle at Mantzikert (19 August 1071) that witnessed the end of the traditional Byzantine army. The battle was the first major clash between the Seljuqs and the West and stands as a good example of the superiority of the steppe nomadic military tradition. Due to the unexpected speed of the Byzantine advance, Alp Arslan (r. 1063–72) was not able to gather all his troops but, with confidence, applied all the standard tactics and techniques of the nomadic military. It also helped that Romanos IV Diogenes was a valiant man but a meagre tactician, and much of his hired soldiery was not to be trusted. Accordingly, an elusive screening force successfully deceived the Byzantines and canalized them into successive ambushes by feigned retreat. An ever-increasing tempo of cavalry attacks supported by deadly arrow showers took their toll, and eventually the Byzantine army lost cohesion. Though the actual losses incurred during the battle were quite limited, affecting largely the emperor's immediate retinue, the real disaster was of a political nature, namely the capture of the emperor and the ensuing civil war, which left much of Anatolia undefended. Much of Anatolia was soon to be overrun by the Seljuq Turks.

The Seljuq expansion in western Iran and Mesopotamia was in part motivated by their desire to liberate the 'Abbasid caliph from the patronage and control of the Shi`a Buwayhids (Seljuq Turks were Sunni converts), an Iranian clan who ruled in the name of the caliph. In this they succeeded in 1055, subsequently eliminating Buwayhid power throughout the region. The Seljuq leader, Tuğrul Bey (r. 1040–63), behaved with more courtesy towards the caliph in providing him with greater financial and political leniency, but it was clear that the latter figure was still mainly a *de jure* ruler. Real power remained in the hands of Tuğrul Bey, who was formally awarded the title of sultan, which up to that time had generally meant 'rule' or 'authority' but henceforth could be understood to mean the *de facto* ruler, ostensibly appointed by the caliph to rule in his name. He was indeed the power behind the caliph's throne, and he now assumed the trappings of a Muslim ruler rather than simple dignity of a Turkish tribal warlord. Henceforth, the Seljuqs presented themselves as the 'defenders of Sunni Islam', and on Tuğrul's death the rule over the unified Seljuq dominions passed to his nephew Alp Arslan. He was a resolute warrior and powerful sultan like his uncle. Under his son, Malik Shah (r. 1072–92), the Seljuq empire reached its apogee, but with the death of Malik Shah the central power of the greater Seljuq sultanate at Baghdad was divided among separate princely houses. In Anatolia itself a separate Seljuq sultanate, that of Rum, was established in the late eleventh century.

It is important at this point, however, to stress that the victorious Seljuqs, as recent converts to Sunni Islam, were in fact far more zealous in their prosecution of *jihad* against the 'heretical' Fatimid Shi`a caliphate than following up their success in Anatolia. Nevertheless, the loss of the eastern themes, and the manpower therein, left the Byzantine empire defenceless in that quarter, and though a new central army soon began to appear in the capital, responsibility for the empire's exposed eastern frontier devolved largely upon an ever increasing number of foreign mercenary units of professional soldiers and warrior tribesmen. Comprising mainly Norman, German and Latin knights, and Seljuq, Uze, Cuman or Pečeneg horse archers, Anna Komnene refers to these mercenaries in her father's time as 'horsemen and footmen coming out of all lands'.[55] Despite the high cost of their maintenance, their constant readiness and mobility made the employment of mercenaries an attractive option. The Macedonian trend had become a Komnenian necessity.

Mercenaries have often been associated by modern scholars with political and military failures. They have been viewed as less reliable and less loyal than native soldiers. Yet with their services Alexios was able to stabilize the empire externally (by repelling the Italo-Normans with the help of Venice and re-conquering the most fertile western parts of Anatolia in the slipstream of the First Crusade) and internally by establishing his own family and its members in the central positions of powers and in the centre of a network of related aristocratic clans. Thus, 'he rebuilt imperial government as an aristocratic connection; family business might be a more accurate description'.[56] Under Alexios and his successors John II (r. 1118–43) and Manuel I (r. 1143–80) Byzantium re-emerged as a great power in the eastern Mediterranean, in the possession of the most productive areas in the west and at the coasts of Anatolia and the major part of south-eastern Europe.

'Sons of Turks'

Both the Byzantines and the Seljuqs incorporated into their respective armies soldiers of mixed ethnic origin (called *mixobarbaroi* in Byzantine sources) who were half-Greek and half-Turk. Anna Komnene comments on several *mixobarbaroi* present in the Seljuq army. These, she reports, were bilingual, and while some of them scoffed mockingly in Greek at their Byzantine opponents,[57] others were found praying in Greek during a dangerous Byzantine attack. Some among them were not loyal to their Seljuq commanders and betrayed them by informing the Byzantines of Turkish battle tactics.[58] Anna also points to the presence of *mixobarbaroi* in the Byzantine army, one of whom, she recounts, made use of his knowledge of the Turkish tongue in trying to bribe and persuade the inhabitants of Nicaea to yield the city to the Byzantines during the First Crusade.[59]

Frankish chroniclers of the First Crusade mention too the presence of contingents called *Turcopoli* (Gk. *Tourkópouloi*, 'sons of Turks') in the army of Alexios I Komnenos. The eyewitness Raymond d'Aguilers describes these Byzantine *Tourkopouloi* as skilled archers who 'were either reared among Turks or were the offspring of a Christian mother and a Turkish father',[60] while the cleric

Albert d'Aix (*fl.* 1100) reports that 'the impious race of the *Turcopoli*, who were said to be Christians only by name but not by their deeds, were born of a Turkish father and a Greek mother'.[61] These references to *mixobarbaroi* and *Tourkopouloi* are very suggestive because they point to a rather early date for the occurrence of intermarriage between Turks and Byzantines in Anatolia during the reign of Alexios I Komnenos.

On the other hand, we are also presented with those examples of Byzantine *Tourkopouloi* who were Turkish converts or sons of Turkish converts. It is thus reasonable to assume that in the second half of the eleventh century, when Byzantium first started to make use of Turkish troops on a large scale and Christian Turks were something of a novelty, the term '*Tourkópouloi*' was applied to all Christian soldiers of Turkish origin — offspring of mixed-marriages and converts — and perhaps to deserters as well. Subsequently the term might have altered its meaning somewhat.

One question that immediately comes to mind in connection with mixed marriages between Turks and Byzantines is whether they were accompanied by religious conversions in either direction. Since it was the Seljuq Turks who came to Anatolia as conquerors, one would expect conversions to Islam to predominate – and in the long run, they did predominate. However, during the period with which we are concerned, there is no evidence of any large-scale conversion of the Byzantine population until at least the reign of Kılıç Arslan II (r. 1155–92).

Conversely, during the first two centuries of the Seljuq presence in Anatolia, the conversion of Turks into Christianity, though not on any grand scale, is also attested, particularly among soldiers, and it was not necessarily a phenomenon resulting only from mixed marriages. This was no new thing, for in the tenth century it was Byzantine policy to grant tax exemptions to Arab prisoners of war who had been converted to Christianity and installed on plots of land as soldier farmers.[62] We do know that several Seljuq Turks among those who served at the Byzantine court or in the Byzantine army were baptized as Christians. According to Anna Komnene, who records not a few of these cases, it was one of her father's greatest ambitions to convert the whole Islamic East to Christianity. At least within the framework of Anatolia, the ambition seems to have persisted with John II Komnenos, who converted to Christianity a large group of Turks he took captive during a campaign in 1124, before incorporating them into his army.

Likewise, Manuel I Komnenos was driven by a desire to increase the number of converts from the Islamic faith to Christianity, as he proposed in 1180 to delete the customary formula of abjuration of Islam from catechetical texts, which inhibited conversions due to a statement in it rejecting the 'God of Muhammad'. However, the patriarch of Constantinople Loukas Chyrsoberges (r. 1156–69) and some of the bishops were vehemently opposed to this measure. The emperor's conflict with the ecclesiastical authorities was finally resolved by the replacement of the anathema against the 'God of Muhammad' with one against the prophet himself and his teachings. Even so, John Kinnamos, secretary to Manuel, mentions by name Turks who were raised by Byzantines or were in Byzantine service. Specially named are John Axouchos, Prosouch, Ishaq, Bairam, John Ises, and one Michael formerly known as Ishaq.[63] The phrase 'Roman upbringing and education' used by John Kinnamos is elusive but it does imply a conversion to Christianity, especially when a Christian name is given as in the cases of John Axouchos, John Ises, and Michael.

As we would expect, *Tourkopouloi* were mounted on swift mettlesome horses. Without the caparison of the 'heavy' cavalryman, they were equipped with only a mail shirt, a helmet, and a diverse array of offensive weapons, with the recurve composite bow being prominent. Talking of Frankish *Turcopoli*, William of Tyre, the Latin chronicler and archbishop of Tyre (1175–86), describes them as '*levis armature*',[64] the same term he uses to describe Turkish mounted archers ('*armature levis equitibus*', '*levioris armature milites*'),[65] and at least on one occasion William makes it clear that *levis armatura* means bows, since he claims that the strength of the Seljuq Turks lay in their swift horses '*et armorum levitate, arcuum videlicet et pharetrarum*'.[66] In his account of an attack on an Egyptian caravan in June 1192 by Richard Cœur de Lion, Ambroise says that the king sent the *Turcopoli*, archers and crossbowmen to harass the Muslim column, in order to delay it, and that they showered it with arrows 'as thick as the drops of dew'.[67]

Whether Byzantine or Frankish, *Tourkopouloi / Turcopoli* were therefore unsuited for 'shock action'. However, heavy armour may have been a mark of distinction, but for the *Tourkopouloi* it was only a burden; for them victory was not won by a concentrated charge at lance point, but by being highly mobile. This made them excellent scouts, guides and raiders. One cannot avoid using modern phrases, but we must be aware of the dangers of using modern definitions of 'heavy' and 'light' cavalry when dealing with late antique and early mediaeval horsemen.

The first encounter of the crusaders with these *Tourkopouloi* occurred when Byzantine forces, including *Tourkopouloi*, came to the rescue of the survivors of the Peasants' Crusade.[68] The encounters which followed were less cordial in nature. *Tourkopouloi* formed an important part of the Byzantine forces that attacked the crusaders on several occasions during the First Crusade, namely, the assault on the contingent of Godfrey of Bouillon near Constantinople;[69] the attack on Bohémond's contingent during the crossing of the river Vardar;[70] and the murder of Baldwin of Hainault.[71] After the emperor and the crusaders settled their differences, the *Tourkopouloi* began to play a more helpful rôle in the crusades: they participated in the capture of Nicaea in 1097;[72] in the invasion of Cilicia by Tancred de Hauteville;[73] and in the army which Alexios I Komnenos supposedly attempted to lead to succour the crusaders, when the latter found themselves in dire straits at Antioch.[74]

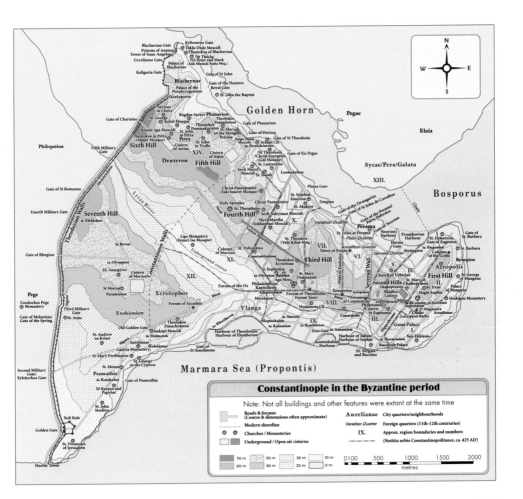

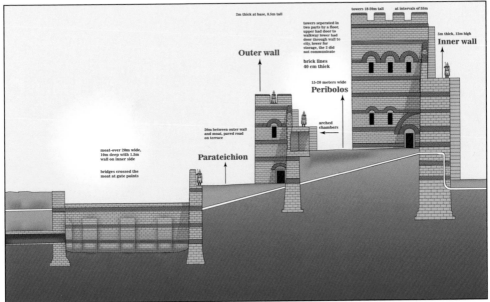

Section and restoration of the Theodosian walls.

Second Bosporus Bridge, looking south down the Bosporus, which spans the narrowest point (700 m) of the straits. This bridge officially opened in the summer of 1988 exactly 2,500 years after Dareios constructed his bridge of boats across the same stretch of water. Perhaps here too Io, in her white cow guise, crossed from Europe to Asia in her desperate attempt to flee the gadfly of Hera. Just beyond the bridge on the European side is the Rumeli Hisarı, the Ottoman fortress that once dominated the straits. (© *Nic Fields*)

The Golden Horn, view looking towards its northern shore and the district of Karaköy, formerly the town of Galata, which had been granted to the Genoese in 1261. This natural sea harbour is a scimitar-shaped, 7.5 km-long inlet of the Bosporus, joining the strait just before it flows in to the Sea of Marmara. In the centre background is the Galata Tower, which took its present form under the Genoese. (© *Nic Fields*)

What now serves as a car park for the Grand Bazaar was once the Forum of Constantinus, an oval colonnaded portico. In the forum's centre Constantinus I erected this column to celebrate the dedication of his city as the capital of the empire on 11 May 330. On the column's summit there was a large capital, upon which stood a statue of the emperor exhibiting attributes of Sol Invictus, the Slayer of Darkness. Originally 50 m tall, the column was constructed of cylindrical porphyry blocks, seven of which still stand, and goes by the local appellation of *Çemberlitaş*, the Hooped Column. (© *Nic Fields*)

A reconstruction of Constantinople with its (near) impregnable land and sea defences. Occupying the site of the Greek *polis* of Byzantion, the city founded by Constantinus was built on a hilly promontory, surrounded on three sides by water with fast-flowing currents, which made it difficult to attack from the sea. On the landward side, it was sealed off by a triple line of defences, the most important of which was the inner, main wall studded with ninety-six towers spaced at regular intervals. (© *Nic Fields*)

The Theodosian walls of Constantinople, on the site where Istanbul is today, looking northwest towards the triple line of defences between the Golden Gate (right) and the Second Military Gate (left). In this particular stretch of the land walls all the eleven towers that guard the inner, main wall are still standing, as are all but one of those in the outer wall: a tribute to Roman engineering genius. However, little remains of the moat; apart from this watery section here, it has mostly been filled in. (© *Nic Fields*)

A laconic bilingual inscription on Proconnesian marble slabs, outer entrance of the *Yeni Mevlanihane Kapısı*, what was then known as the Gate of Rhegion. It records the remarkable feat of renewal (and addition) of the earthquake-damaged Theodosian walls in 447: 'In sixty days, by order of the sceptre-loving emperor, Constantinus the eparchos added wall to wall' (Greek); 'By command of Theodosius, in less than two months, Constantinus erected triumphantly, these strong walls. Scarcely could Pallas have built so quickly so strong a citadel' (Latin). The Greek text merely gives the facts, the Latin one is more boastful with mention of the goddess of war, Athena Pallas. (© *Nic Fields*)

The Byzantine sea walls still standing below the Topkapı Sarayı with the Sea of Marmara beyond. Constructed initially under Constantinus I, the sea walls once extended along the shores of the Golden Horn and the Marmara, to join up with the Constantinian land walls at both ends. They were extended to meet the new Theodosian walls. During the reign of Theophilos (829–42) the Marmara walls (partly seen here) were almost completely rebuilt so as to strengthen the city's maritime defences against the Arabs. The Marmara defences consisted of a single line of walls 12–15m high, studded with 188 towers at regular intervals. These walls stretched a total distance of 8 km, and were pierced by 11 sea gates. (© *Nic Fields*)

The Delphic Column, Hippodrome, Istanbul. Taking the form of a bronze column representing three intertwined serpents, the missing heads of which once supporting a golden tripod. On their lower coils can still be seen the names of thirty-one Greek peoples that 'warred the war' against Xerxes. It was dedicated from the Persian spoils of Plataia (479 BC) to Apollo at Delphi. The tripod had long gone when the column was taken from Delphi by Constantinus I. (© *Nic Fields*)

The Obelisk of Karnak, Hippodrome, Istanbul. This granite monolith was originally commissioned to celebrate the victories of Thutmose III (ca. 1549–1503 BC): it is carved with hieroglyphs glorifying the pharaoh – 'Thutmose, who crossed the great river of Nahrain [Euphrates] as a mighty conqueror at the head of his army'. Added to the *spina* during the reign of Theodosius I (379–95), it still rests firmly upon four bronze cubes, which are supported by a Proconnesian marble plinth carved with bas-reliefs. On three faces of the plinth are seen Theodosius, flanked by his two ineffectual sons Arcadius (with the prominent ears) and Honorius, conducting various activities at the Hippodrome from the *kathisma*: attending a triumph, presiding at the races, and receiving tribute. (© *Nic Fields*)

Marble head (Rome, Musei Capitolini, inv. MC0757) originally from a colossal seated statue of Constantinus I, dating to 313/24 and discovered in the Basilica Nova in the Roman Forum. Only the head, which measures 260 cm, hands and feet, remain of a colossus that once stood some 12 m high. The body of the statue would have been made in wood probably covered in bronze. This is the best-known portrait of the emperor, with his staring hooded eyes and hooked nose, and would have been more imposing when it was crowned with a diadem. (© *Nic Fields*)

East face of the Proconnesian marble plinth supporting the Obelisk of Karnak. In this striking image of imperial power, Theodosius I, the last ruler of a united Roman Empire, is depicted flanked by the adolescent cipher Valentinianus II (left rear), and his sons Arcadius (right) and Honorius (left). He is awarding a victory wreath to an unseen charioteer. Behind the imperial quartet stand Germanic *scholares* (Goths in the East, Franks in the West) of the *scholae palatinae*, while senators (holding *mappae*) stand either side of the *kathisma*. (© *Nic Fields*)

Hagia Sophia, Istanbul, general view of the southwest façade. This was Constantinople's greatest, most glorious building and the sacred heart of the Byzantine empire. The exterior does not exhibit the characteristics of the original sixth-century edifice. The buttresses built to support the outer walls to ensure their endurance over the centuries, and the minarets added during the Ottoman period, have markedly altered its outer appearance. The original architectural characteristics are much more apparent in the interior of the building. (© *Nic Fields*)

Interior panoramic of Hagia Sophia, which provides a good indication of the feeling of space created by the high dome, marble columns and solid masonry arches. Built on a domed basilica plan, the interior of the church has a central nave, northern and southern side naves, two narthexes in the west, and an apse in the east. Only in the central nave, as can be seen in this photograph, is it possible to see all the way up to the dome, its crown some 55.6 m above the floor. A second storey, the gallery, was constructed over the two side naves and the inner narthex. (*Ronan Reinart*)

Gold tesserae mosaic panel, southern vestibule of Hagia Sophia, depicting the Blessed Virgin enthroned on a bejewelled throne, holding the Christ child on her knees. Two emperors on either side are holding models in their hands. On her left, Constantinus I offers her a replica of Constantinople, and on her right Iustinianus I offers her a replica of Hagia Sophia. Both emperors are wearing their ceremonial dress. The mosaic dates to the second-half of the tenth century. (© *Nic Fields*)

(*Above*) Gold tesserae mosaic panel, south gallery of Hagia Sophia, depicting Jesus Christ enthroned and offering (the viewer) the benediction. On his left is Zoë Porphyrogenita (979–1050), who is holding a scroll; the words above the head of the empress read 'Zoë the most pious Augusta'. To the right of Christ is her *third* husband (note his face is not the original one), Constantinus IX Monomachos (r. 1042–55), who is offering a money bag. The words 'Sovereign of the Romans, Constantinus Monomachos' are written above his head. His name too is not the original one. (*Myrabella*)

(*Left*) Apotropaic full-length portrait of Joshua of Navê, one of the great leaders of biblical Israel, in the garb of a Byzantine officer, fresco dated to the second half of tenth century, on the outer face of the north wall of the narthex to the church of the Theotókos, monastery of Hosios Loukas, central Greece. The inscription beside Joshua may refer to the re-conquest of Crete in 961; this event had been prophesised by Hosios Loukas twenty years previously. (© *Nic Fields*)

Gold on enamel icon (Berlin, Kunstgewerbemusuem, inv. W3) of Saint Demetrios dated to the twelfth century. The military saint is depicted as a Byzantine cavalryman, and wears a silk or cotton surcoat, *epiloríkion*, over a lamellar corselet, *klibánion*, while his forearms and lower legs are protected by splint-metal vambraces, *cheiropsella*, and splint-metal greaves, *podopsella*, respectively. A helmet would normally be worn, but saints are invariably bareheaded in icons. Note also his horse's tail is tied. (*FA2010*)

Ivory icon (New York, Metropolitan Museum of Art, inv. 1970.324.3) of Saint Demetrios, dating to 950/1000. The military saint is depicted as a Byzantine *skutatos*, and wears a hip-length lamellar corselet, with *pteruges* at shoulder and waist. Additionally, splint-metal vambraces protect his forearms and splint-metal greaves his lower legs. In his left hand he grasps the rim of a large oval shield, *skoútarion*. A scabbard, which is suspended from a baldric, can be seen behind his right arm. This would house a straight double-edged long sword, *spathíon*. The sash tied around his chest is an indication of senior rank. (*Marie-Lan Nguyen*)

An eighteenth-century egg-tempera on wood icon (Athens, private collection), provenance unknown. The image shows the siege of Constantinople by the Turkic Avars in 626, who are depicted here as Ottoman Turks. The destruction of the city by the Avars was averted only by the military skills of the soldier emperor Heraclius (r. 610–41) or, as was otherwise claimed and clearly alluded to in this icon, the Blessed Virgin Mary and Christ Pantokrator. The central figure is Sergios I, the patriarch of Constantinople. (© *Nic Fields*)

An illustration (Madrid, Biblioteca Nacional, Codex Matritensis Græcus, Vitr. 26-2, folio 34v) from the twelfth-century illuminated manuscript Codex Skylitzes Matritensis. The scene depicts Greek fire being fired from a bronze siphon against the fleet of the rebel Thomas the Slav, who besieged Constantinople during the winter of 821/2. The caption above the left-hand ship reads: 'the fleet of the Romans setting ablaze the fleet of the enemies'. (*Amandajm*)

A fragment of a much larger mosaic depicting the Latin sack of Constantinople, April 1204. Dated to 1273, the mosaic once served as part of the pavement of the Basilica de San Giovanni Evangelista, the oldest church of Ravenna, Italy (it had been commissioned by the empress Galla Placidia in fulfilment of a vow made in 424 during a storm at sea). Here a crusader, armed with a sword and wearing a hauberk, escorts three Byzantine prisoners, presumably aristocrats being held to ransom. To the left is the city, while above is the Latin caption COSTATINO / POLIM. (© *Nic Fields*)

One of the bombards of Mehmet II at the Rumeli Hisarı, the Ottoman fortress colloquially known as *Boğazkesen*, the 'Throat Cutter', rapidly constructed between April and August of 1452. It was then garrisoned by a force of Janissaries, whose bombardiers trained three huge cannons on the Bosporus, warning foreign shipping not to try and get through to Constantinople from the Black Sea. One Venetian captain tried his luck, but his vessel was sunk by a stone shot from a bombard much like this one. Taken prisoner, the sailors were decapitated and their captain impaled. (© *Nic Fields*)

Painting (Vareia, Lesvos, Theophilos Museum) by the Greek folk painter Theophilos Hatzimihail (d. 1934), dated to 1932. When Constantinople fell, Constantinus XI Palaiologos was last seen fighting at the city walls (seen here on the white charger), but the actual circumstances of his demise have remained surrounded in myth. In the years that followed it was said that he was not dead but sleeping – the 'immortal emperor' miraculously turned to marble, who would one day be awakened by an angel and drive the Turks out of his city and empire. (© *Nic Fields*)

A modern bronze statue representing Constantinus XI Palaiologos (there is no contemporary likeness of him), facing the Metropolitan Cathedral of the Annunciation, Athens. The last Byzantine emperor had a sad and tumultuous life, coming to the throne on 6 January 1449 with one singular purpose: to stave off the almost inevitable conquest of Constantinople by the Ottoman Turks, and keep alive the shrivelled stub of the Byzantine empire as long as possible. (© *Nic Fields*)

View of the interior façade of the Golden Gate, the Roman triumphal arch built by Theodosius I in 391. Here we see the large central archway of the original monumental edifice bricked up, of which at least two phases of this process are clearly discernible. When Theodosius II decided to extend the city two decades later, the Golden Gate was incorporated within the new land walls. Michael VIII Palaiologos (r. 1259–82) was the last emperor to ride in triumph through the Golden Gate after Constantinople was regained from the Latins. The last two centuries of the empire were ones of military decline and by then the gateway had been walled up for good. (© *Nic Fields*)

A direction sign, Kavalla, northern Greece. The names Istanbul and Stamboul are corruptions of the Greek εις την πόλιν, *eis tîn pólin*, meaning 'into the city', or 'to the city', a phrase that is still used today by Greeks when referring to the Christian imperial capital once known as Κωνσταντινούπολις, Constantinople. (© *Nic Fields*)

Night time silhouette of Stamboul, that part of Istanbul that was once called Constantinople. This is the First Hill, as viewed from the Sea of Marmara, and from left to right we see the idiosyncratic outlines of Sultan Ahmet Camii (Blue Mosque), Hagia Sophia and Hagia Eirene. The latter Byzantine church never served as a mosque (hence no minarets) after the conquest, being enclosed within the outer walls of Topkapı Sarayı and serving as an arsenal for the Janissaries. (*Sinoplu diyojen*)

During the minor crusade of 1101 we are informed, for the first time, of a *Turcopoli* unit forming an integral part of a crusader army. These were the 500 Byzantine *Tourkopouloi* whom Alexios I Komnenos presented to Raymond de Saint-Gilles, and who served as guides for the crusader army.[75] However, they did not distinguish themselves in the battle of Mersivan, where they were the first to turn tail and flee, thus commencing the disastrous rout of the crusaders. To make matters worse, the following night Raymond and the *Tourkopouloi* abandoned the shattered army, and rode hell for leather to Sinope.[76] Despite the poor performance of Raymond's *Tourkopouloi*, these troops probably gained the respect of the crusaders, who very soon began to raise their own *Turcopoli*. But that is another story.

Enter the Varangians

It was, according to Blöndal/Benedikz,[77] the emperor Basil II (r. 976–1025) who formed the Varangians into a regular *tagma* of his personal lifeguard, having received as many as 6,000 Scandinavian mercenaries from Vladimir (ON *Valdamarr*), prince of Novgorod, grand prince of Kiev and sovereign of Kievan Russia (r. 980–1015) who, as part of the deal, was to convert to orthodox Christianity and marry Basil's sister, the *porphyrogénnêtê* princess Anna, a mature spinster by now, an honour the royal princess tried hard to avoid. According to the Mesopotamian scholar Izz ad-Din Ibn al-Athir (1160–1233), Anna 'refused to hand herself over to one whose faith differed from her own',[78] which is quite understandable, yet there was also the rumour of the 800 or so concubines and slave girls the prince apparently maintained in various Kievan Rus' towns. In the words of an earlier Muslim chronicler, Yahya ibn Sa'īd of Antioch (d. *c.* 1066), an Egyptian Melkite Christian:

> Emperor Basil later sent a Metropolitan [Theophylact, the former Metropolitan of Sebaste in Byzantine Armenia] and bishops to them [viz. the Kievan Rus'] and they baptised the king [prince Vladimir] along with all who lived in his land. He also sent his sister [Anna] to him; she had many churches built in the Rus' lands.[79]

It was rumoured, too, that the pagan Vladimir had investigated other faiths before his conversion to the Orthodox faith. For instance, it is said he had sent a ten-man delegation to the king of the Volga Bulghars, but Islam was rejected because 'drinking is the joy of the Rus', we cannot exist without that pleasure'.[80] Whether or not the use (or abuse) of alcohol was the real issue here, having married the purple-born Byzantine princess, the future Saint Vladimir spent the rest of his life converting the Kievan Rus' to Christianity and building churches.[81] And so began the celebrated Varangian Guard, *tagma tôn Varangôn*.

The truth of such a claim is difficult to establish: the origin of the Varangian Guard is veiled with some ambiguity. What we do know for certain is that in the year 987 Basil was having problems with a veteran usurper, a warlord called Bardas Phokas.

The Phokas clan had its origin in Kappadokia and for several generations had enjoyed high repute in the empire as soldiers. The father of Bardas Phokas was that Leo who had won military fame under Romanos II (r. 959–63), the father of Basil. His uncle Nikephoros was an even greater soldier and was himself to ascend the throne in 963, when he married Theophano, the mother of Basil. Actually, this was the second time Bardas Phokas had rebelled against his lawful monarch, which came to a head on 15 August 987 when he proclaimed himself emperor at Chresianus and promptly marched on Constantinople. Soon after, with Phokas absent, Basil II destroyed his army at Chrysopolis with the aid of those 6,000 Scandinavian mercenaries.[82] Apparently, these mercenaries surprised the rebels at table, drinking. The following year, with his surviving men, Phokas tried to take Abydos – the key to controlling the Hellespont – which Basil came to relieve.[83] Phokas, after twice falling from his horse, rode forward and issued a challenge to single combat (which Basil was unlikely to take up). Phokas then suffered a sudden dramatic stroke, falling dead from his horse mid-battle, which was unfortunate for him. His body was cut in pieces and the head presented to Basil.[84]

It was back in 971 when Bardas Phokas had rebelled for the first time. This was against John I Tzimiskès (r. 969–76), with the help of his brother Leo (the younger) and their father. He was actually proclaimed emperor at Caesarea in Kappadokia, but the rebellion was crushed by another warlord and rival, Bardas Skleros, and the whole Phokas family was sent into exile on the island of Chios.[85] Believe it or not, Phokas was brought out of exile by Basil, now emperor, to counter the rebellion of Bardas Skleros,[86] who had won two battles against Basil in 978 at Pankaleia and Basilika Therma. The rebel Skleros went on to capture Nicaea (İznik) and besiege Constantinople. The following year, at Aquae Seravenae (24 March 979), Phokas defeated his hated rival in single combat, splitting Skleros' head with a sword. So ended the first revolt against Basil. Skleros survived and escaped to the 'Abbasid caliphate where he was to become a prisoner in Baghdad, until his captors released him in 987. With Baghdadi support, he proclaimed himself emperor again. Phokas was sent against him, but he, too, betrayed the emperor, first inviting Skleros to a parley, then treacherously clapping him in irons and declaring against Basil himself.

On the death of Phokas, Skleros, now almost blind, was released by Phokas' widow. He submitted to Basil and was allowed to retire, dying soon afterwards (6 March 991). Apparently he advised Basil not to allow too much power to governors and generals, and admit no woman to the imperial councils.[87] In the words of Michael Psellos:

Basil was well aware of the disloyalty among the Romans, but not long before this a picked band of Scythians [i.e. Rus'] had come to help him from Taurus.[88] These men, fine fighters, he had trained in a separate corps, combined with another mercenary force, divided by companies, and sent them out to fight the rebels.[89]

It must be emphasized at this point that the distinct impression we get from the Russian *Primary Chronicle* is that Vladimir was only too happy to be rid of these Scandinavian mercenaries. For the prince sent messengers ahead of what appears to be a dangerous band of freelancers each bearing the following communication:

See, Varangians are on their way to you. Do not keep them in the City [Constantinople] for then they will only give you trouble, as they have given me, but divide them up into many places, and do not let one man come back here again.[90]

In 977, when the fratricidal war erupted between Yaropolk and his younger brother Oleg, Vladimir had fled to his kinsman Hákon Sigurðsson, ruler of Norway, to enlist mercenaries to aid him to win the princely crown from Yaropolk. When his father Sviatoslav died at the hands of the Pečenegs, Vladimir and his brothers fought savagely among themselves to enlarge the third share of Kievan power he had appointed for each of them. Yaropolk slew Oleg, and then perished in his turn, and it was the third son Vladimir who, with the help of these Scandinavian mercenaries, survived this fratricidal feud to succeed to all the lands of the Rus'.

Vladimir may have wanted to get the Scandinavian warriors out of his own hair, but in doing so eventually there came into being the élite body of heavily armed northerners famous for using long shafted, broad bladed axes, which they 'bear on their shoulders'.[91] But we must leave the Varangians there. They are a whole subject on its own to which justice cannot be done within the limited confines of this book. However, this is a topic to which we shall return in a book of its own.

A good emperor

Basil was to enjoy one of the longest reigns of all, and enjoy it in the fullest sense. For it was, on the whole, a reign of success, despite a start against the odds. Basil, in his youth, had witnessed the gruesome murder of Nikephoros II Phokas (his mother Theophano had snuck her lover John Tzimiskès in through the palace window to murder her husband the emperor), and suspected John I Tzimiskès death, reputedly from typhoid fever, to have been caused by poisoning.[92] Understandably, this made him fully conscious about the dangers around him, particularly as there were members of the aristocracy related to the previous emperors who felt that they had better claims to the throne of Constantinople.

Both Nikephoros and John had, in effect, seized the throne, and had been able to legitimate their position only through marriage to the widow of Romanos II – the father of Basil and his brother Constantinus – who had died in 963. Furthermore, Basil needed to challenge the pre-eminence of military magnates around the eastern themes who could compete against his own dominance over the empire. As discussed above, it was a leading member of one of these ambitious eastern noble clans, Bardas Skleros, who rebelled against Basil shortly after his succession in 976;[93] and it was another leader of an even more prestigious clan, Bardas Phokas, whom the emperor had to call to his assistance in 978.

There is a full-length portrait of Basil in the Basil II Psalter, to be found in the Biblioteca Nazionale Marciana in Venice,[94] which corresponds exceedingly well to the description of the soldier emperor given by Michael Psellos.[95] In it the emperor holds a spear in his right hand and a sheathed sword in his left, while an imperial crown is being handed down from heaven by Christ and an angel. Commissioned by the emperor himself, the portrait shows Basil as a Christian ruler and Roman soldier. The prostrate figures at his feet are identified as various ethnic groups that at one point or another posed a threat to the empire during Basil's long reign. Basil's supreme power is clearly advertised by the Greek inscription flanking his torso: 'Basil in Christ pious emperor of the Romans'.

Purportedly one of the most effective and competent of the Byzantine rulers, Basil was a superb soldier, so much so that later legend has it that at the very appearance of his banner the foe used to flee, shrieking, and 'Fly, the Emperor comes!'[96] It was he who frustrated the territorial ambitions of the Bulghars, and by the mid thirteenth century the image of Basil as Bulghar-slayer, Βουλγαροκτόνος, by which he is still popularly known, was well established. According to the chronicler George Pachymeres, in 1260, the Byzantine army under Michael VIII Palaiologos (r. 1259–82) advanced to Constantinople and placed the Latins under siege. The Byzantine soldiers approached the ruins of the Hebdomon palace, and there, in the church of Saint John the Evangelist, they found upright in a corner a corpse with a shepherd's flute in its mouth. An inscription on the sarcophagus next to it allowed the men to identify the dead body as that of 'Βασίλειος Βουλγαροκτόνος'.[97]

This familiar, albeit barbarous, epithet came about for a notorious atrocity (hence the title). According to John Skylitzes, Basil supposedly blinded all but one in every hundred Bulghar prisoners, whom he left with one eye each to guide the rest back to their tsar Samuel.[98] Whether the tale of wanton cruelty is true is hard to know, although there is probably some element of truth to it. At any rate, Samuel had a seizure of some kind when he saw the state of his once proud army, and died on the spot. Michael Psellos, a source much closer to the time of Basil, said of him that 'he was more of a villain in wartime, more of an emperor in time of peace'.[99] Psellos does not mention Basil's macabre moniker.

Additionally, Basil scored victories over Armenians, Georgians, Arabs and Italo-Normans. His rule marked the apogee of the Byzantine empire. The emperors, regarded by many of their subjects as closer to heaven than earth, understood the importance of pomp and power. In front of their subjects they appeared in all the scintillating splendour of their imperial office: heavy purple robes, bejewelled diadem, pearl earrings and gem encrusted shoes. This helped to maintain the fiction that the godlike emperor was closer to heaven than earth. Basil, on the other hand, was no effete and pampered ruler. In fact, he was unglamorous and one of the least attractive of the emperors in terms of physical appearance, lack of cultural interests, and utter distain for the trappings of power, but he was trusted by the army and the people alike.

To wrap up that Bulghar-Slayer story from George Pachymeres, the chronicler tells that Michael VIII Palaiologos, upon hearing his soldiers had discovered the mortal remains of Basil, had the corpse moved to his camp across the Golden Horn in Galata. There he placed it next to his bed. Shortly afterwards, Basil's remains were transferred to the monastery of the Saviour in Selymbria 'and the empire was restored'.[100]

Chapter 16

Christian Frontline

Quite how the rise of a new religious movement in the Hejaz, in western Arabia, turned into a wave of conquests that embraced much of the eastern and southern shores of the Mediterranean is not easy to understand, not least thanks to the limited and partisan nature of the surviving evidence relating to the earliest phases of the rise of Islam. One of the pertinent issues here was the fact that the Muslim historians writing in Egypt, North Africa and al-Andalus from the later ninth century onward often worked backward from contemporary conditions and practices and tried to find an explanation for their existence in terms of what had happened in the past. In practice this could often mean inventing a past that was able to make sense of the present. The lack of early written sources made such a topsy-turvy approach to historical writing virtually inevitable. In other words, the traditional account of the life of Muhammad is set in early seventh-century Mecca and Medina, *but* there is no contemporary literary or archaeological evidence to support this.

So, what we have are what ninth, tenth and eleventh-century historians *thought happened* or what they thought *ought to have happened* in *seventh*-century western Arabia. It is according to this retrospective literary evidence that on Mount Hira near Mecca a forty-year-old merchant by the name of Muhammad received a divine message from the archangel Gabriel and embarked on his rôle as the prophet of Allah. For the next dozen years or so Muhammad stayed in Mecca (Makka) and gradually built up a following, although his success increased tensions with the polytheists who remained the majority. It appears that his initial preaching to his own tribe, the Quraysh, not only fell on deaf ears but as custodians of the pagan shrine they opposed him. In 622, Muhammad and his followers moved north to Yathrid, an event, *hijra*, which marked the start of the Islamic era. Henceforth, the town was called Medina, the City. In Medina he found openly favourable conditions for his teachings. It appears the inhabitants of Medina were at odds with the aristocracy of Mecca and were readily prepared to take the field against them. So, in that year Muhammad transformed, as if by magic, a cluster of Medina tribes into a warlike people. After a number of skirmishes between the forces of the two towns at last the Muslims, as the followers of the prophet were called, succeeded in capturing Mecca and Islam was launched. Bursting out of the desert, an Arab empire was formed with astonishing speed, stretching from the Ebro to the Indus and on to the oasis cities of Merv, Tashkent, and Samarkand.[1]

The speed of the Arab conquest still astonishes. To use the words of John Pickard, 'the establishment of an *Arab* empire is not contestable, but the tradition of an "Islamic" empire most certainly is'.[2] Whatever forces may have led the tribes of the Arabian peninsula into a series of largely unexpected attacks on their powerful settle neighbours to the north, their spectacular military expansion, which according to the traditional Islamic account had begun with the unification of Arabia under Islam, took the Arabs to territories formerly controlled by the Byzantine and Iranian Sasanian empires. The real significance of the year 622, or Year 1,[3] emerges as the beginning of the Arab era because it was in that year that the Byzantine empire, after twenty long years on the back foot, launched its military counteroffensive against the Sasanian Persians with the result that the Sasanian empire collapsed like a house of cards. In the vacuum that resulted from the Sasanian collapse, Arab military units, which had been on the payroll of both superpowers, were able to assume control of most of Syria, Mesopotamia and Egypt, where Byzantium's position was still weak after the decades of war with Persia, and with them presumably two thirds of the revenues of the empire.

Before Muhammad

Certain Arabic-speaking family dynasties had been Christian converts since the last quarter of the fourth century. It all started when at some indeterminate date, probably about 377 not long after the Arab warrior queen Mavia (Ar. *Mawiyya*) took over the leadership, *phylarchate*, of the 'Saracen' allies of Rome on the death of her husband al-Hawari (d. 375), who had ruled over a confederation of nomadic Arab tribes and sub-tribes in southern Syria. The contemporary monk Rufinus of Aquileia writes, 'Mavia, the queen of the Saracens, began to rock the towns and cities on the borders of Phoenicia and Arabia with fierce attacks'.[4] The fifth-century church historian Sozomen (Salminius Hermias Sozomenus), who was based in Gaza, reports the queen led 'her troops into Phoenicia and Palestine' and got as far as Egypt.[5]

This posed a considerable danger to the empire, as Sozomen says: 'this war was by no means a contemptible one, although conducted by a woman'.[6] Eventually, Mavia agreed to make peace, and an alliance with Rome, but only if a certain ascetic eremite called Moses from the desert of Sinai, himself an Arab, was consecrated bishop of her people.[7] The new Christian hero after the saint and the martyr, the monk who renounced the world and came to live in what the Arabs considered their natural homeland, the desert, especially appealed to them and was the object of much veneration. Despite Moses being a Nicene Christian, the Arian Valens

(r. 363–78) agreed to this investiture, and when this was done, he is said to have converted many Arabs to orthodox Christianity.[8] Notwithstanding later Christian glossing, Mavia herself was not a Christian until this treaty was made.

The pragmatic Valens possibly focused on the Arabs' conversion rather than their choice of bishop. The balance between the desert and the sown was evidently shifting, especially in southern Palestine, causing Arab raids to become a major headache for Rome. The empire's initial response was to increase the number of forts and military installations throughout the frontier zones, but alliances with Arab tribes in southern Palestine and elsewhere were also a feature of fourth-century imperial policy, and a fifth-century law dated to 443 refers to payments of *annona*, food supplies, to Arab *foederati*.[9] So, in return for allowing Mosses to become bishop (he had no fixed see after his consecration, hence his title 'Apostle of the Saracens'), Valens probably demanded Arab auxiliaries to fight against the Goths in Thrace. Mavia honours her bargain at and after Adrianople (9 August 378). It was these Arab auxiliaries that had helped save Constantinople from the Goths in the aftermath of that disastrous battle. Sozomen writes, 'in this emergency, a few of the confederate Saracens sent by Mavia, together with many of the populace, were of great service'.[10]

Though the Arabs *en masse* had suddenly become actors in history, it is interesting to note that Ammianus, a contemporary of these eastern events, completely ignores the revolt of Mavia, which, as we can now appreciate, was a major event. Not only did her defeat of a Roman army allowed the queen to dictate the peace terms to Valens, but it also allowed her to arrange a political marriage between her daughter and the *magister equitum* Victor. Ammianus negatively viewed Romans with a barbarian heritage. Ammianus mentions *comes* (later *magister equitum*) Victor guardedly – both had served under Iulianus during the emperor's invasion of Persia in 363. Victor was repeatedly referenced, but without title. Victor was a successful Romanized and Christianized Sarmatian general and Mavia was a Christianized Arab. Victor and Mavia personified two elements that Ammianus viewed with disfavour; they were both barbarians and both Christians.[11]

It should be mentioned that the most important source for information about Arabia just before Islam is pre-Islamic Arabic poetry. Much was recorded in Islamic times and from it we see the overwhelming importance of tribal society. Oral in its original form and epic in its tenor, the poetry is mainly concerned with tribal warfare, with lonely camel trips on the desert, or the longing for one's paramour. The way to glory, the ancient sages said, is through the palace; to riches, the marketplace; but the only way to wisdom is through a desert.

Meccan trade

By the seventh century the eastern coast of the Red Sea had become the most popular trade route from south to north. The town of Mecca flourished because it was both a centre of the caravan trade and a shrine with the cult object of a great meteorite, the black stone known as the Ka`bah, which is still venerated there today by Muslims. The leading tribe of the city, which had become sedentary, was the Quraysh to which the prophet Muhammad belonged. In his time trade had developed more than in the previous centuries and large camel caravans plied the routes to a number of places, above all to southern Syria, bringing local skins, leather, woollen clothing, and other pastoralist products. The spices and aromatics in which Quraysh have long been assumed to trade were the right kind of commodity from the point of view of low in bulk and weight and could be sold at very high prices, but the idea that the Quraysh traded in such goods has turned out to be what is nowadays called an Orientalist myth.[12] Admittedly, there may have been some trade in gold dust from Africa. Of Muhammad himself, we are told he traded in hides. In return, from Syria came cotton and linen textiles, manufactured objects such as weapons, household wares, and olive oil for lamps. The trade was highly profitable and brought wealth to Mecca. In this milieu, Muhammad was born in 570, or thereabouts, the Year of the Elephant.

All of south Arabia was then ruled by the kingdom of Aksum of Ethiopia, a Christian state, which set up a Christian viceroy 'Abraha al-Ashram over the land. 'Abraha consolidated his rule and gained control of trade, which was the main objective of Ethiopian interest in south Arabia. Indeed, according to Patricia Crone, 'by the sixth century, it was the Ethiopians who conducted most of the eastern trade of the Byzantines'.[13] 'Abraha built a church in San'a (now Sana'a, the largest city in Yemen), and in order to attract pilgrims (and traders) to his centre he sent Ethiopian missionaries to different regions of the Arabian peninsula. At that time Mecca was a place of pagan pilgrimage and 'Abraha sought to divert pilgrims from visiting the Ka'bah to San'a to his Christian shrine. It seems that pilgrims would go to a shrine, pagan or Christian, simply because it was a consecrated or holy place. When someone from the north (it is claimed he was a man from the Quraysh) defiled his church 'Abraha marched against Mecca with an army that included war elephants, thirteen in number according to Islamic tradition. That year was recorded as the Year of the Elephant, and it is mentioned in the Qur'an,[14] but 'Abraha was unsuccessful in his endeavour to raze Mecca from top to bottom and turned back south.

But hides, leather and other pastoralist products were heavy and bulky, and though camels would be self-transporting, all these goods were widely available in the desert areas of Syria itself. As Patricia Crone rightly asks: 'How could Quraysh have made a living by laboriously carrying coal to Newcastle?'[15] It has long been known that the Romano–Byzantine army swallowed up colossal amounts of leather. The army needed leather for tents, scabbards, shields, shield covers, baggage covers, kitbags, purses, horse armour, saddles, reins and other horse gear, boots, belts, wineskins, water skins, as well as diverse slings, strings, laces and straps for use in arms and clothing.

Just to give some idea of demand for leather, the plastic of the age, in a communiqué cited in the *Scriptores Historiae Augustae*, the emperor Valerianus (r. 253–60) orders his procurator of Syria, Zosimus, to furnish the *legio* V *Martia* with annual supplies including 'thirty half score of hides for the tents':[16] we know that at a later date *legio* IIII *Martia* (there was no V *Martia*) was stationed at Betthorus (today's El-Lejjun, Jordan) in Arabia.[17] It has been estimated that a single legion of the classical type (about 5,000 men of all ranks) required the hides of some 65,700 goats simply for the tents it used in the field.[18] So in southern Syria, the 5,000 regular soldiers of *legio* IIII *Martia* alone required some 65,700 goats just to equip themselves with tents. As for any irregulars serving Constantinople in southern Syria, though they were more lightly equipped we do know that even the Bedouin used tents of leather, as well as of hair, in those days, and the opponents of the prophet also made 'the hides of the cattle (tents for) dwelling', which they use on their travels.[19]

To be brief about the matter of possible numbers of soldiers, sixth-century Syria and Mesopotamia accommodated some 18,000 men (according to Kaegi) or twice or three times that number (according to Whitby),[20] all in regular need of food, clothing and a large variety of products manufactured from the skins and hides of sheep, goats, and camels, which were also required for the upkeep of the many forts in the region and for the acquisition of which they will have been in competition with their Sasanian counterparts. Some 5,000 or more of these men were to be found in the three provinces of Palestine and Arabia, which constituted the southern part of Roman Syria. Against this background it is easy to see that it could have been highly profitable to transport leather, hides, woollens, foodstuff and other commodities produced by the pastoralists beyond the imperial frontier for sale in Syria, whether to the imperial authorities or private manufacturers and/or distributors, or directly to the soldiers themselves.

The army was by far the single largest item of public expenditure in the Byzantine empire on the eve of Islam, and no doubt the same was true of the Sasanian empire too; and as Brent Shaw reminds us, 'the largest proportion of this military expenditure was directed (or redistributed) to the periphery of the empire, indeed mainly to the war zones on the frontiers where most of the military establishment was located'.[21] But did the Quraysh make their wealth by organizing supplies to the Romano–Byzantine army? As things stand, a case can be made for it, but not proved.

There are two places in which the Quraysh are regularly said to have been active, namely Bosra in southern Syria and Gaza on the Mediterranean.[22] Bostra (Busra), the capital of the Roman province of Arabia, a garrison city housing *legio* III *Cyrenaica* (which has left numerous inscriptions), raised to the status of metropolis by Philip the Arab (r. 244–9), a native of Shahba (which he later renamed Philippolis) in the

Hauran who rose through the army to become praetorian prefect under Gordianus III (r. 238–44), and then emperor after having murder his commander-in-chief.

Bostra was also the site of a famous fair which Muhammad himself is said to have visited, both as a child and as the agent of Khadija: this was where the monk Bahira spotted him. The Islamic tradition casts Hashim, Muhammad's great-grandfather, as the founder of Meccan trade,[23] but how seriously this should be taken is uncertain. Even so, by Hashim's time, legions were much smaller than in the Principate and typically consisted of some 1,000 to 1,500 men, so it was not an enormous market. But it was not negligible either, and it did have a weapons industry: blades from Bostra are vaunted in pre-Islamic poetry. It was a city in which the makers of goatskin bags were sufficiently wealthy to have reserved seats in the theatre, and it was also famed for products such as wine and grain, which were exported to distant destinations, by sea all the way to India and by caravan to the Arabian peninsula; perhaps they were among the goods carried back by the Quraysh.

As for Gaza, this is where Hashim is said to have died. Muhammad's own father, Abdullah, is envisaged as being on his way back from Gaza with merchandise when he died in Medina, and many other Qurashis are said to have traded there.[24] It does not seem to have had either an armoury or a military presence, though the sixty soldiers from Gaza allegedly martyred by the Muslims are presented as its garrison. However, it was a flourishing port from where the products brought by the Quraysh could have been exported to other cities, such as Caesarea and Alexandria, and it was also a centre of the pilgrim traffic.

Old game, new players

The wars between Byzantium and Persia have often been considered an important factor facilitating the Arab victories in the sense that they left the two empires financially ruined, militarily depleted and, in the Sasanian case, politically disorganized as well. What has not been considered before is the possibility that the wars affected the Arabs themselves, allowing them to gain wealth, organizational skill, and knowledge of imperial ways, and eventually to use this knowledge against the by now ruined and disorganized empires. This is what Patricia Crone, a leading scholar of Islamic studies, proposes.[25]

Ironically, Arabia had seldom been the central concern of either the Byzantines or the Sasanians, but the protracted military struggle between the two superpowers had a definite impact on the peninsula in the decades preceding Muhammad's birth. Both empires, hoping to outflank the other, tried in various ways to extend their own influence over key regions of the peninsula and to thwart the influence of their rival. On the northern fringes of Arabia, the two superpowers established special ties with powerful Arab-speaking families, whose leaders they recognized as 'kings' and supplied with monetary subsides and weapons. The Jafnid family of the tribe of Ghassan, based at al-Jabiya in the Jawlan (Golan) plateau overlooking the Sea of Galilee, were as early as 502 recognized by Constantinople as *foederati* of the empire. Later Islamic sources suggest that the Ghassanids were by origin a south Arabian tribe, which had migrated to the western edge of the Syrian desert and displaced those who were already there.

The Jafnid chieftains emerged from these encounters with the strength and acumen to negotiate with the Constantinople for an alliance.[26] It was the emperor Anastasius I (r. 491–518) who saw fit to appoint the Jafnids (presumably leading the rest of the Ghassanids) as defenders of the Byzantine marches against the Sasanians. Iustinianus (r. 527–65) saw an opportunity to use the Jafnid leader al-Harith ibn Jabala (d. 569) to tackle the ongoing problems caused by the irritating raids of the pro-Sasanian Nasrid leader al-Mundhir (see below).[27] Al-Harith was already a *phylarchos*, and Iustinianus now gave him what Prokopios refers to as the 'dignity of king',[28] probably an honorific and some funding to support his position on what was the fringe of Byzantine territory.

As well as defending Byzantine's eastern frontier in Syria, the Jafnids were also, on occasion, required to furnish contingents to the Byzantine army when it went on campaign against the Sasanians. In Iustinianus' time, the Jafnids, under their 'king' al-Harith ibn Jabala, played an important rôle at the disastrous battle of Callinicum,[29] fought on Easter Sunday 19 April 531, and in Belisarius' deep raid into Assyria ten years later. The Jafnids also warded off and fought against the Sasanian clients, the Nasrids; once (570) they even burned the Nasrid capital at Hira (today's al-Hirah, southern Iraq) on the Euphrates.

With the rise of the Nasrid dynasty and its support of the Sasanian empire in the sixth century, we are informed by Prokopios that Constantinople met its 'most difficult and dangerous enemy'.[30] The Nasrids, who were part of the tribe of Lakhm, became allied to the Sasanians from at least the end of the third century, as the Paikuli inscription from Kurdistan indicates, referring to an individual named 'Amr of Lakhm in a list of Sasanian vassals.[31] Like their rivals, the pro-Byzantine Jafnids, they too were of south Arabian origin and likewise faithful to their new religion and readily built monasteries and churches. Neither of these Christian allies, however, were heirs of the earlier Arab principalities of the caravan cities such as Palmyra and Hatra, but rather they maintained their Bedouin background and customs. They were warriors rather than traders and this contributed to the belief that north Arabia during this time was in a state of nomadization and decline. The Jafnids and the Nasrids fought for supremacy many times against each other. This was done with or without Byzantine or Sasanian encouragement.[32]

Desert song

Let us return to the seventh-century Arabs. The Jafnid and Nasrid forces were probably aided by footloose raiders from deep in the great peninsula called Arabia on the map, a land in which no foreign race had kept a permanent footing and where the Arabs had a long history before the advent of Islam, and a restless one. In some areas of more formal settlement towns had developed and had become centres of mercantile activity and of worship. The bulk of the peninsula, however, was occupied by nomadic tribes of Bedouin, whose way of life was the *ghazw* (corrupted into *razzia*), the raiding of settlements and the seizing of caravans and their merchandise. Accordingly, the nomadic Bedouin lived on what he could extract from the stranger on his desert trails or lift from the town beyond his desert domain; and the desert dweller and the town dweller bore each other a perpetual grudge. Pre-Islamic Arabia was a complex ecology of settled and nomadic tribes, which, while economically and culturally inextricably interdependent, maintained a fierce political and social independence.

The Bedouin was no gypsy roaming aimlessly for the sake of roaming. He represented the best adaptation of human life to desert conditions. Wherever the grass grew, there he goes seeking pasture. In a word, nomadism was a reasonable and stoic adjustment to a hostile environment. Even so, though sheep and camel rearing, and to a lesser degree horse breeding, were his regular occupations, and to his mind the only occupations worthy of a man, for him pillaging was the time-honoured means of survival. He led a precarious and hard life – the keen competition for water and pasturage split the desert populace into warring tribes – and was always prone to the lure of booty. For this reason he would descend like a jackal on a caravan of goods moving through his desert. Jerome (d. 420), in one of his many Christian writings, has left us an eyewitness account of one such robbery by a small band of marauders:

On the road from Beroë to Edessa [al-Ruha'] adjoining the highway is a waste over which the Saracens roam to and fro without having any fixed abode. Through fear of them travellers in those parts assemble in numbers, so that by mutual assistance they may escape impending danger. There were in my company men, women, old men, youths, children, altogether about seventy persons. All of a sudden the Ishmaelites [i.e. Bedouin] on horses and camels made an assault upon us, with their flowing hair bound with fillets, their bodies half-naked, with their broad military boots, their cloaks streaming behind them, and their quivers slung upon the shoulders. They carried their bows unstrung and brandished their long spears; for they had come not to fight, but to plunder. We were seized, dispersed, and carried in different directions.[33]

Jerome's experience corresponds closely to Ammianus' opinion of the mode of warfare conducted by the Bedouin, a people who were like 'rapacious kites' and 'fitted for clandestine acts of war'.[34] His perceptions were shared by other contemporaries with direct experience of this part of the world, such as the emperor Iulianus, who regarded the 'Saracens' as no more than 'bandits'.[35] Naturally, this begs the question of whether these 'bandits' were internal or external.

The solemn creed of the desert meant living off the fear and bounty of his desert neighbours. Raids and counter-raids for booty, revenge and glory were the highest endeavours of life for the Bedouin warrior. For him, the joys of life were a fast camel, the best weapons, and a short sharp crepuscular raid. For him, the three noble spoils were arms, clothes, and riding animals. With particular regards to the last, the camel was the Bedouin's nourisher, his means of transportation, and his medium of exchange. The dowry of a bride, the price of blood, the profit of gambling, the wealth of a chieftain, were all computed in camels. Indeed, the Arabic language is said to include about a thousand names for the camel in its numerous varieties, breeds, conditions and stages of growth, a number rivalled only by the number of synonyms used for the sword. Yet, though always ready for a fight, he was not necessarily eager to be killed. Without a doubt his strength was the strength of a man geographically beyond temptation: the poverty of his environment, with its dry air and salty soil, made him simple, continent, enduring, and an example of contentment to those slaves of unnecessary appetite.

Around the Mediterranean Sea and in the Fertile Crescent empires had come and gone, but in the barren wastes of Arabia the Bedouin remained forever unchanged. Yet, the Arabs in general and the Bedouin in particular had looked always to the Mediterranean Sea, not the Indian Ocean, for their cultural sympathies, for their enterprises, and above all for their expansions. Now their targets were greatly weakened by a long war they had fought between themselves, which had commenced in 602 and ceased only in 628, and which had seen virtually all of the eastern provinces of the Byzantine empire overrun by the Sasanians in the years 610 to 615; Jerusalem had fallen in 614, as had Egypt in 616. Ten years later, in 626, an Avar and Slav army besieged Constantinople, while a Sasanian one waited on the Asiatic shore of the Bosporus, poised to assist in what might have been the carve up of the Christian empire. By the traditional chronology, the prophet Muhammad had died in 632, and it was under his first successor as leader of the Muslim community, the caliph Abu Bakr al-Siddiq (r. 632–4) that the newly united Arabs stirred. And so bloomed their beautiful sensual poetry and cruel spiritual wars.

Out of Arabia

Saracen means Arab or – in a much older use of the word – a Muslim who fought against the Christians. Go back even further, beyond Muhammad, and you find that it once meant a wanderer, a nomad. In the words of the second caliph, 'Umar (r. 634–44), the Bedouin 'furnished Islam with its raw material'.[36] That all being said, the Muslim forces that burst out of the restricted and closed orbit of the Arabian peninsula in the six-thirties were composed almost exclusively of Arab tribesmen, not all of whom, however, where nomadic Bedouin, being as they were settled oasis-dwellers and townsfolk. Led by capable commanders and faced with enemies in relative disorder, these forces succeeded in the space of a generation in conquering Syria, Egypt, Mesopotamia, Iran, and much of the Caucasus and North Africa.

It must be said that today many Muslims attribute their success in conquering a vast expanse of territory in a relatively short period of time to faith. This typically fuels *jihadist* rhetoric as present-day Muslims fail to understand the mechanics of early Muslims' tactical achievements. After all, Arab warriors had trained from childhood in tribal warfare. In pre-teen years, many rode camels and horses, wielded swords, threw spears, and were proficient in the use of the lance and archery.

Because of their plasticity, many of these Arab armies did not need to exceed 20,000 warriors. Horse warriors operated in a tip-and-run fashion against the enemy's cavalry or an exposed flank in preference to charging home, while foot warriors fired arrows into the enemy formation, threw javelins, and fought hand-to-hand with spears and swords; a preferred tactic was to make repeated charges and withdrawals known as *karr wa farr*, using spears and swords combined with arrow volleys to weaken the opposition and wear them out.

Contrary to perceived wisdom, women played an active part in these early Arab armies, accompanying the military expeditions and often administering aid to wounded warriors as well as the *coup de grâce* for those wounded enemies left on the battlefield. Normally, women would bring up the rear of an advancing Arab army, collecting weapons, armour, and anything else of value along the way. However, tradition has is that five women fought alongside Muhammad in the battle of Uhud, and one, Umm Ahmara, died while engaging a Meccan with a sword.[37]

The Persian chronicler Ibn Jarir al-Tabari (839–923) offers an account of how early conquest armies were organized and fought. Components of an early conquest army included the following:

- The Guides *(al-Adilla' or al-Ada)*, scouts who studied the lay of the land and the approaches to the battlefield.
- The Eyes *(al-Ayun)*, specialists in mounted reconnaissance.
- The Stuffers *(al-Hashir)*, who brought up the rear of an army.
- Those of Action *(al-Fa`alah)*, labourers who fixed bridges and dug trenches.
- The Poets *(al-Shu`ara)*, who motivated the warriors prior to battle.[38]

He also informs us that these Arab armies of the early conquest period were articulated on the decimal system within each tribe, with commanders for each ten, one hundred, and one thousand men.[39]

The Arabs did not devise any notable military technological innovations; their success relied on speed, deception, flexibility, and the use of threats, negotiation, truces, duplicity, patience, and violence. Their weaponry was not advanced. Indigenous to the Arabian heartland were bows and arrows, spears, lances, and a straight sword, with the high quality patterns being forged in Yemen using Indian iron. Swords were usually carried from the shoulder in a baldric, in the Byzantine style, rather than from a sword belt as in the Sasanian fashion, with daggers as a personal protection. References are made to women who fought with tent poles (as lances) in defence of their tents, while on another occasion Byzantine soldiers were met by sword-wielding women, again defending their camp. However, once they advanced beyond the Arabian peninsula, the Arabs adopted the technical know-how of their enemies, particularly the use of battering rams, mangonels, towers, mining, and Greek fire, which were employed in the Byzantine art of war.[40]

As E. Rehatsek comments in his discussion of late pre-Islamic and early Islamic arms:

> *Rumh* is the lance, the chief weapon of the Arabs; because they could wield it better on horseback than the sword. The head or blade of the lance had a variety of shapes, and it varied also in length, but the shaft was generally of uniform thickness; it was never thrown like the javelin.[41]

A good material for lances was reed, which has very similar properties to bamboo.

Late pre-Islamic mounted warriors used the horse and camel in tandem, the horse being far too valuable to use other than in battle. Again it is Rehatsek who notes that 'warriors were so careful to fight with horses unexhausted by fatigue that each man rode on a camel ... and led the horse which he was to ride in the battle, without any load by his side ... whilst even the saddle was placed on the camels, so that the horse should arrive quite unfatigued on the battlefield'.[42] Just this sort of combined use of horse and camel is shown on an early second-century BC bronze bowl fragment from Mleiha in the emirate of Sharjah, which depicts a horse and camel mounted by riders. Whereas the cameleer wields a camel stick with which he directs his mount, the horseman is shown in the act of thrusting his lance at an opponent on foot, the arm and shield of whom can just be seen on the right hand of the scene engraved on the interior of the bowl fragment.[43]

Arab tribesmen were hit-and-run raiders, mounted upon fast horses or dromedaries. While this may have been true in the main, the possibility that this may not always have been the case is suggested by the large number of references to body armour (less so to helmets and shields) in pre-Islamic Arabic poetry, which preserves a rich lexicon of terms for different sorts of mail shirts (Ar. *dera'*).[44] There we read statements such as the following: 'We have coats of mail that glitter like lightning, the plaits of which are seen in wrinkles above our belts', or 'They are the people who whether dressed in cuirasses of rings or of leather thongs are like leopards'.[45] On the other hand, the Muslim force that captured Mecca in 630 was called the 'dark army' because it wore so much armour.[46] An ambivalent attitude to armour is reflected in another saying from caliph 'Umar, who describes mail as 'keeping a horseman busy, a nuisance for the infantry, yet always a strong protection'.[47]

As for the use of shields, these are clearly shown on the engraved bronze bowls from Mleiha, mentioned above. The shield on one is circular, with concentric sections, while that on the other is probably rectangular. The model for the latter shield, however, need not have been made of wood and leather. Sasanian soldiers, such as the one found beneath Tower 19 at Dura-Europos, Syria, carried rectangular wicker shields made of cane and of a size comparable to a mediaeval pavis.[48] Smaller, circular shields were probably constructed out of camel hide.

Under the 'Umayyads (661–750) Arab forces remained mainly Arab, but were increasingly professionalized and limited to troops from Syria, the stronghold of the dynasty – the Syrian Arabs tended to look down upon those of Arabia, whom they called 'lizard and gerbil eaters'. The coming of the 'Abbasids, whose armed revolution (747–50) against the 'Umayyads was successfully launched from Khurasan in north-eastern Iran, heralded a fundamental change in the composition of the army, with Khurasani-Arabs taking preference over Syrian Arabs. For the next two hundred years, the balance of power between Europe and the Islamic world remained decisively in the hands of the Muslims, who enjoyed massive economic growth and whose culture flowered in spectacular fashion.

The 'Abbasid caliphate was moulded by Perso-Islamic culture and government and increasingly sustained by the support of Turkish military slaves (Ar. *mamluks*). The great early expansion of the Arabs brought them into Transoxania, the lands beyond the river Oxus. This was the borderland of the Turks of Central Asia, and Arab generals formed Turkish bodyguards from prisoners of war and men brought to them by slavers. In the course of time such military retinues came to form a substantial component of 'Abbasid armies. Because they were foreigners in terms of ethnic origin and geography they did not have any local power base and relations with the local population. They did not have families to look after and were free to allocate all their time to the needs of the military. Their minds and bodies were moulded according to the needs of their patron. Entirely attached to their patron, therefore, these slave warriors were more loyal and dependable than freeborn Arab warriors who were individuals with pride in their tribal traditions. Moreover, it was these tribesmen who had brought the dynasty to power, and from which the dynasty soon wished to distance itself.

Preference for Turkish rather than Arab troops was clearly displayed when the 'Abbasid caliph al–Ma'mun (r. 813–33) included large numbers of Turks in his army, and pursued what was effectively a systematic immigration policy by levying revenue from the eastern border provinces partly in slaves. His soldier brother and successor, al–Ma'tasim (r. 833–42), continued to recruit Turkish military slaves, and in 836 he transferred them *en masse* from the turbulent capital of Baghdad to a new city, 125 kilometres north on the east bank of the Tigris. Samarra (officially *Surra man ra'a*, 'he who sees it is delighted') consisted essentially of the caliph's palace and the cantonments of his *mamluks*, but it inevitably superseded Baghdad as the administrative centre of the caliphate and continued to do so until the closing years of the ninth century.

Thus, it was the 'Abbasid caliphs who created the basis of the *mamluk* system, which was to have an everlasting effect on all Islamic military systems thereafter. There were two key elements: military expertise and loyalty. The candidates were trained rigorously – including religious training – as an individual and as a part of their unit. They were isolated physically and culturally from everybody except the ruler and their unit. After this hard training and isolation, they became loyal only to the ruler and to their unit, which in a sense also became their family. Thus, isolation and training were the important parts of creating a trained and loyal army.

After Muhammad

Muhammad was succeeded by a long line of initially elected caliphs (caliph, Ar. *khalifah*, 'successor'), the first being his disciple Abu Bakr (r. 632–4) who conquered and united the Arab tribes. Or so accepted Islamic tradition says. The notion of *jihad* was important here in that the conquest of the infidel, or non-believers, was considered a duty in the name of Allah – *jihad* is the Arabic word for both spiritual struggle within the individual believer and war in the service of Allah, and has often been called the sixth pillar (*rukn*) of Islam. However, Abu Bakr formulated a detailed set of rules for Islamic conduct during war. He gave the following instructions to an Arab army setting out for Syria, which was then part of the Byzantine empire:

Stop, O people, that I may give you ten rules for your guidance in the battlefield. Do not commit treachery or deviate from the right path. You must not mutilate dead bodies. Neither kill a child, nor a woman, nor an aged man. Bring no harm to the trees, nor burn them with fire, especially those which are fruitful. Slay not any of the enemy's flock, save for your food. You are likely to pass by people who have devoted their lives to monastic services; leave them alone.[49]

Previously, Muhammad had forbidden indiscriminate killing too: 'It is narrated on the authority of Abdullah that a woman was found killed in one of the battles fought by the Messenger of God. He disapproved of the killing of women and children'.[50]

The second caliph and revered companion of Muhammad, 'Umar ibn al-Khattab (r. 634–44), again according to the Islamic tradition, transformed the nascent Arab state in a growing empire by his conquest of Syria (635) and Palestine (638), Egypt (640), and Iran (642). Early Islam assumed many of the institutions and structures of the Byzantine milieu, and while Byzantine administrators obviously decided to abandon the lost eastern provinces, some of them were kept on to serve the new order.

The third caliph was 'Uthman (r. 644–56), a member of the 'Umayyads from Mecca, a family that had been Muhammad's most bitter opponents. He saw fit to continue these conquests, and by doing so came into direct conflict with Constantinople in Anatolia. 'Uthman, however, was killed by Muslims who were angry at his concentration of power in the hands of fellow 'Umayyads and he was succeeded by `Ali ibn Abi Talib (r. 656–61). `Ali was a cousin and son-in-law of Muhammad and had considerable support; the Sunni look upon him as the fourth, and last, of the rightly guided caliphs. Mu`awiya, the nephew of 'Uthman, was outraged by the murder of his uncle and fellow 'Umayyad, and insisted that the assassins be handed over for due punishment.

Mu`awiya had the support of powerful Muslims, such as Muhammad's widow Aisha, but `Ali refused, saying that he was unable to do this. Mu`awiya refused to recognize `Ali as caliph and in response `Ali demanded that Mu`awiya give up his office as governor of Syria. The mutual accusations turned speedily into mutual menaces, and the personality clash turned into a full-blown civil war. `Ali defeated Aisha's forces at the battle of the Camel in Mesopotamia, but was unable to defeat Mu`awiya's forces at the battle of Siffin in Syria. After a stalemate, the two men agreed to arbitrate the dispute. Shortly thereafter, `Ali was assassinated due to dissention in his own camp, and Mu`awiya, now in a very powerful position, convinced `Ali's son Hasan to give up any claim to the caliphate and to retire quietly from public life.

Mu`awiya now declared himself Commander of the Faithful (*amir al-mu'minin*, a title held by the caliphs) in Jerusalem and established the 'Umayyad dynasty (661–750) in hereditary control of the Muslim caliphate, inaugurating what was to be, in true, the first unified Arab state, extending Islamic power right into the Iberian peninsula to the west and Afghanistan to the east. Mu`awiya, a late convert to the new religion, was not a likely candidate to be the leader of the Islamic community. But his skill and intellect, combined with a lot of luck, enabled him to build the first Muslim dynasty. He is also the *first* caliph attested by external (i.e. non-Islamic) historical evidence.

Mu`awiya was also famed for his self-control and careful thought before any important action, one of which was his creation of a strong and somewhat centralized government. Though Jerusalem, which every Semitic race had made holy and was a religious centre for believers in all three major monotheistic faiths,[51] was a place of pilgrimage as the third Holy City of Islam, the 'Umayyad capital and administrative centre was to be established at Damascus. Whereas to Christians Jerusalem was the place where Christ walked, talked, lived and died, to Muslims it was the setting for the *Mi'raj*, Muhammad's night journey and ascent to heaven,[52] later marked by the magnificent Dome of the Rock, and would be the site on which the Resurrection would take place on the Last Day.

Nonetheless, Mu`awiya gave Christians, especially former Byzantine officials, positions in his own government, using their expertise in governing the provinces, and adopting Byzantine financial and administrative systems. Mu`awiya also attempted to conquer the rest of the Byzantine empire. The Arab conquests had been temporarily interrupted by the civil war, but Mu`awiya set them in motion again. He achieved some successes, but his ultimate goal was Constantinople. He launched the first Arab siege of Constantinople, but the attack failed. Mu'awiya was forced to sign a treaty with Constantinople in which he agreed to pay the Byzantines an annual subsidy and refrain from further attacks. He died soon after, in 680.

Mu`awiya had broken convention my naming his son Yazid (r. 680–3) his successor. Because he made rule of the caliphate hereditary— passed down from father to son – Mu`awiya is said to have begun the first Islamic dynasty. Many Muslims felt that this was wrong. Some felt that the new caliph should be chosen by members of the community, rather than inheriting the title. Others believed that the caliph should be from the family of Muhammad, which neither Mu`awiya or his son could claim. A rebellion broke out immediately after Yazid's succession. `Ali's son Hasan had agreed to give up all claims to the caliphate and retire, but his younger brother Hussein had made no such agreement. Opponents of Yazid flocked to Hussein to support him in his bid to become caliph. However, Yazid was eager to remove this threat before it could mature. He despatched an army to surround Hussein and his family as they were travelling. In what became known as the battle of Karbala, though in truth it was little more than a massacre, the army of Yazid slaughtered Hussein and his family, including his six month-old infant son. This was a major event in the Shi`a-Sunni split, and uprisings from Shi`a supporters of `Ali's family would continue to plague the 'Umayyads.

Many Muslims continued to oppose the passing down of the caliphate from father to son. A new and more dangerous opponent of the 'Umayyads appeared in 'Abd Allah ibn al-Zubayr, son of one of Muhammad's closest companions. Ibn al-Zubayr established his powerbase in Mecca and claimed to be the true caliph. Yazid sent an army against Mecca. It besieged the sacred city, severely damaging the Ka`bah in the process, but failed to take it. Yazid prematurely died soon thereafter, and was succeeded by his young son Mu`awiya II. With this, the resistance to Ibn al-Zubayr fell apart. Many Muslims were unhappy with the 'Umayyads and most of their provinces turned to Ibn al-Zubayr and accepted him as caliph. Mu'awiya II was weak and unwilling to fight. He abdicated the throne and died soon thereafter.

World empire, state religion

This was not the end of the 'Umayyad dynasty, however, not by a long chalk. A new 'Umayyad, Marwan, from a cadet branch of the family, took the throne and opposed Ibn al-Zubayr, claiming power for the 'Umayyads. As a result, a second civil war broke out, this time between Marwan in Damascus and Ibn al-Zubayr in Mecca. Marwan did not survive long, ruling only about a year, but he was succeeded by his son, 'Abd al-Malik, who would be remembered as the most important 'Umayyad caliph. In the meantime, another uprising broke out in Mesopotamia as the Shi'a Muslims, acting as guerrillas, began killing anyone they thought responsible for Hussein's death. In due course 'Abd al-Malik rallied his hard pressed forces and defeated the Shi'a guerrillas. He then sent a fresh army to the Arabian peninsula to besiege Mecca. After a bitter siege, the 'Umayyad army stormed the city, and Ibn al-Zubayr was to die fighting while he and his followers while making their last stand at the Ka'bah. With that armed opposition to 'Abd al-Malik was crushed, and an 'Umayyad ruler was once again in firm control of the caliphate.

'Abd al-Malik was the *first* caliph to emphasize the importance of the new faith of Islam to the state, with Muhammad beginning to be featured as the centrepiece of Islamic theology. He also asserted his rôle as leader of the Muslims, as well as that as ruler of an Arab empire. He was the first to develop a centralized system of government, taxation and administration required for running a world empire. With a stable and regular source of revenue he was able to utilize state money to build mosques, and to that end was to be responsible for one of the most important buildings in Islam – the Dome of the Rock.

The Dome of the Rock is not really a mosque, but a magnificent monument built upon the Temple Mount in Jerusalem. Its location has great symbolic meaning. It was upon this spot that the Jewish Temple stood until it was destroyed by the Romans in AD 70. This is also the spot where Muslims believe Muhammad ascended to heaven. The Dome may have been built by 'Abd al-Malik as a pilgrimage site, since the Ka'bah was for some time in the hands of his rival, Ibn al-Zubayr. But it was also meant to show Islamic domination over Jerusalem, and that Islam had surpassed Christianity and Judaism. Indeed, it may have been built to overshadow the basilica of the Holy Sepulchre, and it was decorated with a broad blue band – one within the inner octagon of the building and the other around the outside – bearing verses from the Qur'an in gold lettering, some of which directly rebut Trinitarian

Christian beliefs. For example, one polemic inscription on the Dome says: 'All the praises and thanks are to Allah, Who has not begotten a son (or offspring), and Who has no partner in (His) Dominion, nor He is low to have a helper. And magnify Him with all magnificence, Allah is the Most Great'.[53]

The Christology of Arab monotheism is clearly aligned with those Christian traditions that had taken root in this region, namely those Christians who never accepted the Nicaean Creed or the Trinitarian concept of Constantinople. The Christology of the early Islamic followers was based on the idea that although Jesus was a messiah, as he is described in the Qur'an, the interpretation of this title is closer to the idea of messenger or prophet than to the son of God.

It was a further means of legitimization of his imperial rule that 'Abd al-Malik also initiated a programme of the Arabization of Islam and the Islamization of the Arab polity. The Arabic language was declared to be the official language of the empire and all official documents, treaties, laws and trade agreements were to be written in Arabic. Like all ruling elites, the Arab élite sought to justify its existence, in this case by a dramatic and historic shift in the form and content of Arab monotheism so it could stand as a rival to the Christianity of the Byzantine empire. It was around this time, too, that traditions began to be created about Arabic being the language of Heaven and other languages (sometimes Greek, sometimes Pahlavi) being spoken in Hell.

'Abd al-Malik solidified control of Iran and Iraq after his victory in the civil war. He also continued the rapid expansion of the Arab empire. He sent armies to complete the conquest of North Africa, and in 695 his forces captured Carthage, the crown jewel of Byzantine North Africa, and when the caliph died ten years later, the 'Umayyad caliphate was stronger than ever before. Islam had been successfully placed at the centre of the state at a time when the Byzantines were weak and vulnerable.

Under 'Abd al-Malik's son and successor, Walid (r. 705–15) the 'Umayyad state was to expand even further. Having taken North Africa from the Byzantines, Islamic forces set their sights to the invasion of Europe. In 711, a Muslim army crossed the Pillars of Herakles and entered the Iberian peninsula. At the time Iberia was ruled by the Visigoths, a Germanic nation that had taken the peninsula from Rome, but who had gone on to embrace Roman culture and become orthodox Christians. The Visigothic kingdom rapidly collapsed under Islamic attack, and within four years Iberia was successfully integrated into the 'Umayyad caliphate.

The advance of Islam was to be checked by four factors: the defeat of the second Arab siege of Constantinople (717), the defeat of Muslim forces in Francia (732), the ability of the Khazars to keep the 'Umayyads at bay, and the great plague of the seven-forties, which, together with yet another civil war (744), decimated 'Umayyad manpower. The borders of the Arab empire became fixed, and in many ways it was already far too large to effectively govern. In many ways, the 'Umayyads defined how an Islamic, as oppose to an Arab, empire would be ruled. Nonetheless, their lack of descent from Muhammad, their controversial practice of handing down power from father to son, and their mistreatment of non-Arab Muslims made them a controversial dynasty, a topic of debate among Muslims even to this day and ultimately led to their fall.

It was that hard on the heels of these major setbacks for Islam that the 'Umayyad caliphate was overthrown by the 'Abbasid dynasty (750–1256), which witnessed the rise of Persian influence in the caliphate, especially after the transfer of the capital to Baghdad in 762. Persian and Byzantine court ceremonial replaced the more democratic Arab customs, and the replacement of the 'Umayyads by the 'Abbasid house would bring some new and capable Arab rulers to the throne too.

From ships of the desert to ships of the sea

There is that Arab proverb, 'It is preferable to hear the flatulence of camels than the prayers of fishes',[54] which expresses well the Arab distrust and dislike of the sea. However, once in possession of Syria and Egypt, with great ports, shipyards and maritime resources there, the Arabs began to cast their desert eyes seaward. Though evidently not a seafaring people, the Arabs were not slow to appreciate the importance of naval power, especially after a Byzantine attempt to retake Alexandria in the year 645 demonstrated Arab vulnerability to seaborne attack. Thus, they came to understand that development on their part of sea power was both essential for holding the Mediterranean littoral they had won, as well as the key to further conquest beyond. Credit for this broadening of perspective is due primarily to the new Arab governor of Syria and future caliph, Mu'awiya. The 'Umayyad caliphate of Damascus therefore acquired a fleet from the earliest years of its existence, taking advantage of the shipyards and maritime skills of its new, and in many cases disposed, subjects.

The fledgling 'Umayyad navy was quick to achieve a major success with the destruction of the Byzantine fleet under Constans II (r. 641–68) at the battle of the Masts (or Dhat al-Sawari) near Cape Gelidonya (Cape Teşlik) in 655. The outnumbered Arabs had seen fit to chain their ships together so as to prevent their line being broken. The 'Umayyad caliphate was to go on to lay claim to the coastal regions and the islands of Anatolia, including Cyprus, to occupy Byzantine North Africa, and to threaten Constantinople itself before the seventh century was out. The Mediterranean had ceased to be *mare nostrum*, 'our sea', and became an area of conflict and threat.

By the year 700, central North Africa was firmly in Arab hands, and caliph 'Abd al-Malik sent a thousand Coptic shipwrights to Musa bin Nusayr (d. 716), the governor in Carthage, and ordered him to establish a naval base and shipyard in North Africa. Musa established his base inland from the old port, at Tunis, which could be more easily defended from Byzantine attack. By 704 Tunis was home to a sizable war fleet that exercised sufficient control over the western Mediterranean that Musa was able to complete the conquest of the western portion of North Africa. From there, the Arabs, reinforced by Berbers, were able to cross the Pillars of Herakles and begin the conquest of the Iberian peninsula.

In 717, the Arabs equipped an armada for battle and holy war, succeeding to besiege the Constantinople by land and by sea for a second time. The European side was simultaneously under attack by the Bulghars. Yet the Queen of Cities was saved by Greek fire (see below). It was a triumph in the tradition of 626. The Arabs' first great tide of conquest had ebbed, and their navy was never to be sighted again before the sea walls of Constantinople.

In spite of that, the Arabs were to return to the sea in force under the 'Abbasid caliphs. In 827 footloose Muslim warriors, who had been initially expelled from al-Andalus and some years later from Alexandria, raised a fleet and sailed on Crete, which they managed to capture in short order. For a century and a half they were the scourge of Aegean commerce and a perpetual threat to Byzantine power, despite numerous attempts to dislodge them. In even a more disastrous development for Constantinople, the year 827 also marked the beginning of the Arab conquest of Sicily, the key to the control of the western Mediterranean and the gateway to Italy. The process was slow (Taormina, the last pocket of resistance, did not fall until 902), as Byzantine land forces and fleets forced the conquerors to pay heavily for each span of each port. By 831, Palermo was in use as an advance base for further Arab attacks on Sicily, and ten years Arab corsairs were raiding the Italian mainland and into the Adriatic. It is in this period that there is the first mention of Arab vessels (Ar. *harraqatv*, 'fire ships') equipped with Greek fire.[55] Due partly to its use, Byzantine fleets sent to relieve Sicily were defeated in 840 and again in 859. Byzantine naval supremacy in the Mediterranean was broken, never to be fully restored, and Muslim ships, many of them independent pirates, controlled most of the Mediterranean outside of the Aegean and northern Adriatic seas. Arab attacks on the Italian mainland led to the establishment of pirate bases in Calabria and Apulia.

The best of enemies

In the eighth century the Arabs made a number of attempts by land and sea to take Constantinople. Their failure marked a watershed. Thereafter, the great surge of conquest receded in the lands that bordered Christendom: the Byzantine empire on the one hand and the kingdoms of northern Spain on the other. The Muslim rulers opted for consolidation rather than conquest. On the Byzantine-Islamic borders, both Christians and Muslims continued to be active, and lines of forts were built or rebuilt to strengthen the frontiers. It became the practice for both empires to engage in annual campaigns, described in the Islamic sources as *jihad*, but these gradually became a ritual, important for the image of the caliph and emperor, rather than being motivated by a vigorous desire to conquer new lands for their respective faiths. The boundaries between Islamic and Christian worlds remained more or less stabilized and from the later eighth century onwards it was deemed more important to defend existing frontiers than to extend them; the 'Abbasid-Byzantine frontier had largely stabilized along the crest of the Amanus mountains, through eastern Anatolia to Georgia on the Black Sea.

The rule of Harun al-Rashid (r. 786–809), the fifth 'Abbasid caliph, is considered to be the golden age of the Arab empire, which now stretched from the Iberia peninsula in the west to northern India and Central Asia in the east, and his court in Baghdad, renowned for its science and luxury, is idealized in the *Arabian Nights*. Though the *Arabian Nights* portrays Harun as almost dormant in Baghdad, the caliph was dynamic, repeatedly visiting the provinces of his domain, nine times performing the pilgrimage to Mecca, and eight times invading the territories of the Byzantines – the history of Byzantine warfare during much of the eighth and ninth centuries is rather a depressing one. It was Harun who sent to Charlemagne an Indian elephant, complete with exotic trappings, as a congratulatory gift on being crowned Holy Roman Emperor. His vizier, and frequent boon companion, was Ja'far ibn Yahya Barmaki (767–803), to whose family (Persians from Balkh) Harun delegated the administrative duties of the caliphate. However, in 803, Harun so spectacularly and inexplicably removed the Barmakids from power – it is possible they had overreached themselves. Ja'far was suddenly arrested and beheaded and virtually his entire clan exterminated.

In 838 caliph al-Ma'tasim (r. 833–42) led his army deep into Byzantine territory where it captured and sacked the provincial capital of the Anatolikon theme, Amorion. Thousands of Christian prisoners were marched sixty-odd kilometres along a waterless road in the scorching August sun. Around 6,000 of them died on the way. By the tenth century, however, the pendulum would swing the other way as the 'Abbasid caliphate began to decline and lose its grip on its vast territories, by which time Constantinople could begin to retake the initiative in the region. In 962 Nikephoros Phokas, the future emperor, descended on Syria and, it was said, destroyed everything in his path with fire and sword, ravaging fields and taking captives the populations of Aleppo and other Syrian towns. In 975 his successor, John I Tzimiskès (r. 969–76), pushed even further south, extorting large sums of cash from Muslim communities along his warpath. He came close to capturing Jerusalem, more than a hundred years before the First Crusade.

As we can appreciate, Byzantine relations with the Arabs were often tense on a military level, and both sides justified these brutal campaigns against one another as righteous wars against the infidels. In Islamic accounts successful expeditions were always accompanied by the formula 'Allah gave the victory', while John I Tzimiskès declared that because of his raid deep into Syria 'the Holy Cross of Christ has been expanded'.

In despite of the violence and hot rhetoric, however, there existed a sense of belonging to a common cultural historical continuity. This shared heritage helped to differentiate eastern Orthodox relations with Islam from those of the Roman Catholic Church during the crusades, which was far more intolerant of the Muslims. See how the patriarch of Constantinople Nikolaos I Mystikos (r. 901–7, 912–25) addressed the caliph in the early tenth century:

> It is right that all of us who have obtained power among men, even though there should be nothing else to promote our mutual contact… should not omit to make contact with one another, both by letters and by emissaries… There are two lordships, that of the Saracens and that of the Romans, which stand above all lordship on earth, and shine out like the two mighty beacons in the firmament. They ought… to be in contact and brotherhood and not, because we differ in our lives and habits and religion, remain alien in all ways to each other, and deprive themselves of correspondence carried on in writing.[56]

This was not one of those diplomatic documents mainly filled with theological abuse. For Nikolaos believed that Constantinople and Baghdad, even if divided by religion, were distinguished through their knowledge and wisdom from other cultures. Although their languages and their religions were different, they shared an admiration for the literature and philosophy of classical Greece. It is not at all surprising that Byzantine intellectuals looked to classical Greece for inspiration, but why Islamic ones?

When the Arabs overran the Byzantine eastern provinces they came into possession of several centres of Greek culture, notably Alexandria, and with their repository of scrolls dating back centuries. They exploited this resource in a rather different way than the Byzantines, for their main interests lay in the philosophy, mathematics and medicine that those scrolls contained rather than their linguistic and literary qualities. The caliphs, especially Harun al-Rashid, encouraged their translation into Arabic so that they could be studied more easily by Islamic scholars. Harun's son, al-Ma'mun, took a personal interest in ancient Greek science and in geometry in particular. In some fields Islamic scholars made considerable advances on the ancient Greeks, notably in mathematics, where they developed the numerals that have now become universal. Military theory was also highly developed, with tactical manuals being translated not only from Greek, but Latin, Persian and Sanskrit too.

Converts to Islam

It must be said, however, though neither as a rebellious heretic in Mecca, nor as head of an exile community in Medina, was Muhammad very tolerant of opposition, yet (perhaps because he had himself been subjected to hatred, persecution and violence) he acknowledged the right of Jews and Christians and other 'Peoples of the Book' (*ahl al-kitab*, i.e. the Manichaeans and other dualists) to worship in their own way and indeed to enjoy all personal rights except those of bearing arms (which would have given them power to oppose). With that, the Old Testament, the Jewish Torah, and the Christian Gospel are recognized by the Qur'an as divinely inspired scriptures, although at the same time Jews and Christians are condemned for having deviated from these scriptures and revelations. Muslims rarely forced people to convert to their religion, often preferring to levy a special tax on minority communities instead. So, forced conversions, if indeed they occurred, were reserved for pagans not 'apostates'.

Yet the stunning success of Arab armies could create a context in which other people found it prudent to convert, or in which they were attracted to the religion simply because of its manifest power and triumph. In other instances, Islam spread through more spontaneous conversions as people learned of it through trade and missionary activity. The religion was clearly attractive, with an explicit set of beliefs about what to do and what not to do in order to win access to heaven and avoid a lamentable eternity in hell. It appealed to lower order groups because of its commitment to charity and spiritual equality; it also legitimated merchant activity more than did most belief systems at the time, and so could attract traders. The cultural and political achievements of Islam drew people eager to advance their societies in a variety of ways, including religious ones.

As well as suffering major losses of real estate, the Byzantine empire also suffered major losses of converts to Islam, who found it less oppressive than the ultraconservative Chalcedonian Church. In many ways Islam was a livelier, more promising religion, especially in the eyes of those converts who felt abandoned by Christianity. An anonymous Syriac chronicler, writing no later than 775, bemoaned the lack of faith of some of his fellow Christians with the following diatribe:

> The gates were opened to them to [enter] Islam... Without blows or tortures they slipped towards apostasy in great precipitancy; they formed groups of ten or twenty or a hundred or two hundred or three hundred without any sort of compulsion... going down to Harran and becoming Muslims in the presence of [government] officials. A great crowd did so... from the districts of Edessa and of Harran and of Tella and of Resaina.[57]

We can also add that the Egyptian Copts welcomed the Arab conquest as liberation from Byzantine persecution, though nowadays Coptic Christians in Egypt, with the Muslim Brotherhood at the helm, would be less inclined to agree.

Chapter 17

Celestial Fire

Henry V of England is reputedly to have once remarked that 'war without fire is like sausages without mustard'.[1] If true, then the grim and purposeful English king made a good, albeit brutal, point. For the use of fire in land warfare is as old as war itself, and probably in naval warfare too. After all, it was Homer who sang 'the Trojans threw weariless fire on the fast ship, and suddenly the quenchless flame streamed over it'.[2]

Earthenware or glass pots (Gr. *kútrai*) of Greek fire,[3] horsetails of smoke marking the trajectory of these small but lethal containers as they gracefully arced across the sky before breaking on impact and their jelly-like contents spilling to ignite on their targets. Such fire pots first appear in our period of study only to disappear with the arrival in the West of that other pernicious concoction, gunpowder. The fire pots were thrown by hand, by means of a staff sling, or by machines known as mangonels. These pots were used to set on fire anything wooden – gates, barricades, walkways, ships, siege engines, and so forth. In his account of the Seljuq siege of Mantzikert in 1054, Michael Attaleiates describes a mangonel operated by a large number of men, which fired an immense stone against which the defenders were helpless. They were saved only when a Latin mercenary grabbed a pot of Greek fire, dashed out through the besiegers, and set the machine on fire.[4]

Something new

The origin of Greek fire is surrounded by Christian fable. According to Constantinus VII Porphyrogenitus (r. 913–59), an angel whispered the formula 'to the great and holy first Christian emperor Constantinus', and he warns his son and heir, Romanos II (r. 959–63), to never reveal the secrets of its formulation, as that angel bound the first Constantinus 'not to prepare this fire but for Christians, only in the imperial city and never anywhere else'. As a warning to his son, he adds that one Constantinopolitan official, who was bribed into handing some of it over to the empire's enemies, was struck down by a 'flame from heaven' as he was about to enter Hagia Sophia.[5]

The plausibility of such a fabulous origin notwithstanding, the exact ingredients of Greek fire[6] even today are not known for certain and remain a matter of much debate. We do know, however, that naphtha had been an incendiary tool of siegecraft since Assyrian times, where we witness the use of liquid fire on their bas-relief artwork, while in a passage in the Greek Old Testament the word 'naphtha' is used to refer to a miraculously flammable liquid.[7] Strabo, discussing the naphtha to be found in Babylonia, says that 'if you smear a body with it and bring it near to the fire, the body bursts into flames; and it is impossible to quench these flames with water (for they burn more violently), unless a great amount it used, though they can be smothered and quenched with mud, vinegar, alum, and birdlime'.[8] The eccentric Roman polymath, the elder Pliny, makes the same learned observations about naphtha too, adding that 'it has a close affinity with fire, which leaps to it at once when it sees it in any direction'.[9]

A thirteenth-century Muslim source records a recipe that combined naphtha, olive oil and lime, distilled several times.[10] Liquid naphtha could be somewhat stabilized with heavier oils, tars, or pitch, but, of course, those additives are themselves flammable. The use of soaps and other gelling agents to thicken and stabilize naphtha and/or petroleum is what led to the formulation of the hydrocarbon incendiary weapon napalm in 1942, and allowed it to adhere to targets and burn at very high temperatures over a prolonged time. The term 'napalm' is a combination of two of the constituents of the gelling agent, naphthenic acid (from naphtha) and palmitic acid (from soap).

However, the aforementioned Muslim recipe was rather inexact and, compared with the original Byzantine incendiary substance, was relatively weak. The tenth-century Islamic writer al-Tarsusi, a judge (*qadi*) in Ma'arrat al-Nu'man and Kafartab, wrote a work (now lost) entitled *Siyar al-thughur* ('Ways of Life along the Frontiers'). In it he describes various recipes for making Greek fire. One of his recipes is well worth quoting in full and runs as follows:

> Take ten pounds of tar, three pounds of resin, one-and-a-half pounds each of sandarac and lac, three pounds of pure, good quality sulphur, free from all soil, five pounds of melted dolphin fat, the same quantity of liquefied, clarified fat from goats' kidneys. Melt the tar, add the fats, and then throw in the resin after having melted it separately. Then grind the other ingredients, each one separately, add them to the mixture, put fire under it, and let it cook until it is thoroughly mixed. If you wish to use it in time of war, take one part, add about a tenth part of the mineral sulphur called naphtha, which is greenish and looks like oil, place the whole in a skillet and boil until it is about to burn. Take the pot, which should be earthenware, and a piece of felt. Then throw it with a mangonel against whatever you wish to burn. It will never be extinguished.[11]

The resulting liquid may have had a similar consistency and effect to modern napalm, and would have been every bit as devastating as the mediaeval sources suggests. It rarely seems to have failed.

Besides distilled naphtha, other possible thickening agents included pitch, resin, sulphur and, as mentioned by al-Tarsusi, dolphin fat. It is possible that the incendiary contained saltpetre, which added to the intensity of its burning. Whatever its actual constituents, this deadly cocktail was mixed in proportions that were a tightly guarded state secret, so much so that the exact formula was apparently not put into writing but passed on by word of mouth. One who could have possibly known the constituents of Greek fire was Anna Komnene. She says the following:

> Now this fire was chemically prepared in the following manner. From the pine and other similar evergreen trees they gather resin, which burns easily. This is rubbed with sulphur and introduced into reed tubes. A man blows on it with a strong sustained breath, as though he was playing a pipe, and it then comes in contact with the fire at the end of the tube, bursts into flames and falls like a flash of lightening on the faces in front of it.[12]

Our princess, however, has forgotten to mention one vital ingredient: naphtha.

Proto-napalm

One of the many colourful names given to Greek fire was 'sticky fire' (Gr. *pýr kolletikón*). Indeed, burning fiercely, this mediaeval version of napalm would cling to any surface on which it landed and would even burn on water, which made it burn more violently. Clearly effective against the hulls and sails of ships, Greek fire was an extremely lethal weapon against the fleets of the 'enemies of Christ'. Only sand or earth could suffocate it. This terrible combustible liquid substance would be spewed out from swivelling, bronze nozzles situated in the prows of imperial warships against hostile ships, so burning and scattering them.

Though the actual pumping mechanism still remains a matter of some speculation, Anna Komnene gives an excellent description of these bronze nozzles and their aggressive employment against enemy vessels,[13] and in the Madrid manuscript of John Skylitzes' *Synopsis historiôn* we find an outstanding illustration showing how the fire was projected.[14] An imperial warship (probably a δρόμων, *dromôn*, the workhorse of the Byzantine navy) is about to incinerate the hostile ship representing the rebel navy of Thomas the Slav (d. 823) about to attack Constantinople in 821/2. An immense flame from a tube in the prow is almost engulfing the rebel ship. Two men, specialists called *siphônatores*, are operating the flamethrower or siphon (*síphôn*), while another two (*kôpêlatai*) are attending the oars. In the middle of the ship the fighting crew is represented by a marine with a long spear, while in the stern the helmsman (*prôtokarabos*) is operating the steering oars (*pêdalia*). The wind fills the unfurled lateen sail. The crew onboard the hostile ship is represented by three men, two of them pulling the oars. They are more or less concealed behind the long red flames.

This technology of pumping pressurized, liquid death through siphons mounted on ships' decks, however rocking and rolling, was allegedly the brain child of Kallinikos (*fl.* 670). He was an artificer from Heliopolis in Syria who had fled the Arab occupation of his homeland and found refuge in Constantinople. The emperor Constantinus IV (r. 668–85) was thus able to station 'large biremes carrying fire cauldrons and *dromôns* carrying *siphônes*' in preparation to defend the small harbour of Caesarius against the Arab armada *en route* to beleaguer Constantinople (673–9).[15]

Dominance and defence

Obviously, the main aim of the besieged was to bring the besieger under a deadly fire as he sought to cross the fosse that usually constituted the outermost defences. The mechanical artillery of the day was quite capable of doing this, the larger calibres being able to discharge by counterweight stone shot of sixty kilograms or more, the heavy stuff to crush men, other coarse-textured and explosive to slice or penetrate. Returning to the Seljuq siege of Mantzikert referred to above, an Armenian account makes mention of a huge mangonel, originally built for Basil II, which weighed some 2,000 kilograms and had a pulling crew of 400 men and which could fire stones weighing up to 200 kilograms.[16] The Arab Syrian patrician Usama ibn Munqidh (1095–1188) mentions the Byzantines, when they were besieging Shaizar in 1138, using mangonels that were capable of throwing 'a stone to a distance further than the distance covered by the arrow [over 200 m], their stone being twenty to twenty-five *ratls* [c. 64 to 80 kg] in weight'.[17] During the second siege (April 1204) of Constantinople by the crusaders of the Fourth Crusade, the Byzantines hurled stones 'so large that a man could not lift them from the ground'.[18] Similar machines in western Europe were throwing stone balls of one hundred to 300 *livres* over more than one hundred *toise* (45 to 124 kg over 200 m).

Throwing machines worked on one of two basic principles. Either they were powered by torsion, or they worked like a see-saw. A mangonel was a counterweight machine, which unleashed stones and other projectiles by rocking a long throwing arm, rather like a playground see-saw, but with the pivot very close to one end of the arm. The old Romano-Byzantine form of single-armed torsion powered small stone-throwing machines, *petrareai* and the like, had gradually fallen out of use.[19] Lever-arm artillery had originated in China and came to Europe via the Muslim world in the ninth century. They took the form of a beam pivoted between two uprights. To operate it, a team of men would heave on a set of ropes that hung from the short end of the arm, sending the long end up into the air at speed, hurling a projectile skywards from a scoop-like structure or a separately attached sling. A metal counterweight system was introduced to improve the performance of these stone-throwing machines. The counterweight (or counterpoise) was fitted to the end of the short end of the arm.

Though their particulars are obscure, all these machines seem to be variations of a basic standard type of machine which employed a throwing arm drawn down against torsion tension. When released, this arm propelled a projectile, with direction and range of fire governed respectively by pointing the machine toward the target and by controlling the tension. There are no surviving originals from the mediaeval period, but we do have pictures in illuminated manuscripts and low-relief carvings from churches and tombs. The Madrid manuscript of John Skylitzes' *Synopsis historiôn* depicts similar counterweight machines,[20] called *manganikôn* in the Greek (from *manganon* meaning crush or squeeze, i.e. 'a crusher'), and modern experiments with full-scale replicas show that, with a trained team of eight to sixteen artillerists,[21] stone balls of three to twelve kilograms can be hurled forty to sixty metres with remarkably consistent accuracy even at a quick firing rate of one load per minute.

Naturally, such small stones did little damage to stout fortifications, but they did have a devastating effect on the human body. Heads in particular offered no more resistance than rotten apples to these roaring rocks. At the siege of Toulouse in June 1218, according to the Old Occitan epic poem *Chanson de le croisade albigeoise*, Simon de Montfort the elder died after being struck by a stone shot: the blow to his great helm smashed his eyes, brain, upper teeth, forehead, and jaws to pieces.[22] Branded 'the scourge of the Albigenses', Simon was a notorious and fanatical crusader whose cruelties were remarkable even in that cruel age. In the name of faith he had drenched southern France in blood and massacre, regardless of the victim's age or gender. Fittingly, in the eyes of the Cathar heretics that is, the mangonel that shot the shot that spattered Simon was operated by the 'ladies and girls and women' of Toulouse.[23]

What the mediaeval French called a *biffa*, modern tests by Renaud Beffeyte have shown that a one-kilogram stone shot can reach its target travelling at a speed of 140 kilometres per hour.[24] The surprising thing is not the speed but the noise – or rather, the lack of it. Instead of the explosive charge of a cannon, and the whistling of the cannonball, there is just a scrape as the stone shot moves from under the uprights, a shudder as the throwing arm is stopped in its spin, and then nothing. The stone shot sails through the air towards its target in total silence.

From other contemporary literary sources we learn that not only stone balls were thrown, but even iron balls, pieces of iron, beehives full of bees, poisonous snakes, scorpions, powdered quicklime and the like were hurled. Sometimes literature even mentions the hurling of unpleasant missiles over the walls of a besieged city, such as lifeless carcasses of horses, still conscious spies, or – as in the panegyric poem of Theodosios Diakonos, an otherwise unknown poet, celebrating the recapture of Crete from the Arabs in the year 961 by Nikephoros Phokas – a living jackass. The general placed the animal in the sling and ordered the artillerists to launch it, 'a living jackass for the jackasses'. The operators stationed among the braided ropes then sent the poor beast skywards.[25] We can safely assume that such sentient missiles were not at all silent. All the same, it was rotting animal carcasses that proved to be a popular type of ammunition in mediaeval siege warfare. It had long been a tradition to insult or humiliate the enemy you were beleaguering, but putrid animals (especially pigs, which were deemed the more aerodynamic) were also intended to spread both disease and despondency.

Siege and sack

Siege warfare was another important dimension of military action during our period of study. Apart from waiting it out and allowing starvation to take its slow but inevitable course, the besiegers had the choice of three physical options for gaining their goal, namely, mining under, battering through, or going over the walls they were operating against. Generally, however, in siege warfare the besiegers normally adopted a strategy that was applied slowly and methodically since they knew that their most powerful allies – dearth and discouragement – were to be found inside the city they were besieging. As long as time allowed, it was generally seen as much better to starve the enemy out – and thus keep one's own losses to a minimum – than to engage in outright assaults, which cost lives and materials and might in the event be unsuccessful.

As for the besieged, they normally put their faith in one or more of three possibilities. They might be saved by a relief force despatched by their own side or by a foreign ally; they might hold out until such moment as the besiegers were forced, through shortage of food or time, to give up what had turned into a protracted, grinding siege and take themselves off elsewhere; or they might themselves stage a breakout and defeat the besiegers in a hot, pitched battle. The last option, of course, was rather risky as the besiegers might well enter the city over the bodies of its men. The besieged also knew, if they were to fail in their endeavours, the problems of discipline and control at the end of a successful siege were always great. The besiegers had been subjected to physical hardships, boredom, and often peculiar dangers outside the walls. They had been deprived of other opportunities by a period of enforced inactivity; they had often found themselves trying to live off an increasingly despoiled countryside. If an assault had been necessary this would have inevitably been a good deal bloodier than regular fighting in the open field, and even the siege itself would have given opportunities for the besieged to inflict unusually high casualties on the besiegers.

Still, for the Constantinopolitans Greek fire was a key military resource, and above all for their navy, and the effective use of this incendiary weapon was clearly a principal factor in the longevity of the Queen of Cities. However, it should be said that the last mention of its use comes in 1173 during the aftermath of the anti-Venetian pogroms. John Kinnamos, who took up the task of writing the history of the Komnenoi where Anna Komnene left off, says that the Byzantine fleet that pursued the fleeing Venetian vessels across the Aegean was equipped with it.[26] After 1185 the navy was run down and effectively withered close to extinction.

Sea fire

One of the chief causes of the fall of Constantinople to the Fourth Crusade in April 1204 was this deterioration of the once proud Byzantine navy. The Byzantines lost control of the seas to the Italians, especially the Venetians, and thus they were no longer in command of their own destiny. Niketas Choniates singles out John of Poutzê as being responsible for this lamentable turn of events. He purposely diverted in the treasury the contributions collected by naval expeditions, which were, destined to support the fleet and largely eliminated the warships needed to defend the empire, since the enemy comes by sea as well as by land, arguing that such ships were not always needed and that expenditures made on their behalf were too heavy an annual burden. The result of this ill-advised policy, notes Niketas, was that pirates ruled the seas and harassed the empire's maritime provinces.[27]

Indeed, the contrast between the proud fleet of more than 230 ships sent to invade Egypt in 1169 and the dismay array of rotting hulks and fishing vessels that lined up across the Golden Horn in June 1203 could not be starker. Greek fire was certainly not deployed in January of the following year when the Latins and the Venetians were preparing to fight the Byzantines. For on this occasion a fire-fleet was used in an attempt to destroy the crusader fleet, the Byzantines despatching ghostly, unmanned incendiaries against the precious navy of the Venetians as it lay at anchor in the waters of the Golden Horn.[28]

As discussed above, the Byzantine navy used Greek fire in close combat from ship to ship, bringing both tactical advantage and the element of surprise. The development of Greek fire and of the means of projecting it for some distance out over the bow allowed Byzantine ship designers to do away with the projecting waterline ram since Greek fire effectively fulfilled the ram's sole function – destruction of the enemy ship. Nonetheless, we must heed the comments of Liudprand of Cremona that calm winds and seas were necessary if the *siphônes* were not to become a menace to their own ships.[29] And, obviously, any wind would have to be astern. If an enemy fleet managed to gain the weather gauge with the wind behind it, the *siphônes* would have become useless.[30] Moreover, fixed weapons would have been almost unusable in the varying conditions encountered at sea. There is no doubt that the term *strepta*, 'swivels', was used for weapons. This explains why Liudprand observed that in 941 the Byzantine fleet driving off the Rus' assault on Constantinople 'threw the fire all around'.[31]

And then there was the psychological element too, an application that was fearsome as it was militarily significant: that the Byzantines could control fire and water must have made a marked impression on those assailing Constantinople, knowing that they could project it almost at will at your vessels. We do have a description of experiencing Greek fire, namely that of Jean de Joinville (d. 1317), the constant companion and biographer of Louis IX of France, the future Saint Louis. During the Seventh Crusade (1248–54) Sire de Joinville was once on the receiving end of the deadly viscous flammable stuff shot from Muslim engines of war:

> This was the fashion of Greek fire: it came on as broad in front as a vinegar cask, and the tail of fire that trailed behind it was as big as a great spear; and it made such a noise as it came, that it sounded like the thunder of heaven. It looked like a dragon flying through the air. Such a bright light did it cast, that one could see all over the camp as though it were day, by reason of the great mass of fire; and the brilliance of the light that it shed.[32]

According to the eyewitness account of Usama ibn Munqidh, at Kafartab (known as Capharda to the crusaders), in 1115, one of Muslim soldiers, a Turk, approached a tower and threw a bottle of Greek fire at the crusaders on the top of it: 'The *naft* (Greek fire) flashed like a meteor falling upon those hard stones, while the men who were there threw themselves on the ground for fear of being burnt'.[33] The use of *naft* seems to have been the favoured Muslim response to the problem of dealing with crusader siege machines, namely the siege tower (*burj*) and the penthouse (*dabbaba*). It is worth citing the example of the Muslim use of *naft* at the siege of Acre (1190–1) against a crusader *dabbaba*, as related in an eyewitness account by Saladin's Kurdish biographer, Baha' al-Din ibn Shaddad (1145–1234):

> The enemy had constructed a large terrifying *dabbaba* of four storeys. The first storey was of wood, the second of lead [viz. covered in sheets of], the third of iron and the fourth of copper. It was higher than the wall and warriors rode inside it. The inhabitants of the town were very afraid of it and resolved to ask the enemy for safe-conduct. They [the crusaders] had brought it [the *dabbaba*] near the wall so that there was at a glance a distance of only five cubits between it and the wall. The people began to throw *naft* at it continuously by night and by day until Almighty God decreed that it should be burnt.[34]

Much earlier, at the siege of Durazzo (Dürreš) in 1081, the Venetians themselves had apparently learned the secret of Greek fire. In a sea fight off the city the Venetians, fighting against the Italo-Norman fleet of Robert Guiscard,[35] 'blew that fire, which is called Greek fire and is not extinguished by water, through submerged (?) pipes and thus cunningly burned one of our ships under the very waves of the sea'.[36] On this particular occasion the Venetians were, of course, fighting for the Byzantine empire. Even so, eventually western Christendom, too, learned how to use Greek fire.

The first recorded use of Greek fire in western Christendom was by Geoffroy V d'Anjou at Montreuil-Bellay in 1151. This learned count placed it in a heated iron jar and hurled it from one of his mangonels. The great keep of Montreuil-Bellay went up in flames and was promptly destroyed after a three-year siege.[37] Geoffroy – nicknamed the *le Bel* (a *'grand chevalier e fort e bel'*) and *Plantagenêt* – was the paternal grandfather of Richard Cœur de Lion.

The anonymous author of the work entitled *Richardi Regis Itinerarium Hiersolmorum*, written around 1222, tells how Richard Cœur de Lion, on his sea voyage from Cyprus to Acre, captured an Arab ship loaded with all kinds of artillery such as *ballistae*, besides bows, arrows, spears and an abundance of Greek fire contained in glass bottles, the author here using the term Greek fire: *'oleo incendiario quod ignem Græcum vulgus nominant ...'* He continues by saying that it is a fire that burns with a vivid flame, smells abominably, consumes even stone and iron and that it cannot be extinguished by water, but only by sand, though vinegar to some extent can subdue it.[38]

In a how-to manual bearing the rather macabre title *Liber ignium ad comburendos hostes* ('Book of Fires for the Burning of Enemies') written between 1280 and 1300 by a certain Greek of Constantinople or an Iberian Arab who called himself Marcus Græcus, Mark the Greek, there is the earliest known recipe for Greek fire in the West, though, of course, the substance had clearly been in use in Europe for over a century. Written in Latin, his recipe was as follows:

> You will make Greek fire (*ignem Græcum*) in this way. Take live sulphur, tartar, sarcocolla and pitch, boiled salt, petroleum oil and common oil. Boil all these well together. Then immerse in it tow and set it on fire. If you like you can pour it out through a funnel as we said above. Then kindle the fire which is not extinguished except by urine, vinegar, or sand.[39]

The vinegar was presumably sour wine (Gr. ὄξος, L. *acetum*), the drink of the ordinary soldier as proffered to Christ on the cross.[40] Sand would obviously smother the fire and extinguish it by starving it of oxygen. However, why either vinegar or urine may have been effective, when water was not, is unknown.

Chapter 18

Deus Vult

In March 1204, the Christian army of the Fourth Crusade turned on their Byzantine hosts, finding their territories offered easier pickings than the designated target, Egypt, the then current centre of Muslim power in the Near East. Geoffrey of Villehardouin, as a leading member of the Fourth Crusade, saw things from the top. According to him, there was a secret agreement amongst the leaders of the Fourth Crusade that the expedition would initially sail to Egypt rather than to the Holy Land. As he himself admits, this plan 'was kept a closely guarded secret; to the public at large it was merely announced that we were going overseas'.[1] Geoffrey's careful choice of the word 'overseas' was a clever deceit because to the average potential crusader, it automatically meant the Holy Land. As another Christian author put it, 'the keys of Jerusalem are to be found in Cairo'.[2]

By 15 April, after three days and nights of terrible violence and looting, Constantinople, the centre of Christendom, was firmly in the grip of the crusaders. The city's fall to the Latins, after almost nine centuries during which it had been considered invincible, shattered the self-confidence of the Constantinopolitans. Understandably there was fear of the Latin conquerors after the three days of brutality that followed the conquest. The morale of the orthodox population was also affected by the Latin destruction of sculptures and monuments, many of which were revered. The massive Latin seizure of relics, the expropriation of orthodox ecclesiastical institutions, and the attempts to enforce the submission of the Orthodox Church to the papacy presumably alienated the majority of the Constantinopolitans and induced some them to leave. There was also a reluctance to live under the rule of the 'beef-eating Latins', a sentiment so cattily expressed by Niketas Choniates – a man with a deeply engraved love of, and pride in, his mother city.[3]

Constantinopolitan Diaspora

Some Constantinopolitans fled to Byzantine provinces still under Byzantine rule, namely Thessaly, Thrace, Epeiros, Paphlagonia in the newly established Byzantine state of Trebizond, or even to Turkish territories. On the other hand, some Constantinopolitans reached provinces already occupied by the Latins, such as the islands of Corfu and Euboia. The patriarch of Constantinople, John X Kamateros (r. 1198–1206), took up residence in the provincial city of Didymotheichon, where he was to end 'his days as a vagabond and exile'.[4] However, many if not most great Constantinopolitan families headed toward western Anatolia and rallied around Theodore I Laskaris (r. 1204–22), the brother of the one-day emperor Constantinus Laskaris who established a state-in-exile that ensured the continuity of Byzantium, the so-called empire of Nicaea.[5] It was here, for instance, that Niketas Choniates had gone after he experienced the sack of Constantinople at firsthand. His own house, 'incomparable in beauty and immense in size', had been burnt down,[6] and much to his credit, he had risked his own life to prevent the rape of a young girl by one of the victorious crusaders.[7]

Other Constantinopolitans went to Epeiros where a scion of a family that had once ruled Constantinople, Michael Doukas (r. 1205–15), set up a rival imperial court. The Despotate of Epeiros, as this break-away Byzantine state was called, extended over most of the western coast of modern Greece and Albania and at times included central Greece. The capital was at Arta. Michael's son and successor, Theodore I Doukas (r. 1215–30), conquered Thessaloniki from its Latin ruler in 1224 and proclaimed himself lawful emperor, thus coming into conflict with the claims of the Laskarids in Nicaea, finally falling to the Nicaean emperor John III Vatatzes (r. 1222–54) in 1246. The Doukai claims to the imperial title were irreversibly damaged by the outcome of the battle of Pelagonia in October 1259, which Epeiros roundly lost together with its Latin allies to John Palaiologos, brother of the Nicaean emperor Michael VIII Palaiologos (r. 1259–82). Much of the western knighthood was despatched in rags and chains to do homage to the emperor, an amazing triumph for Michael, which sent shockwaves through Europe. The Despotate of Epeiros was to linger on in one form or another till it was absorbed into the Serbian kingdom in 1348.

Yet other Constantinopolitans fled to the important port city of Trebizond on the Black Sea coast of Anatolia, where the remnants of the imperial family of the Komnenoi had already with Georgian support established an independent seat of empire. It more or less followed an independent existence as an anomaly in Anatolian affairs, managing to survive until 1461 when it fell to the Ottoman Turks.

Constantinople was obviously crucial to any emperor, the sign of his power and legitimacy. With Constantinople in the hands of the Latins, it was, in fact, difficult to establish legitimacy for any particular Constantinopolitan family. And so, the validity of the Laskarid claim fell, ironically enough, on the fact that the exiled Orthodox patriarch of Constantinople was, from 1208, universally recognized as having his seat in Nicaea. Moreover, no rival patriarchate was ever established in the rival break-away states. With the patriarch at their court, the Laskarids had a very strong claim indeed to the Queen of Cities.

But for the Laskarids it was not to be. Following a palace coup in 1258, in which Theodore II Laskarids (r. 1254–8) was deposed and blinded, Michael Palaiologos became regent. In the following year, he was crowned along with the boy emperor John IV Laskaris (r. 1258–61), whom he would later depose, blind and imprison. As God's representative on earth the emperor needed to maintain his corporeal perfection. Blinding, castration and *rhinokopia* (cutting off the nose) all served as effective methods to incapacitate one's rivals. Régime changes invariably are abrupt and deadly.

Frankish defilement

Count Baldwin IX of Flanders was elected the first Latin emperor of Constantinople on 9 May 1204. His coronation, which took place a week later, was held in Hagia Sophia. Though various trappings recalling Byzantine coronations appeared at the Latin ceremony,[8] presumably to lend some sort of legitimacy to the rule of Baldwin I (as he was now acknowledged), the inescapable truth was that the Great Church had been mercilessly plundered by the Latin crusaders and their Venetian ally, who had systematically stripped it of its gold, silver, gems, icons and holy relics.[9] Niketas Choniates describes the despoiling of Hagia Sophia and claims that a prostitute danced on the *synthronon* while it was in progress.[10] He makes full use of supreme irony that so-called soldiers of Christ who had taken a vow to fight the infidel and liberate the holy places were busily looting a Christian city, and he sarcastically contrasts their behaviour with the generosity of Saladin when he had captured Jerusalem in 1187. 'They were exposed as frauds', concludes Niketas.[11]

Hagia Sophia, that heaven on earth, that throne of the glory God, had been desecrated, by the 'forerunners of the Antichrist, chief agents and harbingers of his anticipated ungodly deeds'.[12] The Fourth Crusade demonstrates what private enterprise could do in an age of faith, the loot being spread all over Europe, some even ending up in England, though the best place to see Byzantine treasures today is in the Basilica di San Marco in Venice. One prize, for example, was the *quadriga* of ancient Greek bronze horses from the Hippodrome, which ended up atop the façade of San Marco. Though to be fair to the Venetians, they did possess (in common with their fellow Italians the Pisans and the Genoese) a potent mix of religious zeal and driving commercial ambitions.

The Latins took over at least twenty churches and thirteen monasteries, most prominently of course Hagia Sophia, which became the cathedral of the Latin patriarch of Constantinople. However, for the most part, the Latin occupiers were too few to maintain all of the public buildings of Constantinople, both secular and sacred, and many became targets for vandalism or dismantling. Bronze and lead were removed from the roofs of abandoned buildings and melted down and sold to provide money to the chronically underfunded empire for defence and to support the empire. Buildings were not the only targets of officials looking to raise funds for the impoverished Latin empire of Constantinople, as it was known. As a result, the monumental sculptures that adorned the Hippodrome and fora of the city were pulled down and converted into worthless copper coins. Among the masterpieces destroyed were monumental figures of Hera, Paris Alexandros, standing with Aphrodite and presenting her with the Golden Apple of Discord,[13] and a colossal statue of Herakles, 'mighty in his mightiness', attributed to the fourth-century BC sculptor Lysippos, who had a passion for the large.[14] Along with these master works went the immortal goddess-like bronze of Helen of Troy, so passionately portrayed by that passionate Constantinopolitan Niketas Choniates.[15] One of the grandest victims of this Latin vandalism was the Great Palace.

The Great Palace on the First Hill of Constantinople had served as the main royal residence of Byzantine emperors from 330 to 1081 when Alexios I Komnenos chose as his residence the palace of Blachernai, a peaceful spot away from the hustle and bustle of the capital situated as it was in its north-eastern corner. From that time on the Blachernai palace became the favourite residence of the imperial family, gradually supplanting the Great Palace. Still, the new palace's remoteness made it a prime target for any external attack, so there was a constant need to review the land defences in this quarter and, if necessary, enhance them. Additions were therefore made, and the walls that now surround the Blachernai palace area are the walls built under Manuel I Komnenos (r. 1143–80). According to the eyewitness testimony of Niketas Choniates, during their first siege of the city in July 1203 the armies of the Fourth Crusade:

> [P]itched a camp divided in part into trenches and wooden palisades around a hill from which the buildings of the Blachernai palace complex that faced west were visible. At the foot of this hill there lies an open courtyard that extends southwards to the wall erected by Emperor Manuel to safeguard the palace and touches the sea in the direction of the north wind.[16]

In spite of that, however, the Great Palace complex continued to be used as the primary administrative and ceremonial centre until the three-day sack of Constantinople in April 1204.

The first Latin emperor Baldwin of Flanders did use it as his residence, but his Latin successors lacked sufficient resources for its maintenance and they let it fall into disrepair, a metaphor of the Latin empire's impotence. Indeed, the situation in this respect serious worsened during the long reign of Baldwin II (r. 1228–61), who was chronically indebted. His expedients for raising money included pawning the Crown of Thorns, worn by crucified Christ, to a Venetian merchant for 13,134 gold pieces. When he could not redeem the debt, the relic was taken by agents acting for the saintly Louis IX of France, who was so delighted with this treasure that he constructed the magnificent Sainte-Chapelle in Paris especially for it. By 1257 so impoverished was the Latin empire that Venetian creditors required Baldwin's son Philip as surety for a loan, and even the lead joints stripped from the roofs of buildings within the imperial complex were being sold to generate cash.[17]

The second Baldwin was actually staying in the Blachernai palace, his preferred residence, when a local sympathizer opened one of the gates to a Byzantine advance party quietly waiting outside. On 25 July 1261 a handful of Byzantine troops led by Alexios Strategopoulos overpowered the Latin guards at the Gate of the Pege and forced their way into the city, thus opening up the way for its recapture. The Latin interlopers were bundled unceremoniously out of Constantinople with barely a struggle having been its masters for less than six decades. Other territorial spoils of the Latin victory in 1204 – such as the principality of Achaea and the island of Crete – remained in western hands but the principal achievement of the Fourth Crusade was wiped out. On 15 August 1261 Michael VIII Palaiologos, the ruler of Nicaea and victor at Pelagonia, processed into Hagia Sophia where, in an elaborate ceremony that masked the wreckage he had usurped, he was anointed emperor of Constantinople. Broken down though she was, the Byzantines had happily reclaimed the Queen of Cities.

After 1261 the Great Palace was largely abandoned, the Blachernai palace being used as the imperial residence instead. Indeed, even before that date Constantinople was a city far gone in the humiliating weaknesses and dangerous vanities of senile decay. Large sections of the city were mined, destroyed in the three terrible fires of 1203 and 1204, whole quarters abandoned or given over to allotments for cultivation. Constantinople had been transformed from the greatest city in Christendom to a scarred and ragged shadow of its former splendour. Thus, by the time Constantinople was conquered by the Ottoman Turks in 1453, the palace complex was completely abandoned. Indeed, their triumphal ingress into the city must have picked its way across a landscape of desolation and ruin. Yet in its time the Great Palace had no equal in the world, and mediaeval travellers have left awed descriptions of its splendours.

The monumental maze of residences, offices, churches, baths and barracks of the Great Palace were separated by peristyle porticoes alternating with open courtyards and ornamental gardens. The porticoes were decorated with gold tesserae mosaics, the courtyards and gardens with marble statuary and ornate fountains. Visiting the city as a tourist in the summer of 1203, the crusading knight Robert de Clari claims 'there were 500 halls, all connected with one another and all made with gold mosaics'. He continues, saying there were more than thirty chapels alone in the palace complex. He also saw two large pieces of the True Cross 'as thick as a man's leg and a fathom [6 feet/1.83m] in length', some of the iron nails driven into Christ's hands and feet, a vial of his blood, the Crown of Thorns, a swatch belonging to the robe of the Virgin Mary, and the head of John the Baptist,[18] displayed in such stunning and sumptuous locations.[19] Similarly, his fellow crusader Geoffrey of Villehardouin could hardly believe the number of holy relics contained in the city, exclaiming 'as many as in the rest of the world'.[20] When Geoffrey got to enter the Great Palace after the second siege of the city (April 1204), he could hardly describe the riches on display: 'there was such a store of precious things that one could not possibly count them'.[21] It was these precious relics that had made Constantinople such a spiritual powerhouse.

A much earlier (and more peaceable) foreign visitor, Liudprand of Cremona, had equally marvelled at the palace complex, subsequently gushing forth: 'The palace of Constantinople surpasses not only in beauty but also in strength any other fortification that I have set eyes on'.[22] Surrounded by its own fortification wall, the Great Palace was a vast conglomeration of domicile, devotion and defence. In its glory days, it had been a world of glitter, glorification and menace.

The crusading spirit

Today, when sensibilities and habits of thought have changed, it is no longer considered desirable that such military endeavours as the crusades be viewed in a positive light. Indeed, it would be wrong of us to write in celebration of the crusades – there were at least eight of them – or to lend support to the ideology that brought them about. That said, though the word 'crusade' signals to a western European sensibility something special about these warriors, we must refrain as far as is possible from making value judgments based on modern perspectives. The crusaders, it could be argued, were simply a product of their times, as we are the product of our own times. Or more accurately, we are products of our parents' times, and architects of our own. Therefore in mediaeval terms, rather than our own, the Latins, the self-styled soldiers of Christ, were an inextricable mixture of deep piety, vibrant fanaticism, lust for battle, and land hunger. The last of course, land hunger, was a big drive with crusaders, the way their Old Testament God intended.

With the many and various judgements of the colossal epic of the crusades we are not concerned. All that will be said is that it is important not to view the crusades (and western Christianity for that matter) through the prism of the early twenty-first century – neither religious zealot nor the imperialist image works extremely well – but to remember they were holy wars fought against those who perceived to be the external or internal foes of Latin Christendom, for the recovery of Christian property or in defence of the Roman Catholic Church. There is indeed no doubt that religion played a large part in the whole crusading enterprise. Crusaders were thus waging defensive war in order to re-establish Christendom's rightful possession of the 'patrimony of Christ', and to provide protection for persecuted Christian communities.

Furthermore, as these wars were waged on ecclesiastical authority they were, by definition, just. The First Crusade,[23] for example, was seen less as a joint religious undertaking between the Latin West and the Orthodox East and more as a pathway to the kingdom of Heaven. Salvation and the return of the Holy Land (above all, Jerusalem) was more of a forceful argument for the crusaders than was rescuing fellow Christians in the Byzantine empire from the Islamic conquests.[24] For the Church of Rome, with its dreams of world domination, religion was a means to decide who went on the kill-list. Victims would include Muslims, pagan Slavs, Mongols, Orthodox Christians (Greeks, Russians and Serbs), heretics (Cathars, Bogomils and Hussites), and of course political opponents of the papacy, especially those in Italy.

What the Church fathers say

Marcion AD 80 (80–155) had once taught that the Old Testament God was different from the God described in the New Testament. Marcion and his followers saw the Old Testament God as cruel and barbaric, whereas the New Testament God was full of love and compassion. His teachings did not necessarily catch on with many in the Early Church, Marcion himself being considered a 'heretic' by those claiming to be 'orthodox'. The theory of holy Christian violence had been formulated by intellectual Christian theologians of the fourth and fifth centuries. Its starting point was that violence was not evil but morally neutral and drew moral colouring from the *intention* of the perpetrator, which could be benign. Thus, any perpetrator of Christian violence had to have the *right intention*. He also needed a *just cause*, because violence could only be resorted to in response to a previous *injury* in the forms, for instance, of aggression, menaces, tyranny, or the invasion and occupation of land that rightly belonged to an earlier possessor.

We now think of Christ's life as a paradigm of non-violence and, indeed, early Christianity had rejected war *in toto*. The command to 'turn the other cheek', attributed to Jesus, made it extremely difficult for a Christian to be a Roman soldier at all; and there had been numerous specific instances of men who, after embracing Christianity, felt unable to serve in the Roman army any longer. Let us take just one example, Martin of Tours (d. 397). He asked to be released from the army because 'I am Christ's soldier: I am not allowed to fight'.[25] And when taxed with cowardice, he was said to have volunteered to stand in front of the battleline armed only with a cross. But then, according to his hagiographer Sulpicius Severus (d. 420), who had known the future saint personally, the enemy surrendered immediately, so that no such gesture proved necessary.

Such pacifism was not, however, due to any explicit prohibition of war in the New Testament. It derived instead from an effort to apply what was taken to be the mind of Christ. And it offered a new vision of peace that centred on well-being and security, but without physical characteristics. Christian peace was the absence not only of war but of contention. The earliest forms of Christian pacifism had as much to do with rejection of politics and worldliness and with abhorrence of violence itself. Politics only concerned itself with interest and profit in the eyes of a true follower of Christ.

Christianity in its ideas was never the art of the possible, and after Constantinus the clear separation of the Church and the world ceased to exist, and Christianity could no longer be pacifist in the same way it had been. The Church had long concerned itself with attempting to reconcile the teachings of Christ to the realities of defensive or aggressive war, and the concomitant need to define the status of the soldier in society by such means as just war theory. As a result, the Church began to focus on the evil of violence itself, and to attempt some reconciliation of Christian ideals with the necessity of using armed force in governance. The general solution, perhaps not surprisingly, appears to have been to take refuge in the theology of the Old Testament prophets rather than the much more pacific gospels.

Against this background by the early fifth century Augustine (354–430), the bishop of Hippo Regius and font of Christian authority, formulated a doctrine centred on the twin themes of permission and limitation. Now Augustine could not accurately be described as a pacifist at all. The saying 'turn the other cheek', he pointed out, can only be regarded as metaphorical, since to take it literally would be fatal to the welfare of the state. Wars were sometimes, he believed, a grim necessity, and might even be just, and in any case, he continued, Jesus never told soldiers not to serve and fight.

So, Christians, whether acting as individuals or collectively in war, could engage in violence only under circumstances that met key criteria: right authority, just cause, right intention, proportionality, last resort, and the end of peace.[26] On the whole, as he did believe that some wars at least were a necessary evil, Augustine appears to have retreated into the issue of motivation to distinguish between good and evil, just and unjust. A just ruler would only countenance warfare where it was just; what distinguished good from evil in warfare was the motivation behind it:

The real evils in war are the love of violence, revengeful cruelty, fierce and implacable enmity, wild resistance, and the lust of power, and such like; and it is generally to punish these things, when force is required to inflict the punishment, that, in obedience to God or some lawful authority, good men undertake wars, when they find themselves in such a position as regards the conduct of human affairs, that right conduct requires them to act, or to make others act in this way.[27]

Augustine's approach to thinking about war was based on his concept of the imperfection of temporal government and on his view that war – a phenomenon of an essentially sinful world – was inevitable.[28] Thus, the Augustinian dialogue rendered it right and proper for the state to direct its military power at its own subjects or at outsiders. Recourse to war – to the violent coercion of large numbers of people – was justifiable.[29]

Be all that as it may, early Christianity proved rather reluctant to accept Augustine's justification for the *legitimacy* of war under certain specified conditions. Indeed, this Augustinian moral gloss did not silence the one unending question: Can one spill blood for what is perceived as the greater good?

Some two centuries later, Isidorus of Seville (d. 636) would divide warfare into four different types: just, unjust, civil and private. The bishop's description of just war resembled that earlier proposed by Augustine, although expanding the justification for such violence: 'A just war is that which is aged in accordance with a formal declaration and is waged for the sake of recovering property seized or of driving off the enemy'.[30] Isidorus also pointedly included 'the repulsion of violence by force' as an instance of natural law.[31] By Constantinus' gift, Christianity was both officially established and *fatally* compromised.

Soldiers of Christ

Yet, the concept of Holy War went well beyond the Augustinian notion of the Just War (viz. violence can be justified as a means to secure peace, justice and order), for not only was it considered not offensive to God, but it was thought to be positively pleasing to Him. The Redeemer's power of love accordingly became the love of power. Thus, it was a militant religious faith that energized the moral of the crusaders.

Moreover, the mediaeval Christian belief system was one that had not yet matured into compassion for all, and followed an established Church policy of filling the front lines of Christianity with its most delinquent elements, a policy most exemplified by the plan of pope Urban II (r. 1088–99) for reducing unlawful violence in late eleventh-century Europe by persuading knights to serve as *milites Christi* overseas. Then, he had preached:

> You, the oppressors of children, plunderers of widows; you, guilty of homicide, of sacrilege, robbers of another's rights; you who await the pay of thieves for the shredding of Christian blood – as vultures smell fetid corpses, so do you sense battles from afar and rush to them eagerly. Verily, this is the worse way, for it is utterly removed from God! If, forsooth, you wish to be mindful of your souls, either lay down the girdle of such knighthood, or advance boldly, as

knights of Christ, and rush as quickly as you can to the defence of the Eastern Church.[32]

Private wars and feuds were the blight of Europe, which the First Crusade was subconsciously invented by the pope to relieve by providing a vent for the habitual aggression of the military élite.

For Latin Christendom the Holy War, which Urban II had successfully launched in November 1095, between the papacy and Islam, was to be a very long one. In fact, it turned out to be the longest war in history, since it did not finally end until 13 June 1798 when Napoléon, in command of a French expeditionary force destined for Egypt, captured the corsair island of Malta and so effectively brought to a close the seven centuries of Christian crusading against Muslims.

The small, rockbound island of Malta was a strange anachronism in a Europe riven by the Protestant Reformation and increasingly dominated by nation states, a republic of aristocrats whose rationale was to fight *la guerra eterna*, the eternal war against Islam. The Order of the Hospitaller Knights of Saint John had first ruled Rhodes from 1306 to 1522 before making their base on Malta. The Knights of Malta, as the Hospitaller brothers were now called, had survived a titanic Turkish siege in 1565 and inspired a remarkable victory over an Ottoman fleet at the battle of Lepanto in 1571. Their continuing existence on the island served as a long-lasting relic of the original crusading conflict. While the modern world seems to have no shortage of ideological zealots, even a cursory look at the past shows we have never suffered from such a shortage. One such group, bent on religious conversion through colonization and conquest through the steel of their swords, had once been the *raison d'être* of Hospitaller Order. However, the game changed. When maritime commerce with Muslims flourished, zeal for their massacre declined. The Holy War had long lost its thrust with the frequent use of crusade against so-called internal heretics, and lately with the rise of Protestantism. Nonetheless, the infidel, like the heretic, was still feared by Catholic Christendom as a figure of genuine menace.

The Knights of Malta themselves were the younger sons and younger brothers of the aristocratic families of Roman Catholic Europe, young men bred up to the ideals of chivalry and military glory whose promotion within the Order depended on serving four *caravans* or terms of six months in the galleys of the Order. There were normally around six or eight of these, the strongest and best equipped galleys in the Mediterranean, and they set out on two or three cruises every year searching for Turkish or Barbary shipping and especially the Ottoman-endorsed Barbary corsairs, making the occasional raids ashore to pick up unsuspecting Muslim men, women and children going about their everyday business, and providing part of any more general Catholic maritime force against the Ottomans, such as at the Christian triumph at Lepanto.

Were the Knights of Malta crusaders, or corsairs? A good case can be made for either. They were eager to swing a sword for Christianity, but anxious to make a paying business of it at the same time. So, in truce and war, the Knights of Malta passed back and forth from piracy to service under the papal banner without missing a beat or changing their style. Certainly, the career of these knights brings into sharp relief the difficulty of distinguishing between the two.

Yet, people generally get the wrong idea when you say it was a Holy War, as if two siblings from the same house join up in different churches and start fighting. It does not happen like that. A person is born into a religion. Will wars ever end? Not until the earth becomes Paradise. The origin of wars, according to its fourteenth-century codifier Honoré Bouvet (also called Bonet), lay in Lucifer's war against God, 'hence it is no great marvel if in this world there arise wars and battles since these existed first in heaven'.[33] Accordingly, Bouvet not only claims that warfare is a phenomenon beyond human nature, but also assumes that is approved by God. For this Provençal Benedictine prior the laws and customs of war, and, inevitably, of its moral and spiritual effects, could be critically analysed through a series of chaptered yes/no questions. Before that, however, Bouvet starts with an explanation of the nature of warfare and why men fight battles with each other. The essential justification for warfare is the evidence found of its origins in the Old Testament. As war is not only permitted but also ordained by divine law – 'not merely that He permits war, but that He has ordained it'[34] – Bouvet maintains that war cannot be an evil thing. On the contrary, he finds it a good thing that comes from God for the punishment of the evil. Through every discussion his governing idea was that war should not harm those who do not make war. Clearly most of his ideas proceed from Augustine and his notion that wars were approved by God as long as they were directed towards good.

Truth, whose mother is history, the rival of time. When *L'arbre des batailles*, dedicated to Charles VI of France, appeared in 1387, Bouvet did not suffer for its blunt truths. On the contrary, he was invited to the court and appointed to pensions and positions. Like other prophets of peace, his fate was to be honoured – and ignored. For us moderns Christianity might be the religion of peace, but Constantinus had chosen the Christians' deity as an Old Testament God, the 'lord and governor of battles', an aggressive and intolerant individual noted for its blood-spattered altar of absolutism. After all, had He not commanded Joshua of Navê to wage war against his enemies, and to set an ambush to defeat them? In a lightning campaign 'one and thirty kings' are slain and one Canaanite city after another falls to the Israelites. The most famous, of course, is the city of Jericho,[35] a topic that brings us back to the Byzantines.

Byzantine biblical hero

Adorning the east wall of the north entrance to the Theotokos church, monastery of Hosios Loukas at Steiris, near Delphi in central Greece, can be seen an apotropaic full-length portrait of Joshua, one of the great leaders of biblical Israel. He depicted in the rig of a tenth-century Byzantine soldier. Armed and ready for battle, Joshua is standing before the archangel Michael, of whom only the curve of a wing and tip of a sword survive. The fresco was once part of the pictorial decoration of the façade of the west wall of the original Theotokos church, founded during Hosios Loukas' lifetime, in 946.

Joshua wears the standard hip length lamellar corselet, *klibánion*, with *pteruges* at shoulder and waist, and a red sash tied round his chest, an indication of senior officer rank. He is armed with a long thrusting spear, *kontárion*, and a straight double-edged sword, *spathíon*. It will be recalled that God had given Joshua the following message: 'Do not be afraid of them; I have given them into your hand. Not one of them will be able to withstand you'.[36] The fragmentary inscription beside Joshua proclaims the archangel's presence as ἀρχιστράτηγος, or commander, of the armies of the Lord who has come 'to strengthen' Joshua, and may refer to the Byzantine re-conquest of Crete from the Arabs in 961 by the general Nikephoros Phokas (soon to be the emperor, Nikephoros II Phokas). According to the *Vita* of Hosios Loukas (896–953) this victory had been prophesied by him nineteen years before the actual event.[37]

Whether or not Hosios Loukas actually made such a prophecy concerning the island of Crete is not really of great importance here. What is important, however, is that a contemporary text made the connection between the holy man, his monastery and the Byzantine victory on Crete. The island of Crete had been lost to the empire in 827, following the appearance in Mediterranean waters of a fleet carrying 10,000 Muslim warriors who had first been expelled from al-Andalus and some years later from Alexandria, which they had captured in 818. Once more on the loose in the Mediterranean, they seized Byzantine Crete. After its seizure, the island served as a base for constant raids along the shores of the eastern Mediterranean. No Christian seaside settlement was safe from these swift Saracen corsairs; many Aegean islands were taken over or abandoned. Perhaps the worst of these disasters was the sack of Thessaloniki, the second city of the empire, in the summer of 904. The pirates remained in the city for ten days, slaughtering its inhabitants and pillaging.[38] Thousands of prisoners – around 22,000 in all, mostly youths – were crammed onto boats and carried off to the slave markets of Crete and Tarsus.[39]

The military enterprise headed by Nikephoros Phokas in the summer of 960 was the eighth such attempt to retake Crete since the island's loss to the empire. In his retelling of the Nikephoros' campaign, John Skylitzes says for 'seven months in all he employed every kind of siege engine' for besieging the towns of this island.[40] In the Madrid manuscript of the *Synopsis historiôn* there is an illumination that presents a portrayal of Nikephoros' fleet and siege camp outside the capital of the Emirate of Crete, *rabd al-handaq* – the Arabic means 'castle of the ditch', which was hellenized as *Khándax*, while in the West it was known as Candia; today, Herakleion.[41] This illumination ties in tidily with what Leo Diakonos has to say about this naval expedition. A contemporary of these Cretan events, he says Nikephoros arrived at Crete, used ramps to disembark fully armoured cavalry, the *katáphraktoi*, and successfully drove the Arab defenders back into the fortifications of *Khándax*. He then pitched camp and anchored his ships in a safe harbour.[42]

One of the best literary sources for the history of Byzantine warfare in the second half of the tenth century must be Leo Diakonos, who wrote a narrative in ten books of the reigns of Romanos II (r. 959–63), Nikephoros II Phokas (r. 963–9), and John I Tzimiskès (r. 969–76), with useful digressions into the reign of Basil II (r. 976–1025). Leo was ordained a deacon sometime after 970, and he became a member of the palace clergy after Basil's accession to the throne. He certainly participated (perhaps as a member of the imperial retinue) in the disastrous Bulgarian campaign of 986, at which time he narrowly escaped being captured or killed by the enemy during the battle of Trajan's Gate.[43] There is no suggestion in the *Historia* as we have it that Leo lived beyond the year 1000. At any rate, even as a man of the cloth Leo definitely had firsthand experience of Byzantine warfare and obviously knew and admired our man Nikephoros Phokas.

A general's general – gifted in the military arts, tireless, fearless, physically strong, highly intelligent and above all, deeply religious – Nikephoros Phokas embraced a monastic lifestyle, associating in his off-duty hours with no one but holy men, and was a strict vegetarian to boot. Even at war Nikephoros went into battle with the prayers and the presence of monks. This deeply spiritual, monk-loving general was responsible for the establishment of organized monasticism on the northern Aegean peninsula of Mount Athos, still home to nearly three dozen Orthodox monasteries where he is memorialized as a saint by the monks. In his lifetime he certainly proved himself worthy of his name (literally, 'bringer of victory' in Greek) in battle with Muslims.

In his eulogy to the general, Leo Diakonos describes him 'as strict and unbending in his prayers and all-night standing vigils to God, [keeping] his mind un-distracted during the singing of hymns, never letting it wander off to worldly thoughts'.[44] Despite the modern scepticism this panegyric comment invites, it is clear that Nikephoros Phokas embodied the distinctly Byzantine fusion of war and religion: a monkish ascetic with a flair for fighting. It is George Kedrenos who says that just before the final assault in March 961 this pious Christian soldier invoked the Virgin Mary (as Theotokos), along with the holy warriors and the ἀρχιστράτηγος Michael, supplicating all these glorious saints and Christ with them to make the towers and walls of *Khándax* fall down as formerly those of Jericho crumbled before Joshua.[45] Thus, this contemporary Joshua fresco may be regarded as a prayer of thanks for the Cretan victory over the Arab 'infidel', asserting the biblical parallel of Joshua's divinely aided conquest of Canaan.

The Joshua fresco is remarkably similar in style to manuscript illustrations on the Joshua Roll, a parchment scroll depicting narrative events from Joshua's conquest of Canaan. It is now housed in the Vatican Library and dates from exactly the same period as the Hosios Loukas fresco. The royal theme of conquering Joshua would undoubtedly have appealed to the Macedonian dynasty, fighting as it was to push back the Arabs and the Bulghars and regain lost lands. Only discovered in 1964, today the fresco appears to be freshly painted, for it was covered shortly after completion with marble panels of the newly constructed interlocking, and adjoining the *katholicon*, the main church of the monastery.

Chapter 19

Last Crusade

We may have forgotten the Ottoman empire's glory days, but by the time of the Ottoman siege of 1422, a fight that was to be the dress rehearsal for the fatal siege of 1453, the Turks had their own artillery train. In an eyewitness source covering the 1422 siege, John Kananos describes how the Turks used falcons (short, stout cannons firing a one-kilogram shot) along with other cannons and the usual panoply of siege warfare, towers and tortoises.[1] They also turned their hand to the time-honoured means of overcoming fortifications, mining.[2] The Byzantine defenders had cannon too,[3] so the Turkish besiegers built barricades in order 'to receive the arrows from the bows and crossbows of the Romans and the stones from their bombards'.[4]

It is important to understand that the besieged Byzantines had roughly the same level of technology as the besieging Ottomans. Indeed, it is strangely true that artillery contributed perhaps more to the defence of cities than it did to their assault. Cannons permanently mounted on the walls of a city could be supplied much more efficiently than the cannons of the besiegers hauled up into temporary emplacements from many kilometres away. Yet, the eventual lifting of the 1422 siege was credited not to the success of the wall-mounted Byzantine artillery, but to the miraculous intervention of the Virgin Mary, who appeared on the walls of the city and inspired the defenders.

Gratitude to the Virgin is described by John Kananos in his colourful and dramatic portrayal of the 1422 siege. On that occasion she had appeared on the walls during an attack, and greatly inspired the defenders:

The Romans though exhausted from fatigue, leapt and were glad. They clapped their hands and rendered special thanks to God. They shouted hymns to the Most Holy Virgin,[5] glorifying her from the depths of their hearts, saying, 'This is in truth a rich, celebrated, memorable, extraordinary and remarkable miracle worthy of admiration'.[6]

The miracle was even confirmed by the enemy, every Turkish contingent even swearing under oath they had seen a mysterious woman clad in purple robes on the city battlements:

The army of the Turks confirmed by an oath sworn to the Mersaita [the *sufic* sheikh],[7] spoken of by all at the hour of battle, that on arriving at the walls of the city with an irresistible force to scale them and pursue the Romans and conquer the city, they saw a woman dressed in purple robes walking on the ramparts of the outer fortifications, and having seen her shudders and fright immediately entered everybody's soul. So because of the woman fear overtook them and the city was liberated.[8]

For the Constantinopolitans, this was Christianity prevailing over Islam; it was their God and their Theotokos who had saved their city. Indeed, many of them considered the Virgin Mary to be their go-between with her Son and the Almighty. The holy Mother of God would never allow a city dedicated to her to fall into infidel hands. There remained to that city, however, only thirty years of continued Christian existence before it fell to the Ottoman Turk, an event that would bring an end to the millennial empire of Byzantium.

Osman's dream

The people known as the Ottomans (or Ottoman Turks) were the last and destined to be the most enduring wave of warrior nomads who had swept across the long horizons of the Eurasian steppes. They had emerged sometime in the mid-thirteenth century as a Turkic tribal group of nomadic pastoralists under the leadership of a chieftain called Ertuğrul Bey (d. 1281). His son, Osman Ghazi (r. 1281–1326, sultan from 1299), established the Osmanlı dynasty (the Europeans corrupted the name to Ottoman) that centred on the borders lands stretching eastwards from the Bithynian Olympus. Originally, the Ottomans had been settled on the Anatolian shores of the Black Sea as vassals of the preceding Seljuq Turks and *ğazis*, meaning roughly 'fighters for the faith', in which capacity they acted as guardians of the Seljuq frontier in that region. The chronic warfare in Anatolia along the frontiers of the Christian and Muslim dominions was an affair of raids and counter-raids, an occupation much to the liking of these horse warriors. When the Seljuq empire crumbled under the Mongol invasions, the hard fighting bands of the border warlord Osman declared their independence of Seljuq overlordship, and rose on the ruins of their predecessors.

The general geography and environment of northern Anatolia had important effects on the Ottoman military. It was a suitable place for agricultural and semi-nomadic lifestyles but not suitable for genuine nomadic life. The available pastoral fields were unable to accommodate and feed the many horses required by a genuine nomadic army, and some of the followers of Osman Ghazi were already sedentary or semi-nomadic people. Moreover, the religious scholars and former officials of the

Seljuqs brought sedentary traditions with them, and coexistence and cohabitation with the Byzantine villages and towns also had their affect upon the newcomers. Consequently, more and more of the warrior nomads began to settle and change their lifestyle drastically, which also affected the military and political system.

In twenty-five years, with all the brutal energy of a people on the way up, the Ottomans conquered key cities and large tracts of Anatolia and mastered the Asiatic shore of the thin blue straits separating Asia from Europe. Across the straits on the European side stood Constantinople, capital of what was left of the Byzantine empire. Pushed back into Europe, it was a shrunken scrap of former splendour, its naval and commercial supremacy lost to the Genoese and the Venetians, its social fabric weakened by the Black Death, economic disruptions, religious dissent, peripheral wars and ferocious feuds around the throne. Eventually, these dynastic feuds were to provide the opening through which the Ottoman Turks entered Europe.

It was not all plain sailing, however. In 1304 the Catalan Company, which the emperor Andronikos II Palaiologos (r. 1282–1328, d. 1332) had hired the previous year used their warlike efficiency to curtail the rising power of the Ottomans. The Catalans were to prove their worth more than once, defeating the Ottomans in a number of engagements, subsequently driving back Osman from the western Anatolian littoral. But even defeat turned into gain when a suspicious Andronikos had Rutger von Blum (better known as Roger de Flor), the disgraced Knights Templar who led the Catalans, murdered on 5 April 1305.[9] As we might expect, the enraged mercenaries turned on their perfidious employer. What is unexpected, however, by doing so they dragged the Byzantines into a decade of dynastic civil war. Their rugged homelands had made them hardy warriors, patient of climate and privation, and it was above all their prowess as agile foot soldiers that made them such devilish opponents. The wandering Catalan mercenaries went on to terrorize the inhabitants of central Greece, and even to rule Athens from 1311 to 1388. During those years of civil war not only did numbers of Ottoman horse warriors, hired either by the embattled emperor or by the rampaging Catalans, move to and fro across the Hellespont (Dardanelles), but Osman was able to consolidate his hold on northern Anatolia as far as the Sea of Marmara.

As a consequence, the Byzantines increasingly depended on the services of Ottoman mercenaries for their own internecine fights and even against their enemies to the northwest, the Serbians and the Bulgarians. They initially hired private bands, but after the 1320s they began to deal directly with leaders of the Anatolian emirates, including the Ottoman sultan whose warriors began to repeatedly appear as a mercenary presence in the Byzantine army after 1345. In this process Ottoman warriors learned the weakness of the Byzantines and the Balkan states and became familiar with the terrain. Moreover, whatever the outcome of the particular campaign, the mercenaries looted and destroyed everything, without regard to friend or foe, and in this way contributed greatly to the internal unrest of the Balkan peninsula.

In 1321 another family dispute broke out in Constantinople, causing a rift between Andronikos II and his grandson, also named Andronikos. Subsequently, when the emperor attempted to increase the size of his army, and imposed taxes upon the Byzantine nobility in order to pay for that expansion, he forfeited much support. The grandson proclaimed himself Andronikos III Palaiologos (r. 1328–41), which resulted in open warfare when the new emperor attempted to enter Constantinople and was repulsed. Undaunted, the younger Andronikos instead seized the empire's second city, Thessaloniki. Meanwhile, most of the Byzantine forces in Europe declared for the grandson, and in May 1328 he finally entered Constantinople and forced the abdication of his grandfather.

Andronikos III fought successfully against the Ottoman Turks, Serbs, Genoese, and Bulghars. He also finally defeated the Despotate of Epeiros, reintegrating it into the empire in 1339, and two years later managed to bring to heel the Frankish principalities that still clung to parts of the Peloponnesus. He also took steps to reattach the small but strategically important state of Trebizond to the empire. He died suddenly in 1341, leaving behind as heir his nine-year-old son John, proposing in his will that the grand domestic (in effect the commander-in-chief) John Kantakouzenos, a competent soldier and trusted confident, be made regent. Although Kantakouzenos was a good friend of the late emperor, he had made a bunch of powerful enemies in the court, including Andronikos' widow the empress Anna of Savoy (d. 1365), and the patriarch of Constantinople John XIV Kalekas (r. 1334–47). Kantakouzenos thus found it expedient to decline an offer made by the grand admiral of the imperial navy, the *megas doux* Alexios Apokaukos (d. 1345), to become co-emperor with John V Palaiologos (r. 1341–91), but he did assume the title of regent. Before he could effectively assume his regency, however, his opponents accused him of treason. Proscribed as an enemy of the state and the church, Kantakouzenos fled in fear of his life to Serbia. It was here that he raised the banner of revolt and planned his comeback. By 1343, with Serbian support, Kantakouzenos overran most of Epeiros, and began to advance into Thrace, besieging Thessaloniki as he did so. By the following year, he held most of Thrace. In 1345 he took Adrianople. The Serbs, in the meantime, had withdrawn their support for Kantakouzenos, who now looked elsewhere for aid to continue his struggle against Constantinople.

Ruin of empire

The Ottoman empire really starts with Osman, but it was his eldest son, Orhan Ghazi (r. 1326–59), who took the city of Bursa, as the Turks called Prusa (Gr. *Proûsa*), set on the northern slopes of the Bithynian Olympus and a few kilometres from the Sea of Marmara, and then in 1329 the historic city of Nicaea, which like Prusa had been isolated for years, surrendered to him. Orhan's next target was the seaport of Nicomedia. It resisted him for nine years, receiving supplies and reinforcements by sea. But when he managed the blockade the narrow gulf on which it stood, it was forced to capitulate in 1337. With Nicomedia in his hands, the sultan, as Orhan now officially styled himself, was able to command all the hinterland up to the Bosporus. In 1346 Orhan personally led his warriors across the Hellespont into Europe, establishing the Ottoman dynasty as a force to be reckoned with. In 1353 Orhan seized Gallipoli, the key of the Hellespont, and in so doing entered Europe for good. Although the Byzantines were to regain Gallipoli with the aid of count Amadeus VI of Savoy (nephew of Anna of Savoy) in 1366, by then it was far too late to turn back the Ottomans, who had already established a strong foothold in Thrace. Eleven years later, the Byzantines would abandon Gallipoli without a fight.

In Constantinople, now a sad and lonely city, they could hear the sound of the 'infidel' pounding on the gates. Orhan had taken full advantage of the current civil war in Byzantium, offering his assistance to John Kantakouzenos and marrying his daughter Theodora Kantakouzene in a Muslim ceremony, thus setting up an excellent excuse for invading the fast shrinking empire. Like other great actors in history, Kantakouzenos had no vision of the consequences inherent in his acts. Having been deposed as regent for John V Palaiologos, the child heir to the throne, for near six years Kantakouzenos fought his way back to power, the Bulgarians, the Serbians, and the Turks 'involved on both sides as the instruments of private ambition and the common ruin'.[10] In 1345 the assassination of the ambitious Apokaukos, whose talents and ruthlessness alone upheld the cause of the young emperor, tipped the scales in Kantakouzenos' favour. Two years later he was able to reach an agreement with the surviving supporters of John V, declaring himself joint – in reality, rival – emperor as John VI (r. 1347–54).

It was though these years of civil war that he regained and then maintained his hold by purchasing the services of the hardy, and now disciplined Ottoman forces. When Orhan crossed the straits it was, in Gibbon's knell, 'the last and fatal stroke in the fall of the ancient Roman empire'.[11] Some years later, when he was blamed for having brought the Ottoman Turks into the empire and so forced to abdicate, the once grand domestic became a monk and retired to write in cloistered calm a chronicle of the times he had done so much to embroil, the resulting four-volume

Historia serving 'not a confession, but an apology, of the life of an ambitious statesman'.[12] Kantakouzenos died in 1383 at Mistra aged eighty-eight.

Incurable civil discord at Constantinople gave the Ottomans the means to exploit their gateway at Gallipoli. Upon Kantakouzenos' abdication, his former ward, John Palaiologos, regained the throne (which accounts for the strange succession of John VI by John V) only to plunge into a vicious family struggle in which sons and grandson, uncle and nephew over the next thirty-five years deposed, imprisoned, tortured, and replaced one another in various combinations with the sultan Murad I (r. 1362–89), who gladly assisted the Palaiologi toward their mutual destruction. John V Palaiologos reigned for fifty years, but he was dethroned no fewer than three times, once by his father-in-law, once by his son, and once by his grandson, though in the end he did manage to die on the throne. While the Byzantines twisted and grappled in internal feuds, in 1365 Murad shifted his capital from Bursa to Adrianople (Edirne), on the border between Thrace and Bulgaria and some 180 kilometres inside Europe. Constantinople was entirely encircled by his dominions.

The Ottoman dynasty continued to steadily expand under the wily Murad and his son Bayezit I (r. 1389–1403), the latter reputedly by his contemporaries to be bold, enterprising and avid for war, and nicknamed *Yıldırım*, the Thunderbolt, for the rapidity of his strikes. Chosen sultan on the battlefield of Kosovo Polje – his father had been assassinated by a dying Serb after his victory – he began his reign by strangling his brother with a silken bowstring, and proceeded at once to the business of shaking the Byzantine throne by assisting John VII Palaiologos (r. 1390, d. 1408) to overthrow his grandfather. When John in turn was overthrown by his uncle, Manuel II Palaiologos (r. 1391–1425), Bayezit blockaded Constantinople for seven years.

This blockade of Constantinople was first interrupted by the Crusade of Nikopolis in 1396, the last crusade of any consequence in the mediaeval period, and then terminated due to the battle of Ankara (28 July 1402). It was here that Timur-i-Lenk (1336–1405), the little lame man known in English drama as Tamburlaine,[13] stole the great sultan's thunder when he crushed his army and took Beyazit captive. One of those sudden conquerors who flash up from time to time in steppe history, Timur had turned Central Asia into the wasteland it has been for the past few centuries, levelling towns, destroying irrigation systems, and erecting his trademark pyramid of skulls; his legacy was a single exquisite city, the fabled oasis of Samarkand. Before he turned his baleful attention on the Ottoman Turks he had just completed the conquest of Iran, so becoming the belligerent neighbour of their empire. Apparently kept in a wagon fitted with iron bars, Bayezit was dragged along the Mongol path of conquest until this redoubtable Ottoman sultan died of misery and shame in March of the following year. This is the Beyazit who Christopher

Marlowe makes introduce himself as the Turkish emperor: 'Dread Lord of Affrike, Europe and Asia, / Great King and conqueror of Grecia, / The Ocean, Terrene, and the cole-blacke sea, / The high and highest Monarke of the world'.[14] But a few scenes later we find Tamburlaine entering in triumph and 'two Moores drawing Bajazeth in his cage, and his wife following him'.[15] The iron cage is almost certainly a fable.

Whereas the vast empire of Timur proved a short-lived creation, the Ottomans revived to create a state that endured into the twentieth century. Initially, however, the sons of Bayezit immediately engaged in a civil war, and the empire unofficially divided into three parts. The interregnum period continued for twelve years with vicious internecine fighting within the house of Osman until Mehmet I (r. 1413–21) re-established the stability and unity of the empire. Mehmet, whom his contemporaries surnamed *Çelebi*, a word best translated here as 'gentleman', had shown himself a fine warrior but was by temperament a man of peace. In this respect he remained all his life on terms of cordial friendship with Manuel II Palaiologos. Apart from two inconclusive wars, one with Venice in 1416 and the one with Hungary in 1419, Mehmet spent most of his time consolidating his empire and beautifying his cities. The exquisite *Yeşil Cami*, Green Mosque, at Bursa is a lasting memorial to this serene and cultivated potentate. The mosque got its name from the wonderful green tiles that at one time covered the dome and tops of the minarets, and it shows clearly the sophistication and beauty of Ottoman architecture before it was exposed to the influences of Byzantine Constantinople. The seventeen-century Ottoman traveller and chronicler Evliya Çelebi compared them to emeralds sparkling in the sunlight.[16] Such sophistication surely earns Mehmet a place in history as a patron of the arts if not as a conqueror.

Under Murad II (r. 1421–44, 1446–51) the dynasty prospered, the sultan regaining most of the Anatolian territory lost after the Ankara *débâcle* and undertaking a period of expansion in the Balkans (to be mentioned presently). Obviously, the latter enterprise had been at the expense of the Byzantine empire, which had been whittled down to Constantinople, ruled by Constantinus XI Palaiologos, and the Morea, under his feuding brothers, Thomas and Demetrios. However, Murad's attempt to conquer Constantinople, as we discussed above, ended in failure. Nonetheless, it appears the sultan may have considered another crack at the city. In his *Epistola de crudelitate Tucarum*, dated from Constantinople in December 1438, the Franciscan friar Bartholomaeus gives a long and harrowing description of the devastation caused by the Ottomans, and the sufferings of Christian captives, and the iniquities of Christian slave dealers. He then gives a warning that Murad is preparing an attack on Constantinople for the following year.[17] The warning turned out to be premature.

Hungarian hope

A few major battles and several small campaigns in a time span of only thirteen years shaped the destiny of the Balkans and Europe forever. One of these was one of those milestones in history, the fall of Constantinople in 1453.

By the middle of the fifteenth century, it had become clear that help had to be provided, and the Byzantines asked for it. The condition imposed by western Christendom was to reunite the churches. At the Synod of Ferrara in 1438 (the following year it moved to Florence), under the emperor John VIII Palaiologos (r. 1425–48), a reluctant Byzantine delegation agreed to the Union, although the people, monks and lesser clergy in Constantinople, proud of their faith and their traditions, bitterly disagreed. It was to isolate the Constantinopolitans from the higher echelons of the Church and the court more than any other policy. Officially, however, the Union had been proclaimed, so the West had to provide military help. The Franciscan friar Bartholomaeus de Jano, so named from his birthplace, Giano near Spoleto, was one of the papal envoys employed by pope Eugenius IV (r. 1431–47) in the matter of the Union. He accompanied the emperor to Ferrara, and returned to Constantinople.

Eugenius in Rome called for a crusade in 1440. As many western knights and rulers of western Europe were emphasizing their deep faith and will to wage holy war, there would, theoretically, be no problem to gather a large army in order to defeat the Ottomans in the Balkans and throw them back over the Hellespont into Asia, as everyone bragged. In reality, France and England were busy fighting each other – as so often before – Spain was busy fighting the Moors in the Iberian peninsula, the jealous and distracted states of Italy fought each other, and the German states had other problems. All the powers of western Europe were at war. Besides, the memory of the crushing defeat of the crusader army at Nikopolis in 1396 was still alive in the minds of many.

Thus, only the eastern countries remained on the frontline against the Turks. Poland, although involved in the struggle against the Teutonic Order, was directly interested in keeping the Ottoman Turks at bay and would send troops. The two Romanian principalities, Moldavia and Wallachia, could provide limited help, but were unreliable, and had their own goals. Also, they too were Orthodox, and a huge western army approaching their territories might have been regarded as being more dangerous than the Muslim Turks, who only wanted some loot and the annual tribute. The only state to actually combat the Ottomans was the Hungarian kingdom. It had the longest border with the Ottoman empire and was the most directly threatened. Luckily, it held a good chain of fortifications in the south, and especially Belgrade, the mighty fortress on at the confluence of the Danube and the Sava, which could resist an Ottoman invasion, although raids could simply bypass them. To the south lay Serbia, since Kosovo the loyal Ottoman subject. So Hungry stood virtually alone in the path of the Ottomans.

The Hungarian commander was a talented and battle hardened warlord of Wallachian origin, János Hunyadi of Transylvania (d. 1456). A wise military man, he was the first European soldier who understood the inherent weakness of the Ottoman military at the operational and tactical levels. He launched attacks on the European domains of the Ottomans using a window of opportunity created by the seasonal nature of the Ottoman campaigns and demobilization. In brief, geography and political centralization limited Ottoman expansion. The sultan's personal household troops, the *kapıkulu*, were the foundation of his invincibility, and he could only fight on one front. As his dominions grew, the campaigning season, when grass was available, grew shorter.

Hunyadi, however, earned his battlefield fame by employing the Hussite *hradba vozova*, war wagons, widely against Ottoman cavalry charges. The *wagenburg* or wagon fortress, which had been perfected by the Hussites in Bohemia during the Hussite wars (1419–36), was a defensive arrangement of war wagons chained together. The Hussites under Ján Žižka (d. 1424) had manned their wagons with some twenty crossbowmen and handgunners per wagon, and also protected them against cavalry assault by heavy wooden shielding and light bombards. According to a Czech mercenary who participated in the 1443 campaign, Hunyadi had 600 of these war wagons.[18] These mobile fortresses made of war wagons equipped with bombards and handguns proved very effective against the lightly armoured Ottoman horsemen and their arrow showers. The presence of heavily armoured foot soldiers strengthened the Christian battle formations, but even the smart Hunyadi underestimated the pragmatism and adaptability of the Ottomans. Consequently, he was to suffer two crushing defeats at their hands.

The anti-Ottoman league at this time was under the official command of Władysław III, the young king of Poland (also Ulászló I of Hungary), but Hunyadi acted as *de facto* commander. Their army consisted of Hungarians, Poles and Wallachians, the latter contingent led by Micrea II, the eldest son of Vlad II Dracul. In the previous year the Christian assault had fallen victim to the scorched earth policy of the Ottomans and the cold weather, which proved to be a fiercer enemy than the Ottomans. So this time they tried to follow rivers in order to have secure logistical support. The Byzantines, officially allies of the Hungarians, failed to send them information about the movements of the Ottoman army. The meeting at Varna, on the shores of the Black Sea, between the Christians and Ottoman Turks was a total surprise for the former.

Murad II had marched directly to Varna since he had received good intelligence about the plans of the Hungarians from some captured cavalrymen. Arriving near Varna on 10 November 1444, he manoeuvred his troops to get between the

Christians and their possible line of retreat. Thus, he left them no choice but to fight. Murad and his commanders had learned the hard way that they somehow had to lure the enemy into an attack by abandoning their defensive superiority.

Both Ottoman wings attacked but collapsed against the well-entrenched, heavily armoured Christians. They then conducted a hasty retreat that provoked the enemy centre to follow. Władysław now decided that 'it was fit for a king to fight as a king'.[19] Thus, Władysław led the attack, which crashed headlong into the Janissaries standing firm behind their sharpened stakes and ditches. After a bitter struggle the Janissaries managed to encircle the enemy command group and cut down the horse of Władysław. Unhorsed, the king's head was cut off by a veteran soldier. It was raised at once on the tip of a spear for all to see. The death of the valiant young king and the sudden return of the fleeing Ottoman horsemen caused panic and rout. Hunyadi managed to escape, but many of his comrades were not so fortunate.

Varna had even greater political consequences than what the losses would indicate. It virtually ensured Ottoman domination of most of the Balkans and the eventual fall of Constantinople. If there ever was a chance to save the Byzantine capital from Ottoman conquest, it was at Varna. After that, it was only a matter of time for the Queen of Cities to fall to the Ottoman Turks.

The second encounter took place on the famous battlefield of Kosovo. Hunyadi managed to bring together his old allies and some western mercenaries, including Czech and German handgunners, though official western support was decidedly lacking. The Ottoman army met the Christians on their way to join forces with their Albanian ally Skanderbeg (George Kastriota) on 17 October 1448. This time the battlefield roles were reversed. The Ottoman army remained on the defensive behind a line of stakes and a ditch that covered its entire front. In addition to this defensive measure, the centre, which included the famed (and feared) Janissaries, employed the same kind of war wagons that Hunyadi was renowned for. In fact, the Ottomans established a specialized military unit to man war wagons equipped with light bombards, *Top Arabacıları Ocağı*. The *tabur*, as the Ottomans called it, after the term *szekér tábor*, the Hungarian name for *wagenburg*, followed the Hussite model but were entirely used for static defence. They did, however, refine their wagons by including 'ultra light' guns for the crews. The *tabur* made an ideal platform for these oversized handguns as their long loading times made them too vulnerable out on the open battlefield. Their heavy shot and 'blunderbuss' close range blasts made them defences to be feared.

The first day of the battle was spent with the two sides starting the game by skirmishing. On the second day Hunyadi mainly attacked the left wing of the Ottomans without achieving much success. Next, his inspired night attack against the Ottoman centre was shattered against the war wagons. The Ottoman wings were pulled back as if to reorganize after the previous day's attacks, and the centre was left alone on its original position as a ruse to lure the enemy. Hunyadi tried his chances and attacked. The concealed wings of the Ottoman army encircled the attackers, and the Wallachians and Serbians switched sides at this crucial moment. Most of the Christian forces were annihilated and the survivors took refuge in their fortified camp. The next day Ottoman units captured the camp easily, but discovered that their archenemy Hunyadi had already made good his escape.

The Ottomans had defeated not simply an ordinary commander but one of the best practitioners of tactics of the age. Indeed, the second battle of Kosovo convinced the Europeans of the invincibility of Ottoman military might and of the impossibility of recapturing the Balkans. From now on all their efforts would focus on checking the Ottoman advance into central Europe. Constantinople was now isolated and vulnerable, and soon only its walls would delimit the frontiers of the once mighty empire. Second Kosovo was also a turning point for the Ottoman military. This was the first time that the Ottomans employed up-to-date battle tactics, such as war wagons and firearms, on a large scale while ingeniously combining them with their traditional cavalry tactics. Had it not been for the advent of gunpowder and cannons the massive land walls of Constantinople might never have been breached. At Second Kosovo a young Mehmet had faced battle for the first time, but it was to be at the siege of Constantinople where Mehmet would win his 'spurs' as a sultan. Yet, the victory at Kosovo would have alerted him to the value of the different types of gunpowder weapons. After all, Mehmet was a young man of great curiosity and intelligence.

Chapter 20

The Fall

The sultan Mehmet II (r. 1444–6, 1451–81) devoted his career to incessant military activity and empire building, which deservedly earned for him the title *Fatih*, the Conqueror, and it was his conquest of Constantinople that set the tone for his thirty-year reign. Within two years of his (second) accession Mehmet's men were sniffing gunpowder. The significant date to be remembered here of course is 1453, when his cannons, belching fire and destruction, had breached the Theodosian walls of the Queen of Cities and brought about the final extinction of the Christian Roman empire. Those massive machicolated land walls had stood for a thousand years and had resisted more than one siege in the past – though that was before the days of such artillery as Mehmet now commanded.

On the Eurasian steppes, men learned to ride, hunt and shoot. Mounted on tough, shaggy steppe ponies, they were the perfect material to be moulded into an army with exception mobility and flexibility. But the Ottoman Turks had gone well beyond the usual pattern of mixing nomadic and sedentary troop types. One hundred and fifty or so years in Anatolia and endless encounters with the Byzantines and others had put their armies on the leading edge of gunpowder technology as well, which was to play an important rôle at the siege of Constantinople.[1] E.C. Antoche underlines the speed with which the Ottomans created an artillery train.[2] They had virtually no gunpowder weapons at the battle in Varna in 1444, but four years later they won a victory over the Hungarians at Second Kosovo thanks in large measure to their field artillery.

Devil's distillate

A deeply rooted misconception in the West holds that the Chinese never used gunpowder for war, that they employed one of the most potent inventions in the history of humankind for idle amusement and festive fireworks. This received wisdom is false. One of the earliest accounts of gunpowder appeared during the Song dynasty of China. The suitably entitled *Wujing Zongyao* ('Collection of the Most Important Military Techniques'), a massive military encyclopaedia compiled in 1044 at imperial behest, contains two practical prescriptions for making *huo yao*, 'fire drug'.[3] Both mixtures were low in saltpetre (about 55 per cent), which meant that they relied on rapid combustion, not explosion, for their effects, and at this stage gunpowder was being employed only in the form of incendiary balls flung from mangonels. Even so, a hissing, fire-spurting sphere made a fearsome weapon. Fire starting was an obvious jumping-off point for gunpowder technology and such uses for this unconventional weaponry fit neatly into the long Chinese tradition of incendiary warfare.

So European knowledge of gunpowder originated in China, though the route and date of this transfer is not known. We do know, however, that one of the earliest European written references to gunpowder is found in the *Opus Majus* from 1267, a universal scientific treatise written by the English theologian, philosopher and Franciscan friar Roger Bacon (d. 1292). Therein Bacon writes of the:

[T]oy of children which is made in many parts of the world, namely an instrument as large as a human thumb. From the force of the salt called saltpetre such a horrible sound is produced with the bursting of so small a thing, namely a small piece of parchment that we perceive it exceeds the roar of sharp thunder, and the flash exceeds the greatest brilliancy of the lightning accompanying the thunder.[4]

Bacon was of the conviction that the mysticism of Christianity could be supported by natural sciences and vice versa. As for the oldest known written recipes for gunpowder in Europe, these were jotted down in that aforementioned how-to manual entitled *Liber ignium ad comburendos hostes* by the alchemist calling himself Marcus Græcus.[5] 'Another flying fire is made from saltpetre (*sal petrosus*), sulphur and charcoal from grape wood or willow', the mysterious alchemist informs his readers in one of his recipes, giving proportions that amount to nine parts of saltpetre, three parts of charcoal and one part of sulphur, which would have formed a relatively strong and explosive powder.[6]

A few words about the mysteries of combustion are warranted. Briefly, things 'burn' or are oxidized when a material (fuel) is raised to the ignition point in the presence of oxygen so that combustion occurs, releasing heat, gas, particles, and light. Substances vary in their combustibility, the temperature at which the reaction becomes self-sustaining as the heat being released adequately warms the contiguous material. Substances that burn extremely rapidly but without exploding when unconfined, often with sparking, hissing, and the evolution of large quantities of gas, are said to deflagrate. Because of the rapidity of the pressure wave front and high temperatures generated, such substances provide ideal materials for incendiary warfare. Now, all incendiary materials require an oxidizing agent, a chemical that emits oxygen when heated. Saltpetre, otherwise known as potassium nitrate (KNO_3) or nitre, is one such chemical, for as it burns it releases virgin oxygen. The oxygen accelerates the process of deflagration. In the nitrate radical $(-NO_3)$ that is the crux of saltpetre; three oxygen atoms are fastened to one of nitrogen. When exposed to heat of 335°C, the normally stable salt breaks down, letting loose the oxygen atoms that had been bound up with the nitrogen. This property makes saltpetre the key ingredient of gunpowder.

The remarkable mixture known as gunpowder deflagrates when all the components are present in less than the proper portions, seventy-five parts saltpetre to fifteen parts sulphur to ten parts charcoal, with the type of charcoal surprisingly affecting the burn rate (willow or alder being preferred). Even when perfectly balanced, only weak explosive effects will be achieved unless the mixture has undergone such a thorough process of pre-grinding, sifting, premixing, mixing, wetting, pressing or rolling, and finally grinding that a uniform, fine powder with high surface area results whose combustion properties are said to approach those of a compound rather than a composite mixture. Centuries of painful experience and experimentation were required to evolve the craft knowledge and production techniques necessary to maximize gunpowder's explosiveness, enabling it to provide the required force for cannons and handguns.

Slow beginnings

The innovation responsible for challenging and finally transforming mediaeval warfare practices was gunpowder, which opened up the way for new, more powerful types of weapon, capable of achieving a far more devastating impact than that of their traditional counterparts. Though it must be emphasized that although as a propelling agent gunpowder was far superior to the mechanical forces of tension, twisting and gravity on which the firing of traditional weapons had relied, neither cannon nor handgun achieved the instant success that might have been expected, taking quite some time to become established as serious rivals to the mechanical weapons that they finally displaced. Thus, between the first recorded appearance of cannon in Europe during the siege of La Réole in September 1324,[7] and the last reference to a counterweight war machine during the siege of the Aztec capital Tenochtitlán in May to August 1521,[8] these two types of artillery existed side by side as a result of the slow development of the former, and the technical excellence of the latter.

In hindsight it is hardly surprising that cannons had made a very hesitant and relatively insignificant entrance upon the battlefield. Gunpowder was still sufficiently awe-inspiring to dominate the military imagination, while the handling of this volatile and unpredictable material must have been extremely dangerous in these pioneering days. Furthermore, gunners were often of rough origins. Miguel de Cervantes Saavedra (1547–1616) suffered three gunshot wounds at the great naval engagement of Lepanto, 7 October 1571, one of which permanently maimed his left hand. When he wrote some thirty years later, he spoke through the character of Don Quixote his own indictment on gunpowder: 'Happy were those blessed times that lacked the horrifying fury of the diabolical instruments of artillery, whose inventor, in my opinion, is in hell, receiving the reward for his accursed invention, which allows an ignoble and cowardly hand to take the life of a valiant knight...'[9] All in all, this made the practice of gunnery a jealously kept secret of an exclusive craft. More to the point, the cannons of the age had virtually no tactical mobility, their rate of fire was exceptionally slow, and their bombardment by no means accurate. While these disadvantages did not seriously impede their use in sieges, though they and their gunners had to be protected with mantlets and palisades from counter-bombardment and sortie, it made them utterly ineffective in pitched battles. All these factors have to be borne in mind in assessing the impact of the introduction of cannons on warfare and in particular siege warfare.

Though this new weapon would grow in importance over time, the Florentine writer and political theorist Niccolò Machiavelli (1469–1527), writing as late as the second decade of the sixteenth century, could still belittle the importance of gunpowder in modern warfare, being half inclined to banish cannons from the battlefield altogether, while to the harquebuses he contemptuously assigns the rôle of overawing the peasantry.[10] However, having said that, it is important to realize that Machiavelli, like many humanists, was not a soldier by profession and took no interest in the practice of war for war's sake. On the contrary, war, in his view, was the handmaiden of politics. He took a philosophical survey of the art of war, studying it at a distance in Florence with a view not so much to unveiling the secret of victory as to appraising the possibilities and limitations of armed force.

Mehmet's monster

Mehmet actually used the conquest of Constantinople as pretence to strengthen his position and to transform the Ottoman military. During his first and brief reign after the voluntary abdication of his father Murad II (1444–6), the twelve-year-old sultan faced strong opposition from some of the leading viziers, especially grand vizier Çandarlı Halil Paşa, and from aristocratic Turkish families. These opposition groups tried every method to block his reforms and ambitious plans and, in the end, incited the Janissaries to mutiny and dethroned him.

During his forced exile, Mehmet prepared a detailed plan to deal with the politicized and unruly elements within the Ottoman military. After his reinstatement to the throne he immediately sacked key military commanders, including the *ağa* of Janissaries, Kazancı Doğan, and appointed trusted lieutenants to these positions. His next step was to enforce wide-scale disciplinary measures and harsh punishments, but even these measures did not satisfy him. In order to control the Janissary corps more completely and to insure its loyalty, he increased the Janissaries' pay and numbers, gave them improved weaponry, and made them the core of the Ottoman army. After effectively curbing the Janissaries, Mehmet turned his attention to the technical corps of the army, in particular the artillery. His fascination with military technology was instrumental in the re-foundation of the artillery corps, which previously was an ad hoc unit with a very loose organizational structure. He first turned the artillery into a salaried standing army unit, *topçu ocağı*, which allowed him to deploy it quickly to distant points. To modernize the artillery he employed European cannon founders and technicians like Urban (or Orban), the legendary iron founder and engineer from Brassó, Transylvania, in the kingdom of Hungary. The sultan also mobilized all available local military technicians, craftsmen, and gunsmiths, and Edirne (formerly Adrianople) became a large foundry locus where various groups of salaried founders and technicians (both Muslim and Christian) refined their designs under the personal supervision of Mehmet. All this was in sharp contrast to most of the sultan's European adversaries, in whose realms the gunner remained a master craftsman who had special relationship to his weapon.

Some of these cannons threw shots of 240, 300, and 360 kilograms. The chief Ottoman artillery gunner, a man named Sarıca, cast a large piece weighing approximately 16,200 kilograms. This must have been similar to the large cast bronze piece on display in the Askeri Müze in Istanbul, which is 424 centimetres long, weighs fifteen metric tons, has a bore diameter of sixty-three centimetres, and fired shots about 195 to 285 kilograms in weight.[11] Other similar Ottoman guns are on display in front of the walls of Rumeli Hisarı on the European shore of the Bosporus. According to recent measurements and estimates, these are 427 and 423 centimetres long, have bore diameters of sixty-eight and sixty-four centimetres, and could have fired cut stone balls of 375 and 310 kilograms in weight respectively.[12] Even these, however, were surpassed by the sultan's largest bombard, designed and cast by Orban.

The *Basilika*, as some modern scholars sardonically christened Orban's masterpiece,[13] was a monster, its length of barrel was estimated to be forty spans, and the circumference of the barrel four spans at the rear, twelve at the mouth, and capable of firing a stone ball weighing 600 kilograms over the distance of two kilometres.[14] One of a growing band of technical mercenaries who plied their trade across the Balkans, initially Orban had offered Constantinus XI Palaiologos one of the most highly prized skills of the age: the ability to cast large bronze guns. Constantinus was extremely interested in Orban's offer and authorized a small stipend to detain him in Constantinople. But Constantinus had few funds available for the construction of new wonder weapons. Bronze cannons were ruinously expensive, well beyond the means of the cash-strapped emperor. Orban's niggardly allowance was not even paid regularly, and the supply of metal available for fashioning cannon meagre. As the year of 1452 wore on, the master artificer became destitute and despondent; so later that same year he decided to try his luck elsewhere. Feeling no loyalty to the Christian cause, he made his way to Edirne to seek an audience with Mehmet. With the flexibility of all arms dealers, Orban was now happy to hire himself out to the Ottoman sultan instead.

After two long years of preparation, Mehmet and the main part of the army arrived at Constantinople just after the siege train on 6 April 1453, which had been dragged to the city with infinite trouble. He carefully positioned his troops against the massive Theodosian walls. Most of the siege train was positioned in the centre under the direct command of the sultan himself. Mehmet arranged his cannons in four batteries along the land walls, each battery consisting of at least one large and two to three smaller pieces. The smaller pieces were used to test the proper range of fire for their bigger sisters. The Ottoman gunners fired at the walls with multiple cannons so that the hits would form a triangle. The application of this effective firing technique demonstrates the prowess of the sultan's artillery gunners, among whose ranks were both Muslims and Christians.

Why did Constantinople fall after withstanding dozens of sieges over a thousand years? The common answer is because of super-cannons such as the *Basilika*. We know that one of the most important shortcomings of the unsuccessful 1422 siege was lack of heavy cannons. We also know that Mehmet's siege artillery destroyed the lands walls and demoralized the defenders. But, mainly because of immobility, slow cleaning and reloading, long cooling, and difficulty of aiming these gargantuan guns, it is also obvious that the defenders managed to close the breaches (using baskets and barrels filled with earth and lashed together) and repair damaged walls quickly and effectively, and for a brief time regained their confidence. Regardless of the merits of the Ottoman cannons, the real reason behind the victory was the leadership of Mehmet (portaging some seventy smaller ships overland from the Bosporus into the Golden Horn, and the surprise attack on the weakest section of the defence), prowess in siege warfare (mining, 'triangle' firing technique, and the use of mortars) and the efficient Ottoman military machine that he created. While the Ottoman military previously made use of the capabilities of cannons, Mehmet utilized them properly and even involved himself personally in designing, manufacturing and firing. However, it was his flexible leadership style that capitalized on innovation that turned the tide. Without the dynamic presence of Mehmet himself Constantinople in all probability might have stood yet another siege.[15] Mehmet had wanted Constantinople, he took Constantinople, and that was that.

Mehmet's deadly white caps

The final assault on Constantinople started before dawn on Tuesday, 29 May 1453. According to the established practice in Turkish siegecraft at that time, the storming columns were arranged in three waves. The first wave consisted of mercenaries and volunteers who bore the brunt of the attack and were virtually annihilated as they dashed themselves against the defences, but at the same time wore out the defence further. The irregular Azabs (literally 'bachelors'), who served for whatever loot came their way, attacked as a second wave and nearly scaled the walls. At this critical moment Mehmet ordered the final wave of Janissaries to attack. According to Ottoman tradition the final charge of the Janissaries was led by a giant of a man named Ulubatlı Hasan (b. 1428), a *timarlı sipahi* who hacked his way up onto one of the towers of the outer wall. The courageous colossus was slain, and seventeen of his thirty comrades perished with him, but the remainder then forced their way across the *peribolos* and over the main wall into the city. The defence collapsed after a last stand, and the Ottomans poured into the city.[16]

The élite body of the Ottoman army, the Janissary corps, *jeniçeri ocağı* – literally new army/soldiers – was at first composed of recruits drawn from the fifth part (*besinci*) of the human booty, which according to Ottoman law, belonged to the sultan. Replacements of Christian prisoners of war forced to Islam or Christian volunteers who later converted to Islam proved insufficient for meeting the manpower demands of the growing corps. Thus, the infamous child tribute system called the *devşirme* (literally 'to collect') was imposed on the subject Christian populations in Anatolia and the Balkans. The boys and youths (usually between the ages of six and fourteen) were circumcized and brought up as Muslims. Laonikos Chalkokondyles tells of their three-year training including the learning of the Turkish language and culture, and the rules of Islam.[17] Michael Doukas, who served the Genoese Gattilusio family as an ambassador to the Ottomans in the fourteen-fifties, writes of their indoctrination in the Islamic faith, of their fanatical loyalty to the ruler of the day, and of their distinctive white headgear, in Turkish *ak börk*.[18] The latter, what Latin writers call *mitra* or *pileus*, was a conical cap of white felt, stiff enough to stand up above the crown of the head, but so long that the upper part then bent back and fell down behind the nape of the neck. Its idiosyncratic form is nicely recorded for us in Gentile Bellini's drawing of a Janissary composed in 1480/1.[19]

From the military perspective, the reasons for early enlistment were obvious. Originally prisoners of war or slaves captured during the raids were trained and organized as Janissaries, but these were already mature men who were not very responsive to Ottoman military training. For example, the training of the main weapon of the Janissary, the recurve composite bow, was very demanding and time consuming. In addition to training, loyalty was also a key issue. Most of these forcefully recruited soldiers, who already had undergone hard training and who lived in prison-like conditions, were unwilling to work for a foreign power, so a substantial percentage of them were ready to desert the army at any suitable opportunity. The *devşirme* was a brutal but efficient solution to these problems.

After their initial training the trainees embarked upon a demanding training régime under heavy discipline and spartan conditions. Trainees learned to fight as infantry by using different weapons – especially the ubiquitous Turkic recurve composite bow – under challenging conditions and learned to obey absolutely the orders of their superiors. Loyalty to the sultan was the key theme of the training. The constant evaluation and harsh discipline was instrumental in the selection of the future élite soldiers of the sultan. If their curriculum included the study of the Qur'an and the *hadith*, the emphasis, not surprisingly, was on the arts of war. But the religious dimension of the military education of the Janissary was crucial. His identification with his new faith of Islam complemented his superb skills in the arts of war. In return the sultan provided a career, a status and a salary for life. An alternative to the erratic Turkish levies, these professional soldiers were the sultan's most powerful single weapon; their very name was to become feared from the banks of the Euphrates to the gates of Vienna. The corps was headed by the *ağa* of Janissaries who would serve as the chief of police in Constantinople and would sit with the ministers and the *ulema* (scholar–jurists–theologians) at the Hall of the Divan (*kubbealtı*), situated in the Second Court of the Topkapı Sarayı. In war he accompanied the sultan and commanded his troops in battle.

The Janissaries remained foot soldiers until the very end of their history. Initially, all were equipped with recurve composite bow and sword, and they were always extremely handy with the crooked dagger that each man carried at his belt. They also used a short spear, battleaxes, and other infantry tools of the trade but only as secondary weapons. Over time the Janissaries acquired some of the weapons of their adversaries as preferred weapons, the Mamluk sword, Damascene knife, and European battleaxe, for example. In all probability handguns (*tüfek*) were introduced into the corps during the first half of fifteenth century under Murad II.[20] We should be careful, however, not to overstate the importance of the Janissaries' use of firearms and consider the destructiveness of archers, whose arrows could cause more damage among the enemy than gunfire. Even as late as the turn of the seventeenth century, as was the case in the first phase of the battle of Mezőkeresztes (26 October 1596), the single major battle of the long Habsburg-Ottoman war of 1593–1606, the skills of the Janissaries in archery and the enduring effectiveness of non-gunpowder weapons in their hands was still paramount.

As noted earlier, the Ottoman sultans came to understand the potential and importance of firearms in a remarkably short time. The strict discipline of the Janissaries was frequently mentioned by contemporary eyewitnesses, and the corps had developed one of the most effective methods of training and drill in firearms and other weaponry, as well as in tactics, long before the long Habsburg–Ottoman war. However, the sultans insisted on keeping the recurve composite bow while most European nations – a notable exception was the English insistence on keeping the longbow until the Privy Council by their Ordinance of 1595 decided archers should no longer be enrolled in the train bands – discontinued the old missile weapons that required long and continuous training because they could replace them with easily learned firearms.

A rare blend of pragmatism and conservatism played an important rôle in this decision. The Ottomans had great faith in the capability of their traditional main weapon. Moreover, though it took only a few hours to learn how to use a handgun, early firearms were often faulty, unreliable, and slow. In comparison, composite bows were accurate, reliable, and had a high rate of fire (nine to ten shots per minute against one shot per two to three minutes). A well-trained archer also had greater effective range of up to 300 metres, whereas hitting a target with a firearm farther than seventy metres was pure coincidence. Obviously, casualties inflicted by projectile weapons were significant, because they were cheaply bought in terms of tactical effort, and they could favourably affect the battle's outcome before the clash of opposing forces. We know that the Janissaries preferred several rows of deep formations and achieved a continuous barrage of fire by rotating rows forward.[21] They were able to maintain this formation even against heavy enemy fire because of their discipline, courage, and training.[22]

For the Janissaries, however, missile weapons were preliminary to the main business of a battle. A Janissary assault was relentless, the advancing ranks shouting their battle-cries and calling upon Allah to give them victory. Later Christian commanders would note that the Janissaries would advance into an inferno of fire, climbing over their own dead, and would instantly exploit any flaw or weakness in the opposition's defence. If the first assault failed, a second and a third would follow.

It was at the battle of Nikopolis (Niğbolu, Bulgaria) when, for the first time, the Janissaries showed their presence and affected the outcome of the battle by successful defensive infantry tactics. These tactics integrated the use of volleys of lethal arrows and sharpened stakes planted with the points at the height of a horse's belly to annihilate the Franco–Burgundian assault. This mixed army of western Christians, consisting chiefly of Hungarian and Franco–Burgundian knights, was decisively defeated due to the reckless and uncoordinated attack of the Franco–Burgundian commander, comte de Nevers, who was lured by a successful feigned retreat and ambush by the Ottomans on 25 September 1396. For his reckless courage that fatal day, Nevers was to earn the cognomen *sans peur*. Captured alive, he was to be spared and eventually ransomed. The large number of Christian losses included many celebrated knights, and subsequent horrendous accounts by the participants, convinced western European monarchs to stay away from the Balkans and what was left of the Byzantine empire, leaving this region to the mercy of the Ottomans. So, in one sense, Nikopolis turned out to be the last real crusade, at least for westerners.

At the time of Nikopolis, however, the Janissaries were still nothing but a small corps of personal slave-guards, *kapukulu* (literally 'slaves servitors of the [sultan's] gate'), closely attached to the sultan's person, and not more than a thousand strong. At the battle of Ankara in 1402 most of the Janissaries perished in a last stand, and their sultan Bayezit I *Yıldırım* himself was captured by the enemy. Still, Bertrandon de la Broquière (d. 1459), who visited the court of Murad II in 1433, speaks of them in one place as around 3,000 in strength, but in another passages says that these *jehainicères*, who are the only infantry of value in the sultan's army, may be as many as 10,000.[23] The origins of this military institution are somewhat obscure,[24] but its rôle in Ottoman expansion, in Europe and in the Near East (and later Ottoman history up to the Janissaries' disbandment in 1833), was significant. Statistics are slippery beasts, but, as a rough indication of its importance, the Janissary corps comprised less than 15 per cent of the mobilized Ottoman army, yet, at critical moments, their discipline and endurance proved crucial.

So it was at the siege of Constantinople. Mehmet had purposefully allocated the prestigious final victorious assault on the crumbling walls of Constantinople to the Janissaries and publicized their rôle in public. The unfortunate Azabs and other auxiliary troops were decimated in order to wear down the enemy and received no public acclaim.

The last emperor

Omens and prophecies about the ultimate fate of Constantinople had been heard for many years. The Constantinopolitans were given to bouts of fatalistic gloom and pessimism concerning their Queen of Cities. It was widely believed that the end would come in the seven-thousandth year from the Creation, in 1492, which meant that there were still thirty-nine years to run. Tragically for them, it was not to be so. The Virgin Mary too, who had always been the heavenly patron of Constantinople, seemed to be wavering in her affections. When the most hallowed of her icons was brought out to be paraded round the streets, it slipped off the framework on which it was being carried aloft; and almost at once a thunderstorm broke out and the city was deluged with torrents of rain and hail. Such a coincidence would have made the Constantinopolitans anxious at the best of times. In their present state of terror and credulity it moved them to hysteria. The heavens themselves seemed to be saying that resistance was futile.

Among the defenders of Constantinople was a young novice called Nestor. He had been abducted by an Ottoman artillery unit somewhere in Moldavia, where the stonemasons of the unit were carving stone balls for their cannons and handguns in preparation for the siege of Constantinople. Nestor was forcibly converted to Islam and enrolled in the unit. Since he had some education, Nestor, renamed İskander, was employed in the Ottoman military administration. He accompanied the Ottoman unit from Moldavia, arrived at their encampment west of the city walls some weeks before the onset of the siege on 4 April 1453, and then ran away, 'that I might not die in this wretched faith'.[25] He entered Constantinople where he remained until its fall. The fact that he acquired a substantial knowledge of and familiarity with Ottoman artillery and its deployment is evident in his vivid descriptions of the usage of artillery, artillery barrages, and assaults along the Theodosian walls. His account of the siege may have been written many years later when he was a monk in a Greek monastery, but it has the quality of a lived experience, a firsthand account of what he witnessed as a non-combatant. It has been suggested that he was attached to the forces of the Genoese condottieri Giovanni Longo Giustiniani at the Gate of Saint Romanos and helped them to identify the Ottoman commanders and their weaponry.

Also among the defenders was George Sphrantzes (1401–77). He was a courtier in the Byzantine empire, and had served as an important diplomat and ambassador for a number of emperors. He had been a close friend to Constantinus XI Palaiologos since childhood. Towards the end of his life, Sphrantzes composed a chronicle, known as the *Chronicon minus*, which is partly an autobiographical work and includes the author's personal experiences at the siege, fall, and sack of Constantinople in 1453. On the night of 28 May the emperor, accompanied by Sphrantzes, had stopped briefly at the Blachernai palace after returning from his last visit to Hagia Sophia. According to Sphrantzes, Constantinus assembled the members of his household and said goodbye to each of them, asking forgiveness for any unkindness he might have shown them. The emperor then left the palace and rode with Sphrantzes down to the Gate of the Kaligaria. They dismounted there and the Sphrantzes waited while Constantius mounted one of the towers nearby, whence he could hear the sounds of the Ottoman army preparing for the final assault. After about an hour he returned and mounted his horse once again. Sphrantzes then said goodbye to Constantinus for the last time and then watched as the emperor rode off to his command post on the Murus Bacchatureus.

Of the dramatic turn of events of the following morning, 29 May, George Sphrantzes was to later write:

On Tuesday, 29 May, early in the day, the sultan took possession of our City; in this time of capture my late master and emperor, Lord (Gr. *kúrios*) Constantinus, was killed. I was not at his side at that hour but had been inspecting another part of the City, according to his orders. Alas for me; I did not know what times Providence had in store for me![26]

The struggle was fiercest at the gateway called the Gate of Saint Romanos. Apparently it was there that the emperor was last seen just before the Theodosian walls were breached, fighting valiantly beside a Castilian who claimed to be his cousin, Francisco de Toledo, and his own cousin Theophilos Palaiologos and his close comrade-in-arms, John Dalmata. He had thrown away his regalia. He was very likely killed fighting like a common soldier to stem the flood of infidels pouring into his Christian city.

As Leonardo of Chios (d. 1482), the Greek-born Latin archbishop of Lesbos, very properly observes, the Turks, had they known the emperor, would have made every attempt to save and secure such a prize captive. He had been present during the last weeks of Byzantine Constantinople and in a long letter he reported to pope Nicholas V (r. 1447–55) some six weeks after the capture of the city while his memory was still fresh and thus represents one of the earliest accounts of this event.[27] On the other hand, Niccolò Barbaro (1420–94), a Venetian ship's surgeon and resident of Constantinople, wrote in his journal that it was said the last emperor hanged himself at the moment when the Turks broke in at the Gate of Saint Romanos.[28] All in all, Constantinus' ultimate fate remains a mystery.

Though we generally refer to the last emperor as Constantinus XI Palaiologos, he actually preferred to be known by his mother's surname of Dragaš or Dragases, which she inherited from her Serbian father. On the death of his older brother John VIII (he had no children), Constantinus arrived in Constantinople in early 1449, and after a brief succession struggle with his younger brothers Thomas and Demetrios, was acclaimed emperor by the Constantinopolitans. It was Helena, his mother, who was instrumental in securing the throne for Constantinus over his other brothers. The empress mother lived on as a widow (Manuel II had died in 1425) and a nun until 23 March 1450, shortly after his accession. Just as when reading Shakespeare's *Hamlet*, the reader of any biography of the emperor knows that Constantinus is doomed from the beginning. He stops being an emperor and starts being a tragic hero. An emperor without an empire, Constantinus was to reign for only four years and nearly five months.

The emperor's disappearance during the last hours of the fighting heightened the mythology of the fall of Constantinople. Although a head was solemnly presented to the sultan and a corpse given to the Greeks for formal burial, the body of Constantinus was never found. As a result, many popular tales of his escape and survival circulated. For instance, there was a widely held belief in Ottoman Constantinople, that the last Christian emperor of the city had been taken up by angels when the Ottoman Turks breached the walls. The heavenly messengers turned the valiant man into stone – marble, to be exact.[29] He was then placed into an underground chamber somewhere just outside the Golden Gate. When the sins of the Christians were remitted the angels would awaken the emperor, restore to him his sword, and burst open the Golden Gate. Single-handedly, Constantinus would cast the Turks out of his city and his lands, restoring once more the Christian Roman empire.[30]

This was not just some wives' tale or the desperate dream of a conquered people. It was widely believed by Greeks and Turks alike. And why not? It seemed to be well confirmed by the oracles of Leo VI Sapiens, a collection of popular mediaeval drawings that purported to tell the future. Oracle thirteen depicted a sleeping man bound up in bandages from head to foot and attended to by angels.[31] After 1453 this image was always associated with Constantinus in his cave. According to Greeks interviewed by the French folklorists Henry Carnoy and Jean Nicolaïdès, the Turks had several times searched for the petrified emperor's subterranean chamber but had been unable to find him. There is good reason to believe that this may have been the case – or at least that the danger was understood at all levels of Turkish society in Constantinople.[32]

In the days of the Ottoman empire there was a Greek perspective that held Turkish rule as equivalent to the Babylonian captivity. As with the Jews, God would one day relent from his punishment of the Greeks and restore to them their own Jerusalem – the New Jerusalem of Constantinople. There is that aphorism 'The man who was once future is past'; there were once those who believed this did not apply to Constantinus XI Dragases Palaiologos.

Turk triumphant

From his father Murad II, Mehmet had inherited a well-ordered and flourishing empire, complete but for Constantinople, the Queen of Cities. He was determined therefore to turn the illustrious and strategic metropolis into the jewel of his empire. He was patient but violently moody, notorious for his cruelty but equally famous for the delicacy of his poetry. Yet, upon entering the ruin and the decay that was once the Great Palace of Constantinople, the conquering sultan must have pondered upon the fate of the ancient empire and the fate of its last emperor, for he apparently muttered the lines from a melancholy distich by the Persian poet Saadi Shirazi (b. 1210):

The spider weaves the curtains in the palace of the Caesars; / the owl calls the watches in the towers of Afrasiyab.[33]

Though Mehmet saw it silent, deserted, inhabited by ghosts, the great landmark still inspired awe. In its glory days the Great Palace had been a sprawling complex, not a single structure. Covering the Marmara slopes of the First Hill, it was almost a small city within the city, a sort of Byzantine Forbidden City or Kremlin.

The Byzantine empire had been Greek in both language and religion. Mehmet and his successors built upon this legacy, organizing a military theocracy modelled upon the Byzantine one: *pax Ottomanica* replaced the much earlier authority of Rome. Yet, the academic Francis Bacon, who did a stint as Lord Chancellor of England (1618–21, d. 1626), described the Turks as 'a cruel people, who nevertheless are kind to beasts, and give alms to dogs and birds',[34] yet are 'a nation without morality, without letters, arts or sciences... where Ottoman's horse sets his foot, people will come up very thin'.[35] To Renaissance Europe, in general, the Ottoman domination over much of the eastern half of the continent became associated with arbitrary rule and the barbarous massacres of Christians: religious tolerance, not ruthless persecution, was more typical of Ottoman overlordship. The oriental luxury of the sultan's court was equated with a decadent sensuality, cruelty and deceit, incorporating the harem, eunuchs, and unspeakable sexual practices: the court of Süleyman I the Magnificent (r. 1520–66), better known to the Turks as *Kanuni*, the Lawgiver, was the scene of a great artistic and flowering rather than of debauched perverse activities, and Turkish social convention was marked by kindly and hospitable good manners, not by an intensive and habitual cruelty. Süleyman, a model ruler, processed the gift of being able to temper severity with justice, and warlike accomplishment with a love of culture and thus eased the strictures on the non-Muslim subjects of his realm, which, incidentally, stretched from Baghdad in the east, to Algiers in the west, from lower Egypt to the southern border of imperial Russia. During the apogee of the empire the sultans ruled over thirty kingdoms, and drew taxes from all of them. It was his father, Selim I *Yavuz*, the Grim (r. 1512–20), who had assumed the title of caliph of Islam. Selim also brought from Mamluk Egypt, after the conquest of that country in 1517, the relics of the prophet – hairs from his beard, one of his teeth, his footprint, his bow, his staff, his seal, and his black camel hair mantle, as well as the swords of the first four caliphs. With the title and these sacred emblems of Islam, which were quickly installed in the Topkapı Sarayı, the Ottoman sultans assumed the unquestioned leadership of the Islamic world.

Yet the Ottoman empire did not interfere with the traditional practices of its subjects: it merely taxed them, Muslim and non-Muslim alike, with increasing vigour and efficiency. This matter-of-fact Ottoman benevolence is expediently exemplified by the fate of that pinnacle of Byzantine monumental architecture, Hagia Sophia. Mehmet II, now Constantinople's first sultan and proudly bearing the cognomen *Fatih*, was a classic blend of cultivated connoisseur and ruthless conqueror; even going so far to identify himself with that ace conqueror, Alexander the Great.[36] Mehmet is said to have spoken or understood, apart from his native Turkish, five languages: Arabic, Persian, Hebrew, Latin and Greek.[37] In his world, everything and everybody moved at his command. Though stamped with the touching traces of decline, he issued orders that Hagia Sophia be promptly converted into the great imperial mosque of Ayá Sófiyah.

Having entered the long-desired city in the late afternoon of Tuesday 29 May 1453, Mehmet had ridden slowly through the streets of despoiled Constantinople. According to the Venetian observer, Niccolò Barbaro, 'blood flowed in the city like rainwater in the gutters after a sudden storm, and the corpses of Turks and Christians were thrown into the Dardanelles, where they floated out to sea like melons along a canal'.[38] On rode the sultan until he had reached Hagia Sophia. He dismounted at the door of the mother church of Orthodox Christianity and bent down to take a handful of earth, which he sprinkled over his turban as an act of humility before his God. The fall of Constantinople was of course Mehmet's passport to fame and the Ottoman traveller and chronicler Evliya Çelebi exploits this victory to the full:

Sultan Muhammad [Mehmet] II, on surveying more closely the church of Ayá Sófiyah, was astonished at the solidity of its construction, the strength of its foundations, the height of its cupola, and the skill of its builder, Aghnádús [Ignatius?]. He caused the ancient place of worship to be cleared of its idolatrous impurities and purified from the blood of the slain, and having refreshed the brains of the victorious Muslims by fumigating it with amber and lign-aloes, converted it that very hour into a *jámi* (mosque) by erecting a contracted *mihrab*, *minber*, *mahfil*, and *menareh*, in that place which might rival Paradise. On the following Friday, the faithful were summoned to prayer by the *müezzins* (criers), who proclaimed with a loud voice this text [Qur'an 33:56]: 'Verily, God and his angels bless the Prophet'. Ak-Shemsu-d-din and Karah Shemsu-d-din [two holy men] then arose, and placing themselves on each side of the sultan, supported him under his arms; the former placed his own turban on the head of the conqueror, fixing in it a black and white feather of a crane, and putting into his hand a naked sword. Thus conducted to the minber he ascended it, and cried out with a voice as loud as David's, 'Praise be to God the Lord of all worlds' [Qur'an 1:1],[39] on which all the victorious Muslims lifted up their hands and uttered a shout of joy.[40]

According to the author's own testimony, his 'great-grandfather, then his [Mehmet's] standard-bearer, was with him at the conquest of Islámból (Constantinople)'.[41] We shall assume, therefore, that he was an eyewitness to the inaugural Friday prayers in Ayá Sófiyah.

At first, the Latin belfry served as a makeshift minaret, and then a wooden one was erected over the turret on the west façade. In due course four independent minarets were set up. The ambo was removed and a *mihrab*, the niche facing Mecca (southeast in Turkey), was cut in to the apse. Also erected was a carved *minber*, a form of pulpit from which the imam could read passages of the Qur'an, gripping in the other hand a sword as was correct for a captured city; this was set against the south column of the apse. The marble floor was covered in carpets. In 1650 an inscription in praise of Allah was written in the centre of the dome: 'In the name of God the Merciful and Pitiful; God is the light of Heaven and Earth. His light is Himself, not that which shines through glass or gleams in the morning star or glows in a firebrand'.[42]

Gradually, over time, all the mosaics showing the human figure were carefully covered in plaster and a coat of whitewash, a salutary reminder that the Ottoman Turks were not the uncompromising iconoclasts they are often assumed to be. Indeed, something of the reverence that was accorded to Hagia Sophia under Ottoman rule can be gathered from the fact that five sultans are buried in its precincts. These five imperial Ottoman tombs, *türbes*, are located in the gardens just to the south of the church. The five sultans are: Selim II the Sot (r. 1566–74), Murad III (r. 1574–95), Mehmet III (r. 1595–1603), Mustafa I the Mad (r. 1617–18, 1622–3), and Ibrahim the Mad (r. 1640–8) – it was customary among the Turks to name people for some fault or virtue that they had, hence the proliferation of 'Grim', 'Sot', 'Mad'. Other imperial *türbes* contain the remains of three sultanas and 140 children, 103 of which stemmed from the fertile loins of Murad III, nineteen of whom were executed when their eldest brother Mehmet III achieved the throne – this bloody code of the Ottomans was to ensure the peaceful accession of Mehmet. Murad III was the epitome of the new, sedentary style of sultan. Insatiable for sex not victory, he rarely left Constantinople. Though loving his chief wife Safiye, a beauty from Venice, he finally yielded to the temptations placed in his way by his sister Ismihan, the wife of the grand vizier Sokollu Mehmet Paşa, and his mother, the valide sultan Nur Banu.

The harem was much misunderstood by the Christian West, who conceived of it only as a furnace of lust, in which sultans indulged their passion, and the women gratified each other's desires. In fact, its origins arose from Islam's preoccupation with female purity, which meant that women were to be separated from all men except their husbands and young sons. The world of women was forbidden, *haram*, to all other males. In the hands of the Ottomans this system of seclusion became a political and social institution as well. Naturally, the imperial harem was designed for the sexual gratification of the sultan. At some moments the rooms – some 300 of them, almost all surprisingly small – of the Harem of the Grand Seraglio was home to a couple of thousand women and girls in various stages of training; it is, however, noticeable that those who attracted the attentions of the ruler and bore children were scarcely ever Turkish.

By male descent the later sultans were no doubt derived from Osman Ghazi, but the percentage of actual Turkish blood in their veins was negligible. Ever since the days of the Conqueror the cruel law of fratricide had prevailed, whereby a new sultan, on his succession, put to death all his brothers to avoid the possibility of dispute or civil war; the loss of a prince or two was less to be deplored than that of a province, and indeed the Ottoman empire was noticeably free of internal strife. As alluded to above, at the death of Murat III in 1595, his son and successor Mehmet III consigned no fewer than nineteen brothers to be strangled by mutes with a silken bow-string, the most honourable form of death. Gradually in the seventeenth century the practice changed to the comparatively honourable confinement of the cadets of the dynasty within the Topkapı Sarayı, where in the Harem were a series of apartments known as the Cage (*kafes*). On too many occasions a bemused or inexperienced prince had to be released from the *kafes* to assume the throne of a dead brother, destined to become little more than a mere cipher in the hands of his manipulative ministers. This grotesque emasculation of the line meant that power was often a prize to be squabbled over by the valide sultan (mother of the sultan), the chief black eunuch – the Ottomans having inherited the Byzantine practice of employing eunuchs – the grand vizier and the Janissaries.

Epilogue

To end our story we cut to 1934, for in that year Mustafa Kemal Atatürk (1881–1938) judiciously decreed that the sacred monument of Hagia Sophia would become a secular museum, which was formally opened on 1 February the following year. Now all practice of religious worship ceased, and this fabulous, enduring shrine welcomes today not the worshippers of Christ, nor the followers of Muhammad, but the curious, the tourist, and the learned. Once a highly charged piece of sacred space, it now stands for all of us, one of the most fabulous pieces of architecture and living history preserved in our time. If the truth be told, Atatürk actually hated religion. He said so, in terms that would earn him a *fatwa* these days in many Muslim countries:

> I have no religion, and at times I wish all religions at the bottom of the sea. He is a weak ruler who needs religion to uphold his government; it is as if he would catch his people in a trap. My people are going to learn the principles of democracy, the dictates of truth and the teachings of science. Superstition must go. Let them worship as they will; every man can follow his own conscience, provided it does not interfere with sane reason or bid him against the liberty of his fellow-men.[1]

The paradox here, of course, is that modern Turkey, founded on secularism, is now aggressively Islamic and hurtling towards fragmentation, with the Turkish military serving as the guardians of the republic's secular heritage embodied by Atatürk.

One of the greatest political leaders of the twentieth century, Atatürk was born Mustafa Kemal in Thessaloniki, then part of the Ottoman empire. At the outbreak of the First World War, he advocated neutrality, but distinguished himself in the defence of Gallipoli in April 1915 by personally inspiring the men with his bravery to hold their lines, even at great cost. He earned the epithet Atatürk, 'Father of the Turks', by taking back the entire Anatolian peninsula – after their defeat in the war Ottoman rule had been limited to Istanbul and the northern part of Anatolia – against pretty much the whole world. The Allies wanted to hand western Anatolia to the Greeks – and the Greeks made a good case that the Mediterranean coastal region was and always had been Greek.

The peace settlement of Lausanne (July 1923) gave Kemal a Turkey in Asia free of foreign troops and with essential control of the Dardanelles, and provided for exchanges of populations between Greece and Turkey. Exasperation at the shabby and defeatist rôle of the sultan safely ensconced in Istanbul led Kemal to work for the abolition of the Osmanlı sultanate in 1922, the proclamation of the republic with Ankara as its capital in 1923, and the abolition of the caliphate in 1924; thus the rule of the Ottoman Turks was terminated and for the first time in sixteen centuries Constantinople was no longer the capital of an empire. As the first president of the Republic of Turkey, he advocated a programme of literacy, equal rights and the emancipation of women, as well as secularisation and state investment in infrastructure. He even introduced surnames, the Latin alphabet, and abolished the fez, the traditional male headgear, as too redolent of the Ottoman past, to which he attributed much of the backwardness of his homeland. Atatürk died, still at the helm, in Istanbul on 10 November 1938.

Religion, faith, belief, call it what you will, is a private matter, in the head and the heart, and within the home. It is not a battle cry, not a badge of identity, not something to parade, not a demand on a nation, and certainly not a mark of segregation or sanction. Whatever your tribal allegiance, we should live under the same civilized laws, buy into codified human rights, and foster bonds of universal citizenship.

Notes

Chapter 1

1. Pierre Gilles, *De topographia Constantinopoleos* 4.11.
2. Dionysios Byzantii, *Anaplus Bospori*, 3.2.7–9. One *stade* = 625 Roman feet or 606¾ English feet.
3. Herodian, *Historiae* 3.1.6, cf. John Zonaras, *Epitome historiarum* 13.3.
4. Pausanias, *Guide to Greece* 4.31.5.
5. According to the pagan historian Zosimos (*Historia nova*, 2.30) the new city of Constantinus was enclosed by walls cutting off the isthmus from sea to sea fifteen *stadia* beyond the walls of old Byzantium. However, Zosimos' text is probably referring to the size of Constantinople as it stood in the time of Theodosius II and not of Constantinus. See, on this, Pierre Gilles, *De topographia Constantinopoleos* 1.3.
6. In fact, Ἑλληνικῆς had already lost all 'ethnic' significance in late Roman times and had assumed the more general meaning of 'pagan' or 'non-Christian' (e.g. Michael Psellos, *Chronographia*, Michael VI 7.41), a usage to which the fourth-century church father Gregory of Nazianzos had objected strongly (*Orationes*, 4.5.79–81). In our period of study, the word 'Greek' was used only by westerners.
7. *Skjald* A I 385, B I 355, cf. *Heimskringla: Haralds saga Sigurðarsonar*, 2.
8. Obolensky 1971: 84, 160.
9. In Old Norse: *Greklands Gud så himmelsrik skrudar*, Å. Ohlmarks (ed.), *Snorres kungasagor* (1961), p. 208.
10. *Laxdæla saga*, 77. The Old Norse word *skarlet* is somewhat deceptive as the cloth could be red, but also dark brown, blue or grey.
11. *Heimskringla: Haralds saga Sigurðarsonar*, 16, 17, *Morkinskinna*, 8, 14.
12. *Ágrip af Nóregskonúngasögum*, § 55, *Morkinskinna*, 62, cf. *Heimskringla: Magnússona saga*, 12. Alexios I Komnenos (r. 1081–1118) is the Byzantine emperor named most frequently in Icelandic sagas, whether the events narrated take place during his reign or not. In the sagas he is called 'Kirjalax', which derives from the emperor's common title, Κύριος Ἀλέξιος, Kyrios Alexios or Lord Alexios. However, it should be noted that his Icelandic name of Kirjalax is one that became attached to more than one emperor, in particular to his son and successor John II Komnenos (r. 1118–43).
13. Tyerman 2006: 22.
14. Beeler 1971: 250.
15. Benjamin of Tudela, *Sefer Masa'oth* ('Book of Travels') 23 Adler.
16. Robert de Clari, *La prise de Constantinople* par. 101.
17. Fulcher de Chartres, *Historia Hierosolymytana* 1.9.1. Born in 1059, Fulcher was present when pope Urban II (r. 1088–99) preached the First Crusade on 27 November 1095 at the close of the Synod of Clermont. The Vicar of Christ was one of the political powers of the world, and held a politician's weapon in the monopoly of propaganda. Little wonder, therefore, Urban's thunderings produced an immediate and widespread response among the peoples of France, Germany and the Low Countries. The cleric himself left Europe with the army of Robert of Normandy, Stephen of Blois, and Robert of Flanders,

accompanying it as far as Edessa, where he joined Baldwin, brother of Godfrey of Bouillon, duke of Lower Lorraine. It was Godfrey who was to rule (1099–1100) as the first king of Jerusalem (although he refused the title 'king' as he believed that the true king of Jerusalem was Christ, ruling thence as *Advocatus Sancti Sepulchri*, 'Defender of the Holy Sepulchre'). In spite of a short reign as king of Jerusalem in all but name, Godfrey's reputation was soon mythologized and he was shortly to become one of the most celebrated figures in the whole of Christendom. As for Baldwin, Fulcher remained his chaplain until the king died in 1118, when Fulcher may have become prior of the Mount of Olives. Intended for the church but chose to crusade instead, the Lorrainer Baldwin, who had been born Baldwin of Boulogne, certainly had a remarkable career as a second son. Godfrey and Baldwin were of course the sons of Eustace II of Boulogne, one of the chief allies of William of Normandy at Hastings, and Ida of Lorraine (d. 1113), popularly recognized as a saint soon after her death. As a final point of interest, once Jerusalem fell to the crusaders, the kingdom was carved into three great principalities besides the royal territory – this was the county of Tripoli, the principality of Antioch and the county of Edessa. A crusader-Armenian kingdom was also formed north of Antioch. But even by the time of Baldwin's accession, the Franks maintained only a precarious hold over the greater part of the Muslim Levant.

18. Prokopios, *Wars* 6.30.1–5, Agathias, *Historiae* 5.20.5.
19. Anon., *Gesta francorum et aliorum Hierosolymitanorum apud RHC occidentaux* iii, 494.
20. Benjamin of Tudela, *Sefer Masa'oth* 20 Adler.
21. Geoffroi de Villehardouin, *La conquête de Constantinople* par. 58.
22. Quoted by Sumner-Boyd and Freely 2010 [1972]: 2.

Chapter 2

1. Pierre Gilles, *De Bosporo Thracio* 1.4.
2. Ibid. 1.5.
3. Aischylos, *Prometheus Bound* lines 733–4, *Persians* lines 723, 746, Ephoros 70 F 157, Polybios, *Historiae* 4.43, Arrian, *Bithynica* 156 F 20b, Appian, *Mithridatica* 101, Ammianus Marcellinus, *Res Gestae* 22.8.13, etc.
4. Apollodoros 2.1.3, Dionysios Byzantii, *Anaplus Bospori* 4.2.13–17, cf. Herodotos, *Historiae* 1.1.2.
5. There are many accounts of and references to the Argonauts in classical literature; the two fullest versions are both called *Argonautica*, one a Greek epic poem by Apollonius Rhodius, and the other a Latin epic poem by Caius Valerius Flaccus.
6. E.g. Aischylos, *Supplicants*, line 594, *Anthologia Palatina*, v 16, xii 53.
7. Cicero, *In Verrem* II 4.129.
8. London, British Museum, inv. 1012.
9. *CIG* ii 3797 = *Anthologia Palatina*, i 108.
10. Polybios, *Historiae* 4.39.6.
11. Pompeius Mela, *De situ orbis libri III* 1.101.
12. Timothenes of Rhodes apud scholiast Apollonius Rhodius, *Argonautica* 2.532.
13. Dionysios Byzantii fr. 47 Muller.
14. Ibid. fr. 48 Muller.
15. Herodotos, *Historiae* 4.87–8.
16. Thucydides 1.128.1–3.
17. Diodorus Siculus 11.44.3, Pausanias, *Guide to Greece* 3.17.7–9, Nepos, *Pausanias* 3.1–3.
18. Thucydides 1.131.1–2, 134.1–3.
19. Ibid. 1.94.2, 95.1–2, 8.80.1–3, cf. Xenophon, *Hellenika* 1.1.36.
20. Plutarch, *Alcibiades* 31.2–4.
21. Xenophon, *Anabasis* 7.1.16–25.
22. Xenophon, *Hellenika* 4.8.31, cf. Demosthenes 20.60.

23. Isokrates 5.53, Diodorus Siculus 15.78–9.
24. Demosthenes 8.14, 10.68, 18.71, 73, 87–9, 139, 244.
25. Diodorus Siculus 16.74.2–76.4, 77.2–3, Plutarch, *Phokion* 14, Arrian, *Anabasis* 2.14.5, Pausanias, *Guide to Greece* 1.29.10, Justin 9.1.2–7, Polyainos 4.2.21, Frontinus, *Strategemata* 1.3.4, 4.13.
26. Menander, *Auletris* fr. 67 Koch.
27. Polybios, *Historiae* 4.46.5–47.6. Aristotle (*Eudemian Ethics*, 8.1247a20) talks of a 2 per cent duty being levied by the Byzantines in his day.
28. Polybios, *Historiae* 4.52.5.
29. Ibid. 4.38.1–3, cf. 4.44.
30. The English name is a direct translation of its ancient Greek name *Chrysokéras* (Pliny, *Historia naturalis* 9.51), the linguistic derivation of which is obscure. An inlet of the Bosporus, the scimitar-shaped Golden Horn (Tk. *Haliç*) is some 11 kilometres long; at is broadest part it is 750 metres in width; and it reaches a maximum depth of thirty-five metres where it joins the Bosporus at Saray Point to flow into the Sea of Marmara.
31. Prokopios, *De aedificiis* 1.5.10.
32. Pierre Gilles, *De topographia Constantinopoleos* 1.4.
33. Herodotos, *Historiae* 4.144, cf. the sixth-century historian John the Lydian (*De magistratibus populi Romani*, 3.70) who states that the colony was founded at the time of the thirty-eighth Olympiad, viz. 628/625 BC, by a certain gentleman named Zeuxippos.
34. Stephanos Byzantii apud Eustathius of Thessaloniki, *Commentarii ad Homeri Iliadem Pertinentes* 3.3.66.6–7, Dionysios Byzantii, *Anaplus Bospori* 12.2.1–17, 13.2.1–4.
35. Herodotos, *Historiae* 4.144.
36. Strabo, *Geographia* 7.6.2, Tacitus, *Annales* 12.63.1.

Chapter 3

1. Theodore Synkellos, *Homily on the Avar Siege of Constantinople* sect.19. Synkellos (Gr. *súnkellos*, literally 'living in the same cell') is an office in the Orthodox Church roughly equivalent to that of an episcopal vicar in the Roman Catholic Church. In the Early Church it was a term used for those monks or clerics who lived in the same cell with their bishops and whose primary duty was to be witness to the purity of their lives. Later, in the Orthodox Church, they became the confessors and councillors of patriarchs and bishops. It is perhaps in this rôle that we can see Theodore Synkellos, which would thus make him an excellent eyewitness to the pious actions of patriarch Sergios on Tuesday 29 July, 626.
2. In Greek: Ὁδηγήτρια, literally 'One who leads the Way'. Here the Virgin Mary is depicted holding Christ Child in her left arm and gesturing towards Him with her right hand as the source of salvation of mankind. Thus, the Hodegetria activates the power of the Virgin to pull up and lead mankind back to the light of God.
3. The Luke legend was a creation of the Iconoclasm, appearing in such ecclesiastical works as the anonymous *The Letter of the Three Patriarchs* (38–9) and Symeon Metaphrastes (apud *PG* vol. 115, col. 1136B, vol. 117, col. 113D). See, on this, Pentcheva 2014 [2006]: 124–7.
4. Theodore Synkellos, *Homily on the Avar Siege of Constantinople* sect. 15.
5. Ibid. sect. 17. The collapse of the 626 siege broke the power of the Avars and removed them as a direct threat to the empire. Their realm contracted to the area of modern Hungary, from which they continued to be the scourge of at least central Europe until they were finally destroyed by Charlemagne in the seven-nineties (*Annales regni Francorum*, under 791, 796).
6. Pentcheva 2014 [2006]: 41.
7. Ibid. 41–2.
8. Pentcheva 2002:5.
9. Anon., *Chronicon paschale* 716–26.

10. Ibid. 725.
11. Theodore Synkellos, *Homily on the Avar Siege of Constantinople* sects. 14–15, 17, 33–9, 51, 52.
12. See, on this, Pentcheva 2014 [2006]: 117–29.
13. According to Christian tradition, the outer veil, or *maphorion*, of the Virgin Mary was preserved by the apostle Thomas after the Assumption. In 451, the relic was transferred to Constantinople and deposited at the church of the Virgin Mary of Blachernai (Pentcheva 2002: 20). The Blachernai was among the oldest Marian foundations in Constantinople and boasted of a powerful array of relics.
14. Photios provided two sermons during and following the Rus' attack on Constantinople in which he portrays the Rus' as terrifying and violent savages. He states 'Woe is me, that I see a fierce and savage tribe fearlessly poured round the city, ravaging the suburbs, destroying everything, ruining everything, fields, houses, herbs, beasts of burden, women, children, old men, youths, thrusting their sword through everything, taking pity on nothing, sparing nothing. The destruction is universal' (*Homilies of Photios patriarch of Constantinople*, homily 4, sect. 4).
15. George Kedrenos, *Compendium historiarum* 2.551, Zosimos, *Historia nova* 2.162. See also, Pentcheva 2002: 21.
16. This was, of course, the banner of Adhémar de Monteil, bishop of Le Puy-en-Velay, who had been named apostolic legate and appointed to lead the First Crusade by pope Urban II. At the time, no one knew what crusade was. Crusade was the new business of the Vicar of the Prince of Peace and warrior order of western Europe. Adhémar had been the first to take the crusading vow at the town of Clermont in November 1095. Adhémar travelled with Raymond IV of Toulouse (also known as Raymond de Saint-Gilles) and helped give unity to the First Crusade. Before he reached Constantinople he was wounded and captured by Pečenegs, though released when found to be a bishop. He died on 1 August 1098 of disease (probably typhoid) at Antioch, a tragic loss to the continuing unity of the First Crusade.
17. Michael Psellos, *Chronographia*, Basil II 1.16.
18. Niketas Choniates, *O City of Byzantium* I, p. 10 [15] Magoulias.
19. Michael Psellos, *Chronographia*, Romanos III 3.10.
20. Michael Attaleiates, *Historia* 152–3 (on Romanos IV Diogenes). As a toponymic name, *Blachernitissa* only pinpoints the location where the icon was kept, not the actual icon; the Blachernai church had a number of miraculous Marian icons. See, on this, Pentcheva 2014 [2006]: 76–7.
21. Michael Psellos, *Chronographia*, Romanos III 3.10–11, Michael Attaleiates, *Historia* 153 (on Romanos IV Diogenes), Niketas Choniates, *O City of Byzantium* II, bk. 5, p. 90 [158] Magoulias.
22. Niketas Choniates, *O City of Byzantium* VIII, p. 312 [567] Magoulias.
23. Geoffroi de Villehardouin, *La conquête de Constantinople* par. 228.
24. Robert de Clari, *La prise de Constantinople* par. 89.
25. Ibid. par. 62.
26. Bertrandon de la Broquière, *Le Voyage d'outremer* 150–65.
27. Tisset-Lanhers 2.52.
28. Quicherat 4.89.
29. The name is very similar to the Roman fort of *Vinovium* at Binchester, County Durham. Land's End, *Caer Guidn* in the Brythonic tongue, has also been proposed.
30. This quote suffers from the same problems as that for the battle of Badon in the *Annales Cambriae*: the Welsh words for shield (*ysgwyd*) and shoulder (*ysgwydd*) being confused. Geoffrey of Monmouth explains that Arthur bore armorial bearings of both the Cross and the Virgin: the arms later adopted by Glastonbury Abbey.
31. Nennius, *Historia Brittonum* 56.

32. Pelikan 2011 [1990]: 129.
33. Matthew 1:18–25, Luke 1:26–38.
34. The Dormition of Mary is not to be found in the four gospels or any other New Testament book; it is a late apocryphal, homilic and hymnological Christian tradition.
35. For the sake of convenience the following terms have been used throughout this book: Chalcedonian Church = the Christian communities that recognize the Fourth Œcumenical Synod (Chalcedon in 451) where Christ was proclaimed fully human and fully divine in one incarnate *hypostasis* or manifestation; the Orthodox Church = the group of Christian communities belonging to the Eastern Orthodox or Chalcedonian Church of the Byzantine empire; the Roman Catholic Church = the Chalcedonian Church of the West that recognizes the supreme authority of the pope of Rome as the Vicar of Christ.
36. John Mauropous, *Poemi*.
37. Akathistos stanza 23, verses 10, 12–15.

Chapter 4

1. Olympiodorus, fr. 3.
2. An inscription found in 1993 suggests that the project may have already begun under Arcadius. See, on this, Asutay-Effenberger 2007: 2.
3. Χρυσεία Πύλη, *Chryseía Pylê* (Gr.), *Porta Aurea* (L), *Altınkapı* or *Yaldızlıkapı* (Tk.). In a distant historical tribute to Constantinople, the entrance to San Francisco Bay California acquired a new name. In a letter to Captain Wilkes USN, Colonel John Charles Frémont wrote, "Give to the entrance of San Francisco harbour the name of Chrysopylae – GOLDEN GATE – and place it on the map. On the same principle that the harbour of Byzantium (afterwards Constantinople) was called Chrysokéras – GOLDEN HORN" (*Memoirs of my life*, p. 17). Frémont was a nineteenth-century polymath: soldier, politician, statesman, explorer, and, some would say, a military hero of appreciable accomplishment.
4. Based on archaeological and literary evidence, Jonathan Bardill (1999B: 671–96) made the convincing case that the arch was used for Theodosius' triumph of 10 November 391 to celebrate his defeat of Magnus Maximus in 388.
5. Apparently these elephants had been removed from the temple of Ares in Athens by Theodosius II (George Kedrenos, *Compendium historiarum* 1.567). Robert de Clari claims (*La prise de Constantinople*, par. 108–9) to have seen two of these elephants when he saw the city during the summer of 1203.
6. None of these bas-reliefs survive on the Golden Gate, although some of the cornices and pilasters that once framed them are still in situ, having seen them myself. Pierre Gilles certainly saw twelve of them when he was busy exploring Constantinople (1544–7), but he only describes the south side sculptures in detail (*De topographia Constantinopoleos*, 4.9).
7. Zosimos, *Historia nova* 4.46.
8. Priscus fr. 43 apud count Marcellinus, *Chronica*, under 447.
9. Attila apparently styled himself *flagellum Dei*, 'the Scourge of God'. According to Lupus, bishop of Troyes (383–478/9) and later saint, when asked who he was, Attila came back with a smart *bon mot*, in impeccable classical Latin of course, "*Ego sum Attila, flagellum Dei*". Whether or not he actually said this to the good bishop, and one of our most important eyewitnesses, Priscus of Panium, is certainly ignorant of this savage by-name, Attila was more than just part of God's housekeeping of the world, to cleanse it of evil, corruption and decay. See, on this, Fields 2015.
10. Janin 1964: 202.
11. The notion that there were five (named gateways) used by the general public, the other five (numbered gateways) reserved to the military, is a modern convention first established by the Belgian scholar Philipp Anton Déthier in 1873.

12. *ILS* 823. The *Yeni Mevlanihane Kapısı* takes its name from a *tekke*, or headquarters, of Mevlevi dervishes that once stood outside the gateway.
13. *Anthologia Palatina*, ix 690.
14. John Zonaras, *Epitome historiarum* 15.27.
15. For an itinerary of these gateways, see Çelebi, *Seyâhatnâme* ('Narrative of Travels') 1.4 apud von Hammer-Purgstall i, 14–16. Evliya Çelebi was a Turk born in Istanbul in 1611, and much of his narrative is a description of his native city as it was in the mid seventeen century, an extremely interesting, lively and humorous depiction of life in the Ottoman capital as it neared the end of its golden age.
16. Al-Mas'udi, *Muruj al-dhahab wa ma'adin al-jawhr* § 465.
17. The recent discovery of an inscription by Neslihan Asutay (2003: 1–4) points to the Gate of Saint Romanos being identical with the Fourth Military Gate. It was named *Topkapı* after the great Ottoman cannon, the *Basilika*, which was placed opposite it during the 1453 siege (Niccolò Barbaro, *Diary of the Siege of Constantinople 1453* par.14).

Chapter 5

1. Gibbon, *D & F* vol. 3, ch. 71, p. 803.
2. The *Scriptores Historiae Augustae* was probably composed by an anonymous author in the last quarter of the fourth century, while pretending to be six different authors writing in the late third and early fourth centuries.
3. *Scriptores Historiae Augustae*, Carus 18.4.
4. Anonymous Valesianus, *Origo Constantini* 4, Socrates Scholasticus, *Historia ecclesiastica* 1.2.1, cf. Lactantius, *De mortibus persecutorum* 24.8.
5. In 2012, with a potpourri of civic pride, football populism and political conviction, the then mayor of Rome (2008–13), Gianni Alemanno, a politician with a neo-fascist background, organized the celebrations for the 1700th anniversary of the battle of Pons Mulvius. 'That battle', stressed Alemanno, 'represents an epochal transition not only for Rome, but for the whole of Christianity, regarded as the bedrock of European civilization and identity' (*Ponte Milvio, celebrazioni per i 1700 anni della battaglia*, http://terpag.blogspot.it/2012/10/ponte-milvio-celebrazioni-per-i-1700.htm). According to the mayor, 'such an important event in the history of humanity' had to be remembered not in an 'oversimplified way' but 'with uprightness, seriousness and sobriety' (Anno 312, Costantino vince a Ponte Milvio il Campidoglio celebra l'anniversario, *La Repubblica*, 25 October 2012, http://roma.repubblica.it/cronaca/2012/10/25/news/alemanno - 45300935.htm).
6. Eusebius, *Vita Constantini* 1.28–9.
7. Most scholars agree that Eusebius is describing the *labarum* as it appeared after 326, based on the description that he gives at *Vita Constantini* 1.30–1; specifically, the mention of the head-and-shoulders portrait of Constantinus and his sons in some relation to the tapestry hanging from the transverse bar.
8. Eusebius, *Historia ecclesiastica* 9.9.5–6.
9. Jerome, *Chronicon* 230 e, *De viris illustribus* 80.
10. Lactantius, *De mortibus persecutorum* 44.5–6.
11. Anon., *Panegyrici Latini* 12(9) passim.
12. Anon., *Panegyrici Latini* 12(9).2.4, 2.5, 4.1, 4.2, 4.5, 13.2, 16.2, 22.1, 26.1.
13. Ibid. 3.3.
14. Eusebius, *Historia ecclesiastica* 9.9.2.
15. Anon., *Panegyrici Latini* 12(9).17.2.
16. Paris, Bibliothèque national, Codex Græcus 510, folio 440.
17. Weiss 2003: 250.
18. Ibid. 249, cf. Bhola 2015: 28–37, 41–2, 48–9. The Latin term *corona*, while meaning 'crown' (here, *laureae coronae*, 'laurel crowns'), was used to describe solar halos, usually referring to a ring or points of light around the real sun; see, for example, Pliny *Historia naturalis* 2.28.

19. Eusebius, *Historia ecclesiastica* 10.5, Lactantius, *De mortibus persecutorum* 48.
20. According to the eyewitness testimony of Lactantius (*De mortibus persecutorum*, 48), the decree refers to 'the Christians' and 'all who choose that religion', and though it refers to God and 'the Deity', it is written as if referring to an all encompassing spiritual figure.
21. Zosimos, *Historia nova* 2.22–8, Lactantius, *De mortibus persecutorum* 47–50.
22. Zosimos, *Historia nova* 2.28, Eutropius, *Breviarium ab urbe condita* 10.5, cf. Eusebius, *Vita Constantini* 2.58–9.
23. Philostorgius, *Historia ecclesiastica* 2.9.
24. Sozomen, *Historia ecclesiastica* 2.3, cf. Iulianus, *Orationes* 1.8.
25. There is no reference to the Virgin Mary being chosen by Constantinus as the patron saint of his city in the contemporary documents relating to the early centuries of Constantinople. Indeed, for a century or so there was a bitter controversy concerning the issue of the virgin birth, the status of Mary, and therefore her title. It would not be until the Third Œcumenical Synod, held at Ephesos in 431, that Mary would be official recognized as the Theotokos, the one who brought forth or gave birth to God.
26. Anon., *Origo Constantini imperatoris* 6.30.
27. Eutropius, *Breviarium ab urbe condita* 10.8.
28. Socrates Scholasticus, *Historia ecclesiastica* 2.13.
29. Themistius, *Orationes* 3.47, Zosimos, *Historia nova* 2.108.
30. Sozomen, *Historia ecclesiastica* 2.3, Zosimos, *Historia nova* 2.30, cf. John Zonaras, *Epitome historiarum* 13.3.
31. As witnessed by John Sanderson, ambassador of Elizabeth I of England to the Ottoman court, who visited Troy in 1584 and 1591, as did Richard Wragg in 1594.
32. *Iliad*, 12.30 Lattimore.
33. The exact number of porphyry blocks is disputed, but common figures range from seven up to as many as eleven. Pierre Gilles (*De topographia Constantinopoleos*, 3.3), for example, opts for eight blocks, while Edward Gibbon (*D&F* vol. 1, ch. 17, p. 441) plumbs for ten.
34. Aurelianus had attributed his eastern victories to the assistance of Sol Invictus and had erected a temple in his god's honour in Rome.
35. John Zonaras, *Epitome historiarum* 13.3, cf. Anna Komnene, *Alexiad* 12.4.5.
36. See, on this, George Kedrenos, *Compendium historiarum* 1.564–5.
37. Virgil, *Aeneid* 2.166.
38. On the Forum of Constantinus and the column, see Janin 1964: 62–4, 79.
39. Luke 7:37, cf. Matthew 26:7.
40. Gregory I of Nazianzos the Theologian, *Homily* XXXIII.
41. Paul VI, Second Vatican Synod.
42. Luke 7:36–50.
43. Pausanias, *Guide to Greece* 1.24.5–7.
44. Diodorus Siculus apud Eudocia, *Violarium* 322.
45. Apollodoros, *Epitome* 5.9–14.
46. Ovid, *Fasti* 6.434–5.

Chapter 6

1. John 19:19, cf. Matthew 27:37.
2. Ambrose of Milan, *De obitu Theodosii oratio* 40–9, cf. the later Greek account in Socrates Scholasticus, *Historia ecclesiastica* 1.7, which was repeated later by Sozomen and Theodoretos of Kyrrhos.
3. Rufinus of Aquileia, *Historia ecclesiastica* 10.7–8.
4. Theodoretos of Kyrrhos, *Historia ecclesiastica* 17.
5. Isaiah 60:13 NIV.
6. A. Frolow, *La relique de la Vraie Croix; recherches sur le développement d'un culte* (Paris, 1961).

7. Prudentius, *Contra orationem Symmachi*, lines 486–8, cf. Eusebius, *Historia ecclesiastica* 10.4.16.
8. Eusebius, *Vita Constantini* 1.28.2.
9. Ibid. 1.29.
10. Ibid. 1.30–1.
11. Cameron & Hall 1999: 207.
12. Eusebius, *Historia ecclesiastica* 9.9.2.
13. Ibid. 9.9.10–11.
14. Eusebius, *Vita Constantini* 1.40–41.1.
15. Theophanes Continuatus 6.10, George Kedrenos, *Compendium historiarum* 2.363, John Zonaras, *Epitome historiarum* 5.6, Leo Diakonos, *Historia* 1.3, 4.5, 8.1.
16. Quoted by Pentcheva 2014 [2006]: 219 n. 71.
17. Psalm 45:5 NIV. This psalm has frequently been interpreted as a Messianic prophecy.
18. Constantinus VII Porphyrogenitus, *De ceremoniis aulae byzantinae* 485 Reiske, George Akropolites, *Opera* 1.19–20.
19. Theophanes Continuatus 4.15. In addition many pectoral crosses have been found in the excavations of fortresses.
20. Theophanes Continuatus 5.42, George Kedrenos, *Compendium historiarum* 2.211, 5.11.
21. In Greek: *nikopoiós*, Theophanes Continuatus 5.89.
22. Quoted by Pentcheva 2014 [2006]: 70.
23. Eusebius, *Vita Constantini* 2.8.2–9.3.
24. John Zonaras, *Epitome historiarum* 13.8.17, Iulianus, *Orationes* 1.36, 2.59, Cyril of Jerusalem, *Letter to Constantius* apud *PG* vol. 33, coll. 1165-76 at col. 1172.
25. Ps.-Zachariah of Mytilene, *Historia ecclesiastica* 9.17.

Chapter 7
1. Prokopios, *De aedificiis* 1.1.10.
2. Prokopios, *Wars* 8.33.27.
3. Agathias, *Historiae* 1.6.8, 22.6.
4. Evagrius Scholasticus, *Historia ecclesiastica* 4.214–15.
5. Agathias, *Historiae* 2.12.2–6.
6. Prokopios, *Wars* 8.31.9–10.
7. Paris, Musée du Louvre, inv. OA9063.
8. John the Lydian, *De magistratibus populi Romani* 3.42, 68.
9. In Greek: *Haghía Sophía*, which honours Christ as the Holy Wisdom of God, *not* to an individual saint named Sophia.
10. Sozomen, *Historia ecclesiastica* 8.20–2.
11. Prokopios, *Wars* 1.24.37.
12. Prokopios, *De aedificiis* 1.1.21.
13. John the Lydian, *De magistratibus populi Romani* 3.70.
14. Prokopios, *De aedificiis* 1.1.24.
15. Anon., *Narratio de aedificatione templi Sanctae Sophiae* 27, apud T. Preger, *Scriptores originum Constantinopolitanarum* i, 105. The *Narratio*, however, is late and largely legendary.
16. In fact, this is the second dome, built by the son of one of the original architects, Isidore the Younger. The original dome had crashed to the ground in May 558 after a very large earthquake had seriously weakened it in the previous year (Theophanes Confessor, *Chronographia*, annus mundi 6050, Agathias, *Historiae* 5.3.1–6.9). A Constantinopolitan lawyer, Agathias would have lived through the 557 earthquake at Constantinople, so his observations are firsthand. He would have also witnessed the octogenarian Iustinianus re-inaugurate the repaired Hagia Sophia on Christmas Eve of 562.
17. Prokopios' famous description of Hagia Sophia is in *De aedificiis*, 1.1.27–78.

18. By way of comparison, the dome of Christopher Wren's Saint Paul's in London stands sixty-seven metres, but its main nave is only 13.41 metres across compared with Hagia Sophia's main nave of 32.27 metres across, which is even larger than that of Saint Peter's in Rome.

19. For a good, firsthand account on the interior of Hagia Sophia, see Paul the Silentiary, *Descriptio Sanctae Sophiae* apud Otto Veh, *Prokopios Werke* v, 306–58. The contemporary Agathias refers his audience to Paul's famous description of Hagia Sophia: 'If anyone who lives far from the capital wishes to get a clear and comprehensive a picture of the church as he would if he were there to view in person, then he could hardly do better than to read the poem in hexameters of Paul the son of Cyrus and the grandson of Florus' (*Historiae*, 5.9.7). Paul the Silentiary wrote an *ekphrasis* of Hagia Sophia recited during the rededication ceremonies held between 24 December 562 and 6 January 563 in the imperial and patriarchal palaces.

20. Prokopios, *De aedificiis* 1.1.65.

Chapter 8

1. Eusebius, *Vita Constantini* 4.56, 62.

2. Ibid. 4.67.

3. Socrates Scholasticus, *Historia ecclesiastica* 1.40.1–2, cf. John Zonaras, *Epitome historiarum* 13.23, 58.

4. John Chrysostomos, *Contra Iudaeos et gentiles quod Christus sit deus* 9.

5. Pierre Gilles, *De topographia Constantinopoleos* 4.2. A grandiose cruciform edifice with multiple domes, completed by Iustinianus (r. 527–65) in 550, replaced the original church, which had fallen into decay (Prokopios, *De aedificiis* 1.4.9–24). Most emperors were buried in the heroön until the eleventh century. This church was demolished in 1462; its bricks serving as a quarry for the *Fatih Camii*, the enormous mosque complex of Mehmet II the Conqueror that now stands on the spot. A miniature in the Vatican Library gives some idea of the building's magnificence (Vaticanus Græcus, MS 1162, folio 2b), while the best-known 'replica' of the Holy Apostles is the eleventh-century Basilica di San Marco, the famous church of the doges in Venice.

6. Iulianus, *Caesares* 336 A–B.

7. Voltaire, *Dictionnaire philosophique*, sv Baptême.

8. Zosimos, *Historia nova* 2.29.2.

9. Ibid. 2.29.1.

10. Anon., *Panegyrici Latini* 6(7).21.3–7, 22.1.

11. Eusebius, *Vita Constantini* 1.28–32.

12. Acts 26:13 NIV.

13. The story of the vision of Paul occurs three times in Acts of the Apostles, at 9:1–19, 22:1–21, and 26:9–21, and although the experience in not told in exactly the same way each time, all three versions have strong continuities.

14. See, on this, Bhola 2015: 167–75.

15. Theodoretos of Kyrrhos, *Historia ecclesiastica* 1.1.

16. Alföldi 1948: 33.

17. 2 Chronicles 1:3.

18. Eusebius, *Historia ecclesiastica* 9.9.10–11, *Vita Constantini* 1.39.

19. Ibid. *Vita Constantini* 3.54.4, 55, 57.4.

20. Thompson 2014: 14.

21. At some point, 21 May became the day when the Orthodox Church remembered the emperor and his mother as οἱ ἅγιοι Κωνσταντίνος καὶ Ἑλένη οἱ Ἰσαπόστολοι. In the modern Orthodox liturgy, the *troparion* (Gr. *tropárion*), the short verse chanted towards the close of vespers to set the theme for the services of the coming day, includes the following:

'He saw the image of the Cross in the heavens, / and, like Paul, he did not receive his call from men, O Lord. / Your apostle among rulers, the emperor Constantinus, / was appointed by Your hand as ruler over the imperial City / that he preserved in peace for many years, / through the prayers of the Theotokos, O only lover of mankind'.

22. Ammianus Marcellinus, *Res Gestae* 21.16.18.
23. Quoted by Braudel 2001 [1998]: 354–5.
24. Eustathius of Antioch apud Theodoratos, *Historia ecclesiastica* 1.7. According to the liturgies of the Eastern Orthodox Church and the Coptic Orthodox Church of Alexandria, 318 bishops took part in the Synod of Nicaea I, as was stated by Iustinianus (*Novellae constitutiones*, Novella 131.1 apud Scott 12.125).
25. Eusebius, *Vita Constantini* 3.10.
26. Op. cit.
27. Ibid. 3.12.
28. Rufinus of Aquileia, *Historia ecclesiastica* 10.5.
29. Decree of the First Œcumenical Synod (Nicaea I in 325).
30. *Codex Theodosianus* XVI.10.10 (February 391), 11 (July 391), 12 (November 392).
31. Zosimos, *Historia nova* 4.30, 33, 40, 56.
32. Pacatus, *Panegyrici Latini* 12.22.
33. It is possible that the Frigidus is now known as the Vipava, a left tributary of the river Isonzo/Soča in modern day Slovenia.
34. Rufinus of Aquileia, *Historia ecclesiastica* 11.33. For an in-depth survey of the Christian sources dealing with the Frigidus, see Cameron 2013 [2011] 93–131.
35. Orosius, *Historia adversus Paganos* 7.35. The 'miracle' was actually a katabatic wind known as the Bora, a northern to north-eastern wind that carries high density air from a higher elevation down a slope under the force of gravity. The wind itself is known by various renderings of the name of the mythological Greek figure, Βορέας, the North Wind, such as *bura* in Croatian, *burja* in Slovene, буран in Bulgarian and βοράς in Modern Greek. The most commonly used *Bora* is probably from the Turkish. The Bora is still a recurring feature of the Vipava valley, so much so that it influences the layout and architecture of settlements in the region. Narrow streets bordered by robust buildings with heavy stone roofs predominate in many towns in the path of the Bora and ropes and chains are strung along footpaths should people get caught outside.
36. Zosimos, *Historia nova* 4.58.4, Socrates Scholasticus, *Historia ecclesiastica* 5.25, Philostorgius, *Historia ecclesiastica* 11.2, John of Antioch, fr. 187.
37. Ambrose of Milan, *Epistola* 57.
38. Sozomen, *Historia ecclesiastica* 7.25.
39. Leviticus 18:22 NIV.
40. *Codex Theodosianus* IX.7.6 (May 390).
41. Augustine of Hippo, *De mendacio* 7.10.
42. Theodoretos of Kyrrhos, *Historia ecclesiastica* 5.17.
43. Ambrose of Milan, *Epistola* 51.
44. Ammianus Marcellinus, *Res Gestae* 22.16.12.
45. Both quoted by Grant 1990 [1976]: 162.

Chapter 9

1. Voltaire apud Besterman, *Voltaire's Correspondence* 12362 (5 April 1762).
2. Matthew 22:37–40 NIV.
3. The Gospel of Luke has Jesus say the now famous lines, 'Then give to Caesar what is Caesar's, and to God what is God's' (Luke 20:25 NIV, cf. Romans 13:7).
4. John 18:36 NIV.
5. The Greek word means either *life* or *soul*.

6. Matthew 16:24–5 NIV.
7. Spiridakis 1968: 340.
8. Anon., *Doctrina Jacobi nuper baptizati* 3.8, cf. Theophanes Confessor, Chronographia, annus mundi 6122 [629/30].
9. Acts 9:1–22.
10. Tacitus, *Annales* 15.44.3–8, cf. Suetonius, *Nero* 16.2.
11. Tacitus, *Annales* 15.44.4, 5.
12. *Ascension of Isaiah*, 4.2.
13. Eusebius, *Historia ecclesiastica* 2.25.2.
14. E.g. Sulpicius Severus, *Chronica* 2.28-9.
15. Galatians 3:28 NIV.
16. Romans 6:3–4.
17. Mark 2:10 NIV.
18. 2 Corinthians 5:16.
19. Philippians 2:9–11.
20. Ibid. 2:7–9.
21. Romans 8:17, cf. 2 Timothy 2:12.
22. Cf. Isaiah 53 1:10, though not initially a messianic prophecy, it became to be viewed as such by early Christians.
23. Matthew 26:26–7.
24. At the time of writing, Syria was very much in the news. Hardly surprising when you consider that Syria runs on one of the world's biggest ethnic/religious fault lines, the eastern Mediterranean, what they used to call the Levant. This is where the Euro–Christian tectonic plate has been grinding against the Arab–Muslim plate for 1,400 years, with seismic activity picking up no end just recently. Carthaginians, Greeks, Romans, Byzantines, Crusaders, Ottomans, British, and French – they all had a shot at the coastal strip and the country around Damascus. So, the hills in the west of Syria, along the coastal and a few miles inland, have been fizzing with foreign influence for some two thousand years now. That has led to some complicated tribes and religions developing in those parts. There are the Druze in south-western Syria, a people who adapted to Muslim conquest by insulating their real religion, some kind of quasi-Graeco-Gnostic-Hinduism thing, with a thin outer shell of Islam. There are the Christians who hung on after the Muslim conquest, in their mountain villages, in spite of pogroms and massacres. And most of all, there are the Alawites, Shi`a mountain tribes who were hated by the Sunni Arab majority east of the coastal hills, in the desert, who look south and east to Arabia for their cues. They currently have a little slogan that gives you a nice, clear blueprint for their political program: 'Christians to Beirut, Alawites to the graveyard'. And we have yet to mention the Kurds, 10 per cent of the population, who are Sunni but not Arab, which has made for all sorts of gory complications.

Chapter 10

1. Mark 1:9–11, Matthew 3:1–17, Luke 3:21–2, John 1:29–34 (Baptism), Acts 2:1–4 (Pentecost).
2. Gregory of Nyssa, *Not Three Gods* apud Schaff-Wace, *Nicene and Post-Nicene Fathers* series II, vol. V.
3. Gregory I of Nazianzos the Theologian, *Orationes* 29.6–10.
4. Voltaire, *Dictionnaire philosophique*, sv Antitrinitaires.
5. Ibid. *Poème sur e désastre de Lisbonne* verse 2, line 32.
6. Letter dated October, 'Victor Constantinus, the Great Augustus, to Alexander and Arius', § 5 apud Eusebius, *Vita Constantini* 2.64–72.
7. Exodus 3:1–6.

8. Genesis 28.10–15.
9. Inner Octagonal Arcade, lines 7–10, 15–16.
10. See also Qur'an 4:109, 5:77, 5:116, three verses specifically directed against the Trinity.
11. Qur'an 4:171, 5:74.
12. Ibid. 3:45, 4:157.
13. Ibid.3:49, 5:110.
14. Ibid. 3:46.
15. Ibid. 40:55, 48:2.
16. Maximos Confessor, *Acta* § 100.
17. Ayers 2004.
18. Divine Liturgy of Saint John Chrysostomos.

Chapter 11

1. 2 Corinthians 6:18, cf. Matthew 28.18 NIV, 'Then Jesus came to them [the disciples] and said, "All authority in heaven and on earth has been given to me"'.
2. Revelations 1:8, 4:8, 11:17, 15:3, 16:7, 16:14, 19:6, 19:15, 21:22.
3. Revelations 1:8 NIV, cf. John 19:37.
4. Pentcheva 2006: 631.
5. Basil of Caesarea, *On the Holy Spirit* 18:45.
6. Tolstoy 2014 [1897]: 81.
7. Theodore the Stoudite, *On the Holy Icons* apud *PG* vol. 99, coll. 328–436.
8. So called because it was adorned with gilded bronze sheets. See, for this, George Kedrenos, *Compendium historiarum* 1.563, 656–7. For an in-depth description of the Chalke, see Prokopios, *De aedificiis* 1.10.12–20.
9. Theodore the Stoudite, *On the Holy Icons* apud *PG* vol. 99, col. 1164.
10. Quoted by McLees 2012: 39.
11. Theosteriktos, *Vita Niketas* § 62.
12. Quoted by McLees 2012: 39.
13. *Scriptor Incertus [de Leone Armenio]* , fr. 2.
14. Decree of the Seventh Œcumenical Synod (Nicaea II in 787).

Chapter 12

1. Philotheos, *Kleterologion* p. 165, lines 21–2, p. 167, lines 10, 13–14.
2. It is significant that the common Greek word *logos* had semantic roots in both speech and reason; it can mean 'word', 'utterance', 'story', 'account', 'explanation', 'reason', and 'ratio', among other things. It seems, much like Plato before him, one of Jesus' major and ongoing undertakings was to construct moral models of what it is for an utterance not to just tell a story but to give a reason.
3. See, on this, Acts 17:22 NIV, where Paul at Athens could say, 'I see that in every way you are very religious'. The sermon, however, was not the success he had hoped. For the 'false' virgin Athena, as opposed to the one and only eternal, Virgin Mary, still captivated the city. Of course, there was Saint Dionysius the Areopagite. This Dionysius has a walk-on part in the Acts of the Apostles (17:34), where he is converted by Paul as the apostle preached on the Aeropagos Hill (hence 'Areopagite').
4. Michael Psellos, *Chronographia*, Michael VI 7.1.
5. Leo Diakonos, *Historia* 5.7, John Skylitzes, *Synopsis historiôn* 1.5 [11]. It was toppled by an earthquake in 1532. See, on this, Janin 1964: 101.
6. Constantinus VII Porphyrogenitus, *De ceremoniis aulae byzantinae* 1.51 (42) apud *CSHB* ii, 24–5.
7. Ibid. 1.8 apud *CSHB* i, 50.
8. Liudprand of Cremona, *Antapodosis* 1.7, 3.31.

9. Anna Komnene, *Alexiad* 6.8.1.
10. Ammianus Marcellinus, *Res Gestae* 16.10.10.
11. Libanius, *Orationes* 12.63.
12. Xenophon, *Hellenika* 7.1.38.
13. Sidonius Apollinaris, *Epistolae* 1.2.6.
14. Anon., *Deeds of the bishops of Halberstadt*, apud *Contemporary Sources for the Fourth Crusade*, tr. A.J. Andrea, 2000: 254.
15. Matthew 16:18 NIV.
16. Liudprand of Cremona, *Relatio de legatione Constantinopolitana ad Nicephorum Phocam* 51.
17. Constantinus VII Porphyrogenitus, *De ceremoniis aulae byzantinae* apud *CSHB* i, 108–9.
18. Leo Diakonos, *Historia* 9.12.
19. Ibid. 10.2.
20. John Skylitzes, *Synopsis historiôn* 15.18 [310], cf. Leo Diakonos, who says it was 'the icon of the Theometor, holding the divinely human Logos in her arms, which he took from Mysia [Bulgaria]' (*Historia*, 9.12). For an explanation of the differences in the two accounts concerning the Marian icon, see Pentcheva 2014 [2006]: 53–4.
21. Niketas Choniates, *O City of Byzantium* I, p. 12 [18–19] Magoulias.
22. Ibid. II, bk. 5, p. 90 [158] Magoulias.
23. Jerome, *Epistola* 22 § 32, 'To Eustochium'.
24. Ezekiel 27:24 NKJV. As an aside, my preferred version of the Bible, the New International Version, translates the key word, incorrectly, as 'blue', whereas the New King James Version correctly uses the word 'purple'. While we are on the subject of the Bible, it should be understood that apart from the book of Kings, the Old Testament is not a historical record *per se* – it is a mishmash of factual events, legends and myths drawn from a number of different sources. The Bible, like Shakespeare, will sustain any theory you bring to it, as well or as badly as any other.
25. Pliny, *Historia naturalis* 9.63.137.
26. Prokopios, *Wars* 8.17.1–7.
27. Virgil, *Georgics* 2.121.
28. John Skylitzes, *Synopsis historiôn* 16.3 [317].
29. *Codex*, 11.8.3, apud Scott 15.175.
30. Ibid. 11.8.4, apud Scott 15.175.
31. *Novels*, 80 apud Scott 17.272.

Chapter 13
1. John Zonaras, *Annalium* 12.9, *Epitome historiarum* 13.3.
2. Constantinus VII Porphyrogenitus, *De ceremoniis aulae byzantinae* 2.15 apud *CSHB* ii, 589.
3. Eusebius, *Vita Constantini* 3.54, Zosimos, *Historia nova* 2.31, Sozomen, *Historia ecclesiastica* 2.5.
4. Herodotos, *Historiae* 9.81.1.
5. Fornara 59.
6. Pausanias, *Guide to Greece* 10.13.9.
7. Niketas Choniates, *O City of Byzantium* X, p. 360 [652] Magoulias.
8. According to the sixth-century Roman statesman Cassiodorus (*Variae epistolae*, 3.51) the four colours represented the four seasons.
9. John Malalas, *Chronographia* 16.2.24–25.
10. Cameron 1973: 53.
11. Prokopios, *Wars* 1.24.7.
12. Ibid. 1.24.1.
13. John Malalas, *Chronographia* 16.4.
14. Cameron 1973: 240–52.

15. John Malalas, *Chronographia* 18.71, Theophanes Confessor, *Chronographia*, annus mundi 6024.
16. John Malalas, *Chronographia* 18.99, Theophanes Confessor, *Chronographia*, annus mundi 6039.
17. John Malalas, *Chronographia* 18.138.20–3.
18. Ibid. 18.150, Theophanes Confessor, *Chronographia*, annus mundi 6055.
19. John Malalas, *Chronographia* 18.117.
20. Prokopios, *Anékdota* 7.1–2.
21. Ibid. 7.3.
22. Ibid. 7.4.
23. Ibid. 7.5.
24. See, on this, Agathias, *Historiae* 3.1.4.
25. Menander Protector, fr. 1.
26. Op. cit.
27. Niketas Choniates, *O City of Byzantium* VII, p. 305 [558] Magoulias.
28. Ibid. IV, bk. 2, p. 192–3, 194 [349–51, 352] Magoulias.
29. Agathias, *Historiae* 5.21.4.
30. Anon., *Chronicon paschale* 235–6, Theophanes Confessor, *Chronographia*, annus mundi 6053, cf. Cameron 1976: 91.
31. Prokopios, *Wars* 1.24.5.
32. Ibid. 1.24.3. For a discussion on the difficulties associated with interpreting Prokopios with regard to the circus factions, including dating, biases, and the necessity to read between the lines, see Bell 2013: 8–19.
33. Cameron 1976: 24–44, 74–104, 126–54.
34. E.g. Liebeschuetz 2003: 215, Evans 2005: 17, cf. Bell 2013: 143–5, Main 2013.
35. Cameron 1976: 105–6.
36. See, on this, Main 2013: 31.
37. The earliest reference to a Roman emperor being proclaimed by shield-raising is Iulianus in 361 (Amminianus Marcellinus, *Res Gestae* 20.4.17, Zosimos, *Historia nova* 3.9.4).
38. Theophylact Simocatta, *Historiae* 8.6.2–7.1.
39. Theophanes Confessor, *Chronographia*, annus mundi 6094. According to Theophylact Simocatta (*Historiae*, 8.7.11) the numbers of the faction members were 1,500 Greens and 900 Blues.
40. Cameron 1976: 308.
41. Cameron 1973: 63.
42. Ibid. 256.
43. Niketas Choniates, *O City of Byzantium* X, p. 361 [653] Magoulias.
44. Sidonius Apollinaris, *To Consentius* (Carmina 23.395–415).
45. Ibid. 23.376–8.
46. Ibid. 23.304–427.
47. This can be seen on the Theodosian base (east side) of the so-called Obelisk of Theodosius (Obelisk of Thutmose III), where Theodosius I, standing in the imperial loge, or *kathisma*, and flanked by his two sons, is handing out a wreath of victory to a charioteer.
48. İstanbul Arkeologı Müzelerı, inv. 2995, inv. 5560.
49. John Malalas, *Chronographia* 16.6.
50. *Anthologia Palatina*, xvi 356.
51. Ibid. xvi 340. Alan Cameron has discerned Porphyrios had thirty-two epigrams celebrating his circus exploits (*Anthologia Palatina*, xv 44, 46, 47, xvi 335–62, 380–1).
52. Ibid. xvi 374.
53. Cameron 1973: 209–10.
54. *Anthologia Palatina*, xvi 350.

55. Martial, *Epigrammata* 10.50.7.
56. *CIL* vi 10082.
57. Ovid, *Tristia* 4.8.19.
58. John Kinnamos, *Deeds of John and Manuel Komnenos* 263.17–264.11 Brand.
59. Cameron 1976: 153.
60. Leo Diakonos, *Historia* 1.4.
61. Ibid. 1.6, cf. John Skylitzes, *Synopsis historiôn* 14.19 [276].
62. John Skylitzes, *Synopsis historiôn* 5.10 [96].
63. Ibid. 5.19 [108].
64. Ibid. 5.21 [109].
65. Ibid. 17.1 [370], cf. [371].
66. John Kinnamos, *Deeds of John and Manuel Komnenos* 5.4.
67. Guillaume de Tyr, *Historia rerum in paribus transmarinis gestarum* 22.4.
68. Geoffroi de Villehardouin, *La conquête de Constantinople* par 11.
69. Ibid.
70. Benjamin of Tudela, *Sefer Masa'oth* ('Book of Travels') 24 Adler.
71. See, on this, Jacoby 2014: 149.
72. Benjamin of Tudela, *Sefer Masa'oth* 19–24.
73. Ibid. 22. See, on this, Jacoby 2014: 157.
74. Michel Baudier, *Histoire general du serial et de la cour du Grand Seigneur, empereur des Turcs* 85–6.
75. *Odyssey* 19.422–3 Lattimore.
76. A series of 427 beautifully painted Ottoman miniatures illustrate the imperial festivities of 1582. They are bound in a book entitled *Surnâme-i Hümâyûn* ('Book of the Imperial Circumcision Festival'), which is housed in the Topkapı Sarayı Müzesi (Hazine Ktp. nr. 1344). Executed between 1583 and 1588, the miniatures were skilfully and colourfully painted by the renowned miniaturist Nakkaş Osman and his team.

Chapter 14

1. In Greek: 'Ἐκ γυναικός τα χείρω'. 'Και εκ γυναικός τα κρείπω'. Quoted by McLees 2012: 57.
2. Based on the story from Luke 7:36–50.
3. Divine Liturgy of Saint John Chrysostomos.
4. Prokopios, *Anékdota* 10.5.
5. Gibbon, *D&F* vol. 2, ch. 40, p. 461.
6. Prokopios, *Anékdota* 9.9.
7. At the time of his brother's accession to the throne, Constantinus married Helena, the beautiful daughter of the nobleman Alypios. She bore him three equally beautiful daughters, Eudokia, Zoë and Theodora. Eudokia, badly disfigured by smallpox, had long been packed off to a convent (Michael Psellos, *Chronographia*, Constantinus VIII 2.5). The other two, Zoë and Theodora, were almost equally ill-favoured, both spinsters and well past their prime.
8. Michael Psellos, *Chronographia*, Constantinus VIII 2.10, John Skylitzes, *Synopsis historiôn* 17.3 [374], Yahya ibn Sa'id apud Vasiliev–Kratchkowsky *Patrologia Orientalis*, t. xxiii, fasc. III, 486.
9. Michael Psellos, *Chronographia*, Romanos III 3.5, 17.
10. John Skylitzes, *Synopsis historiôn* 16.45 [367], 46 [369].
11. George Kedrenos, *Compendium historiarum*, 2.733.
12. Michael Psellos, *Chronographia*, Romanos III 3.26, cf. Michael IV 4.5. Assassination by poison was so common that it is never difficult to favour this theory. Poison affords a cloak of anonymity to the assassin: if it was Zoë, we shall probably never know for sure. As so often

happens when female hands touched the reins of power, breathless whispers of innuendo curled around her reputation. George Kedrenos (*Compendium historiarum*, 2.733), for instance, definitely asserts that Romanos was being slowly poisoned by Zoë. According to John Skylitzes (*Synopsis historiôn*, 18.17 [389]) it was John the Orphanotrophos who actually administered the poison. On the other hand, Yahya ibn Sa'ïd (apud Vasiliev-Kratchkowsky *Patrologia Orientalis*, t. xxiii, fasc. III, 536) has Romanos dying of consumption.

13. John Skylitzes, *Synopsis historiôn* 19.2 [392].

14. Michael Psellos, *Chronographia*, Michael IV 4.16.

15. Ibid. Romanos III 3.22.

16. Ibid. Michael IV 4.26.

17. Ibid. Michael V 5.14–15, cf. Michael IV 4.28–9, Michael V 5.6. As Michael Psellos says, for the wicked uncle 'evil followed evil' (ibid. Michael V 5.15); John was blinded in prison on the orders of the patriarch of Constantinople, Michael I Keroularios (1043), and finally put to death on the orders of Constantinus IX Monomachos.

18. George Kedrenos, *Compendium historiarum* 2.750, Michael Psellos, *Chronographia*, Michael V 5.21.

19. Michael Psellos, *Chronographia*, Michael V 5.21. We should remember that Zoë's father was Constantinus VIII, her uncle Basil II, her grandfather Romanos II, her great-grandfather Constantinus VII Porphyrogenitus.

20. Theodora had been exiled to the convent of Petrion during the reign of Romanos III Argyros. To be stripped of office or position and confined to the peace and security of a convent or monastery was a common form of sugar-coated imprisonment among the Byzantines, assuming, of course, you had not been blinded as well.

21. John Skylitzes, *Synopsis historiôn* 21.7 [434].

22. Michael Psellos, *Chronographia*, Michael V 5.26.

23. Constantinus IX Monomachos would die on 11 January 1055 from a chill after staying too long in the bath, and subsequently Theodora, as the only survivor of the legitimate Macedonian dynasty, would find herself once more dragged into the whirlpool of world events and reign alone in name for the next eighteen months. She died on 31 August 1056, at the age of seventy-six (Michael Psellos, *Chronographia*, Theodora 6.21).

24. Venice, Codex Marciana Græcus 524, *Epigrams* 7, poem 10.

25. Michael Psellos, *Chronographia*, Constantinus IX 6.160.

26. Ibid. 6.61.

27. *Iliad*, 3.156–7 Lattimore: 'Surely there is no blame on Trojans and strong-greaved Achaeans / if for long time they suffered hardship for a woman like this one', cf. Niketas Choniates, *O City of Byzantium* X, p. 361 [653] Magoulias.

28. E.g. Constantinus' concave *miliaresion* in silver has on the obverse the Virgin Mary, *orans* and *nimbate*. On the reverse Constantinus is shown standing, wearing a diadem with a cross and pendula, lamellar armour and military cloak. In his right hand he holds a long cross; his left hand holds a sheathed sword. The Greek inscription reads: 'O Lady, preserve the pious Monomachos'. For the coin, see Grierson 1973: III 2, 745–6.

29. Whittemore 1942: 17–20, cf. Oikonomidès 1978.

30. Constantinus Doukas had been originally betrothed to Helena, the daughter of Robert Guiscard.

31. John, Alexios' eldest *son*, had been formally crowned co-emperor in 1092. This was clearly an endeavour by Alexios to secure his newly-founded imperial house, the Komnenoi.

32. Niketas Choniates, *O City of Byzantium* I, p. 8 [10] Magoulias.

33. Gibbon, *D&F* vol. 3, ch. 48, p. 55.

34. Niketas Choniates, *O City of Byzantium* I, p. 8 [10] Magoulias.

35. Anna Komnene, *Alexiad* 14.7.6.

36. John Zonaras, *Epitome historiarum* 18.24, Niketas Choniates, *O City of Byzantium* I, p. 8–9 [10–11] Magoulias.
37. John Zonaras, *Epitome historiarum* 3.763–4, cf. Niketas Choniates (*O City of Byzantium* I, p. 6 [6] Magoulias) who stresses that it was John himself who secretly slipped the imperial ring from the dying emperor's finger. Both authors, however, suggest John's departure from his father's deathbed was venal and self-serving.

Chapter 15
1. Gibbon, *D&F* vol. 2, ch. 46, p. 712.
2. Michael Psellos, *Chronographia*, Michael IV 4.19.
3. Leo VI Sapiens, *Taktiká* 20.12.
4. John Skylitzes, *Synopsis historión* 21.28 [476].
5. Leo VI Sapiens, *Taktiká* 20.22.
6. Usually known by its Latin name, *De administrando imperio*, 'On administrating a realm', was in part derived from the official archives of the Byzantine foreign ministry.
7. Anna Komnene, *Alexiad* 12.5.2.
8. Thietmar of Merseberg, *Chronicon Thietmari* 11, 34.
9. Liudprand of Cremona, *Antapodosis* 1.11.
10. Anna Komnene, *Alexiad* 13.4.6.
11. Ibid. 13.4.7.
12. Ostrogorsky 1968: 365.
13. Anna Komnene, *Alexiad* 13.12.2.
14. Ibid. 10.11.6.
15. Ibid. 14.2.1–4.
16. Constantinus VII Porphyrogenitus, *De ceremoniis aulae byzantinae* 1.86 (77) apud *CSHB* ii, 174.
17. Tzimiskès was a word of Armenian origin referring to John's small statue, he himself being of the Kourkouas clan, which had Armenian blood. John's mother was the sister of Nikephoros Phokas, while his first wife, Mária, was the sister of Bardas Skleros. For the appearance and character of John Tzimiskès, see John Skylitzes, *Synopsis historión* 15.22 [312].
18. John Zonaras, *Epitome historiarum* 13.8.
19. John Skylitzes, *Synopsis historión* 5.24 [113], cf. 6.15 [131]).
20. Leo was the son of either Basil I or Michael III by Eudokia – a beauty who seems to have had a somewhat varied licentious life and was generous with her favours. This probably accounts for Basil's harshness to Leo, eventually having him locked up for three years. Some modern commentators have argued that supporters of Leo may have killed Basil in a hunting 'accident'. He was certainly wounded across the stomach and the emperor died nine days later, probably as a result of peritonitis and gas gangrene. The symptoms peritonitis are fever, vomiting and extreme weakness and patients often also suffer mental confusion, prostration or shock. Basil's was not a glamorous death. It was not the way an emperor was supposed to die.
21. Antioch – present day Antakya in what is now the Turkish province of Hatay – had a history going back to the third century BC, when it was founded by Seleukos I Nikator (r. 321–281 BC), the most able of Alexander's generals, and was the urban centre of outstanding importance in the Roman empire. It had been the empire's traditional base for military campaigns in the East; apart from being the third largest city in the empire, it was strategically important for the eastern frontier, the key to northern Syria. It had fallen to the Arabs during the caliphate of 'Umar (r. 634–44), and would come once more under Muslim rule in 1084, remaining so until the arrival of the First Crusade. The city remained a powerhouse in the Levant until, in 1268, it was sacked and razed it to the ground by an

Egyptian army under the Mamluk sultan Baybars (d. 1277) and all its surviving inhabitants sold into slavery. Antioch was never to recover and slowly sank into the mud that washes down from Mount Silpios.

22. As reported by Liudprand of Cremona (*Relatio de legatione Constantinopolitana ad Nicephorum Phocam*, 10) to the Holy Roman Emperor Otto I after his diplomatic mission to Constantinople in 968. The writings of Liudprand are amongst the most essential sources for both Italy and Byzantium in the tenth century. He was born of a good Lombard family and pursued a successful career in the Church, ending his life as bishop of Cremona. He passed away, in fact, in Constantinople, for his fluency and facility in Greek made him a great asset to Otto, who dispatched him on two diplomatic missions to the capital. Liudprand remains to this day an important eyewitness to events in the Constantinopolitan court during the middle part of the tenth century.

23. In Greek: Βασίλειος Β'. He was known at the time as Basil Porphyrogenitus to distinguish him from his supposed ancestor, Basil I the Macedonian.

24. Michael Psellos, *Chronographia*, Zoë & Theodora 6.1.

25. *Farmers' Law*, § 18.

26. Theophanes Continuatus, 456.

27. Anon., *De velitatione* 217. *De velitatione* ('On Skirmishing') was a text compiled around 975 from notes written by Nikephoros Phokas.

28. According to Treadgold (1995: 119–23) during the tenth century a thematic soldier could hope to earn each year twelve gold pieces.

29. Constantinus V Kopronymos, the arch-iconoclast who was nevertheless victorious against both Arabs and Bulghars, gained his scatological soubriquet because he had soiled the baptismal water in the sacred font at his christening – which for iconodule writers foretold his unorthodox rule (Theophanes, *Chronographia*, annus mundi 6211).

30. Leo Diakonos, *Historia* 6.11. This *tagma* was named after the old Achaemenid Persian unit, the Immortals (Gr. *Athánatoi*, cf. OP *Amrtaka* or Followers) as the Greeks called them, because they liked to believe, falsely, that their 'number was at no time either greater or less than ten thousand' (Herodotos, *Historiae* 7.83.1). First formed by Cyrus the Great (Xenophon, *Kyroupaideia* 7.5.68), this superbly trained élite unit had been composed mostly of ethnic Persian though closely related Medes from northern Iran and Elamites from southern Iran were also known to have been members.

31. Treadgold 1995: 36, 66.

32. Michael Psellos, *Chronographia*, Michael VI 5.1–4.

33. Ibn Rustah, *Kitab al-a'lak an-nafisa* 30, cf. 140 where the author has the Khazar king riding with 10,000 horsemen, 'fully armed, with banners, lances and strong coats of mail', when he goes out raiding. Ibn Rustah wrote a seven-volume encyclopaedia of historical and geographical knowledge, completed in 913, of which only one volume survives.

34. Nikephoros Phokas, *Præcepta militaria* 1.8, 11. For *drouggoi*, see McGreer 2008 [1995]: 203; for *menavlatoi*, see Anastasiadis 1994, McGreer 2008 [1995]: 209–10.

35. According to McGreer (2008 [1995]: 205), this oval shield was no less than 140 centimetres. See also, Dawson 2007: 2–6.

36. Dawson (2007: 19), analysing a soapstone craving depicting a *spathíon*, says eighty-five centimetres, while Parani (2003: 131), citing *Syllogê taktikôn* 38, says infantry swords were ninety-four centimetres long from pommel to point, cavalry swords up to 110 centimetres. For comparison, Carolingian *spathae* were usually between ninety and a hundred centimetres in length, of which the blade represented some seventy-five to eighty centimetres.

37. Leo VI Sapiens, *Taktiká* 6.2.

38. In Greek: ζωστίκιον σπαθίον, *zôstíkion spathíon*, Nikephoros Phokas, *Præcepta militaria* 1.3, 4.

39. Dawson 2009: 84.

40. Michael Psellos, *Chronographia*, Constantinus IX 6.108.
41. Leo VI Sapiens, *Taktiká* 6.
42. Parani (2003: 141) citing the *Syllogê taktikôn*, says arrows were at least seventy centimetres in length.
43. McGreer 2008 [1995]: 68, 207.
44. Decker 2013: 230.
45. Anon., *De velitatione* 17.17–19.
46. Abu at-Tayyib al-Mutanabbi, *To Sayf al-Dawla*, lines 7–8.
47. McGreer 2008 [1995]: 313.
48. Nikephoros Phokas, *Præcepta militaria* 3.4, repeated verbatim in Nikephoros Ouranos, *Taktiká* 60.4.
49. In Greek: *sidhrorábdia*, Nikephoros Phokas, *Præcepta militaria* 3.7, 9.
50. Anon., *Digenes Akrites* 1.148.
51. Nikephoros Phokas, *Præcepta militaria* 3.7.
52. Leo VI Sapiens, *Taktiká* 6.2.
53. The *Taktiká* (c. 1000) often copies the *Præcepta militaria* (c. 969) word for word, but does incorporate tactical changes made during the intervening three decades, as well as other material. Moreover, the work by Nikephoros Phokas apparently heavily borrowed from a slightly earlier work, the *Syllogê taktikôn*, which itself derives from earlier texts.
54. McGreer 2008 [1995]: 317.
55. Anna Komnene, *Alexiad* 15.1.1.
56. Angold 2008: 612–13.
57. Anna Komnene, *Alexiad* 15.5.2.
58. Ibid. 15.6.3.
59. Ibid. 11.2.9.
60. Raymond d'Aguilers, *Historia Francorum qui ceperunt Iherusalem* apud *RHC occidentaux* iii, 246.
61. Albert d'Aix, *Historia Hierosolymitana expeditionis* apud *RHC occidentaux* iv, 434.
62. Constantinus VII Porphyrogenitus, *De ceremoniis aulae byzantinae* 694.22–695.14 Reiske.
63. John Kinnamos, *Deeds of John and Manuel Komnenos* 1.2, 2.14, 3.18, 4.13, 5.13, 7.3.
64. Guillaume de Tyr, *Historia rerum in paribus transmarinis gestarum* 19.25, 22.18 (17).
65. Ibid. 4.7, 21.27 (28).
66. Ibid. 16.22.
67. Ambroise, *L'estoire de la Guerre Sainte*, line 10421.
68. Albert d'Aix, *Historia Hierosolymitana expeditionis* apud *RHC occidentaux* iv, 289.
69. Ibid. iv 307–8, Oderic Vitalis, *Historia ecclesiastica* 9.6.
70. Raoul de Caen, *Gesta Tancredi in expeditione Hierosolymitana* par. 607, Oderic Vitalis, *Historia ecclesiastica* 9.6.
71. Albert d'Aix, *Historia Hierosolymitana expeditionis* apud *RHC occidentaux* iv, 434.
72. Fulcher de Chartres, *Historia Hierosolymitana* 1.10.10.
73. Raoul de Caen, *Gesta Tancredi in expeditione Hierosolymitana* pars. 631, 640.
74. Albert d'Aix, *Historia Hierosolymitana expeditionis* apud *RHC occidentaux* iv, 417.
75. Oderic Vitalis, *Historia ecclesiastica* 10.20, Albert d'Aix, *Historia Hierosolymitana expeditionis* apud *RHC occidentaux* iv, 563–4, 584.
76. Oderic Vitalis, *Historia ecclesiastica* 10.20, Albert d'Aix, *Historia Hierosolymitana expeditionis* apud *RHC occidentaux* iv, 569–70, 573–1.
77. Blöndal & Benedikz 2007 [1978]: 45–6. Their argument rest on evidence in the anonymous late tenth-century Byzantine treatise *De re militari*.
78. Ibn al-Athir, *al-Kamil fi'l-ta'rikh* ('The Complete History') 9.43–4.
79. Yahya ibn Sa'īd apud Vasiliev-Kratchkowsky *Patrologia Orientalis*, t. xxiii, fasc. III, 423. In truth, it is estimated that perhaps a dozen or so churches were built during Vladimir's

reign. The sources of Yahya ibn Sa'id's account are Greek and Syriac chronicles, which he readily found in Antioch, the Byzantine-held city to which he and a number of Egyptian Christians and Jews fled during the persecutions of the rather eccentric sixth caliph of the Shi`a Fatimid empire centred on Egypt, al-Hakim bi-Amr Allah (r. 996–1021), which was to culminate in the destruction of the basilica of the Holy Sepulchre in Jerusalem on 28 September 1009.

80. *Primary Chronicle*, 6494 [986].

81. Churches many or few, by the eleventh century Kiev was no backwoods place, its fame having reached the German and Muslim chroniclers. The German chronicler Thietmar of Merseberg (975–1018) viewed Kiev as a 'great city' with 'more than four hundred churches, eight markets, and an unknown number of inhabitants' as well as underscored its proximity to Byzantium (*Chronicon Thietmari* vii, 72), while the Saxon chronicler Adam of Bremen considered Kiev 'the competitor of the sceptre of Constantinople, the most charming gem of Greece' (*Gesta Hammaburgensis ecclesiae pontificum* ii, 19).

82. 14 September 987, according to Yahya ibn Sa'id apud Vasiliev-Kratchkowsky *Patrologia Orientalis*, t. xxiii, fasc. III, 422. The number 6,000 is from the eleventh-century Armenian historian Stepanos Asoghik (*Universal History*, vol. 2, 164–5). However, Stepanos uses the same number on other occasions to denote a large army (ibid. 156).

83. 13 April 989, according to Yahya ibn Sa'id apud Vasiliev-Kratchkowsky *Patrologia Orientalis*, t. xxiii, fasc. III, 424.

84. Michael Psellos, *Chronographia*, Basil II 1.15–18.

85. John Skylitzes, *Synopsis historiôn* 15.7 [292–4].

86. Ibid. 16.8 [324].

87. Michael Psellos, *Chronographia*, Basil II 1.28.

88. Hence the Greek term *Tauroskuthai*. *Scythia* is a geographical concept of impressive durability. As a name for the part of Europe north of the Black Sea from the Danube to the Don, it was already well-established when Herodotos wrote about it in the fifth century BC. A thousand years later, it had the same meaning when Jordanes (*Getica* 30–2, 45, 123–5) wrote about the Goths in the middle of the sixth century. During these first Christian centuries, it is certain that the term 'Scythians' had started to be attributed to any group beyond the Danube coming into contact with the Roman world. For instance, the Goths are said by Prokopios (*Wars*, 4.5–6) to have been called Scythians previously, because all groups who lived in that area were called Scythians. In our own period of study, the Russian *Primary Chronicle*, under the year 907, mentions the Varangians first among the peoples that the Greeks counted as being part of *Scythia*.

89. Michael Psellos, *Chronographia*, Basil II 1.14.

90. *Primary Chronicle* 6488, [980].

91. Anna Komnene, *Alexiad* 2.9.4, 2.12.4, 3.9.1, 4.6.2, 9.9.2, 12.6.3, Niketas Choniates, *O City of Byzantium* II, book 5, p. 98 [172] Magoulias, cf. Michael Psellos, *Chronographia*, Zoë & Theodora 6.3, Constantinus IX 6.87, Michael VI 7.22, Romanos IV 7.19.

92. Though it is no means certain that John I Tzimiskès was poisoned, this is the version of events offered by John Skylitzes (*Synopsis historiôn*, 15.22 [312], cf. Leo Diakonos, *Historia* 10.11).

93. Bardas Skleros was the brother-in-law of John I Tzimiskès, who had married his sister Mária. He had expected to succeed John, for he had been promised the throne by the emperor on his deathbed.

94. Venice, Codex Marciana Græcus 17, folio IIIr.

95. Michael Psellos, *Chronographia*, Basil II 1.35–6.

96. John Skylitzes, *Synopsis historiôn* 16.40 [356], George Kedrenos, *Compendium historiarum* 2.466.

97. George Pachymeres, *Historia* 1.174–7.

98. John Skylitzes, *Synopsis historiôn* 16.35 [349], cf. 38 [353].
99. Michael Psellos, *Chronographia*, Basil II 1.34.
100. George Pachymeres, *Historia* 1.176.

Chapter 16

1. Crone & Cook 1977 offer a somewhat extreme reinterpretation, but give a powerful presentation of the problems of the evidence.
2. Pickard 2013: 353.
3. We have to remember that the Arabs numbered their years from 622, the year Muhammad and his supporters move from Mecca to Medina. This migration is known as the *hijra*, whence each numbered year is designated AH for the Latin *anno Hegirae*, 'in the year of the *hijra*'. The Islamic calendar is lunar and therefore the *hijri* year is eleven days shorter than the solar year.
4. Rufinus of Aquileia, *Historia ecclesiastica* 2.6.
5. Sozomen, *Historia ecclesiastica* 6.38. See also Shahid 1984: 142–52.
6. Op. cit.
7. Theodoretos of Kyrrhos, *Historia ecclesiastica* 4.23.
8. Sozomen, *Historia ecclesiastica* 6.38 with Socrates Scholasticus, *Historia ecclesiastica* 4.36 apud Rufinus of Aquileia, *Historia ecclesiastica* 2.6.
9. *Codex Theodosianus, Novellae Theodosianus* 24.2.
10. Sozomen, *Historia ecclesiastica* 7.1.
11. Shahid 2006 [1984]: 142–75.
12. Crone 1987: 93–7, 137.
13. Ibid. 40.
14. Qur'an 105:1–5.
15. Crone 2007: 65.
16. *Scriptores Historiae Augustae*, Divus Claudius 14.3.
17. *ND Or.* 37.22.
18. See, on this, Crone 2007: 65–6.
19. Qur'an 16:80.
20. Kaegi 1992: 39–41, Whitby 1995: 73–4.
21. Shaw 2001: 141.
22. 'Ikrima apud al-Suyuti, *Kitab al-durr al-manthur fi 'l-tafsir bi'l-ma'thur* viii, 638, *ad* 106:2.
23. See Crone 1987: 98, and the sources cited there.
24. *Encyclopaedia of Islam²*, sv Ghazza. See also Crone 1987: 110, 115 n. 21, 118.
25. Crone 2007: 88.
26. Ibn Habib, *Kitab al-muhabbar*, 370–1, Ibrahim ibn Ya'qub, apud Qazwini, *Athar al-bilad wa akhbar al-'ibad* ('Monuments of the Countries and Histories of their Inhabitants') 233–5.
27. Prokopios, *Wars* 1.17.46.
28. Ibid. 1.17.47.
29. Prokopios (*Wars*, 1.18.30–50), a source noted for its hostility towards al-Harith ibn Jabala, states that the Arab *foederati* betrayed the Byzantines and fled their position on the right wing, thereby costing Belisarius the battle. John Malalas (*Chronographia*, 18.60), however, reports that while some Arabs indeed fled, Harith stood firm.
30. Prokopios, *Wars* 1.17.45.
31. Humbach, et al., *Sassanian Inscription* 3, 71, § 91.
32. E.g. Prokopios, *Wars* 2.28.12–14.
33. Jerome, *The Life of Malchus, the Captive Monk* 4.
34. Ammianus Marcellinus, *Res Gestae* 14.4.1, 23.3.38.
35. Iulianus, *Orationes* 1.21b.

36. Ibn Sa'd, *Kitab al-Tabaqat al-Kabir* ('Book of the Major Classes') apud Eduard Sachau vol. iii, pt. I, p. 246, 1.3.
37. Al-Bukhari, vol. 6, bk. 60, *hadith* nos. 344–416.
38. Aboul-Enein & Zuhur 2004: 26.
39. Ibn Jarir al-Tabari, *Tarikh al-Rusul wa' l-muluk* ('The History of the Prophets and Kings'), vol. 3, p. 8.
40. Bosworth 1976: 202.
41. Rehatsek 1879: 235.
42. Ibid. 229.
43. Potts 1998: 188, fig. 3.
44. Rehatsek 1879: 233.
45. Quoted by ibid. 234.
46. Nicolle 1993B: 6.
47. Quoted by ibid. 11.
48. James 2010: 31–9.
49. Quoted by Aboul-Enein & Zuhur 2004: 22.
50. Muslim, bk. 19, *hadith* no. 4313.
51. Ibn al-'Arabi, *Rihla* § 65. The relevancy of this particular holy city is best encapsulated by the Palestinian poet Mahmoud Darwish (1940–2008) in his *Memory for Forgetfulness* (1995): 'I love Jerusalem. The Israelis love Jerusalem and sing for it. You love Jerusalem. Feiruz sings for Jerusalem. And Richard the Lion-Hearted loved Jerusalem' (p. 41).
52. Qur'an 17:1.
53. Ibid. 17:111.
54. Quoted by Phillips 2005 [2004]: 69–70.
55. In 835, according to Ibn al-Athir, *al-Kamil fi 'l-ta'rikh* 6.289.
56. Nikolaos I Mystikos, *Letters* § 251.
57. Quoted by Pickard 2013: 393.

Chapter 17

1. The Armagnac chronicler Jean Juvénal des Ursins (*Histoire de Charles VI Roy de France*, 561) on Henry firing of the district around Meaux in October 1421. This heavily fortified Armagnac town was some thirty-seven kilometres east of Paris, currently controlled by an Anglo-Burgundian régime, and its garrison had long been a thorn in the capital's side. It fell after seven months of siege, through the grimmest of winters, in early May 1422.
2. *Iliad*, 16.122–3 Lattimore.
3. E.g. Theophanes Confessor, *Chronographia*, annus mundi 6164. It should be noted, years are reckoned from 5509 BC, annus mundi, i.e., according to the biblical beginning of time or Creation, as calculated by the Byzantine system. With that, elaborate computations had established the first year of creation to have been 1 September 5509 BC – 31 August 5508 BC, that is, 5509 years before the birth of Jesus Christ. The Byzantine calendar year began on the first day of September. Thus, for mediaeval Christians, history was finite and continued within comprehensible limits. If it began with Creation, it was scheduled to end in a not indefinitely remote future with the Second Coming, which was the hope of afflicted mankind, followed by the Day of Judgement.
4. Michael Attaleiates, *Historia* 46.8.
5. Constantinus VII Porphyrogenitus, *De administrando imperio* 13.
6. Although the term 'Greek fire' has been in general use in most European languages since the crusades, in the original Byzantine sources (e.g. Theophanes Confessor, *Chronographia*, annus mundi, 6164, 6218, 6305 etc.) it is called by a variety of descriptive names, such as 'sea fire' (Gr. *pýr thalássion*), 'Roman fire' (Gr. *pýr rhomaïkón*), 'wet fire' (Gr. *pýr hygron*) or

'war fire' (Gr. *polemikòn pýr*). For a full discussion on Greek fire, see Pryor-Jeffreys 2006: 607–31.

7. 2 Maccabees 1:19–22.
8. Strabo, *Geographia* 16.1.15.
9. Pliny, *Historia naturalis* 2.108.
10. Ibn al-Athir, *al-Kamil fi't-Ta'rikh* 6.289.
11. Al-Tarsusi, *Siyar al-thughur* ('Ways of Life along the Frontiers') 20–1.
12. Anna Komnene, *Alexiad* 13.3.6.
13. Ibid. 11.10, 13.3–4, cf. 14.2.10, Leo VI Sapiens, *Taktiká* 19.51, 57.
14. Madrid, Biblioteca Nacional, Codex Matritensis Græcus, Vitr. 26–2, folio 34v.
15. Constantinus VII Porphyrogenitus, *De administrando imperio* 48.20, Theophanes Confessor, *Chronographia*, annus mundi 6164–5. Writing about the middle of the twelfth century George Kedrenos (*Compendium historiarum*, 1.765) uniquely reports Kallinikos was from Heliopolis of Egypt rather than Syria.
16. Dennis 1998: 108.
17. Usama ibn Munqidh, *Kitab al-I'tibar* ('Book of Learning by Example') 143 Hitti. A *ratl* was a measure of weight, which in Syria was equivalent to 3.202 kg.
18. Robert de Clari, *La prise de Constantinople* par. 95.
19. Romano-Byzantine literary sources mention such machines (Gr. *mêchanaí*) as *órgana*, *petrobóla*, *lithobóla*, *petrareai*, etc., all of them signifying stone-throwing machines, e.g. Anna Komnene, *Alexiad* 4.1.1, 2, 4.5, 6.1.2. Contemporaneous bolt-shooting machines included *cheirobalistrai*, *toxobalistrai*, etc. See, on this, Dennis 1998.
20. Madrid, Biblioteca Nacional, Codex Matritensis Græcus, folios 151, 166, 169.
21. Leo Diakonos says (*Historia*, 10.8) that these machines were useless in the hands of an inexperienced crew.
22. Simon de Montfort the elder was the father of the Simon de Montfort, earl of Leicester, who defeated Henry III of England at Lewes in 1264 and was killed at Evesham the following year.
23. In Old Occitan: '*donas e tozas e mulhers*', *Chanson de le croisade albigeoise*, laisse 205. Ironically, a relief carving in the Basilica de Saint-Nazaire, Carcassonne, originally from the tomb of Simon de Montfort, portrays the siege of Albigensian-held Carcassonne. In the lower right-hand corner of the relief is clearly seen a man-powered counterweight machine.
24. Beffeyte 2008 [2000]: 10.
25. Theodosios Diakonos, *De Creta capta* verses 716–21, cf. 326, 973.
26. John Kinnamos, *Deeds of John and Manuel Komnenos* 6.10.
27. Niketas Choniates, *O City of Byzantium* II, bk. 1, p. 32–3 [54–5] Magoulias.
28. Geoffroi de Villehardouin, *La conquête de Constantinople* par. 89.
29. Liudprand of Cremona, *Antapodosis* 5.15.
30. E.g. *vide* Theophanes Continuatus 5.59, John Skylitzes, *Synopsis historiôn* 6.29 [151].
31. Liudprand of Cremona, *Antapodosis* 5.15.
32. Jean de Joinville, *Histoire de Saint Loys* §§ 203–4.
33. Usama ibn Munqidh, *Kitab al-i'tibar* 104 Hitti. The term *naft* is used in the mediaeval Muslim sources for Greek fire, while the specialists that handled it in battle are called *naffâtûn*, 'naphtha soldiers'.
34. Ibn Shaddad, *Al-nawadir al-sultaniyya wa 'l-mahassin al-yusufiyya* apud *RHC orientaux* iii, 221–2.
35. Robert de Hauteville (1016–85), who quickly won for himself the surname Guiscard, the Cunning, was the most successful of eight remarkable brothers, the sons of Tancred de Hauteville, who had played a leading part in the battles and politics of southern Italy in the first half of the eleventh century. In 1059, pope Nicholas II (r. 1059–61) had invested Robert as his vassal with the dukedom of Apulia and Calabria, also prospectively Sicily,

although the actual conquest of the island from the Arabs was to be achieved by his younger brother Roger (d. 1101). By making himself master of almost all of southern Italy, Robert brought to an end centuries of Byzantine authority in and control of Apulia and Calabria.

36. Gaufredus Malaterra, *Historia Sicula* 3.26 apud Muratori, *Scriptores* v, 584.
37. Jean de Marmoutier, *Historia Gaufredi ducis* 218–19.
38. Anon., *Richardi Regis Itinerarium Hiersolmorum*.
39. Marcus Græcus, *Liber ignium ad comburendos hostes* § 26, cited in Partington 1999 [1960]: 50.
40. John 19:29.

Chapter 18

1. Geoffroi de Villehardouin, *La conquête de Constantinople* par. 35.
2. Quoted by Ehrenkreutz 1972: 233.
3. Niketas Choniates, *O City of Byzantium* IX, pp. 326–7 [594–5], 347–8 [634–5] Magoulias.
4. Ibid. IX, p. 347 [633] Magoulias.
5. Geoffroi de Villehardouin, *La conquête de Constantinople* par. 266.
6. Niketas Choniates, *O City of Byzantium* IX, p. 323 [587] Magoulias.
7. Ibid. IX, p. 324–5 [590–1] Magoulias.
8. Robert de Clari, *La prise de Constantinople* par. 97.
9. It should be noted that in the winter of 1203, in an effort to satisfy the increasingly aggressive demands for funds by their then allies the crusaders, the emperors Isaakos II Angelos and Alexios IV Angelos allowed some of the treasures from Hagia Sophia to be removed and melted down – dozens of silver lamps that hung from the ceiling of the church were gathered together and cast into the flames.
10. Niketas Choniates, *O City of Byzantium* VIII, p. 315 [573–4] Magoulias.
11. Ibid. VIII, p. 316–7 [575–6] Magoulias.
12. Ibid. VIII, p. 315 [573] Magoulias.
13. Ibid. X, p. 357 [648] Magoulias.
14. Ibid. X, p. 358 [649–50] Magoulias, although he wrongly attributes the work to Lysimachos, cf. Pliny *Historia naturalis* 34.40.
15. Niketas Choniates, *O City of Byzantium*. X, p. 360 [652] Magoulias.
16. Ibid. VI, bk. 2, p. 297–8 [543] Magoulias.
17. George Pachymeres, *Historia* 1.213.28–30.
18. What actually became of the head of John the Baptist is difficult to determine. The patriarch of Constantinople Nikephoros (r. 806–15) says (*Historia ecclesiastica*, 1.9) that Herodias had it buried in the fortress of Machaerus (following Josephus, *Antiquitates Iudaicae* 18.5.2). Other writers say that it was interred in the palace of Herod at Jerusalem; there it was found during the reign of Constantinus I, and thence secretly taken to the Syrian town of Emesa (Homs) where it was concealed, the place remaining unknown for years, until it was manifested by revelation in 453 (Marcellinus Comes, *Chronicon*, under 453). Today, several different locations claim to possess the severed head of John the Baptist. The current official place for the Roman Catholic Church is the Shrine of Saint John the Baptist (Nabi Yahya in Arabic) inside the Umayyad Mosque in Damascus.
19. Robert de Clari, *La prise de Constantinople* par. 103.
20. Geoffroi de Villehardouin, *La conquête de Constantinople* par. 76.
21. Ibid. par. 92.
22. Liudprand of Cremona, *Antapodosis* 5.21.
23. The numbering system is actually a creation of eighteenth-century French historians and applies only to the largest of the crusades, although we can now identify several smaller campaigns between (for example) the Second and Third crusades that fulfil the criteria of a papally authorized holy war.

24. It is interesting to note that one strand of the Muslim historical tradition as to why this *unexpected* invasion of the lands of Islam, *Dar al-Islam*, came about blamed the Fatimids (Shi`a Muslims) for inviting the crusaders (or 'Franks', *al-frank*, as all western European Christians were called) to come and attack Syria and Palestine in order to protect Egypt from the Seljuqs (Sunni Muslims). See, on this, Hillenbrand 1999: 44–7.

25. Sulpicius Severus, *Vita Sancti Martini* 4.

26. Today the best known mediaeval treatment of the ethics of war is that of Thomas Aquinas in his *Summa Theologiae* (2.2, *quaestio* 40), who laid down three requirements for a just war: it must have right cause, right intention, and right authority.

27. Augustine of Hippo, *contra Faustus Manichaeum* 22.74. For a time Augustine also belonged to the Manichaeans, a rigorists sect, which followed the teachings of the third-century Mesopotamian guru Mani, according to which there were two gods, an evil creator god who was responsible for matter, and the good god of spirit.

28. Augustine of Hippo, *De civitate Dei* 17.13, 22.22. A vast work of twenty-two books, this was written in part at least to explain why God had allowed the sack of Rome by Alaric in 410. One of his later works, written over a period of about fourteen years and finished in 427, its focus is on Rome, the Roman past and Roman authors.

29. Bainton 1960: 53–100.

30. Isidorus of Seville, *Etymologiae* 18.1.2.

31. Ibid. 5.4.

32. Baldric de Dol apud *RHC occidentaux* iv.

33. Honoré Bouvet, *L'arbre des batailles* par. 81.

34. Ibid. 125.

35. Joshua 6:20.

36. Joshua 10:8 NIV.

37. Anon., *Life and Miracles of Saint Luke of Steiris* § 60.

38. John Kaminiates, *On the capture of Thessaloniki* 72.

39. Ibid. 73.

40. John Skylitzes, *Synopsis historiôn* 12.4 [249].

41. Madrid, Biblioteca Nacional, Codex Matritensis Græcus, Vitr. 26–2, folio 140r.

42. Leo Diakonos, *Historia* 1.3.

43. Ibid. 10.8.

44. Ibid. 5.8.

45. George Kedrenos, *Compendium historiarum* 2.340–7.

Chapter 19

1. John Kananos, *De Constantinopoli obsidone* 6.18, 7.24, 8.2.

2. Ibid. 8.8–16.

3. The word Kananos sometimes uses for cannon is βουμπάρδος, bombard (ibid. 6.13, 7.2), so named from the Greek verb βομβέω, to boom, because of the booming sound it made.

4. John Kananos, *De Constantinopoli obsidone* 6.12–13.

5. Though the most common epithet for the Virgin Mary in Byzantine writings is Theotokos (Gr. *Theotókos*), Kananos uses the word Panayia (Gr. *Panagía*), which means all-holy woman. It was an everyday term for her, and remains so in modern Greece.

6. John Kananos, *De Constantinopoli obsidone* 21.20–5.

7. It was most probably common practice among the Ottoman Turks, as it was with Europeans, for clerics to accompany the armies of the empire on campaign.

8. John Kananos, *De Constantinopoli obsidone* 22.17–23.2.

9. Ramon Muntaner, *Crònica* chap. 215. At the time the knight Ramon Muntaner (1265–1336) was one of the leading members of the Catalan Company, serving as its quartermaster.

10. Gibbon, *D&F* vol. 3, ch. 63, pp. 584–5.

11. Ibid. p. 585.
12. Ibid. p. 577.
13. Timur, a Turco-Mongol, had gained the moniker 'Lame' after being struck by several arrows in a skirmish in 1363: one hit Timur in the right leg, another in the right arm, permanently damaging both. These wounds were confirmed when Soviet archaeologists opened his mausoleum in Samarkand in 1941, shortly before the Germans invaded Russia.
14. Marlowe, *Tamburlaine* part 1, act 3, scene 1.
15. Ibid. part 1, act 4, scene 2.
16. Evliya Çelebi, *Seyâhatnâme* ('Narrative of Travels') 2.5 apud von Hammer-Purgstall ii, 7.
17. Barthomaeus de Jano, *Epistola de crudelitate Tucarum* apud *PG* vol. 158, coll. 1055-67.
18. Alfons Huber, *Die Kriege zwischen Ungarn und den Türken (1440–1443)*, apud *Archiv für österreichische Geschichte*, vol. 68 (1886), pp. 159–207, here p. 198.
19. Quoted in Held 1988: 25.

Chapter 20

1. DeVries 1997, cf. Philippides 1999: 56–60, who expresses the opinion that the cannons of the Ottoman Turks, including the fabled great bombard commissioned by Mehmet II, should not receive the sole credit for the fall of Constantinople.
2. Antoche 2004.
3. *Wujing Zongyao*, part 1, vol. 12.
4. Roger Bacon, *Opus Majus* part 6 'On Experimental Science' apud R.B. Burke, *The Opus Majus of Roger Bacon* vol. 2, p. 629.
5. Marcus Græcus, *Liber ignium ad comburendos hostes* §§ 12, 13, 14 and 33.
6. Ibid. § 33.
7. The fortress of La Réole in 'English' Aquitaine fell after a month's bombardment by '*les bouches à feu*'. Some two years later the first known pictorial representation appears in *De nobilitatibus, sapientiis, et prudentiis regum* (Christ Church, Oxford, MS 47680, folio 44v), a treatise on the duties of a king complied for the future English King Edward III (r. 1327–71) by Walter de Milemete, King's Clerk and later Fellow of King's Hall, Cambridge. It depicts a *pot-de-fer*, a vase-shaped barrel set on a four-legged wooden frame, which is firing a large dart-shaped projectile.
8. Despite the depreciation of gunpowder by which Machiavelli and other writers of the period indulge, during the ten-week siege of the Aztec capital Hernán Cortés (1485–1547), conquistador of Mexico, did deploy gunpowder weapons. These included the harquebus and small cannon, the latter being mounted on thirteen brigantines, one per vessel (Tenochtitlán stood on a 'floating garden' of built up silt in lake Texcoco and was assessed from the mainland by three causeways). Incidentally, in 2013, during the Syrian civil war, forces of the Syrian National Coalition were filmed using a counterweight trebuchet during the battle of Aleppo. The trebuchet was being employed to hurl explosives at government troops. As we well appreciate, the trebuchet was the largest of counterweight machines and the only device truly capable of throwing fortification-threatening missiles. For this reason, it was the principal mediaeval tool for pounding walls.
9. Cervantes, *Don Quixote* part 1, ch. 38, pp. 332–3 Grossman.
10. Machiavelli, *Arte della guerra* bk. II (on harquebuses), bk. III (on cannons). Machiavelli, however, lived to see, if not recognize, the beginning of the change from the mediaeval to the modern view of gunpowder weapons, what we recognize as the change from the mysterious to the scientific, from ritual to empiricism.
11. Ágoston 2005: 66.
12. Smith & DeVries 2011: 50.

13. Most contemporary authors refer to Orban's creation as the 'famous bmbard' and the 'great cannon', or simply as 'the monster', e.g. Michael Doukas, *Historia Turco-byzantia* col. 35, 37, Leonardo of Chios apud *PG* vol. 159, col. 929.

14. Michael Doukas, *Historia Turco-byzantia* col. 307. One span, unit of measurement equal to the distance across a man's outstretched hand between the point of the thumb and that of the little finger ($\equiv$ 223 millimetres). See, on this, Philippides & Hanak 2011: 413–25.

15. DeVries 1997: 345–6.

16. Niccolò Barbaro, *Diary of the Siege of Constantinople 1453* par 52.

17. Laonikos Chalkokondyles, *Historiarum demonstrationes* 2.8.2–9.17, apud *PG* vol. 159.

18. Michael Doukas, *Historia Turco-byzantia*, coll. 920C–921D.

19. London, British Museum, inv. 47033/3.

20. Ágoston 2014: 94–5.

21. This is corroborated by the Ottoman chronicler Celalzade Mustafa (d. 1567), who claimed that at the battle of Mohács (29 August 1526) 'four thousand Janissaries were deployed in nine consecutive rows according to the rules of imperial battles [led by the sultan]' (quoted by Ágoston 2013: 141).

22. See, on this, Uyar & Erickson 2009: 36–44.

23. Bertrandon de la Broquière, *Le Voyage d'outremer* 182–5, 268.

24. See, on this, Palmer 1953, Imber 2011.

25. Nestor-İskander, *Tale of Constantinople* 89.

26. George Sphrantzes, *Chronicon minus* 35.9. Sphrantzes was made a prisoner by the Turks, but succeeded in paying his ransom and retired to Corfu, where in the year 1462 he entered the monastery of Saint Elias, and wrote his memoirs.

27. For an English translation of this Latin letter see Melville-Jones: 1972: 11–42.

28. Niccolò Barbaro, *Diary of the Siege of Constantinople 1453* par 67.

29. In modern Greek the 'sleeping' Constantinus XI Palaiologos is known as ο μαρμαρωμένος βασιλίας, 'the marble/petrified emperor'.

30. The literature on the petrified emperor is vast. See, on this, Nicol 1992: 101–2.

31. *PG* vol. 107, col. 1138.

32. Carnoy-Nicolaïdès 1894: 47–9. A fascinating compilation, *Folklore de Constantinople* covers an assortment of diverse legends and stories, mostly of non-Muslim origins. These stories are related to different places and monuments in Istanbul before and after the Ottoman conquest. For each story, the authors indicate the name of the person from whom the story was collected, his ethnic origin, profession, birthplace, and age. These storytellers (all male) consist of Turks, Greeks, Kurds and Armenians with origins from different parts of the Ottoman empire.

33. Quoted by Runciman 2002 [1965]: 149. Afrasiyab was the fabulous city of the legendary king Alp Ertonga. Many scholars identify Afrasiyab with the ancient Sogdian capital Marakanda where, in the autumn of 328 BC, Alexander the Great, blind drunk and out of control, ran his buddy Kleitos the Black through with a pike. This is now the site of Samarkand in Uzbekistan.

34. Francis Bacon, 'Of Goodness and Goodness of Nature', apud *The Essays of Francis Bacon* (1908), p. 54.

35. Ibid. 'An Advertisement Touching a Holy War', apud *The Works of Francis Bacon* (1827), vol. 7, p. 125–6.

36. Mehmet even went so far as to commission a biography of himself in Greek, from a minor Byzantine functionary on the island of Imbros, Michael Kritoboulos, on the same paper and in the same format as a copy of Arrian's *Campaigns of Alexander*, which he had read to him daily. A man of keen intellect, Kritoboulos entered the sultan's service after the fall of Constantinople.

37. See, for this, Runciman 2002 [1965]: 56.

38. Niccolò Barbaro, *Diary of the Siege of Constantinople 1453* par. 67.

39. Lord: the actual word used in the Qur'an is *rabb*, cognate with Hebrew *rabbi*. There is no proper equivalent in the English language. In essence, it means the One and the Only Lord for the entire universe, its Creator, Organizer, Provider, Master, Planner, Sustainer, Cherisher, and Giver of security. *Rabb* is also one of the thousand names of Allah.

40. Evliya Çelebi, *Seyâhatnâme* 1.11 apud von Hammer-Purgstall i, 45.

41. Ibid. 1.9 apud von Hammer-Purgstall i, 31. Evliya Çelebi's great-grandfather was Yavuz Erisan. It was he who built what is probably the oldest mosque in Istanbul on the land he was awarded as part of his spoils of the conquest. The *Sağrıcılar Camii* the Mosque of the Leather-Workers, so named after the guild that has long had its workshops in this quarter, was founded in 1455. Evliya Çelebi's family remained in possession of the mosque for at least two centuries, living in a house just beside it. Evliya Çelebi was born in this house in 1611, and twenty years later he began to write his *Seyâhatnâme* there.

42. Qur'an 24:35.

Epilogue

1. Cited in A. Mango, *Atatürk: the Biography of the founder of Modern Turkey* (2002), 463.

Rulers of Constantinople

Constantinian dynasty (306–63)
Constantinus I 306–37
Constantius II (f) 337–61
Iulianus (c) 361–3

Iovianus 363–4
Valens 364–78

Theodosian dynasty (379–457)
Theodosius I 379–95
Arcadius (f) 395–408
Theodosius II (f) 408–50
Pulcheria (s) 450–3
Marcianus (m) 450–7

Leonid dynasty (457–518)
Leo I the Thracian 457–74
Leo II Mikros (n) 474
Zeno (m) 474–5, 476–91
Basilikos (m) 475–6
Anastasius I Dikoros (m) 491–518

Illyrian dynasty (518–602)
Justin I 518–27
Iustinianus I (ff) 527–65
Justin II (ff) 565–78
Tiberius II Constantinus (a) 578–82
Mauricius (m) 582–602

Phokas 602–10

Herakleian dynasty (610–95)
Herakleios 610–41
Constantinus III (f) & Heraklonas (f) 641
Heraklonas 641
Constans II (ff) 641–68
Constantinus IV Pogonatos (f) 668–85
Iustinianus II Rhinotmetos (f) 685–95, 705–11

Twenty–year Anarchy (695–717)
Leontios 695–8

Tiberius III Apsimar 698–705
Philippikos Bardanes 711–13
Anastasius II 713–15
Theodosius III 715–17

Isaurian dynasty (717–802)
Leo III the Isaurian 717–41
Constantinus V Kopronymos (f) 741–75
Leo IV the Khazar (f) 775–80
Eirene the Athenian (ux) 780–802 , d. 803
Constantinus VI (f) 780–97, d. 805

Nikephorian dynasty (802–13)
Nikephoros I 802–11
Staurakios (f) 811
Michael I Rangabè (m) 811–13

Leo V the Armenian 813–20

Amorian dynasty (820–67)
Michael II the Amorian 820–9
Theophilos (f) 829–42
Theodora the Paphlagonian (ux) 842–56
Michael III the Sot (f) 842–67

Macedonian dynasty (867–1056)
Basil I the Macedonian 866–86
Leo VI Sapiens (f) 886–912
Alexander (b) 912–13
Constantinus VII Porphyrogenitus (ff) 913–59
Romanos I Lekapenos (m) 920–44
Romanos II Porphyrogenitus 959–63 (son of Constantinus VII)
Nikephoros II Phokas (m) 963–9
John I Tzimiskès (ff) 969–76
Basil II Porphyrogenitus 976–1025 (son of Romanos II)
Constantinus VIII Porphyrogenitus (b) 1025–8
Zoë Porphyrogenita (d) 1028–50

Romanos III Argyros (m) 1028–34
Michael IV the Paphlagonian (m) 1034–41
Michael V Kalaphates (a) 1041–2
Zoë Porphyrogenita & Theodora
   Porphyrogenita 1042
Constantinus IX Monomachos (m) 1042–55
Theodora Porphyrogenita 1055–6

Michael VI Stratiotikos 1056–7
Isaakos I Komnenos 1057–9

Doukai dynasty (1059–81)
Constantinus X Doukas 1059–67
Michael VII Doukas (f) 1067–78
Romanos IV Diogenes (m) 1068–71
Nikephoros III Botaneiates (m) 1078–81

Komnenoi dynasty (1081–1185)
Alexios I Komnenos 1081–1118
John II Komnenos (f) 1118–43
Manuel I Komnenos (f) 1143–80
Alexios II Komnenos (f) 1180–3
Andronikos I Komnenos (p) 1183–5

Angeloi dynasty (1185–1204)
Isaakos II Angelos 1185–95, 1203–4
Alexios III Angelos (b) 1195–1203
Alexios IV Angelos (ff) 1203–4
Alexios V Doukas Mourtzouphlos (m) 1204

**Laskarid dynasty (1204–61) – reigned in
   Nicaea**

Theodore I Laskaris 1204–22
John III Doukas Vatatzes (m) 1222–54
Theodore II Laskaris (f) 1254–8
John IV Laskaris (f) 1258–61

Palaiologi dynasty (1261–1453)
Michael VIII Palaiologos 1259–82
Andronikos II Palaiologos (f) 1282–1328
Andronikos III Palaiologos (n) 1328–41
John V Palaiologos (f) 1341–91
John VI Kantakouzenos (m) 1347–54
Andronikos IV Palaiologos (f) 1376–9
John VII Palaiologos (f) 1390
Manuel II Palaiologos 1391–1425 (son of John
   V)
John VIII Palaiologos (f) 1425–48
Constantinus XI Dragases Palaiologos (b)
   1449–53

Key
(f) Son of predecessor
(b) Brother of predecessor
(p) Uncle of predecessor
(ff) Nephew of predecessor
(c) Cousin of predecessor
(n) Grandson of predecessor
(d) Daughter of predecessor
(s) Sister of predecessor
(ux) Wife of predecessor
(a) Tie through adoption
(m) Tie through marriage

Patriarchs of Constantinople

Alexander 314–37
Paul I the Confessor 337–9, 341–2, 346–51 (+)
Eusebius of Nicomedia 339–42
Macedonius I 342–6, 351–60
Eudoxius of Antioch 360–70
Evagrius 370
Demophilos 370–80
Gregory I of Nazianzos the Theologian 379–81 (+)
Maximos the Cynic 380
Nectarius 381–97
John I Chrysostomos 397–404, d. 407 (+)
Arsacius 404–5
Atticus 406–25
Sisinios 426–7
Nestorius 428–31, d. 451
Maximian 431–4
Proklos 434–6 (+)
Flavianus 446–9 (+)
Anatolius 449–58 (+)
Gennadios I 458–71
Acacius 472–89
Fravitas 489
Euphemios 489–95
Macedonius II 495–511
Timothy I 511–18
John II the Kappodocian 518–20
Epiphanios 520–35
Anthimos I 535–6
Menas 536–52
Eutychios 552–65, 577–82
John III Scholastikos 565–77
John IV Nesteutes 585–95
Kyriakos (Cyril) 595–606
Thomas I 607–10 (+)
Sergios I 610–38
Pyrrhos 638–41, 654
Paul II 641–53
Peter 654–66
Thomas II 667–9

John V 669–75
Konstantinos I 675–7
Theodore I 677–9, 686–7
Georgios I 679–86
Paul III 687–93
Kallinikos I 693–705
Cyrus 706–11
John VI 712–14
Germanos I 715–30
Anastasios 730–754
Konstantinos II 754–66
Niketas I 766–80
Paul IV 780–4
Tarasios 784–806 (+)
Nikephoros I 806–15, d. 827
Theodotos I Kassiteras 815–21
Antonios I Kassimatis 821–36
John VII Grammatikos 836–42
Methodios I 842–6
Ignatius I 846–58, 867–77
Photios I the Great 858–67, 877–86
Stephanos I 886–93
Antonios II Kauleas 893–901
Nikolaos I Mystikos 901–07, 912–25
Euthymios I Synkellos 907–12
Stephanos II of Amasea 925–8
Tryphon 928–31
Theophylaktos 931–56
Polyeuktos 956–70
Basil I Skamandrinos 970–4
Antonios III the Stoudite 974–80
Nikolaos II Chyrsoberges 984–5
Sisinios II 996–9
Sergios II 999–1019
Ephsthatios 1020–5
Alexios Stoudite 1025–43
Michael I Keroularios 1043–59
Konstantinos III Lechoudis 1059–63
John VIII Xifilinos 1063–75
Kosmas I of Jerusalem 1075–81
Ephstratios Garidas 1081–4

Nikolaos III Grammatikos 1084–1111
John IX Agapetos 1111–34
Leo Styppeiotes 1134–43
Michael II Kourkouas 1143–6
Kosmas II Attikos 1146–7
Nikolaos IV Mouzalon 1147–51
Theodotos I 1151–3
Neophytos I 1153
Konstantinos IV Khliarinos 1154–6
Loukas Chyrsoberges 1156–69
Michael III 1170–7
Chariton Eugeniotis 1177–8
Theodosios I Boradiotes 1178–83
Basil II Kamateros 1183–6
Niketas II Moutanes 1187–9
Leontios Theotokites 1189–90
Dositheos of Jerusalem 1190–1
George II Xifilinos 1191–8
John X Kamateros 1198–1206
Michael IV Autoreianos 1207–13
Theodore II Eirenikos 1213–15
Maximos II 1215
Manuel I Haritopoulos 1215–22
Germanos II 1222–40
Methodios II 1240
Manuel II 1240–55
Arsenios Autoreianos 1255–60, 1261–7
Nikephoros II 1260–1

Germanos III 1267
Joseph I Galesiotes 1267–75, 1282–3
John XI Bekkos 1275–82
Gregory II Kyprios 1283–9
Athanasios I 1289–93, 1304–10
John XII 1294–1304
Nifon I 1311–15
John XIII Glykys 1316–20
Gerasimos I 1320–1
Isaiah 1323–34
John XIV Kalekas 1334–47
Isidoros I 1347–9
Kallistos I 1350–4, 1355–63
Philotheos Kokkinos 1354–5, 1364–76
Makarios 1376–9, 1390–1
Neilos Kerameios 1380–8
Antonios IV 1389–90, 1391–7
Kallistos II Xanthopoulos 1397
Matthew I 1397–1410
Euthymios II 1410–16
Joseph II 1416–39
Metrophanes II 1440–3
Gregory III Mammas 1443–50
Athanasios II 1450–3

Key
(+) Later sanctified

Abbreviations

AJA	*American Journal of Archaeology* (Princeton, NJ, 1897—)
Ar.	Arabic
BMGS	*Byzantine and Modern Greek Studies* (Birmingham 1975—)
BSOAS	*Bulletin of the School of Oriental and African Studies* (London, 1917—)
BZ	*Byzantinische Zeitschrift* (Leipzig and Munich, 1892—)
CIG	A. Böckh, *Corpus Inscriptionum Græcorum* (Berlin, 1825–60)
CIL	T. Mommsen *et al.* , *Corpus Inscriptionum Latinarum* (Berlin, 1863—)
CJ	*Classical Journal* (Chicago, IL, 1905—)
CSHB	B.G. Niebuhr, *Corpus scriptorum historiae byzantinae* (Bonn, 1828–97)
D&F	E. Gibbon, *The History of the Decline and Fall of the Roman Empire*, 3 vols. (London, 1890)
DOP	*Dumbarton Oaks Papers* (Washington DC, 1958—)
Fornara	C.W. Fornara, *Translated Documents of Greece & Rome I: Archaic Times to the end of the Peloponnesian War*, 2nd edition (Cambridge, 1983)
Fr.	French
Gr.	Greek
GRBS	*Greek, Roman and Byzantine Studies* (Cambridge, MA, 1963—)
IG	*Inscriptiones Græcae* (Berlin, 1923—)
ILS	H. Dessau, *Inscriptiones Latinae Selectae* (Berlin, 1892–1916)
JHS	*Journal of Hellenic Studies* (Cambridge, 1880—)
JLA	*Journal of Late Antiquity* (Baltimore, MD, 2008—)
JMRC	*Journal of Medieval Religious Cultures* (University Park, PA, 1974—)
JTS	*Journal of Turkish Studies* (Cambridge, MA, 1977—)
JRA	*Journal of Roman Archaeology* (Ann Arbor, MI, 1988—)
JSS	*Journal of Semitic Studies* (Oxford, 1955—)
JWH	*Journal of World History* (Honolulu, 1990—)
L	Latin
ND Or.	O. Seeck, *Notitia Dignitatum in partibus Orientis* (Berlin, 1876)
NIV	New International Version
OP	Old Persian
PG	J-P. Migne, *Patrologiae cursus completus: Series græca*, 161 vols. (Paris, 1857–66)
Quicherat	J. Quicherat, *Procès de condemnation et de réhabilitation de Jeanne d'Arc*, 5 vols. (Paris, 1841–9)
REB	*Revue des études byzantines* (Bucharest and Paris, 1944—)
RHC occidentaux	*Recueil des historiens des croisades: Historiens occidentaux*, 5 vols. (Paris, 1844–95)
RHC orientaux	*Recueil des historiens des croisades: Historiens orientaux*, 5 vols. (Paris, 1872–1906)
RSBN	*Rivista di studi bizantini e neoellenici* (Roma, 1964—)
Scott	S.P. Scott, *The Civic Law*, 17 vols. (Cincinnati, 1932)
Skjald	F. Jónsson, *Den norsk-islandske skjaldedigtning*, A I–II, B I–II (Köbenhavn, 1912–15)
Tisset-Lanhers	P. Tisset and Y. Lanhers, *Procès de condemnation de Jeanne d'Arc*, 3 vols. (Paris, 1960–71)
Tk.	Turkish

Bibliography

Aboul-Enein, Y.H. and Zuhur, S., 2004. *Islamic Rulings in Warfare*. Carlisle Barracks, PA: Strategic Studies Institute, US Army War College.

Ágoston, G., 1994. 'Ottoman artillery and European military technology in the fifteenth to seventeenth centuries'. *Acta Orientalia Scientiarum Hungaricae* 47: 15–48.

Ágoston, G., 2005. *Guns for the Sultan: Military Power and the Weapons Industry in the Ottoman Empire*. Cambridge: Cambridge University Press.

Ágoston, G., 2013, 'War-winning weapons? On the decisiveness of Ottoman firearms from the siege of Constantinople (1453) to the battle of Mohács (1526)'. *JTS* 39: 129–43.

Ágoston, G., 2014. 'Firearms and military adaptation: The Ottomans and the European military revolution, 1450–1800'. *JWH* 25/1: 85–124.

Alföldi, A., 1948. *The Conversion of Constantine and Pagan Rome*. Oxford: Oxford University Press

Anastasiadis, M.P., 1994. 'On handling the *menavlion*'. *BMGS* 18: 1–10.

Angold, M., 2008. 'Belle époque or crisis? (1025–1118)', in J. Shepard (ed.), *The Cambridge History of the Byzantine Empire, c. 500–1492*. Cambridge: Cambridge University Press, 583–626.

Antoche, E.C., 2004. 'Du tabor de Jan Žižka et Jean Hunyadi au tâbur çengi des armées ottomanes'. *Turcica* 36: 91–124.

Arslan, M., 2014 'Byzantion: A foundation legend, from myth into history'. *Actual Archaeology* 10: 38–49.

Asutay, N., 2003. 'Die Entdeckung des Romanos-Tores an den Landmauern von Konstantinopel', *BZ* 96: 1–4.

Asutay-Effenberger, N., 2007. *Die Landmauer von Konstantinopel-Istanbul: Historisch-topographische und baugeschichtliche Untersuchungen*. Berlin: Walter de Gruyter.

Ayers, L., 2004. *Nicaea and Its Legacy: An Approach to Fourth-Century Trinitarian Theology*. Oxford: Oxford University Press.

Bainton, R.H., 1960. *Christian Attitudes toward War and Peace: A Historical Survey and Critical Re-evaluation*. New York: Abingdon Press.

Baker, G.P., 1992. *Constantine the Great and the Christian Revolution*. New York: Cooper Square Press

Bardill, J., 1999A. 'The Great Palace of the Byzantine emperors and the Walker Trust Excavations'. *JRA* 12: 216–30.

Bardill, J., 1999B. 'The Golden Gate in Constantinople: a triumphal arch of Theodosius I'. *AJA* 103: 671–96.

Bartusis, M., 1992. *The Late Byzantine Army: Arms and Society, 1204–1453*. University Park, PA: Pennsylvania State University Press.

Beatson, P., 1998. 'Byzantine lamellar armour: conjectural reconstruction of a find from the Great Palace in Istanbul, based on early mediaeval parallels'. *Varangian Voice* 49: 3–8.

Beffeyte, R., 2008 [2000]. *Les machines de guerre au Moyen Age*. Rennes: Éditions Ouest-France

Bell, P., 2013. *Social Conflict in the Age of Justinian*. Oxford: Oxford University Press.

Bhola, R.K. (PhD thesis), 2015. *A man of visions: A new examination of the vision(s) of Constantine* (Panegyric *VI*, Lactantius' De mortibus persecutorum, *and* Eusebius' De vita Constantini). Ottawa: University of Ottawa.

Birkenmeier, J.W., 2002. *The Development of the Komnenian Army*. Leiden: E.J. Brill.

Blaum, P.A., 1994. *The Days of the Warlords: A History of the Byzantine Empire,* AD 969–991. Lanham, MA: University Press of America.

Blöndal, S., (trans., rev. & ed. B.S. Benedikz, 2007 [1978]). *The Varangians of Byzantium*. Cambridge: Cambridge University Press.

Bosworth, C.E., 1976. 'Armies of the Prophet: Strategy, tactics and weapons in Islamic Warfare', in B. Lewis (ed.), *Islam and the Arab World*. New York: Alfred A. Knopf.

Bozhkov, A., 1972. *The Miniatures of the Madrid Manuscript of Johannes Scylitzes*. Sofia: Bulgarian Academy of Sciences.

Braudel, F., 1998 (trans. S. Reynolds, 2001). *The Mediterranean in the Ancient World*. London: Penguin.

Brett, G., Martiny, G. and Stevenson, R.B.K., 1947. *The Great Palace of the Byzantine Emperors*. London.

Buckler, G., 1968. *Anna Comnena, a Study*. Oxford: Clarendon Press.

Bugarsky, I., 2005. 'A contribution to the study of lamellar armours'. *Starinar* 55: 161–79.

Byrd, K.M. (trans.), 2008. *Pierre Gilles' Constantinople*. New York: Italica Press.

Cameron, A., 1973. *Porphyrius the Charioteer*. Oxford: Oxford University Press.

Cameron, A., 1976. *Circus Factions: Blues and Greens at Rome and Byzantium*. Oxford: Oxford University Press.

Cameron, A., 2013 [2011]. *The Last Pagans of Rome*. Oxford: Oxford University Press.

Cameron, Av. and Hall, S.G., 1999. *Eusebius: Life of Constantine*. Oxford: Clarendon Press.

Carnoy, É.H. and Nicolaïdès, J., 1894. *Folklore de Constantinople*. Paris: É. Lechevalier.

Cheynet, J-C., 2006. *The Byzantine Aristocracy and its Military Function*. Burlington, VT: Ashgate Publishing.

Ciggaar, K.N., 1996. *Western Travellers to Constantinople: The West & Byzantium, 976–1204*. Leiden: E.J. Brill.

Connor, C.L., 1993. 'Hosios Loukas as a victory church'. *GRBS* 33: 293–308.

Crone, P., 1987. *Meccan Trade and the Rise of Islam*. Oxford: Oxford University Press.

Crone, P., 2003 [1980]. *Slaves on Horses: The Evolution of the Islamic Polity*. Cambridge: Cambridge University Press.

Crone, P., 2005. 'How did the quranic pagans make a living?' *BSOAS* 68/3: 387–99.

Crone, P. 2007. 'Quraysh and the Roman army: Making sense of the Meccan leather trade'. *BSOAS* 70/1: 63–88.

Crone, P. and Cook, M.A., 1977. *Hagarism: The Making of the Islamic World*. Cambridge: Cambridge University Press.

Daryaee, T., 2008. *Sasanian Iran (224–651 CE)* . Costa Mesa: Mazda Publishers.

Davidson, Ellis, H.R., 1973. 'The secret weapon of Byzantium'. *BZ* 66: 61–74.

Dawson, T., 1998. '*Kremasmata, Kabadion, Klibanion*: some aspects of middle Byzantine military equipment reconsidered'. *BMGS* 22: 38–50.

Dawson, T., 2007. '"Fit for the task": equipment sizes and the transmission of military lore, sixth to tenth centuries'. *BMGS* 31: 1–12.

Dawson, T., 2009. 'The *Walpurgis Fechtbuch*: an inheritance of Constantinople?'. *Arms & Armour* 6: 79–92.

Dawson, T., 2013. *Armour Never Wearies: Scale and Lamellar Armour in the West, From the Bronze Age to the 19th Century*. Stroud: Spellmount.

DeVries, K., 1997. 'Gunpowder weapons at the siege of Constantinople, 1453', in L. Yev (ed.), *War and Society in the Eastern Mediterranean, 7th – 5th Centuries*. Leiden: E.J. Brill, 343–62.

Decker, M.J., 2013. *The Byzantine Art of War*. Yardley, PA: Westholme.

Dennis, G.T., 1997. 'The Byzantines in battle', in K. Tsiknakes (ed.), *Το εμπόλεμο Βυζάντιο, 9–12 ai*. Athens: Εθνικό Ίδρυμα Ερευνών, 165–78.

Dennis, G.T., 1998. 'Byzantine heavy artillery: the Helepolis'. *GBRS* 39: 99–115.

Dennis, G.T. (trans. & ed.), 2008. *The Anonymous Byzantine Treatise On Skirmishing by the Emperor Lord Nicephoros, in Three Byzantine Military Treatises*. Washington, DC: Dumbarton Oaks Center for Byzantine Studies.

Drake, H.A., 2000. *Constantine and the Bishops: The Politics of Intolerance*. Baltimore, MD: John Hopkins University Press.

DuBois, T.A., 1999. *Nordic Religions in the Viking Age*. Philadelphia, PA: University of Pennsylvania Press.

Ehrenkreutz, A.S., 1972. *Saladin*. Albany, NY: State University of New York Press.

Evans, J.A.S., 2005. *The Emperor Justinian and the Byzantine Empire*. Westport, CT: Greenwood Publishing.

Featherstone, M., 2006. 'The Great Palace as reflected in the *De ceremoniis*'. *Byzas* 5: 47–6.

Fields, N., 2015. *Attila the Hun*. Oxford: Osprey (Command 31).

Fisher, G., 2011. 'Kingdoms or dynasties? Arabs, history, and identity before Islam'. *JLA* 4/2: 245–67.

Flori, J., 2007. *Bohémond d'Antioche, chevalier d'aventure*, Paris: Éditions Payot-Rivages.

Forbes, R.J., 1959. *More Studies in Early Petroleum History*. Leiden: E.J. Brill.

Freely, J., 1996. *Istanbul: The Imperial City*. New York: Viking.

Freely, J., 2009. *The Grand Turk: Sultan Mehmet II – The Conqueror of Constantinople and Master of an Empire*. New York: The Overlook Press.

Freely, J., 2011 (6th edn.). *Blue Guide Istanbul*. London: Blue Guides.

Geanakoplos, D., 1984. *Byzantine Church, Society and Civilization Seen Through Contemporary Eyes*. Chicago, IL: University of Chicago Press.

Goodwin, G., 1997 [1994]. *The Janissaries*. London: Saqi.

Grabbar, A. and Manoussacas, M. (eds.), 1979. *L'Illustration du Manuscrit de Skylitzes de la Bibliothèque Nationale de Madrid*. Venise: Institut Hellénique d'Études Byzantines et Post-byzantines de Venise.

Grant, M., 1990 [1976]. *The Fall of the Roman Empire*. New York: Collier Books.

Greatrex, G., 1997. 'The Nika Revolt: A reappraisal'. *JHS* 117: 60–86.

Grierson, P., 1973. *Catalogue of the Byzantine Coins in the Dumbarton Oaks Collection and in the Whittemore Collection*, vol. III, parts 1 & 2. Washington, DC: Dumbarton Oaks Center for Byzantine Studies.

Haldon, J.F., 1999. *Warfare, State and Society in the Byzantine World, 565–1204*. London: University College London Press.

Haldon, J.F., 2000. *The Byzantine Wars: Battle and Campaigns of the Byzantine Era*. Stroud: Tempus

Haldon, J.F., 2003. *Byzantium at War, 600–1453*. London: Routledge.

Haldon, J.F. (ed.), 2007. *Byzantine Warfare*. Burlington, VT: Ashgate Publishing.

Haldon, J.F. and Byrne, M., 1977. 'A possible solution to the problem of Greek fire'. *BZ 70*: 91–9.

Hernandez, F., 1974. 'The Turks with the Grand Catalan Company, 1305–1312'. *Boğaziç Üniversitesi Dergisi* 2: 25–45.

Harari, Y, 1997. 'The military role of the Frankish Turcopoles: A reassessment'. *Mediterranean Historical Review* 12/1: 75–116.

Harris, J., 2001. 'Looking back on 1204: Nicetas Choniates in Nicaea'. *Mésogeios* 12: 117–24.

Heath, I., 1994 [1979]. *Byzantine Armies, 886–1118*. Oxford: Osprey (Men-at-Arms 89).

Held, J., 1988. 'Hunyadi's Long Campaign and the battle of Varna 1443–1444'. *Ungarn-Jahrbuch. Zeitschrift für die Kunde Ungarns und verwandte Gebiete* Band 16: 10–27.

Hillenbrand, C., 1999. *The Crusades: Islamic Perspectives*. Edinburgh: Edinburgh University Press.

Hoffmeyer, A.B., 1966. 'Military equipment in the Byzantine manuscript of Skylitzes in Biblioteca Nacional in Madrid'. *Gladius* 5: 7–160.

Holmes, C., 2005. *Basil II and the Governance of Empire (976–1025)*. Cambridge: Cambridge University Press.

Hourani, A., 1991. *A History of the Arab Peoples*. Cambridge, MA: Belknap Press.

Humphries, P.D., 1985. '"Of Arms and Men": Siege and battle tactics in the Catalan Grand Chronicles (1208–1387)'. *Military Affairs* 49/4: 173–8.

Imber, C., 2006. *The Crusade of Varna, 1443–45*. Farnham: Ashgate Publishing.

Imber, C., 2011. 'The origin of the Janissaries', in C. Imber (ed.), *Warfare, Law and Pseudo-History*. Istanbul: Isis, 165–71.

Jacoby, D., 2014. *Travellers, Merchants and Settlers in the Eastern Mediterranean, 11th – 14th Centuries*. Farnham: Ashgate Publishing (Variorum Collection Studies series: CS1045).

James, S., 2010. *Excavations At Dura-Europos, 1928–1837, Final Report VII, The Arms and Armour and other Military Equipment*. London: British Museum Press.

Janin, R., 1964 (2ᵉ éd.). *Constantinople byzantine: developpement urbain et repertoire topographique*. Paris: Institut Français d' Études Byzantines.

Jefferson, J., 2012. *The Holy Wars of King Wladislas and Sultan Murad: The Ottoman–Christian Conflict from 1438–1444*. Leiden: E.J. Brill.

Jones, A.H.M., 1964. *The Later Roman Empire 284–602*, 2 vols. Baltimore: John Hopkins University Press.

Kaegi, W.E., 1992. *Byzantine and the Early Islamic Conquests*. Cambridge: Cambridge University Press.

Káldy-Nagy, G., 1977. 'The first centuries of the Ottoman military organisation'. *Acta Orientalia Academiae Scientiarum Hungaricae* 31/2: 147–83.

Kollias, T.G., 1980. 'Ζάβα, ζαβάρετον, ζαβαρειώτης'. *Jahrbuch der Osterreichischen Byzantinistik* 29: 27–35.

Kollias, T.G., 1988. *Byzantinische Waffen*, Wien: Verlag der Osterraischen Akademie der Wissenchaften.

Leithart, P.J., 2010. *Defending Constantine: The Twilight of an Empire and the Dawn of Christendom*. Downers Grove, IL: InterVarsity Press.

Lewin, A.S. and Pellegrini, P. (eds.), 2007. *The Late Roman Army in the Near East from Diocletian to the Arab Conquest: Proceedings of a Colloquium held at Potenza Acerenza and Matera, Italy (May 2005)*. Oxford: British Archaeological Reports International Series 1717.

Liebeschuetz, J.H.W.G., 2003. *The Decline and Fall of the Roman City*. Oxford: Oxford University Press.

Lindow, J., 1976. *Comitatus, Individual and Honor: Studies in North Germanic Institutional Vocabulary*. Berkeley, CA: University of California Publications in Linguistics.

Loud, G.A., 2000. *The Age of Robert of Guiscard: Southern Italy and the Norman Conquest*. London: Longman.

McGreer, E., 2008 [1995]. *Sowing the Dragon's Teeth: Byzantine Warfare in the Tenth Century*. Washington, DC: Dumbarton Oaks Center for Byzantine Studies (Dumbarton Oaks Studies 33).

McLees, N., 2012. 'Byzantine bride-shows and the restoration of the icons: A tale of four iconophile empresses'. *Road to Emmaus* 13/4: 34–69.

Malmburg, S., 2007. 'Dazzling dining: banquets as an expression of imperial legitimacy', in L. Brubaker (ed.), *Eat, Drink and Be Merry (Luke 12:19): Food and Wine in Byzantium*. Farnham: Ashgate Publishing, 75–91.

Main, R.W. (MA thesis), 2013. *Mob politics: The political influence of the circus factions in the eastern empire from the reign of Leo I to Heraclius (457–641)*. Ottawa: University of Ottawa.

Mansel, P., 1995. *Constantinople: City of the World's Desire, 1453–1924*. London: John Murray

Markus, R., 1983. 'Saint Augustine's views on the "Just War"'. *Studies in Church History* 20: 1–14

Melville-Jones, J.R., 1972. *The Siege of Constantinople: Seven Contemporary Accounts*. Amsterdam: Hakkert.

272   God's City

Morillo, S., 2008. 'Mercenaries, Mamluks and militia: Towards a cross-cultural typology of military service', in J. France (ed.), *Mercenaries and Paid Men: The Mercenary Identity in the Middle Ages*. Leiden: E.J. Brill, 243–60.

Necipoğlu, N. (ed.), 2001. *Byzantine Constantinople: Monuments, Topography and Everyday Life*. Leiden: E.J. Brill.

Nicol, D.M., 1992. *The Immortal Emperor: The Life and Legend of Constantine Palaiologos, Last Emperor of the Romans*. Cambridge: Cambridge University Press.

Nicol, D.M., 1993 (2nd edn.). *Last Centuries of Byzantium*. Cambridge: Cambridge University Press.

Nicolle, D.C., 1991. 'Byzantine and Islamic arms and armour, evidence for mutual influence'. *Graeco-Arabica* 4: 299–325.

Nicolle, D.C., 1993A. 'Digenes Akritas and armies of Akritai'. *Military Illustrated* 67: 26–29, 44.

Nicolle, D.C., 1993B. *Armies of the Muslim Conquest*. Oxford: Osprey (Men-at-Arms 255).

Nicolle, D.C., 1995. 'No way overland? Evidence for Byzantine arms and armour on the 10th–11th century Taurus frontier'. *Graeco-Arabica* 6: 226–45.

Nicolle, D.C., 1997 [1995]. *The Janissaries*. Oxford: Osprey (Elite 58).

Nicolle, D.C., 1999. *Nicopolis 1996*. Oxford: Osprey (Campaign 64).

Norwich, J.J., 1993. *Byzantium: The Apogee*. London: Penguin.

Obolensky, D., 1971. *The Byzantine Commonwealth*. London: Weidenfeld & Nicolson.

Odahl, C.M., 2015. 'Constantine and God: imperial theocracy for the Christian divinity in the first Christian emperor's beliefs and policies'. *The Ancient World* 46/1: 25–64.

Oikonomidès, N., 1978. 'The mosaic panel of Constantine IX and Zoë in Saint Sophia'. *REB* 36: 219–32.

Oikonomidès, N., 1997. 'Entrepreneurs', in G. Cavallo (ed.), *The Byzantines*. Chicago, IL: University of Chicago Press, 144–71.

Ostrogorsky, G.A., 1963 (3rd edn. trans. J. M. Hussey, 1968). *History of the Byzantine State*. Oxford: Blackwell.

Palmer, J.A.B., 1953. 'The origins of the Janissaries'. *Bulletin of the John Rylands Library* 35/2: 448–81.

Parani, M.G., 2003. *Reconstructing the Reality of Images: Byzantine Material Culture and Religious Iconography, 11th – 15th Centuries*. Leiden: E.J. Brill.

Partington, J.R., 1999 [1960]. *A History of Greek Fire and Gunpowder*. Baltimore, MD: John Hopkins University Press.

Pelikan, J.J., 2011 [1990]. *Imago Dei: The Byzantine Apologia for Icons*. Princeton, NJ: Princeton University Press.

Pentcheva, B.V., 2002. 'The supernatural protection of Constantinople: the Virgin and her icon in the tradition of the Avar siege'. *BMGS* 26: 2–41.

Pentcheva, B.V., 2006. 'The performative icon'. *The Art Bulletin* 88/4: 631–55.

Pentcheva, B.V., 2014 [2006]. *Icons and Power: The Mother of God in Byzantium*. University Park, PA: Pennsylvania State University Press.

Philippides, M., 1981. 'The fall of Constantinople: Bishop Leonard and the Greek accounts'. *GRBS* 22: 287–300.

Philippides, M., 1999. 'Urban's bombard(s): gunpowder and the fall of Constantinople (1453)'. *Byzantine Studies/Études Byzantines* 4: 1–67.

Philippides, M. and Hanak, W.K., 2011. *The Siege and the fall of Constantinople in 1453: Historiography, Topography, and Military Studies*. Burlington, VT: Ashgate Publishing.

Phillips, J., 2005 [2004]. *The Fourth Crusade and the Sack of Constantinople*. London: Pimlico.

Pickard, J., 2013. *Behind the Myths: The Foundations of Judaism, Christianity and Islam*. Bloomington, IN: Author House.

Pogăciaş, A., 2015. 'John Hunyadi and the Late Crusade', in F. Sabaté (ed.), *Life and Religion in the Middle Ages*. Newcastle upon Tyne: Cambridge Scholars Publishing, 327–34.

Potts, D.T., 1998. 'Some issues in the study of the pre-Islamic weaponry of southeastern Arabia'. *Arabian Archaeology & Epigraphy* 9: 182–208.

Pryor, J.H. and Jeffreys, E.M., 2006. *The Age of the Δρόμων: The Byzantine Navy ca. 500–1204*. Leiden: E.J. Brill.

Purdie, M.H. (MA thesis), 2009. *An Account by John Cananus of the Siege of Constantinople in 1422*. Perth: University of Western Australia.

Rambaud, A., 1912. 'Michael Psellos, philosophe et homme d'état byzantin du XIᵉ siècle', in A. Rambaud (éd.), *Études sur l'histoire byzantine*. Paris: Armand Colin, 109–71.

Rehatsek, E., 1879. 'Notes on some old arms and instruments of war, chiefly among the Arabs'. *Journal of the Bombay Branch of the Royal Asiatic Society* 14: 219–63.

Remensnyder, A.G., 2014. *La Conquistadora: The Virgin Mary at War and Peace in the Old and New Worlds*. Oxford: Oxford University Press.

Riedel, M.L.D., 2015. 'Nikephoros II Phokas and Orthodox military martyrs'. *JMRC* 41/2: 121–47

Riley-Smith, J.S.C. (ed.), 1991 [1990]. *The Atlas of the Crusades*. London: Guild Publishing

Roland, A., 2008. 'Secrecy, technology, and war: Greek fire and the defence of Byzantium, 678–1204', in J. France and K. DeVries (eds.), *Warfare in the Dark Ages*. Farnham: Ashgate Publishing, 655–79.

Różycki, Ł., 2014. 'A soldier's tale through the eyes of a "Polish Janissary"'. *Medieval Warfare* Special Edition 2: 53–8.

Runciman, S., 1962. 'The schism between the Eastern and Western Churches'. *Anglican Theological Review* 44: 337–50.

Runciman, S., 1988 [1929]. *The Emperor Romanus Lecapenus and his Reign: A Study of 10th-century Byzantium*. Cambridge: Cambridge University Press.

Runciman, S., 2002 [1965]. *The Fall of Constantinople 1453*. Cambridge: Cambridge University Press.

Sakel, D. (ed.), 2014. *Byzantine Culture: Papers from the Conference "Byzantine Days of Istanbul" (Istanbul, May 21–23 2010)*. Ankara: Türk Tarih Kurumu.

Schrodt, B., 1981. 'Sports of the Byzantine Empire'. *Sports History* 8/3: 40–59.

Ševčenko, I., 1962. 'The illuminators of the Menologium of Basil II'. *DOP* 16: 243–55.

Ševčenko, I., 1965. 'Sviatoslav in Byzantine and Slavic miniatures'. *Slavonic Review* 24: 709–13.

Ševčenko, I., 1984. 'The Madrid manuscript of the Chronicle of Skylitzes in the light of its new dating', in I. Hutter (ed.), *Byzanz und der Westen, Studien zur Kunst der europäischen Mittelalters*. Wien: Österreichischen Akademie der Wissenchaften, 117–30.

Shahid, I., 1979. 'Byzantium in South Arabia'. *DOP* 33: 23–94.

Shahid, I., 1981. 'Christianity among the Arabs in Pre-Islamic Times'. *JSS* 26/1: 150–3.

Shahid, I., 1995. *Byzantium and the Arabs in the Sixth Century*. Washington, DC: Dumbarton Oaks.

Shahid, I., 2006 [1984]. *Byzantium and the Arabs in the Fourth Century*. Washington, DC: Dumbarton Oaks.

Shahid, I., 2006 [1989]. *Byzantium and the Arabs in the Fifth Century*. Washington, DC: Dumbarton Oaks.

Shaw, B.D., 2001. 'War and violence', in G. W. Bowersock, P. Brown and O. Grabar (eds.), *Interpreting Late Antiquity: Essays on the Postclassical World*. Cambridge, MA: Harvard University Press.

Shepard, J., 1985. 'Information, disinformation and delay in Byzantine diplomacy', in J.F. Haldon and T.A. Koumoulides (eds.), *Perspectives in Byzantine Culture*. Amsterdam: Hakkert, 233–93

Shepard, J., 1993. 'The uses of the Franks in eleventh-century Byzantium'. *Anglo-Norman Studies* 15: 275–305.

Shepard, J. and Franklin, S. (eds.), 1992. *Byzantine Diplomacy: Papers from the Twenty-fourth Spring Symposium of Byzantine Studies, Cambridge, March 1990*. Cambridge: Cambridge University Press.

Smail, R.C., 1995 (2nd edn.). *Crusading Warfare, 1097–1193*. Cambridge: Cambridge University Press.

Smith, R.D. and DeVries, K., 2011. *Rhodes Besieged: A New History*. Stroud: Tempus

Spiridakis, S., 1968. 'Zeus is dead: Euhemerus and Crete'. *CJ* 63: 337–40.

Stephenson, P., 2003. *The Legend of Basil the Bulgar–Slayer*. Cambridge: Cambridge University Press.

Stevens, S.T. and Conant, J.P. (eds.), 2016. *North Africa under Byzantium and Early Islam*. Washington, DC: Dumbarton Oaks Research Library & Collection.

Stewart, M.E., 2015. 'The *andreios* eunuch commander Narses'. *Ceræ: An Australasian Journal of Medieval and Early Modern Studies* 2: 1–25.

Stolz, B.V. and Soucek, S. (trans.), 1975. *Memoirs of a Janissary: Konstantin Mihailović*. Ann Arbor, MI: University of Michigan Press.

Sumner-Boyd, H. and Freely, J., 2010 [1972] (rev. edn.). *Strolling Through Istanbul*. London: I.B. Tauris.

Talbot, A-M and Sullivan, D.F. (trans. & ed.), 2005. *The History of Leo the Deacon: Byzantine Military Expansion in the Tenth Century*. Washington, DC: Dumbarton Oaks Center for Byzantine Studies (Dumbarton Oaks Studies 41).

Talbot Rice, D. (ed.), 1958. *The Great Palace of the Byzantine Emperors: Second Report*. Edinburgh: Edinburgh University Press.

Theotokis, G., 2012. 'Rus', Varangian and Frankish mercenaries in the service of the Byzantine emperors (9th–11th C.): numbers, organisation and battle tactics in the operational theatres of Asia Minor and the Balkans'. *Βυζαντινά Σύμμεικτα* 22: 125–56.

Thompson, G.L., 2014. 'From sinner to saint? Seeking a consistent Constantine', in Smither, E.L. (ed.), *Rethinking Constantine: History, Theology and Legacy*. Eugene, OR: Pickwick Publishing, 5–25

Tolstoy, L.N., 2014 [1897]. *What is Art?* London: The Big Nest.

Toom, T., 2014. 'Constantine's *summus deus* and the Nicene *unus deus*: Imperial agenda and ecclesiastical conviction'. *Vox Patrum* 34 t. 61: 103–22.

Treadgold, W.T., 1992. 'The army in the works of Constantine Porphyrogenitus'. *RSBN* 29: 77–62.

Treadgold, W.T., 1995. *Byzantium and its Army, 284–1081*. Stanford, CA: Stanford University Press.

Treadgold, W.T., 1997. *A History of the Byzantine State and Society*. Stanford, CA: Stanford University Press.

Treadgold, W.T., 2001. *A Concise History of Byzantium*. New York: Palgrave.

Treadgold, W.T., 2006. 'Byzantium, the reluctant warrior', in N. Christie and M. Yazigi (eds.), *Noble Ideas and Bloody Realities*. Leiden: E.J. Brill, 209–33.

Tsamakda, V., 2002. *The Illustrated Chronicle of Ioannes Skylitzes in Madrid*. Leiden: Alexandros Press.

Tuchman, B.W., 1979. *A Distant Mirror: The Calamitous Fourteenth Century*. London: Macmillan

Turner, D.R., 1996. *The East Roman Empire and its Legacy*. Athens: Lake Forest College.

Tyerman, C, 2006. *God's War. A New History of the Crusades*. Cambridge, MA: Harvard University Press.

Uyar, M. and Erickson, E.J., 2009. *A Military History of the Ottomans: from Osman to Atatürk*. Santa Barbara, CA: ABC-CLIO.

Vasiliev, A.A., 1948. 'The monument of Porphyrius in the Hippodrome at Constantinople'. *DOP* 4: 27–49.

Vasiliev, A.A., 1964 (2nd edn.). *History of the Byzantine Empire*, 2 vols. Madison, WI: University of Wisconsin Press.

Volkoff, V., 1984. *Vladimir the Russian Viking*. Woodstock, NY: Overlook Press.

Weiss, P., 2003 (trans. A.R. Birley). 'The vision of Constantine'. *JRA* 16: 237–59 (originally published in 1993 as 'Die Vision Constantins', in J. Bleicken (ed.), *Colloquium aus Anlass des 80. Geburtstages von Alfred Heuss*. Kallmünz: M. Lassleben, 143–69.

Whitby, M., 1995. 'Recruitment in Roman armies from Justinian to Heraclius (ca. 565–615)', in A. Cameron (ed.), *The Byzantine and Early Islamic Near East, III: States, Resources and Armies*. Princeton, NJ: Darwin Press, 61–124.

Whittemore, T., 1942. *The Mosaics of Hagia Sophia at Istanbul. Third Preliminary Report. Work done in 1935–1938. The Imperial Portraits of the South Gallery*. Oxford.

Whittow, M., 1996. *The Making of Byzantium, 600–1025*. Berkeley/Los Angeles, CA: University of California Press.

Wilson, N.G., 1978. 'The Madrid Skylitzes'. *Scrittura e civiltà* 2: 209–19.

Wortley, J., 2005. 'The Marian relics at Constantinople.' *GRBS* 45: 171–87.

Yewdale, R.B., 2010 [1924]. *Bohemond I, Prince of Antioch: A Norman Soldier-of-Fortune and Crusader 1050–1111*. Milton Keynes: Leonaur.

Index

Constantinus (charioteer), 116
Copts of Egypt, 177, 181, 244 n. 24
Crete, island of, 138, 195
    Byzantine expedition against (960–1), 187,
        202–204
    Muslim conquest of (827), 178, 202
Crispus (son of Constantinus I), 31, 33, 55–7
crossbow(s)/crossbowmen, 154, 205, 213
Crown of Thorns, 59, 194, 196
    see also relics
crusades
    First (1096–9), 5, 17, 27, 40, 135–6, 152,
        154, 197, 199–200, 235–6 n. 17, 238
        n. 16, 251–2 n. 21
    Peasants' (1096), 154
    Second (1147–9), 258 n. 23
    Third (1189–92), 258 n. 23
    Fourth (1202–4), 5–7, 99–100, 120–2, 185,
        188, 191–6, 258 n. 9
    Seventh (1248–54), 189
    of Nikopolis (1396), 210, 212, 224–5
    of Varna (1443–4), 213–14
Cyril, patriarch of Alexandria (412–44), 82

Damascus, 41, 56, 70, 90, 174–5, 177, 245
    n. 24, 258 n. 18
Danube, river, 2, 36, 62, 112, 212, 254 n. 88
Dardanelles see Hellespont
Dareios I (the Great), Great King of Persia
    (522–486 BC), 10–11
De re militari, anonymous Byzantine military
    treatise, 253 n. 77
De velitatione, anonymous Byzantine military
    treatise, 140–1, 252 n. 27
Delphi, 14, 105–106, 202
Demetrios Palaiologos, brother of
    Constantinus XI Dragases Palaiologos, 211,
    227
Devol, Treaty of (1108), 136
Digenes Akritas, Byzantine epic poem, 149
Diocletianus, emperor (284–305, d. 311),
    30–1, 48, 98
Dionysios Byzantii, Greek historian, 2, 9
Dionysius the Areopagite (Saint), 246 n. 3
diplomacy, Byzantine, 133–5, 138
doméstikos, 142
    of the East, 143
    of the Scholai, 142–3
    of the West, 143
Donatists, 59–60
Dura-Europos, 171

dromôn, 184–5
    síphôn(es), siphon(s), 184–5
    see also Greek fire
Durazzo (Dürreš)
    Italo-Norman sieges of (1081, 1107), 136,
        190

Eboracum (York), 31
Edessa (Urfa), 167, 181
    county of, 235–6 n. 17
Eirene the Athenian, empress/regent
    (708–802, d. 803), 90–1
Eirene Doukaina, empress and wife of Alexios
    I Komnenos, 131
elephant(s), 24, 163, 179, 239 n. 5
Epeiros, 191, 208
    Despotate of, 192, 208
Ephesos, 1, 21
    Synod of (455), 21–2, 82, 241 n. 25
    see also Œcumenical synods
Ertuğrul Bey, Ottoman chieftain (d. 1281),
    206
Eucharist, 72–3
Eudokia, empress and wife of Arcadius, 49
Eugenius, Flavius, western usurper (392–4),
    62–3, 65
Eugenius IV, pope (1431–47), 212
Euhemeros, Greek philosopher, 68
eunuch(s)
    Byzantine, 6, 46, 99, 102, 126–7
    Ottoman, 229, 232
Euphrates, river, 36, 46, 106, 166, 223
Eusebius of Caesarea Palestinae (d. 339), 41,
    54, 70
    on Constantinus I, 56–7, 60–1
    on Constantinus' vision, 32–3, 42–4, 56
    on the labarum, 44–5, 240 n. 7
Eusebius of Nicomedia (d. 342), 53, 80
Eustace II, count of Boulogne (1049–87),
    235–6 n. 17
Euxine see Black Sea
Evliya Çelebi, Ottoman traveller, 211, 230,
    240 n. 15, 262 n. 41

Farmer's law (Nomos georgikos), 140
Fatima, daughter of Mohammad, 76
Fatimid caliphate, 76, 151, 253–4 n. 79, 259
    n. 24
    see also Shi`a Islam
Fausta, empress and wife of Constantinus I,
    31, 55–7